D1603971

CLEANSING HONOR WITH BLOOD

CLEANSING HONOR
WITH BLOOD

Masculinity, Violence, and Power in the
Backlands of Northeast Brazil, 1845–1889

MARTHA S. SANTOS

STANFORD UNIVERSITY PRESS

Stanford, California

This book has been published with the assistance of the Department of
History and the College of Arts and Sciences of the University of Akron

Sections of Chapters 1 and 3 were originally published as Martha S. Santos,
"On the Importance of Being Honorable: Masculinity, Survival, and Conflict
in the Backlands of Northeast Brazil, Ceara, 1840s–1890," *The Americas*
64, no. 1 (July 2007): 35–57. © Academy of American Franciscan History.
Reprinted with permission.

Library of Congress Cataloging-in-Publication Data

Santos, Martha S. (Martha Sofia), author.
    Cleansing honor with blood : masculinity, violence, and power in the
backlands of Northeast Brazil, 1845–1889 / Martha S. Santos.
        pages   cm.
    Includes bibliographical references and index.
    ISBN 978-0-8047-7456-7 (cloth : alk. paper)
        1. Masculinity—Brazil—Ceará (State)—History—19th century.
2. Men—Brazil—Ceará (State)—History—19th century.   3. Machismo—
Brazil—Ceará (State)—History—19th century.   4. Violence—Brazil—Ceará
(State)—History—19th century.   5. Power (Social sciences)—Brazil—
Ceará (State)—History—19th century.   6. Honor—Brazil—Ceará
(State)—History—19th century.   7. Sex role—Brazil—Ceará (State)—
History—19th century.   8. Ceará (Brazil : State)—Social conditions—19th
century.   I. Title.
HQ1090.7.B6S26   2012
303.6'20811098131—dc23
                                                                        2011032100

Typeset at Stanford University Press in 10.5/13 Bembo

To Sean,
y a mis padres, Galo y Margarita

CONTENTS

Tables

Figures

ACKNOWLEDGMENTS

The completion of this book would not have been possible without the many individuals and institutions that, through the long and arduous process of conceptualizing, researching, writing, and revising this work, offered me their inspiration, support, and encouragement. To them, I would like to extend my deeply felt thanks.

This project began to take shape at the University of Arizona, where the late Nívea Parsons opened the doors to Brazil, its culture, its people, and especially, the *sertanejo* universe of Ceará, many years ago. I am deeply thankful to B. J. Barickman, who constantly challenged me to sharpen my ideas and my writing, and offered insights that helped me navigate both the intellectual and the practical twists and turns of doing research in local archives in the Brazilian Northeast. He generously offered his penetrating and detailed commentary on the manuscript chapters—suggestions that ultimately contributed to make this a better book. To Donna Guy, now at Ohio State University, I owe a debt of gratitude. Her conviction that I could write a gender history of the backlands and her feedback on early chapter drafts helped me not lose sight of gender as I investigated and wrote on the social history of Ceará. I also benefited from the insightful suggestions and encouragement of Kevin Gosner, and the commitment of Bill Beezley to funding my archival research in Brazil. Laura Shelton, James Wadsworth, and Tracy Alexander provided intellectual support and friendship. I am thankful especially to Laura Shelton, now at Georgia Southern University, who offered important commentary on the introduction to this book.

Other scholars have made valuable contributions to this work. I would like to thank Hendrik Kraay, who did a careful reading of the original manuscript and indicated several avenues for improvement and revision. Peter Beattie, Mary Ann Mahony, and Hal Langfur offered useful suggestions on papers based on this research that I presented at CLAH and BRASA conferences over the years. Marixa Lasso, from Case Western Reserve University, has been a keen reader of sections of the manuscript and has provided valuable advice.

I would also like to thank the outside reviewers of my manuscript for their thorough reading, constructive criticism, and the many corrections and suggestions for revision that they presented in their reports. I am particularly indebted to Judy Bieber, who identified herself as one of the reviewers, and whose commentary helped me both understand and sharpen my arguments. At Stanford University Press, Norris Pope has graciously guided me through the publication process. Many thanks to him both for his support to this project from the time we first met and for seeing it through to its completion.

I am deeply thankful to the History Department at the University of Akron, where I have found a very supportive community. Janet Klein, T. J. Boisseau, Lesley Gordon, Steve Harp, and Mike Levin read and commented on different sections of this book. In addition, Connie Bouchard, Walter Hixson, and Michael Sheng as department chairs at various times provided an environment conducive to the conclusion of this project, both by financially supporting research travel and by granting me a one-semester release from teaching duties to work on the revisions to the manuscript. Many thanks to Javier Hernandez Ayala and Kevin Butler, from the Geography Department, for their help in the preparation of the map submitted with this study. The contributions of all of these people, and of others not mentioned here because of lack of space, but not of gratitude, have made the publication of this work a reality. Of course, any errors contained in this book are my responsibility alone.

The research and writing of this study have also been made possible by the financial and logistical support of several institutions. The Tinker Foundation and the Department of History of the University of Arizona, in conjunction with the William and Flora Hewlett Foundation, funded research travel to the Arquivo Público do Estado do Ceará (APEC), in Fortaleza, during the summer of 1999 and the academic year 2001–2. A fellowship from the Harry Frank Guggenheim Foundation supported me financially for one year, as I put together the foundations of this study in 2002–3. The Center for Multicultural Excellence of the University of Denver and the University of Akron provided funds for additional research trips to Fortaleza and to Rio de Janeiro. The Department of History and the College of Arts and Science of the University of Akron supported some of the costs incurred in the publication of this text. The journal *The Americas* published portions of Chapters 1 and 3 in earlier versions. I am thankful to the editors for permission to use and expand on that material.

Many people in Brazil have also contributed to this project, both in direct and indirect ways. I owe a special thanks to the director of the APEC during my research travels, Professor Walda Mota Weyne, and to Cléa Vasconelos, coordinator of the notarial section of the archive, for their support of this project. I appreciate the assistance of all the archive's employees who put up with my unceasing requests for documents. I especially offer thanks to Etevaldo Evangelista, José Carlos Pereira, and Paulo Cardoso de Lacerda. To Vera Lúcia Ramos and Maria Gorete Lira I owe thanks for their friendship and their sense of humor, and for making the countless hours I spent transcribing documents at the Arquivo more enjoyable. At UFC, I would like to thank Professors José Francisco Pinheiro and Frederico de Castro Neves for generously sharing with me their own historical work on Ceará. To my friends in Fortaleza Silmara Chila Meira and Isabela Alencar, and to Saray Chila Meira and Valcides Santana, now of Curitiba, I wish to express my gratitude for their friendship and solidarity in times of illness, and for so graciously sharing with me their homes, Brazilian music, and Sundays at Praia do Futuro. I thank Ingrid Barancoski for her hospitality during my several stays in Rio de Janeiro.

Finally, I would also like to express gratitude to my family, which has supported me through this process in many different ways. I have appreciated my sister Ana's efforts over the years to drive me to various libraries in the state of São Paulo where I decided I needed to consult more dictionaries, dissertations, and theses, even when we were supposed to enjoy our vacation together at her home in Campinas. I would like to thank my parents, Galo Santos and Margarita Padilla de Santos, for the care, encouragement, and *acompañamiento* they have given me and this project over the years, even from a distance. Their belief that I could manage even when I felt it was not possible to work any harder, and their conviction that this book would see the light of day sustained me through difficult times. And my husband, Sean, I cannot even begin to thank for his unceasing support, companionship, and love. Undoubtedly, it has been his comfort and patience through the many sleepless nights of writing and revising, his good food and humor, his editorial assistance, and his willingness to discuss "cotton production," "hegemonic masculinities," and "state formation" again and again with me that have allowed me to complete this project. To him and to my parents I dedicate this book.

A NOTE ON WEIGHTS, MEASURES, BRAZILIAN CURRENCY, AND ORTHOGRAPHY

Weights and Measures

The following list shows Brazilian weights and measures and their closest metric equivalents:

1 alqueire, 36.27 liters, or about one English bushel
1 braça, 2.2 meters
1 légua (league), about 6,600 meters
1 tarefa, an area of 30 braças by 30 braças, or 4,356 square meters

Currency

The basic unit of currency in Brazil during the years 1845 to 1889 was the *real* (*réis* in the plural). The sum of 100 réis was written Rs. $100. Larger sums were expressed in *mil-réis* (literally, 1,000 réis), which was written Rs. 1$000. The figure of 1,000 mil-réis was referred as one *conto de réis*, or simply, one *conto*, and was written Rs. 1:000$000, or Rs. 1:000. A conto was worth about 500 dollars in 1877. Thus, the average price of a pregnant cow in the interior of the province of Ceará in that year was U.S. $8.25, or about Rs. 15$000; the price of a full-grown steer in the same year was U.S. $11.00, or Rs. 20$000.

Orthography

Orthographical rules have changed in Brazil several times since the nineteenth century. In this study, names of persons, places, and other proper nouns are spelled according to the most recent standardized rules. However, in citing the names of authors and titles of older published works, I have retained their original spelling.

ABBREVIATIONS

The following abbreviations are used in Tables, Figures, Notes, and Bibliography:

APEC	Arquivo Público do Estado do Ceará
Arrol.	Arrolamento (postmortem inventory)
Art. (Arts.)	article (articles)
Câm. Mun.	Câmara Municipal (municipal council)
ch.	chapter
Cív.	Processo civil (civil case)
Co. Soc.	Comissão de Socorros (Drought Relief Commission)
Com.	Comandante (commandant)
Cr.	Processo criminal (criminal case)
CSSH	*Comparative Studies in Society and History*
DT	Processo de demarcação de terra (civil case of land demarcation)
est.	estante
fl.	fólio
Freg.	Freguesia (township)
Gov.	Governo (government)
HAHR	*Hispanic American Historical Review*
Inv.	Inventário (postmortem inventory)
liv.	livro
Of. (Ofs.)	oficio (oficios)
Pres.	Provincial President
Prov.	Província (province)
RIC	*Revista do Instituto do Ceará*
RIHGB	*Revista do Instituto Histórico e Geográfico Brasileiro*
RT	Registro de terra (land registry)
Secr.	Secretaria (secretariat)
Tít.	título
UFC	Universidade Federal do Ceará

Introduction

Here they stand, then, with their characteristic garb, their
ancient customs, their strange adherence to the most remote
traditions, their religious sentiment carried to the point
of fanaticism, their exaggerated point of honor, and their
exceedingly beautiful folklore and folk poetry, three centuries old. . . . A strong and ancient race, with well- defined
and immutable characteristics, even in the major crises of
life—at which times the cowboy's leather garb becomes the
jagunços'* flexible armor—sprung from far-converging elements, yet different from all the rest of the population of the
country, this stock is undeniably a significant example of the
importance of those reactions induced by environment.
—Euclides da Cunha, *Rebellion in the Backlands.*[1]

This passage from *Os sertões*, Euclides da Cunha's highly acclaimed treaty
on the history and customs of the Brazilian Northeastern hinterlands and
its peoples, encapsulates one of the most enduring and influential tropes of
Brazilian literature, history, and popular culture: the idea that the *sertanejos*,
or male inhabitants of the semiarid backlands, have been the possessors of a
well-developed sense of honor, and have been conditioned to aggression by
deep-seated cultural traditions that appear fixed in time and landscape.[2] Da
Cunha belonged to the intellectual, coastal elite of the turn of the twentieth
century. This generation condemned rural backwardness—embodied in the
figure of the rude, racially mixed sertanejo—as an obstacle to the attain-

*The word *jagunço* denoted a Northeastern rural gunman or a bandit. However, Euclides
da Cunha applied the term to the armed defenders of the Bahian millenarian community
of Canudos—destroyed by the Brazilian republican army in 1897—whom he described as
mixed-raced descendants of "virile and adventurous" men, whose character had been formed
"in a turbulent society." Da Cunha, *Rebellion*, 78. Unless otherwise noted, all translations from
the Portuguese are my own.

1

ment of progress and civilization.[3] Nevertheless, because *Os sertões* projected the mythical origins of the Brazilian nation into a positive admiration of the physical capacity for adventure and endurance, and even for aggression, among the male backlander population, this work remained influential during the first half of the twentieth century.[4] Paradoxically, while over the past five decades scholarly research on banditry, resistance, and rebellion in the Northeastern hinterlands has called into question da Cunha's positivism and geographic determinism, those studies have failed to challenge the view that describes poor rural men as "quick to become violent," and inured to aggression by a timeless culture of feuding.[5] In doing so, much of the scholarship, in addition to the popular literature, several motion pictures, and even museum exhibits from the rural Northeast have underscored the perplexing survival in this region of a violent culture that originated in a remote past. Likewise, this large body of interdisciplinary production has unwittingly perpetuated the idea that aggression in defense of honor constitutes an inherent and immutable feature of sertanejo masculinity.[6]

Only in very recent years has the stereotype of the belligerent sertanejo been called into question in academic circles. The pioneering work of Brazilian historian Durval Muniz de Albuquerque Júnior examines the artistic and literary construction of the *nordestino macho*—the always brave, virile, and honor-obsessed Northeastern man—as a regional type during the first half of the twentieth century.[7] The author shows that this process of "invention" of a masculine regional identity occurred when a series of transformations, including the aftermath of the abolition of slavery and the adoption of republicanism, incipient urbanization, and industrialization—especially in the Southeast—threatened the power of agrarian notables from the Northeast.[8] Facing these changes as challenges to the "virility" of the Brazilian nation, these elites produced a masculinist regional discourse that created a gendered identity, centered on the cultural image of an always-already violent sertanejo, as the symbol of resistance of the region to the onslaughts of a modernizing, now feminized, republican nation.[9] Yet, for all its contributions to identifying the political uses of the sertanejo macho cliché, Albuquerque Júnior's work only partially contests the idea that propensity to aggression and readiness to fight in defense of honor constitute essential characteristics of backlanders' masculinities. The author's exclusive focus on the invention of the nordestino macho as an idealized representation fails to explain whether or not actual sertanejos in specific locales reproduced a form of manliness centered on the capacity to exercise violence, and if so, for what reasons.

On the whole, neither depictions of the sertanejos as culturally conditioned to violence, nor Albuquerque Júnior's approach to masculinity as mere discourse, answer questions that seem central: did local conditions in different historical periods affect notions of honor and the reproduction of violence in its defense among male backlanders? If violence constitutes a physical assertion of dominance, over whom were archetypically violent sertanejos asserting power in particular contexts? What was the position of women and of femininity in a society purportedly dominated by a timeless masculine concern with honor? Or, were gender and violence in the backlands only rhetorical constructs in service of national and regional disputes? Answering these questions requires both going beyond analysis of the discourses that have popularized these images and examining the variety of factors that have accounted for the conventionalization of specific types of masculine identity in backlands communities. For, as Pierre Bourdieu has shown, the values, discourses, meanings, and symbols that come to define gendered subjects and their identities do not pre-exist, isolated, in the domain of mental structure or ideology. Instead, gender identities are constituted through the daily experiences, rituals, and power relations that take place in social practice itself.[10]

Thus, this book examines the daily experiences of interpersonal violence and the concern with honor among free poor men from the *sertão*, or hinterlands, of the Northeastern province (colonial captaincy and present-day state) of Ceará between the years 1845 and 1889.[11] But unlike much of the recent research, it confronts the stereotype of backlander aggression and fixation with honor by analyzing the effects of broad-ranging structural shifts in the gender politics of sertanejo households and interior communities, and in the cultural meanings of honor. And it explains how and why some free poor *Cearense*[12] men reproduced a violent model of manhood—one that placed a premium on the male capacity to fight and "cleanse honor with blood"—in the interactions, discursive exchanges, and power relations they sustained with women, with their social superiors, and among their peers.[13]

The rapidly changing hinterlands of Ceará of the post-1845 years—a region that has been characterized as menacing—constitute the ideal locale for a study that, in challenging the image of the inherently belligerent sertanejo, also calls into question the enduring depiction of poor Latin American men as obsessively and essentially macho.[14] One of the most populous provinces of the Brazilian Empire, Ceará underwent deep economic and social transformations from the mid-1840s onward, which gradually reshaped the traditionally cattle-raising sertão into an area with a growing market economy based on both commercial agriculture and livestock breeding. Likewise, the second half of the nineteenth century witnessed the consolidation of the Imperial state in the backlands, a process that disrupted established structures of masculine authority and domination at the interpersonal level. These and other shifts transformed the social fabric of Cearense interior communities, reconfigured relations of inequality between men and women and power differences among men, and generated a measure of masculine violence. These conditions, in turn, had powerful implications on the social construction of masculine identities that were focused on the notion of honor, and in the functioning of gender.

My examination of criminal court cases, popular poetry, and contemporary novels from Ceará from the second half of the nineteenth century reveals that a sense of honor was central to the variety of social practices through which free poor sertanejos defined their masculine identities and negotiated both survival and positions of power with a variety of social actors. This collection of sources makes clear that men from this group, like their counterparts in other Latin American contexts, did, indeed, insist on *dar-se ao respeito*—literally, on making themselves be respected by others.[15] Honor functioned through the interplay between a man's conceptualization of his own worth and dignity and the social recognition or acceptance of that estimation by other members of his community.[16] Yet, a concern with honor was not only relegated to masculine arenas of sociability and competition, such as card games, fights, and drinking parties, or to the world of male jealousies caused by romantic attachments. Instead, as the sources from Ceará make evident, lower-class men asserted masculine respectability in their land disputes with poor neighbors as well as with *fazendeiros* (owners of large cattle ranches), in their dealings with slaves and with police authorities, and in their petty trade relations with local women as well as with male merchants from other towns. Clearly, a preoccupation with reputation was not merely a matter of masculine pride or the result of a cultural prescription. Rather, the concept of honor articulated normative ideas of appropriate manhood among the sertanejos with their positions in hierarchical relations with others.

In an effort to build a platform for the analysis of how sertanejo men structured gender identities relationally and in social practice, this study integrates research on the shifting social-economic conditions of the Cearense interior with an inquiry into the strategies of survival among free poor families. This task requires not only calling into question the enduring and often unsupported contention still made by a large body of scholarship that the latifundia system has always been the main landholding pattern in the region, but also reconstructing the agrarian history of the Cearense interior from archival sources.[17] Consequently, I demonstrate that during the period between 1845 and the mid-1860s, the emergence of a land tenure pattern based on smallholdings, in combination with the expansion of commercial agriculture, allowed a substantial class of sertanejo families to gain stable access to land and to achieve a measure of economic prosperity. These smallholding families participated actively and autonomously in the growing provincial economy through the adoption of livelihoods based on a combination of subsistence agriculture and small-scale commercial farming and ranching. Some even managed to purchase one or two slaves who assisted them in their productive activities. Furthermore, I argue that these conditions released the most fortunate of these families from onerous labor obligations toward large landowners or other patrons, and granted male smallholders as household heads a degree of prominence, autonomy, and authority to control their own labor power and that of others. Nonetheless, another series of broad-ranging upheavals from the mid-1860s onward, including changes in the international cotton market that had favored the free poor, the decline of slavery in the region, epidemics, the recruitment of poor men to fight in the Paraguayan War (1864–70), and the devastating Great Drought of 1877–79, undermined the tenuous prosperity and autonomy of this segment of the Cearense interior population. Indeed, those shifts brought downward mobility, dispossession, migration, separation of family members, and alterations in the small farmers and ranchers' means of earning their living.

My investigation into the transformations in the material conditions of smallholding families sets the stage for my analysis of both the corresponding shifts in gender politics within households and the different strategies that free poor men used to assert authority over women, both within and outside their households. This effort sets this book apart from much of the scholarship on the free poor populations of Brazil that has concentrated on what Hebe Mattos calls their "socio-economic agency" but has failed to analyze the connections between that type of agency and the functioning of gender.[18] As the following pages will make evident, sertanejo men exercised patriarchal authority over family women and articulated such power through the language of honor that is familiar to students of Latin American and Mediterranean cultures. Indeed, when they enjoyed a brief moment of prosperity in the years after 1845, male smallholders constructed honor as contingent on their ability to monitor the mobility and sexuality of female kin, and to control women's and children's productive labor within the household. Nevertheless, the dislocating transformations of the last third of the nineteenth century strained this gender order, and the practical possibilities of male defense and protection of the honor of family women. I build this argument on my finding, pieced together from scattered sources, that a significant stratum of free poor women became temporarily or permanently separated from male relatives as a result of the conditions of adversity that smallholding families faced from the mid-1860s onward. In fact, these women remained outside of familial patriarchy, as they earned their living and headed their households independently. I further illustrate the ways in which the very public presence of these autonomous females exposed the disjuncture between the ideal of patriarchal authority and the reality of insecurity in subsistence and familial disorganization affecting many among the poor. In this context, I argue that, as the exercise of private patriarchy became fragile, a public enforcement of patriarchy, often asserted through violence, partially filled that vacuum. This system of public patriarchy, in turn, operated to establish limits to female initiative and to ensure the continuation of some form of male authority in backlands communities living in a state of flux.

But poor rural men did not sustain gendered relations of authority solely over women. As feminist scholars of gender have shown, assertions of dominance and power that in many contexts are understood and legitimized as a masculine prerogative do not take place only in male-female, but also in male-male relationships.[19] Combining these insights with my focus on gender as built-in social practice, this book illustrates how relations of authority among males of all social groups—in charge as they were of defending and managing landed patrimonies—were affected by the intense conflict for control over productive resources that characterized the second half of the nineteenth century. Through analysis of criminal and civil court records and postmortem inventories, this study highlights the contested use of shared resources in joint landholdings, the competitive association between agriculture and ranching in a drought-prone environment, the continuous subdivision of smallholdings caused by partible inheritance, and the inability of the Imperial state in regulating property boundaries as factors that led to tensions among neighbors and coproprietors in the same estates. In those circumstance, claims to masculine respectability based on yardsticks of honor that denoted a degree of material success offered smallholding sertanejos a form of leverage, or social authority, in the face-to-face negotiations they sustained with other men for management of land, water, wood, and livestock. Likewise, this book reveals that during the period of intense hardship—the time when many small farmers and ranchers experienced downward mobility and some, even destitution—the social relations mediated by honor that neighbors and coproprietors used to regulate land issues and resource utilization, eroded. Even more, as poor sertanejos facing extreme urgency of survival could no longer reach compromises with their neighbors, they relied on violence as a strategy to protect their access to tenuously held landed patrimonies, wood, and water, and to retain possession of highly mobile livestock that grazed in the open range.

By focusing on the contradictory and shifting experiences of power of lower-class, rural men from Ceará, this study also analyzes their interactions with Imperial state institutions, as the police and the criminal- and civil-justice bureaucracy expanded into the backlands after the mid-nineteenth century. Inspired by a growing body of scholarship on the functioning of Imperial politics away from the center of power in Rio de Janeiro, my goal is to explore some features of the process of state building in a peripheral region.[20] In this way, I hope to illuminate how elite political projects that originated at the center affected not only a larger political system that extended to the periphery but also the functioning of gender and notions of honor among the less influential subjects of the Brazilian state. Although I leave the examination of partisan politics—a topic that deserves book-length analysis—to other scholars, I investigate some of the ways in which sertanejo men negotiated the paradoxes of the Imperial political system, which combined the practices of patronage, paternalism, and exclusion with the discourses of liberalism and equality.[21] Here, I demonstrate that poor rural men who by virtue of their class, illiteracy, lack of patrons, and racially mixed ancestry occupied an inferior rank within the seigniorial order of the empire, in fact, used the language of the dominant culture to wield a modicum of influence in courtrooms and police stations. As a large body of scholarship has shown, according to the ideology of the seigniorial class, paternalism, honor, and wealth guaranteed some men the enjoyment of political rights and ensured privileged treatment, even from representatives of the state.[22] In this sense, I contend that, in their attempts to outrank their tenuous social positions, Cearense small farmers and ranchers who obtained or retained a degree of material prosperity emphasized their possession of such markers of masculine honor as economic independence, property ownership, and capacity to provide for family members, as rhetorical tools to establish minimum claims to citizenship.[23] Clearly, such claims to honor do not constitute examples of the sertanejos' fixation with reputation or of the survival in the remote backlands of an anachronistic culture of honor. Instead, they represent strategies used by free poor men to assert political, civil, and even property rights, precisely as they inserted themselves and were inserted into the political practice imbued with honor and hierarchy that characterized the functioning of Imperial state institutions from Rio de Janeiro to Ceará.

This study also examines the violent contests for masculine authority that resulted from the accelerated, yet inefficient, consolidation in the Cearense backlands of the centralized criminal-justice and police apparatus. My scrutiny of how these features of an incomplete state formation process affected power struggles among free poor men distinguishes this study from the existing historiographical focus on how the failures of the Imperial state to monopolize the use of violence in rural areas conditioned contests for domination among local and regional elites.[24] Through analysis of manuscript correspondence, criminal records, as well as provincial presidents and police chief reports, I demonstrate that the regulative capacity of these state institutions was extremely weak. Indeed, while state authorities empowered poor backlanders as sources of state authority, these men did not possess the training, discipline, proper weaponry, and most important, legitimacy among the rest of the population to exercise that type of command. These conditions, I argue, generated a measure of aggression, since sertanejos resorted to the use of personalized, disorganized, and disordered acts of violence to impose a superior power—a form of authority that was sanctioned only by physicality—over other men. Predictably, rural men who were at the receiving end of belligerent state interventions also responded with hostility. A significant concern of mine in this regard is to lay bare that, far from being a consequence of the isolation of the backlands, this form of aggression was articulated and shaped by the ineffectual expansion of Imperial institutions that unleashed, and failed to resolve, tensions regarding the exercise of masculine authority and the legitimate use of violence, even among poor rural men.

In analyzing how the assertion of honor and manifestations of violence not only constituted strategies to deal with conflict but also gendered practices in defense of positions of power among free poor Cearense men, I have found R. W. Connell's theory of "hegemonic masculinities" a valuable interpretive approach.[25] According to this application of Antonio Gramsci's concept of hegemony to the study of gender, a hegemonic masculinity includes those strategies, norms, and practices that serve to guarantee men's authority over women and over subordinated masculinities. Equally important, practices and norms of hegemonic masculinity help legitimize the authority of the ruling class and are often reproduced by subordinate groups. Features of this dominant masculinity, as John Tosh describes, "are imposed on other social groups either by compulsion or through the pressure of social prestige," or are reproduced because they yield particular benefits to some men at the expense of the power of women and other men.[26] In accordance with these insights, I contend that in their everyday practice, speech, and postures, free poor backlanders manifested hegemonic masculinities focused on honor as contingent on their success as small proprietors and rulers of households, when they had the means to do so. Arguing that these sertanejos elaborated hegemonic masculinities does not imply that they were always the most powerful members of their families, villages, or ranches. Instead, I demonstrate that these men reproduced this model of masculinity because it not only allowed them to uphold citizenship rights and defend access to resources but also helped them maintain—even if momentarily—positions of authority over women and categories of men that they deemed inferior. In this sense, this book's gender approach allows us to address a persistent problem in the scholarship of the backlands. With a few exceptions, the literature has depicted free poor men—by virtue of their presumed landlessness—as continuously dominated by large landowners, and as incapable of sustaining relations of power or dominance over any other social group.[27]

My inquiry into the manifestation of hegemonic masculinities among free poor Cearense men reveals that some of them also used aggression to uphold the privileges of patriarchy and honorable reputations. Nevertheless, my analysis of these practices of violence as represented in criminal court records shows that belligerence was not an instinctive macho reflex. Rather, when verbal assertions of honor and claims to embody a form of social authority were no longer sufficient to negotiate both positions of power and survival, sertanejos resorted to interpersonal violence to accomplish those very same aims. Even more, as the series of economic, social, and political transformations, particularly of the last third of the nineteenth century, limited the range of strategies to defend the symbolic and material privileges associated with hegemonic masculinities, belligerence became the main tool for these free poor Cearense men to uphold a form of gendered dominance. As Connell has argued, the use of aggression is a meaningful component of systems of domination, but also "a measure of its imperfection."[28] The construction of hegemonic masculinities centered on honor and violence also took place in discursive practices that were not separated, but rather integrated, into the lived experiences of male backlanders. Through an examination of the discourse produced by poor rural men who engaged in fights, by popular bards who celebrated the violent deeds of courageous sertanejos, and by local male authorities who applied criminal laws to exonerate some acts of aggression, I demonstrate that various actors exalted courage as the "natural" masculine endowment that guaranteed a form of power or status. In turn, this discourse contributed to legitimize the use of male violence in service of the reproduction of power imbalances between men and women and within different groups of men.

This study also accounts for the challenges, especially from *sertanejas*, or free poor females, to the reproduction of hegemonic masculinities built on practices of domination and violence against women. In Raymond Williams's words, hegemony does not "passively exist as a form of dominance. It is continually resisted, limited, altered, challenged, by pressures not at all of

its own."[29] My focus on women's actions in opposition to their subordination within the household and to the reproduction of violent patriarchy that
was centered on the public beatings of unprotected females constitutes a
significant step in giving visibility to sertanejas as gendered subjects, a group
that, for the most part, has been virtually ignored in the historical scholarship.[30] Thus, I pay special attention to the use by autonomous women of the
criminal justice system as a strategy to obtain protection from and retribution
against men who physically abused them. Sertanejas did, indeed, denounce
such practices to local authorities and in some cases prosecuted their offenders. Yet, as this book also shows, the exercise of criminal justice played a
contradictory role in that it opened an avenue for women to contest their
victimization and at the same time contributed to the circulation in interior
communities of a discourse that sanctioned the use of masculine violence
in defense of honor and that regarded aggression, even against unprotected
women, as a "natural" male instinct.

While I emphasize the ways in which free poor Cearense men constituted
gender identities, meanings of honor, and violent strategies to assert power
and resolve conflict within a backdrop of change in their material and political environments, this study does not deny that they interacted within a
cultural context in which notions of honor that derived from Iberian models
continued to be central to interpret reality. Clearly, male backlanders drew
on what historian Thomas Miller Klubock has called in a different context
"the cultural resources at their disposal" to build their sense of honorable
manhood.[31] Still, the present research demonstrates that, far from being a
"traditional" system that did not evolve since its establishment during the
colonial period, as much of the historiography on the Northeast argues, the
"culture of honor" accommodated and adapted to the rapid transformations
of the post-1845 period. Accordingly, I understand honor as a cultural system
in a manner that resonates with William Roseberry's elaboration of culture
as at once "socially constituted (it is a product of present and past experience)
and socially constitutive (it is part of the meaningful context in which activity takes place)."[32] Thus, while political developments and material realities,
including landholding patterns and environmental pressures, were key in
shaping specific gender configurations, insofar as they conditioned power
relations in families and communities, it is also evident that sertanejos used
the cultural idiom of honor to make sense of their lives and identities. Just as
important, this book illuminates the ways in which cultural practices that had
honor and masculinity at their center, including ritualized verbal exchanges,
fights, patterns and rhythms of work, games, and everyday interaction, as well
as discourse, reproduced and naturalized patriarchy, re-created the boundar-

ies between masculinity and femininity, and legitimized particular forms of masculine domination in sertanejo communities.

In broader terms, this book uses a study of men and masculinities in the Cearense backlands to challenge the oft repeated stereotype of Latin American *machismo*—the depiction of Latin American men, especially from the lower classes, as essentially intransigent, misogynist, homophobic, and violent—that still abounds in popular culture and even in some scholarly work, both in the United States and Latin America.[33] As anthropologist Roger Lancaster has argued, efforts at dismantling this idea need to account for both the elaboration, within particular circumstances, of variant as well as dominant male ideologies that embody machismo, and the discursive construction of the operation of these gendered systems of power as normal, natural, and even necessary.[34] This book does not claim to locate the origins of the legendary macho, brave, and honor-obsessed masculinity of Northeastern men in the sertão of Ceará in the post-1845 years. But as an illustration of how masculine identities—even those that have so often been depicted as inherent to a particular group—are, in fact, constructed in practice and discourse within particular power relations and historical conditions, this book contributes to undermine the unitary notion of the Latin American macho. In doing so, this study also joins ongoing efforts by a growing body of interdisciplinary studies to replace the ahistorical, anachronistic, and essentialist machismo framework with a better paradigm to understand gender in Latin America—one grounded on the historical, cultural, and geographical specificity of gender patterns in the region.[35]

A Note on Sources and Methodology

Studying the construction of lower-class masculinities as embedded in social practice requires linking two areas of analysis that are often treated as separate entities: the history of social-economic and political structures and the emphasis on the process of formation of meanings and subjective identities that is associated with cultural history.[36] Thus, in this book I have undertaken the task of simultaneously researching aspects of the economic and social history of Ceará that have been poorly understood as well as the rituals, practices, and discourses that constructed hegemonic masculinities in specific locales from its interior. In order to trace the agrarian history that conditioned the strategies of survival of rural families, my research relies extensively on two types of manuscript sources: land registries and postmortem estate inventories. The land registries, a part of the Imperial registration of lands prescribed by the 1850 Land Law, were completed by parish priests throughout the 1850s. They provide a perspective on landholding patterns and property sizes in the townships of São Bernardo de Russas, Icó, São Gonçalo da Serra dos Cocos do Ipu, and Santa Quitéria. Even though they were located in different geographic sections of the province, these townships displayed similar topographies that allowed the development of both cattle ranching and agriculture in small, midsize, and large landholdings. I have verified the information from these localities through analysis of 245 postmortem inventories from the south-central municipality of Jucás, another agricultural and ranching township that possessed a variety of microclimates.[37] These probate records, increasingly used by historians who study the free poor populations in Brazil, list all the goods owned by a decedent at the time of his/her death. While these records do not provide information on the very poor who did not own any assets, since, in all likelihood, they could not afford the required judicial fees, postmortem inventories do offer invaluable data on land-tenure patterns among those who held at least some land as well as wealthier and larger landowners.

This study also relies on estate inventories for information on material conditions and economic activities. Reading these records against other sources, including foreign travelers' accounts and reports from scientific expeditions into interior townships, allows me to describe slaveholding patterns as well as agricultural and ranching practices among the free poor throughout the province. Furthermore, I compare information from data sets organized by decade to reconstruct the effects of social-economic change in the survival strategies of smallholding families over time. Lists of the decedents' creditors and debtors that are regularly attached to the inventories and the existence of postmortem inventories of Cearenses who possessed as little property as one head of cattle or one goat allowed me to document the material ruin and the precarious living conditions of members of the free poor as they faced hardship and environmental calamity.

In its examination of material reality, conflict, and the social construction of gender, this book makes extensive use of 450 criminal court cases from three different municipalities. These include Jucás, Tamboril—a ranching and agricultural township located in the midwestern section of the province—and Itapagé, a municipality with a variety of microclimates situated in the north of Ceará.[38] Criminal records constitute a uniquely rich source with which to gauge the effects of competition for resources in an unforgiving environment on the social relations between neighbors and coproprietors, as well as on other dimensions of tension. In order to determine to what extent the incidents of conflict presented in these cases were exceptional, I complement their analysis with an examination of civil cases and suits for demarcation of lands from the township of Jucás, and with descriptions of the interior by for-eign travelers and other outside observers. Investigation into the depositions of witnesses, plaintiffs, and defendants in criminal cases also puts in evidence the centrality of honor in the sertanejos' strategies to use and maintain access to productive resources. It furthermore illustrates the ways in which rural families organized social relations along the axis of gender.

Criminal court cases are also extremely useful to examine discourses and practices of violence both between men and against women, and the ways in which aggression played a role in the gender politics of sertanejo communi-ties. Several scholars have raised important questions, including the issue of representativeness, when using these cases as sources in the writing of social histories. They have asked if we can generalize from the experiences of the groups one frontier historian has called "the colorful few," who take greater risks, or in the case of violent crime, use aggression and enter the criminal record, to those of "the colorless many," who never appear in such cases. Likewise, historians wonder to what extent formulaic depositions produced in the artificial court setting reflect the true cultural values of people featured in these sources.[39] In order to address these limitations, I have compared the social profiles of plaintiffs, victims, and defendants, including data on occupa-tion, age, literacy, domicile, and social relations, with that of witnesses who also appear in criminal suits. In addition, I have read the depositions presented by various actors in courtroom dramas against information presented in con-temporary novels, foreign traveler accounts, popular poetry, police correspon-dence, and other reports. This analysis has demonstrated that, far from being a trait of social deviants, masculine aggression was inserted into a continuum of discourses and practices that included insults, taunts, physical abuse, and violent acts that were regarded as legitimate and justified in service of mascu-line domination and the establishment of a form of authority. I have also used criminal cases in this manner to study how men constructed understandings about the prerogatives of patriarchy and the challenges that women posed to masculine domination, both within and outside the household.

In the absence of other sources that reveal the cultural world of poor, il-literate backlanders, I have complemented my exploration of the everyday importance of honor, violence, and gendered authority with an examination of popular poetry produced and recited by backlands bards. The popular poetic tradition of the rural Northeast dates back to the colonial period, but toward the end of the nineteenth century, some of the oral songs and poems were written down and have thus survived in the form of published an-thologies. These collections contain the sung verses of *cantadores,* or popular poets, who engaged in poetic challenges, or *desafios,* with one another during the late nineteenth and early twentieth centuries, as well as the narrative poems that they performed in local market fairs and other public venues.[40] Transcripts of desafios are particularly helpful in my examination of the meanings and uses of masculine honor and aggression since this mostly masculine poetic genre chronicled long-standing rivalries between cantadores and included the stylized exchange of personal insults.[41] Critics of the use of oral sources as historical documents point to the existence of standardized motifs, predetermined structures, and conventional plots in manifestations of popular culture, such as poetry and folk tales, and to the difficulties in locating chronologically the cultural views expressed in them.[42] Yet, as historian Robert Darnton has demonstrated, it is possible to tease out historical meanings from oral sources "by relating them to the surrounding world of significance, passing from text to context and back again until the researcher has cleared a way through a foreign mental world."[43] Thus, I have paid special attention to the cantadores' dates of birth and death, to the references to specific late-nineteenth-century developments in their poetry, and to the commentary they offered about particular events of the period under study as a way to situate their poems chronologically. Moreover, I have analyzed the contents of the songs and improvised verses in relationship to the information on social, economic, and political conditions in the backlands gleaned from the well of archival and printed sources used in this study, and have not taken their meanings in isolation. This probing has allowed me to observe how cantadores adapted the inherited themes and structures of the desafio, including the concern with honor and respectability, to the late-nineteenth-century sertanejo audiences that shared an understanding of the specific motives that gave urgency and social value to those preoccupations. Likewise, I have tried to ascertain the ways in which cantadores, as free poor men, had a commonality of experience with other lower-class male backlanders that, in turn, allowed their poetry to communicate an historically specific worldview, and not just the repetition of meaningless traditional themes.[44]

The text that follows obeys a chronological and thematic organization. Chapter 1 examines how structural transformations, including the migration of drought refugees into the interior, the growth of a mixed rural economy, and the emergence of a land-tenure pattern based on small and midsize holdings, brought a degree of economic prosperity to a stratum of free poor sertanejo families during the period between 1845 and the mid to late 1860s. Chapter 2 traces the expansion of centralized state institutions in the Cearense hinterlands from the mid-nineteenth century with the goal of demonstrating the sertanejos' precarious legal position within the political order of the empire, and the ways in which they inserted honor into their political practice. This chapter also focuses on the violent struggles for masculine authority that were unleashed by the process of state-building—a paradoxical result, given the concern with imposing "order" that underpinned the strengthening of the police and criminal justice apparatus in the interior. Chapter 3 analyzes the relationship between, on the one hand, the heightened levels of competition for scarce resources and the inadequate system of land delimitation in the sertão, and on the other, the concern with maintaining honorable reputations demonstrated by poor rural men during the post-1845 years. The chapter also demonstrates how domestic gender arrangements under which males controlled the labor of women and children contributed to a structure of male power and privilege within smallholding families.

Chapter 4 maps out the adverse structural transformations that began in the mid-1860s and that precipitated the end of a period of modest prosperity for smallholding families. Here, I also investigate how pressures in the material and social conditions of free poor families disrupted the practices that were central to the constitution of hegemonic masculinities defined in terms of autonomy and ownership of material resources as emblems of honor. Chapter 5 examines how these changes in the economic fortunes of free poor families affected the lives of women and relations between men and women outside the household during these years of intense hardship. It makes evident that the large-scale absence of free poor men, which took place as a result of male migrations related to drought, army recruitment, and banditry, placed women in the position of household heads. The chapter also explores the use of aggression against autonomous women as a male strategy to reverse the disruption of normative gender roles and power that accompanied familial disorganization during this period. Chapter 6 explores how through the practice of violence in masculine spaces of sociability, young men—who were particularly affected by the devastating changes of the last third of the nineteenth century—constructed masculine reputation and privilege as contingent on violence. The chapter also shows how and why small farmers and ranchers who managed to maintain some property during the years of social-economic upheaval were increasingly unable to negotiate use of resources in nonviolent ways. An examination of the intensification of banditry from the 1870s follows, along with analysis of how the transformation of destitute sertanejos into brigands contributed to the elaboration, in discourse and in practice, of violence as a "natural" attribute of sertanejo masculinity.

Chapter 1

A Brief Moment of Prosperity:
Land, Opportunity, and Autonomy, 1845–70

In 1865, provincial president Lafayette Rodrigues Pereira declared that Ceará had become an "essentially agrarian province."[1] With this statement the highest political authority recognized the great transition that the province had undergone from an exclusive reliance on a pastoral and subsistence economy in the late seventeenth and eighteenth centuries. By the mid-nineteenth century Ceará's economy, and consequently the fortunes of its inhabitants, were more tightly linked to commercial agriculture and to the ebb and flow of international markets. Nevertheless, the cattle economy had not receded; instead, it grew along with agriculture during the 1850s, 1860s, and 1870s, until the calamitous drought of 1877–79 halted these gains and brought heavy losses to the industry.

For free poor sertanejos who had lived precarious existences at the margins of large cattle ranches, the development of commercial agriculture and the expansion of the ranching economy that began in the years following the catastrophic 1845 drought brought an opportunity to escape chronic poverty and extreme insecurity in living conditions. Moreover, as the following pages will demonstrate, by taking advantage of the small landholding pattern that came to characterize the province by the mid-nineteenth century, poor Cearense families were able to develop autonomous, if still vulnerable, livelihoods based on a combination of subsistence farming, small-scale commercial agriculture, and livestock grazing. Some even enjoyed a degree of prosperity that allowed them to purchase one or two slaves who assisted in domestic tasks and in farming and ranching activities performed in small plots of land.

The emergence of a land-tenure pattern based on smallholdings in the backlands of Ceará and other Northeastern provinces, and its implications for the lives of sertanejo families, have received little scholarly attention. This neglect in the historiography can be partially explained by the enduring representation of cattle ranchers and other large landholders as the owners of enormous extensions of land since the late colonial period into the present.[2] Some studies have demonstrated that renters, sharecroppers, and even squatters earned their subsistence as small farmers and ranchers during different historical periods. Nevertheless, even in those cases, the scholarship has tended to emphasize these groups' lack of "socio-economic agency." Thus, the small farmers and ranchers appear in the literature as entirely dependent on fazendeiros for access to land and, consequently, as virtually tied to their economic and political interests through relations of patronage and kinship.[3] As a result of this scholarly approach, little is known about rural cultivators' strategies of survival that did not include patron-client ties with fazendeiros. Just as important, we still need to unveil the position of small landholders and small-scale slaveowners in the organization of labor for the increasing commercial agriculture and ranching industries that developed precisely at the time when the province faced the decline of slavery that resulted from the 1850 cessation of the transatlantic slave trade.[4]

This chapter begins to address some of these questions. It demonstrates that the broad social-economic transformations of the mid–nineteenth century brought poor rural families into a new social position within the hierarchical relations that ruled life in interior communities. As smallholders and, sometimes, small-scale slaveowners, they gained a measure of independence, autonomy, and even authority, both over themselves and over other groups, in particular, slaves. Even more, the poor farmers' active participation in the provincial economy as small-scale producers of subsistence and export crops amounted to a form of competition with large landowners for access to and control over rural labor—their own labor. As we will see, large landowners who faced a shortage of workers clashed with smallholders bent on using their labor power in their own small-scale agrarian activities, instead of in the lands of others, as they sought to take advantage of the economic expansion of the post-1845 years.

The free poor Cearenses' moment of prosperity lasted only a few years. The provincial economy as a whole continued expanding during the second half of the nineteenth century. Nevertheless, as Chapter 4 will illustrate, economic transformations that began in the mid-1860s, including shifts in the international cotton market, coupled with rapid political and social change, would contribute to undermine the new prominence of the small farmers and ranchers. In effect, these shifts brought downward mobility, poverty, and dislocation to poor Cearenses. But the story of this chapter is a somewhat brighter one. It tells of the years when humble sertanejos in Ceará enjoyed a small degree of prosperity, security, autonomy, and perhaps more than anything, hope of a better life even within the hardship that living in the sertão represented for the poor.

Geographic Setting and Settlement of the Cearense Backlands

In order to understand the structural features of rural communities during the second half of the nineteenth century, it is first necessary to examine the topography and the patterns of settlement and colonization of the Cearense interior during the late seventeenth and eighteenth centuries. Geographically, the territory of Ceará is divided into two regions: the littoral—a narrow belt along the coastline that receives regular rainfall—and the broad semiarid backlands, covering the rest of the Cearense territory, conventionally called the sertão.[5] Climatic irregularity characterizes the hinterland. A rainy season extending from January to June may start as early as December or as late as March. Likewise, precipitation can vary enormously, ranging from excessive to insufficient rainfall, including episodic drought. In terms of flora, much of the backlands terrain is covered by tall grass—thus, the development of pastoral activities there since Portuguese occupation—and *caatinga* vegetation—xerophilous thorn shrubs and bushes that are able to withstand the irregular rains.

Two major river systems dominate the province: the southern and central portions of Ceará are influenced mainly by the Jaguaribe River, which originates in two smaller rivers that run downward from the Ibiapaba mountain range, located at the easternmost portion of Ceará. From there, the Jaguaribe cuts through the center to receive the Salgado River in the area of Icó, from where it changes direction toward the north to deposit its waters in the Atlantic Ocean, next to the port city of Aracati. The Acaraú originates in the smaller mountains of Matas and of the Serra das Bestas, cuts between the Meruoca and Uruburetama hills, and continues northward to the Atlantic. These two rivers form very wide valleys, sometimes measuring up to ten kilometers in width, that become completely flooded in rainy seasons. Nevertheless, until construction of large water dams in the twentieth century, the Jaguaribe, Acaraú, and their tributaries remained dry throughout most of the year. These conditions, coupled with the sandy and clayish soil consistency in the wide *várzeas* (valley bottomlands), made it almost impossible for sertanejos to take advantage of river irrigation to cultivate subsistence crops. The only crop capable of adapting to muddy ground during the winter, and

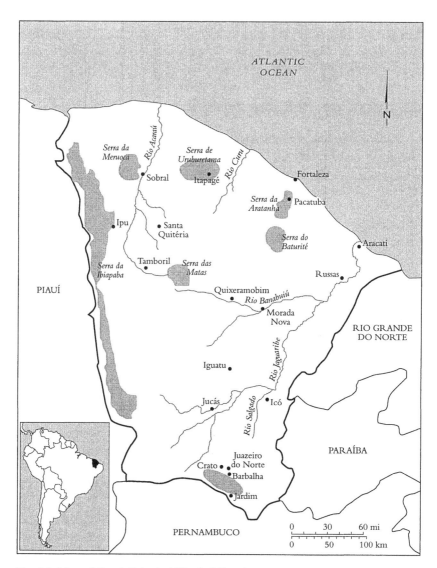

Fig. 1.1. Map of Ceará: Principal Physical Features.

hard, creaking terrains in the summer, was the *carnaúba* palm (*Copernicia cerifera*), which yielded a widely used wax and which grew naturally into true forests in many of the interior municipalities of Ceará. A series of small and fertile hills, or *serras*, such as the Baturité, Meruoca, and Maranguape ranges, lay scattered throughout the sertão. They enjoy regular rains even during the summer months of June to December, and therefore most of their slopes and *ipus* (adjacent terrains irrigated by water currents that descend from the mountains) constitute the best agricultural regions in the backlands.

To a large extent, climate and geography conditioned the patterns of colonization and the slow development of agriculture in the region.[6] Early efforts by Portuguese settlers and Jesuit missionaries to colonize the captaincy proved fruitless in generating settlements in the dry backlands. Severe droughts and constant Indian attacks obliterated the initial expeditions of the 1610s and 1630s. In the decades following the Dutch occupation of Ceará (1637–44), which also failed to translate into hinterland colonization, a few Portuguese settlers established primitive livestock ranches in the higher margins of the Acaraú and the lower Jaguaribe. Nevertheless, the *Tapuia* Indians[7] successfully impeded their permanent settlement by frequently stealing cattle and attacking the *fazendas* (large cattle ranches) and their owners. Effective occupation began around the 1670s and 1680s as an outcome of the great expansion of cattle ranching from the backlands of the colonial captaincies of Bahia and Pernambuco. Established cattle raisers from the middle São Francisco River valley who were seeking better or additional grazing lands reached the Parnaíba River basin in southern Piauí and from there moved eastward, into territories belonging to the captaincy of Ceará. By the 1680s, Bahian and Pernambucan cattlemen began setting up ranches along the headwaters of the Jaguaribe and Acaraú rivers, as they sought to take advantage of the várzeas' natural grasslands.

Central to the colonization of the interior was a generous Portuguese policy of awarding *sesmarias* (royal land grants) of large dimensions to influential settlers who vowed to use the lands they had conquered to raise cattle and to defend those territories from Indian attacks. The progressive establishment of extensive corrals on lands donated in sesmarias turned the Cearense backlands into an important supplier of cattle. Initially, livestock was transported live in *boiadas* (cattle drives) to fairs in the sugar plantation regions of coastal Pernambuco and, to a lesser extent, also to those in Bahia. But by the mid-eighteenth century, cattle raisers began establishing *oficinas* or *charqueadas* (rustic beef-salting factories) in Cearense ports from which they shipped salted beef and hides to various colonial markets in a more profitable and efficient manner.[8]

The expansion of the livestock-raising economy facilitated by the continuous award of sesmarias resulted in the creation of a pattern in which large cattle fazendas spread in the *sertões* (a word that in a restricted sense denotes the pasturelands of river and creek valleys), along with subsistence farming. The serras, or more humid rugged hills, remained mostly unsettled or inhabited by the Indian groups that had managed to survive the intensified warfare practiced against them between the late seventeenth century and the 1720s.[9] The colonization of the Cariri valley, situated in the southernmost portion of Ceará, constituted an exception to this overall pattern of settlement. Sugarcane agriculture developed there from the mid-eighteenth century on. Settlers from Bahia took advantage of the permanent irrigation that a series of streams that run downward from the Araripe mountains provided to the valley's fertile territory and produced *cachaça* (sugarcane brandy) and *rapaduras* (brown sugar cakes) from numerous *engenhocas* (small sugar mills), as well as foodstuffs.[10]

In a paradoxical manner, the droughts of 1777–78 and 1790–92 stimulated the dawn of commercial agriculture throughout the backlands. The severe drop in cattle production and the consequent disorganization of the salted beef industry that followed the droughts first generated an interest in agricultural activities. Moreover, in the late eighteenth century, the expansion of the British textile industry created a growing demand for raw cotton. Coupled with a 1799 decree that allowed direct trade between the captaincy and Lisbon, the growing demand encouraged the cultivation of cotton—especially its arboreal variety—throughout the interior. Indeed, attracted by the adaptability of arboreal cotton to semiarid as well as humid terrains, its short vegetative cycle, and the relatively low labor intensity it required compared with sugarcane, both large cattle ranchers and the sharecroppers who lived in their lands cultivated the crop in the different Cearense microclimates. By 1810, cotton had spread on the slopes of the Baturité, Uruburetama, Meruoca, and Aratanha mountains, as well as the Jaguaribe River valley, and had become the most significant product for the Cearense economy.[11] Even though of short duration (the participation of Brazil in the cotton boom came to an abrupt end in the 1820s, as a result of severe competition from the southern United States), the cultivation of cotton encouraged an expansion in the production of food crops, such as cassava or manioc, corn and beans, and stimulated migratory movements into the hinterland. The available figures indicate that the population of Ceará grew from approximately 61,400 inhabitants in 1782 to 125,800 in 1818.[12]

The period from the 1820s to the 1840s was marked by decline in the interior. Falling cotton prices in the international market and the devastat-

Table 1.1

Population Estimates for Ceará, Selected Years, 1782–1884

Years	Population	Years	Population	Years	Population
1782	61,408	1850	350,000	1872	721,686
1813	149,285	1857	486,208	1877	816,556
1819	201,170	1860	504,000	1879	712,000
1835	223,554	1864	540,000	1884	760,000

Sources: Sousa Brasil, *Ensaio estatístico*, 1: 289; Cavalcante, *Chorographia*, 145.

ing effects of the drought of 1824–26 severely affected the cattle and cotton economies. Political instability, widespread rebellion, and banditry brought additional hardship and dislocation to the poor inhabitants of the backlands. Nonetheless, the region experienced significant population increase during those years. The available estimates indicate that by the mid-nineteenth century the population of the province as a whole had more than doubled in size from what it had been around the late 1810s. (See Table 1.1.) Much of this demographic growth was concentrated in the backlands rather than the littoral. Roger Cunniff has demonstrated that while the coastal ports of Fortaleza and Aracati increased in population from 12,195 to 16,557 and from 8,100 to 8,805 between 1813 and 1837, the population of the township of Icó, in the upper Jaguaribe River valley rose from 1,258 to 9,307 inhabitants, and that of Crato, in the Cariri valley, from 10,747 to 17,199 persons.[13] In particular, the 1825 drought induced further migratory movements, changes in demographic patterns, and an escalating turn toward the planting of subsistence crops in the hillsides and valleys. In the areas in and around Baturité, for example, non-Indian settlers moved after the drought and quickly cleared fields to grow manioc and cereals, crops that they gradually replaced with sugarcane, and beginning in the 1840s, with coffee. The Tapuia Indians, who until the 1820s had been the main inhabitants of these lands, could no longer pose effective resistance, since they experienced near decimation caused by the drought and the subsequent smallpox epidemics of 1826.[14]

By the mid-nineteenth century, migratory movements and the initial expansion of commercial agriculture had already begun to transform the interior of the province of Ceará. The original pattern of colonization that had left vacant the hillsides and mountaintops had shifted. The increasing numbers of newcomers had commenced the processes of displacing the few surviving Indians, settling in serra lands and developing them for agriculture. These changes, in turn, continued attracting other migrants, who came to the hinterland from other Northeastern provinces also assailed by periodic drought and poverty. They were in search of land and better conditions that would allow them to escape the insecurity of landlessness and misery.

Mid-Nineteenth Century Land Tenure Structure

The shift in the pattern of settlement in the interior of Ceará was, in large part, encouraged by rapid transformations in the landholding structure based on large landholdings that began to take place during the late eighteenth century and continued during the nineteenth century. The sesmarias that had been awarded to cattle ranchers throughout the colonial period measured between one to three leagues in length by one league in width, or between 4,356 and 13,068 hectares. Crucially, there were no limits placed on the number of sesmarias that one particular individual could be granted. Celebrated in the history of Ceará for the number of sesmarias that they obtained are Lourenço Alves Feitosa, who possessed twenty-two land grants, José Bernardo Uchoa, who received fourteen sesmarias, and João de Barros Braga, who claimed eleven land grants.[15] Clearly, by the middle of the eighteenth century, notable Cearense families and their descendants held landed properties of enormous sizes. For instance, by 1722, José Gomes de Moura had come to hold five different sesmarias along the Salgado River, three in the sertões of Icó, and two in the mountainous district of Cariri. Each one of the sesmarias measured three leagues in length by one league in width, or 13,068 hectares. The total number of hectares claimed by Gomes de Moura was 65,340.[16]

Nevertheless, while some sesmaria-holding families from the Northeastern backlands were able to hold on to their large properties into the nineteenth century, a process of subdivision seems to have transformed sesmarias in some of the cattle-ranching districts of the region. According to contemporary observers traveling in the semiarid hinterlands along the middle São Francisco River in Bahia, for example, several of the once notorious large fazendas that had been installed in sesmaria lands had fragmented into very small properties as a result of inheritance practices. Portuguese succession laws, which remained valid in Brazil (with minor modifications until 1916), allowed primogeniture only in a few cases. Otherwise, those laws mandated a system of partible inheritance under which all recognized children received equal parts of the paternal and maternal wealth.[17] Accordingly, the British explorer Sir Richard Burton noted in 1867 that a fazenda that originally measured eleven leagues in length along the middle São Francisco had split into numerous landholdings during the course of three generations, and that the "multitudinous descendants of the original proprietor" occupied those small ranches. Some scholars have begun to examine the process of disintegration of sesmarias in backlands districts. For instance, in a study based on postmortem inventories, land registries, and deeds of purchase, Douglas

Araújo demonstrates that, because of inheritance practices, large sesmarias in the present-day municipalities of Caicó and Florânia, in Rio Grande do Norte, began a process of fragmentation in the mid-eighteenth century that continued throughout the nineteenth and twentieth centuries.[18]

While there is a dearth of studies detailing the subdivision of sesmarias in Ceará during the colonial period, Billy Jaynes Chandler's history of the Feitosas family of the sertão of Inhamuns allows us to observe this process in one cattle-grazing region during the nineteenth century. According to Chandler, the system of dividing inheritances worked to break up the sesmarias of large families within two or three generations. In an attempt to confront this trend, families of sesmaria holders and their descendants adopted strategies, such as selling smallholdings to more prosperous relatives or finding marriage partners from within the family, in order to regroup the properties. Despite these efforts, Chandler continues, several of the descendants of the original sesmaria owners could not halt the disintegration of their estates. This can be illustrated by the subdivision of the property of Colonel Antônio Martins Chaves, one of the descendants of Colonel José de Araújo Chaves, originally from Ipu, who received sesmarias in the Inhamuns area in 1717 and 1720, and of Francisco Alves Feitosa, the Feitosa family founder, who began acquiring sesmarias in the Inhamuns in 1707. By the time of his death, in 1873, Antônio Martins Chaves had come to possess seventy-five separate properties, which included a number of very large fazendas in sizes that exceeded 10,000 hectares. However, his descendants could not impede the effects of dividing inheritances, and by the early twentieth century they were impoverished and possessed only the fragments of Martins Chaves's original estates.[19]

Fragmentation caused by dividing inheritances seems to have transformed some of the sesmarias in agricultural regions of Ceará. A recent and still unpublished study by Yony Sampaio, for instance, documents the progressive disintegration of large sesmarias in the municipality of Barbalha, located in the Cariri valley. In 1717, six individuals received a sesmaria grant that measured eighteen leagues in length and that encompassed nearly the entire territory within the current borders of Barbalha. But, from the 1750s onward, sales of portions of the sesmaria began to reduce its size. Equally important were the subdivisions that resulted from inheritance. Thus, by the end of the eighteenth century, as a result of both inheritance and land sales, more than twenty smaller *sítios,* or farms, had been dismembered from the original sesmaria of Barbalha.[20]

In addition to the breakup of a number of sesmarias due to inheritance and sales, the lack of land legislation in the Brazilian Empire until 1850 contributed to the transformation of land tenure patterns in Ceará. The colonial system of sesmaria grants was abolished in 1822, shortly before Brazil's declaration of independence. During the next twenty-eight years, the parliament of independent Brazil failed to pass any legislation regulating the acquisition of land in the public domain as private property. The absence of land legislation, in turn, gave way to a widespread de facto recognition of squatters' possession rights to the *posses* (landholdings alienated through occupation instead of formal grant) they claimed. Although they did not amount to full private ownership, possession rights to land could be sold and bequeathed to heirs. Those possession rights had, in fact, legal precedent on the *Ordenações Filipinas,* the Portuguese law code passed in 1603.[21] It was only in 1850 that, finally, the Brazilian parliament approved a new law regulating the acquisition of land on the frontier. The law prohibited simple squatting and required squatters to purchase land in the public domain. But, by all accounts, the Land Law of 1850 was ineffective in controlling the private appropriation of public lands.[22]

From the available sources, it is impossible to assess the extent of effective occupation of public lands in Ceará. The extent, no doubt, varied, within the province, across regions. But contemporary reports suggest that the mid-nineteenth century witnessed the rapid settlement of previously unoccupied lands. For instance, letters from the president of Ceará to the minister of agriculture stated that there were no more unclaimed lands available for occupation in the municipality of Milagres, whereas, only "a few" public lots were still unoccupied in Baturité and Imperatriz in 1861. The renewed migration into the interior by refugees who had been displaced from their homes in the backlands of other Northeastern provinces during the droughts of the years 1845 to 1847 resulted in further occupation of public lands in the partially populated serras and other humid regions. In fact, according to Tomás Pompeu de Souza Brasil, by the late 1850s, newcomers increasingly found it difficult to obtain hillside lands that could be developed for agriculture. As a result, they began settling in some of the permanently dry regions and even populated the pasturelands previously reserved for cattle ranching, thus coming into conflict with established cattlemen.[23]

In any event, the predominance of the posse regime between 1822 and 1850, the largely ineffective enforcement of the 1850 Land Law, which translated into continued occupation of frontier lands, and the partible inheritance system encouraged the emergence of a fragmented pattern of land tenure in newly occupied regions of the interior. Obviously, migrants to previously unsettled areas could, in principle, lay claim to the possession of sizable stretches of territory. Indeed, two entries from the land registry of the township of Santa Quitéria demonstrate that notable men such as José Rodrigues Veras Júnior and Joaquim Rodrigues Veras, members of the influential Araújo family, obtained some of their properties through squatting. These men recorded in the Santa Quitéria registry two of their posses in the Lugar Paus Brancos, including a landholding measuring 3,267 hectares, which had been acquired through effective occupation in the years 1803 and 1828.[24] But even in such cases, the system of partible inheritance again worked to break up those holdings. Here the crucial variable was the number of children who inherited their parents' wealth. A sample of thirty postmortem inventories carried out in Jucás in the 1830s suggests an average of six surviving children per family. That average seems to match childbearing patterns in other municipalities. For example, the botanist Francisco Freire Alemão commented that the estate of a Pacatuba landholder, encompassing the whole Serra da Aratanha, ended up divided into eight separate smaller sítios among his heirs, who subsequently put them to use independently.[25]

Quantitative analysis of the land registries completed, as a result of the 1850 Land Law, help illustrate the landholding structure that had come to prevail in three backlands parishes by the mid-nineteenth century. Table 1.2 and Figure 1.2 show the distribution of landholding sizes, converted to hectares, in the parishes of Russas, Icó, and Santa Quitéria.[26] The registries contained information on the frontage size of some of the properties measured

Table 1.2

Distribution of Landholding Sizes in Hectares, Townships of São Bernardo de Russas, Icó, and Santa Quitéria, 1855–58

(Number of Properties According to Size, and Percentages of All Properties)

Townships	Agricultural plots (0–100 hectares)	Very small ranching/ midsize agricultural properties (101–500 hectares)	Small properties for ranching (501–1,500 hectares)	Midsize properties for ranching (1,501–4,360 hectares)	Sesmaria-scale properties (4,361–21,800 hectares)
Russas	50 (43.10%)	44 (37.93%)	14 (12.06%)	3 (2.58%)	5 (4.31%)
Icó	143 (30.81%)	213 (45.90%)	60 (12.93%)	40 (8.62%)	8 (1.72%)
Santa Quitéria	38 (26.76%)	29 (20.42%)	20 (14.08%)	36 (25.35%)	19 (13.38%)

Sources: RT, Freg. Nossa Senhora do Rosário da Vila de São Bernardo, 1855; RT, Freg. Cidade do Icó, 1858; RT, Freg. Santa Quitéria, 1855, APEC.

Note: These calculations are based on a sample of entries that contained information on property sizes from each of the three land registries. Not all entries in the land registries specified the measurements of each property. Thus, for Icó, 464 out of a total of 512 entries, and for Santa Quitéria, 142 out of a total of 1,078 registries, provided land sizes. For the township of Russas, 116 of the 133 entries that were available for consultation in my research trip of 2002 provided property sizes.

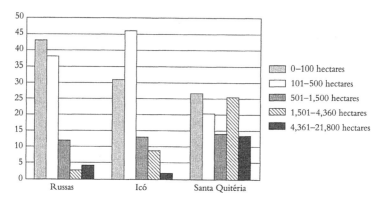

Fig. 1.2. Size of Landholdings in Hectares, Townships of São Bernardo de Russas, Icó, and Santa Quitéria, 1855–58. Sources: RT, Freg. Nossa Senhora do Rosário da Vila de São Bernardo, 1855; RT, Freg. Cidade do Icó, 1858; RT, Freg. Santa Quitéria, 1855, APEC.

in braças and leagues. Most entries, however, failed to specify the depth of the properties. But from information contained in civil suits and other documents, it is more than safe to assume that most properties extended somewhere between a half-league and one league backward from the streambeds where the frontage was estimated.[27] The converted measurements, therefore, result from the assumption that, on average, properties were one league in depth.

The data clearly indicate that small and midsize holdings had come to predominate in the property map of these townships. In Russas and Icó, more than three-quarters of the properties (81 percent and 76.7 percent, respectively) were constituted by small agricultural plots of less than 100 hectares, and very small ranching holdings measuring between 101 and 500 hectares. In the two parishes, around 12 percent of all properties measured between 501 and 1,500 hectares, an area that in the semiarid backlands where cattle-raising continued to represent an important economic activity can be considered small. According to Chandler, at least 1,000 hectares of land were necessary to sustain 50 to 150 head of cattle in years of normal rainfall. This herd size was the minimum needed for a fazenda to constitute a self-perpetuating and viable economic unit.[28] Midsize properties for cattle ranching constituted 2.58 percent and 8.62 percent of all landholdings in Russas and Icó, respectively. All importantly, sesmaria-size properties measuring more than 4,361 hectares represented only a very small minority of the properties in the two townships.

This fragmented configuration of landholding would seem, at first sight, to be derived exclusively from the geographic and environmental conditions of these two townships, which facilitated the development of agriculture in smallholdings. Russas featured slopes with fertile soils, which were well suited for the cultivation of sugarcane and manioc, a natural exuberance of carnaúba palms, arable lands irrigated by dams in the caatinga, and sertão lands for grazing. The quality of land in most of the township of Icó was dry, and appropriate for grazing. Yet, the same land became fertile during the rainy season. Agricultural crops could also be planted along the riverbeds and near water dams. Nevertheless, a similar complex profile of property sizes can be observed in Santa Quitéria—one of the most important grazing townships of the province—located in very dry and flat terrain, where a few scattered rocky serras could not be used for year-round agriculture.[29] There, a more concentrated pattern of distribution of landholding size can be observed, in comparison with the two other townships. Still, almost half of the holdings (47.18 percent) were small agricultural plots and very small ranching properties. Small and midsize properties for ranching constituted another 39.43 percent of the sample. Furthermore, even though sesmaria-scale properties were more numerous in Santa Quitéria, and tended to be larger (the largest property measured 21,800 hectares in Santa Quitéria, 17,424 hectares in Russas, and 13,068 hectares in Icó), they still represented a minority of all properties, at 13.38 percent.

Analysis of some of the individual entries in the land registries permits us to visualize the relationship between a pattern of agrarian organization in which a few large fazendas coexisted with a large number of smaller properties and the complex world of opportunities for a diverse array of inhabitants of the backlands. The land registries do confirm the existence of enormous landholdings and the concentration of those lands in the hands of very wealthy families. For instance, Francisco de Paula Pessoa, originally a merchant from the municipality of Sobral and a prominent member of the Liberal Party, who culminated his political career as a senator of the empire in 1848, held the most numerous and the largest properties of those compiled in the Santa Quitéria registry. He declared possession of thirty-one individual holdings of various sizes. Among them were three leagues of land (approximately 13,068 hectares) that encompassed the Fazendas Santa Quitéria and Pé de Serra, the Sítio das Barrigas, measuring four leagues of frontage (approximately 17,424 hectares), and the five leagues of land (approximately 21,800 hectares) along the Groaíras River, where another three of the senator's fazendas were located. Not all the entries of this individual landholder specified the methods through which he had acquired access to those lands. But the sixteen that did make clear that he had purchased eight landholdings from diverse sellers and had inherited another eight from the estate of his father-in-law, Colonel Vicente Alves. Interestingly, only two of the holdings that he inherited were qualified as sesmaria lands. Biographical information on the senator reveals that he situated most of the large fazendas that he purchased in the township of Santa Quitéria, as he became connected by marriage to the descendants of the Pinto de Mesquita family, whose ancestors had received a number of sesmarias, beginning in 1733.[30]

Nevertheless, the land registries also provide a portrayal of landholding that deviates from the more classical image of the Northeastern backlands as dominated by great latifundia owners and large cattle fazendas. This is possible to observe in the registry for the township of Icó, where information on literacy of the registrants was recorded consistently. There, of a total of 512 entries, 107 were listed by illiterate people. While it is true that illiteracy was common in the backlands, even among the more prosperous men (with a few exceptions, women, even from influential families, were illiterate), it is plausible that at least some of the illiterate claimants of landholdings in the registry were members of the free poor population. This can be determined by the absence of notable families' last names, the lack of names of *procuradores*, or persons with power of attorney who registered the land claims and signed the entries of more prosperous families, and the fact that these registrants claimed ownership or possession of only one small landholding. For instance, João José de Oliveira, an illiterate man, registered one landholding in the Lugar França, measuring 100 braças of frontage (approximately 145 hectares), that he had purchased from Francisco de Paula de Barellos. José Pedro Barroso, another illiterate man, listed one plot "of more or less" 100 braças of frontage that he had purchased in the Sítio Mandacaru from João Evangelista do Espírito Santo. Another illiterate man, Manoel Duarte da Assunção, claimed to be possessor of one landholding of 48 braças (approximately 70 hectares) that he had purchased in the same sítio. These smallholders, in all likelihood, could afford to purchase their plots of land because their prices were relatively inexpensive by mid-nineteenth century. Fertile agricultural lands could cost between Rs. 6$000 and Rs. 1$000 per braça, depending on quality of soil and nearness to sources of water, while grazing lands cost as little as Rs. $500 per braça. Thus, João José de Oliveira and José Pedro Barroso in all likelihood paid either Rs. 50$000 or Rs. 100$000 for their properties measuring 100 braças, if we consider that much of the territory of Icó was made up of dry lands suitable for grazing year round and for agriculture only during the rainy season. By comparison, during the same years, a pregnant cow could sell for up to Rs. 25$000, and a horse for Rs. 80$000.[31]

Table 1.3

Registration of Landed Property in the Township of São Gonçalo

da Serra dos Cocos, c. 1856

Number of holdings[a]	Number of landholders	Percentage of sample total
1	256	60.95
2	77	18.33
3	29	6.90
4	27	6.42
5	13	3.09
6 to 10	13	3.09
11 to 15	3	0.71
More than 15	2	0.47
	Total 420	99.96

Source: RT, São Gonçalo da Serra dos Cocos, Comarca do Ipu, 1856, APEC.

[a] I added the total number of holdings that individual landholders claimed in both single and separate registrations. The total number of holdings in the sample is 856 described in 636 individual entries or registries.

Note: The surviving sample includes 636 entries or registries, filed by 420 different individuals.

Analysis of the number of landholdings for which individuals filed entries in the land registries provides an idea of the proportion of smallholders with access to landed resources. Here, we can begin by analyzing the land registry of Ipu, a township located directly on the Ibiapaba mountain range in northwestern Ceará, which, like Russas, possessed moist areas suitable for agriculture on the mountain slopes, as well as caatinga areas for cattle raising.[32] (See Table 1.3.) The property map of Ipu, as were the cases of Russas, Icó, and Santa Quitéria, was characterized by subdivided properties. In fact, a total of 1,060 entries constitute the entire land registry of this township. Examination of the number of landholdings for which individuals filed entries there demonstrates that 7.4 percent of the landholders declared possession of five or more plots of land of various sizes, while 31 percent claimed two to four pieces of land. Even more important, the land registry entries from Ipu reveal that more than 60 percent of the landholders claimed rights, either jointly or singly, over one piece of land. It is difficult to assess to what extent these data exaggerate the real proportion of holders of one plot, because of the possible reregistration of jointly held lands by different co-owners.[33] Nevertheless, probate records from Jucás, a south-central municipality that, like Ipu, possessed a variety of microclimates, confirm the trend observed in that township. Postmortem inventories from the period between 1830 and the 1850s indicate that 49 percent of landholding families in Jucás declared one plot of land as an inheritable asset, while 5.6 percent declared five or more holdings.[34]

The land registries and postmortem estate inventories clearly show that, by the mid-nineteenth century, a substantial stratum of holders of one small or medium-size land parcel shared control over rural property with a group of more prosperous landholders in five different backlands townships. The vague and variable nomenclature used in these documents makes it impossible to determine the methods through which these smallholders, whether migrants who settled in unoccupied lands or impoverished descendants of original landholding families, had acquired access to their one plot of land. For the most part, the entries do not consistently reveal whether that access was predicated on squatting on public lands, purchase, exchange, or inheritance of landholdings derived from sesmarias. But the documents clearly reveal that free poor smallholders enjoyed a small degree of stability in their occupation and usufruct of those lands. This stability, in turn, explains their appearance as landholders in the land registries of the 1850s and as decedents who left small plots of land as inheritable assets to their heirs, in the postmortem inventories.

Cearenses who did not inherit or occupied landholdings, or who lacked sufficient income to purchase landed property or additional plots, could obtain more or less stable access to arable and grazing land through other methods. Those methods included *aforamento*—a form of emphyteusis—and land rentals. In the municipalities of Jucás and Tamboril, *foreiros* held rights to planting or grazing fields, including inheritance rights, in the form of perpetual leases of lands belonging to the *patrimônios*[35] of the parishes of Nossa Senhora do Carmo and Santo Anastácio, respectively. Contracts of aforamento varied, from the leasing of large tracts of land to small and medium-size plots, as in the case of the illiterate farmer Francisco Fernandes de Oliveira from Jucás, who paid Rs. 12$000 annually for 300 braças of foreira lands in the Patrimônio of Nossa Senhora do Carmo. *Rendeiros,* or tenant farmers, typically rented lands to plant subsistence crops or other staples. Contracts established different lengths of tenure on rented lands, varying from one to six years, payable annually and in cash.[36]

Other land tenure arrangements in place in Ceará also made possible access to landed resources to poor Cearense families. Settled in lands belonging to larger or more prosperous landowners, *moradores,* sometimes called *agregados,* either paid a minimum amount as rent or simply lived and planted beans, corn, and manioc in lands that the landowner yielded them for their own use. In exchange for access to land, moradores sometimes performed services as the landlords requested, or in areas more heavily populated, such as the Cariri, they dedicated two or three days of the week to tend the landowner's fields.[37] In the same region, this relationship could also have a sharecropping component, by which the proprietor had the right to half of the morador's rice harvest.[38] Crucially, recent literature for other regions has indicated that because of the availability of frontier lands, especially during the first half of the nineteenth century, landowners could not force moradores to provide more than a day's labor for themselves. When conditions in the land where they had settled became too onerous, moradores could easily move to other areas, clear some lands, and begin planting subsistence crops. In fact, M. A. de Mornay, the foreign observer who lived in Pernambuco in the 1840s, remarked that moradores were "tenants at will" who did not pay rent.[39] Thus, it is plausible that under similar conditions in the backlands of Ceará, even moradores and agregados enjoyed an amount of control over their own lives, and over their strategies of survival.

On the whole, the available evidence indicates that, by the 1850s, small and medium-size holdings predominated in the interior of Ceará. This land tenure pattern resulted from a series of factors, including the subdivision of sesmarias caused by partible inheritance and land sales, and the rapid settlement of frontier areas, encouraged by the lack of land legislation since 1822. Just as important, this landholding structure allowed a substantial group of rural Cearenses to obtain more or less stable access to land. As we will see below, this group of free poor sertanejos were able to take advantage of the expanding agriculture and ranching economies at the provincial level to develop more secure agrarian-based livelihoods and to reach a degree of autonomy and control over their own lives.

Smallholders and Small-Scale Slaveowners in the Expanding Agricultural and Livestock Economies, 1845–70

By the start of the second half of the nineteenth century, the province of Ceará began to experience a marked growth in its commercial agriculture both for export and for internal markets.[40] This process was facilitated in part by the greater political stability enjoyed at the provincial and Imperial levels and paralleled, albeit on a smaller scale, the overall growth of the Brazilian agricultural export economy.[41] In Ceará, the disastrous effects of the 1845 drought on the cattle-ranching economy prompted a shift toward commercial agriculture with the entrance of new cash crops, including coffee, tobacco, carnaúba wax, and rubber. While coffee and tobacco (twist tobacco being the variety produced in Ceará) were commercialized within and outside the province, the carnaúba wax and rubber that were extracted in the province were sold in overseas markets. The cultivation of sugarcane, cereals, and manioc, products that during the first half of the nineteenth century had been sold mainly in local markets, expanded rapidly after 1845,

Table 1.4
Cotton Exported from Fortaleza, 1845–85 (selected years)

Years	Kilos exported	Price (réis per kilo)	Years	Kilos exported	Price (réis per kilo)
1845–46	124,757		1867–68	4,332,412	$912
1847–48	249,603		1868–69	4,686,300	$1014
1849–50	368,207		1869–70	5,219,147	$780
1851–52	630,337		1870–71	7,253,893	$560
1852–53	991,628		1871–72	8,324,258	$605
1855–56	954,062		1872–73	4,970,064	$567
1857–58	1,128,168		1874–75	5,738,090	
1859–60	1,139,354		1876–77	3,082,420	$377
1860–61	863,479		1877–78	1,314,574	
1861–62	745,828	$855	1878–79	628,948	
1862–63	646,050	1$275	1879–80	683,879	
1863–64	888,290	1$600	1880–81	2,071,625	
1864–65	1,403,261	1$090	1881–82	5,270,269	
1865–66	2,002,114	1$190	1883–84	4,433,771	
1866–67	2,380,838	$770	1884–85	3,072,195	

Sources: Girão, *História econômica*, 218–19; Guabiraba, *Ceará*, 205–6; Cunniff, "The Great Drought," 81.

as the province of Ceará increasingly exported them to its neighbors. Then, in the 1860s, as a result of the interruption of the American supply of cotton to the European textile industry because of the U.S. Civil War (1861–65), a cotton boom again swept the Northeastern hinterland.[42] With increasing international demand and prices, cotton-growing in Ceará experienced a true revitalization; during the years between 1845 and 1871 cotton exports soared, as cultivation of the crop spread to almost all of its different microclimates. (See Table 1.4.) Furthermore, after recovering from the heavy losses of the midcentury drought, the cattle-ranching industry, both for internal consumption and export, also expanded and regained an important place in generating finances for the province.

This diversified agriculture and the expanding livestock industry unleashed a series of other social transformations, not the least of which was a renewed process of demographic expansion and further settlement of partially populated serras and even already inhabited várzeas, hillsides, and sertões. As Table 1.1 indicates, the provincial population had more than doubled in size between the early 1850s and 1877, from 350,000 to 816,556 inhabitants. Most of the Cearenses who participated in the growing commercial agriculture and ranching economies and those coming from neighboring provinces to take advantage of the cotton boom were *pardos* (persons of mixed African and European descent). The 1872 census revealed that pardos constituted 49 percent of the free population of Ceará; 39 percent of the province's free inhabitants were white while free blacks and *caboclos* (racially mixed individuals with Indian ancestry) accounted for 12 percent.[43]

The expansion of commercial agriculture in these years took place within the pattern of small- and medium-size holdings that had come to characterize the province by the mid-nineteenth century. As late as 1879, João Brígido, representative of Ceará to the Brazilian parliament, pointed out that "in the Southern region of the empire, large landholdings are considered effective. Here [in the Southeast], the more profitable agriculture based on smallholdings is unknown." By contrast, in Ceará before the Great Drought, he noted, "[We] sent almost 140,000 sacks of cotton, and we did not have large landholdings, or large [agricultural] fazendas." In 1886, Tomás Pompeu de Sousa Brasil remarked on the peculiar land distribution arrangement in Ceará, where "the fazenda, with a multitude of slaves living in *senzalas* (slave huts) does not exist." This Cearense statistician further pointed out that "peasants [*camponeses*] from the poor class were responsible for most of the agricultural production in Ceará."[44] In effect, as we will see, the transformations in the quarter century after 1845 provided families of rural cultivators with the means to derive more or less autonomous livelihoods based mainly on subsistence and small-scale commercial agriculture and the selling of small numbers of livestock.

Poor Cearenses traditionally grew beans, corn, manioc, and when possible, also rice for family consumption in subsistence plots. In years of abundant rainfall, even the poorest peasants had enough surpluses to sell either in weekly *feiras* (open-air markets) or through personal networks with neighbors, acquaintances, and itinerant merchants. By the late 1840s, however, smallholders had embraced commercial farming of breadstuffs to the point that the provision of these crops at the provincial level depended almost entirely on small farmers. Indeed, contemporary observers noted that as a result of this group's participation in the cultivation, harvesting, and marketing of food staples, the province of Ceará had become self-reliant in breadstuff production. What is more, smallholders turned to the cultivation of even more profitable commercial crops, alongside food staples, during these years. They especially favored crops that required low investment and that could be planted and harvested with the employment of family labor or the use of a few hired workers or slaves.[45] Thus, according to the authors of two articles that appeared in the *Cearense* in 1857, the small farmers' growing "abandonment" of the cultivation of manioc and cereals and their increasing predilection for cotton, tobacco, carnaúba, rubber, and even coffee had contributed to the considerable price increase in food staples during the 1850s.[46]

Of all the commercial crops cultivated or extracted by Cearenses during the years of agricultural expansion, cotton gained the widest preference among small farmers and peasants because of its flexibility (it can be intercropped with food staples), and the relative small labor force required to plant and harvest the trees. Sertanejos favored the arboreal, or tree, cotton from Maranhão, even though British buyers and government officials took some measures to encourage the cultivation of the higher-yielding, better-priced bush cotton. Poor Cearenses preferred the arboreal variety because cotton trees blossomed in a shorter time. Moreover, once planted, a cotton tree could yield two or three harvests, whereas cotton bushes needed to be replanted each year. Thus, cotton, and in particular arboreal cotton, became the "crop of the poor." Contemporaries reported that the cotton rush of the 1860s was a "fever" that "hallucinated" everyone, including manioc and cereal farmers, as well as women who "left the looms behind" in order to cultivate the precious crop.[47]

The cotton boom brought about a new-found, if short-lived, affluence and economic independence to many of the rural poor. That affluence, of course, depended on their ability to market their crop. Free poor sertanejos did, indeed, commercialize their cotton in different ways. Observers at the time described the high traffic of oxcarts loaded with cotton traveling the dirt roads of the interior, as well as the vibrant commercial exchanges that took place in backland towns and in Fortaleza. *Comboieiros* (wagon drivers) and farmers reportedly transported cotton and filled urban warehouses and stores, where they sold their merchandise and bought "necessary as well as superfluous" goods. According to one observer, leather-clad sertanejos who "had never seen the sea" sold their harvest on credit in Fortaleza and bought cloth, thread, rosaries, combs, matches, spices, and other items to take back to their families in the hinterland.[48] Other small cotton farmers sold their product in their own localities to larger landowners, who collected and commercialized it, or who possessed *descaroçadores* (cotton gins) on their land. Intermediary agents from big commercial houses such as Casa Boris from Fortaleza also bought cotton in the interior directly from both small as well as larger-scale farmers.[49]

The provincial livestock economy also expanded rapidly after 1845, despite a temporary decline during the dry years of 1846 and 1847. Yet, contrary to traditional interpretations of the cattle-ranching activities typical of the Northeast, a variety of contemporary sources clearly indicate that smallholders actively participated in the grazing industry.[50] Already in 1808, Antonio José da Silva Paulet observed that small fazendas existed in different regions of the then captaincy of Ceará, with as few as thirty head of cattle, and the largest with about four hundred animals. In the early 1840s, Gardner noted that most of the inhabitants of Várzea da Vaca, in Jardim, whom he called "cattle farmers," possessed herds that ranged from half a dozen head to just over a hundred. The open range type of grazing practiced in Ceará allowed small ranchers with insufficient lands to raise small herds of livestock. For example, Paulet complained that many of the small fazendas that he observed in Ceará in the early nineteenth century were in reality refuges for "vagrants" who, "hiding behind the title of criadores" took advantage of the fields of neighboring fazendas. Smallholders also raised goats and sheep, types of livestock that they referred to as *miúdos*, which they commercialized for small prices or used to feed themselves and their families.[51]

An analysis of estate inventories from the municipality of Jucás provides a view of the ways in which free poor Cearenses in rural areas took advantage of the expanding provincial economy and developed agrarian-based livelihoods to ensure household and family survival. Here, we can begin with families that declared ownership of a single plot of land since they tended to be poorer than those with more than one plot.[52] Of the families in Jucás that claimed only one piece of land as an inheritable asset in the 1860s, 91 percent raised at least a small number of livestock, ranging from four to fifteen head. Typically, their livestock included calves, cows, steers, bulls, and, less often, oxen, both young and adult, as well as goats and sheep. Most families, even the poorest who had two or three cows, kept horses for transportation purposes, while some families obviously raised colts, horses, mules, and sometimes burros either for sale or for use in hauling businesses. Nearly half (47 percent) of families who had access to at least one piece of rural property declared animals as their only significant inheritable assets besides land, while 22 percent of families with one landholding declared fruit trees, and *cargas,* or sacks,[53] of manioc, beans, rice, tobacco leaves, and cotton, besides animals, as items to bequeath to their heirs. In turn, 17 percent of all families with one landholding had as their only inheritable assets a handful of animals and a few simple agricultural implements, such as hoes, scythes, and axes. These figures indicate that most poor families who owned a single piece of land were able to combine subsistence agriculture with small-scale ranching, and that, in some cases, they also managed to cultivate commercial crops. These inventories further demonstrate that even those who engaged in wage labor as day laborers, cowboys, oxcart drivers, ranch-hands, or cattle drovers had small numbers of cows, sheep, and goats to supplement their income, and that, in many cases, they also could grow subsistence crops, which, in turn, granted them a degree of autonomy from exclusive dependence on full-time work for others.

Ownership of or access to an additional plot of land allowed poor rural families to engage more extensively in commercial agriculture. Estate inventories reveal that those families often grew food crops for sale, processed manioc for *farinha* (cassava flour), and also cultivated tobacco, cotton, fruit trees, and even sugarcane. As in the case of the families with one landholding, livestock raising was pervasive among those with two landholdings. Nearly nine-tenths (88 percent) of those families owned livestock. The size of the herds that this group of wealth-holders retained ranged from six to forty animals. Fully 53 percent of these families listed sacks of cotton, beans, tobacco leaves, and sugar cane as inheritable assets as well as banana and coconut trees. Several of the families included in this group declared farinha houses to process manioc as inheritable assets.

The postmortem inventories from the municipality of Jucás also demonstrate that the most prosperous families of small farmers and ranchers possessed slaves as inheritable assets, and that they used their labor in domestic tasks or in complementing family labor in agricultural or small-scale ranching activities. It is true that provincial authorities and contemporary observers often stated that free labor was the most common arrangement in Ceará and elsewhere in the Northeastern backlands in the nineteenth century.[54] Moreover, slavery as an institution began declining around the mid-nineteenth century in these hinterlands; the transfer of slaves from the Northeast to the coffee plantations of the Southeast after the end of the transatlantic slave trade in 1850 and the gradual manumission of slaves by an emancipation fund established in Ceará in 1868 determined a decrease in the number of captives in the province. According to estimates, slaves represented 20 percent of the total population of the province in 1830, 7 percent in the 1860s, and 4 percent in 1872.[55] Nevertheless, the inventories from Jucás reveal that slaveowning was not uncommon among the wealth-holding population that had at least enough assets to merit the expense and effort of drawing up an inventory. Forty-four percent of the total number of analyzed inventories for the 1840s listed slaves as inheritable wealth. This figure rose slightly to 46 percent of the total number of inventories consulted for the 1850s. Of the postmortem inventories for the 1860s, 24 percent listed slaves as part of the total inheritable assets.[56] Even more important, the documentation from Jucás reveals that a sizable stratum of very modest wealth-holders could be counted among the slaveowning population of the municipality. Thus, in the 1840s, half of all slaveholding families in the sample fell into the lowest wealth bracket, which is approximately Rs. 1:000$000. In the 1850s, families from the same group still accounted for a substantial share of all slaveowners (33.3 percent). The slaveowning small farmers and ranchers of Jucás generally owned only a few slaves. Estates from the 1840s and 1850s with an appraised value of Rs. 1:000$000 or less never listed more than four slaves; and, in those few cases where four slaves were listed, that number typically included young children and even infants, along with slave women.[57]

Poor farmers and ranchers obtained credit for these small-scale commercial enterprises from a variety of sources. They often negotiated small loans or received cash advances from family members or neighbors. For instance, the 1853 estate inventory of Miguel Mendes da Silva from Jucás indicates that he and his wife, Francisca da Luz Ferreira, had borrowed a small amount of money, Rs. 2$800, from their son, José Mendes. According to the inventory of Josefa Diniz Maciel, she and her husband, Raimundo Alves Pereira, had received a small loan of Rs. 2$000 from Josefa's mother, Maria.[58] In addition, free poor people arranged loans from larger landowners, who could act as middlemen by buying cotton or other crops from small farmers and by providing them with cash advances. Local elites in Jucás that lent money included the Oliveira Bastos and the Silva Pereira Costa Leal families, whose members held positions in the municipal council and high rank in the local National Guard unit.[59] The estate inventories also indicate that beginning in the 1850s, smallholders increasingly turned to merchants and vendors from the towns of Icó, Aracati, and even Fortaleza as the main sources of credit. Icó merchants that appear regularly in the probate records are José de Azevedo Vilaroca and Cândido Monteiro. Merchants from Baturité and other interior towns also offered credit to small farmers in their districts. Although, as we will see in Chapter 4, the terms of these commercial practices tended to work against the often cashed-starved and illiterate sertanejos, credit sources allowed some among the poor to take advantage of the economic expansion and to enjoy a modest level of prosperity, at least for a few years.[60]

The deep transformations that affected the province and the survival strategies of its inhabitants are further illustrated through analysis of the percentages of occupations presented in the 1872 population census of Ceará. In a province once legendary for its cattle-ranching industry, it is noteworthy that *criadores* (cattlemen) as a group accounted for a very small share of the population (3.2 percent). By contrast, farmers and farm workers combined represented a sizable group (28.2 percent) of the total population.[61] In all likelihood, the category criador referred mainly to larger producers who drew the bulk of their income from ranching. Likewise, it seems entirely plausible that, because of the very small share of the provincial population that cattlemen represented, this category did not include small-scale producers who combined the cultivation of food and export crops with raising a few head of cattle. At the same time, as the analysis of postmortem inventories above demonstrated, agricultural laborers in the province sometimes had access to land to grow subsistence crops and to raise small herds of goats and sheep. Thus, while the figures from the 1872 census demonstrate that large-scale ranchers and their families represented a very small minority within the province's population, those figures also obscure the fact that a substantial group of poor Cearenses held small bits of land where they eked out a living by cultivating a variety of different crops and raising a few sheep, goats, and cattle.

The participation of small farmers and ranchers in the growing commercial agriculture and ranching economies allowed them a certain degree of independence from more affluent landowners. In particular, free poor Cearenses with access to subsistence *roças* (plots planted with food staples) and small numbers of animals enjoyed a measure of freedom of choice in deciding whether or not to work as wage laborers for others. For instance, João Brígido asserted that before the Great Drought of 1877–79, poor "shepherds" and farmers in Ceará were "proprietors" within the increasingly subdivided land tenure pattern of the province. He noted that poor Cearenses were day laborers "sometimes" and "their homes were free from the authority of the *senhorio* (large landowners)."[62] This observation, in fact, seems to imply that many poor Cearenses were free of relations of dependence and labor obligations based on rental contracts with large landowners. Likewise, according to the botanist Freire Alemão, poor caboclos and other mixed-raced peoples planted small quantities of manioc, rice, and corn in their roças and, therefore, were able to hire themselves as workers only from time to time. From the perspective of large landowners and other local elites, the autonomy enjoyed by free poor farmers meant increasing difficulties in meeting their own labor needs through the employment of wage earners. For example, an article from a Crato newspaper asserted that *alugados* (wage laborers) "think of themselves as owners of the situation," and "impose their own laws, working how and when they want to, as if their work was not compensated according to mutual agreements" favorable to both employer and employee. Indeed, an 1872 commentator wrote in the *Cearense* newspaper that because of the decline of slavery at the provincial level, fazendeiros were "subjected to the whims of the free workers."[63]

Such commentary is significant because it also illustrates the ways in which the social and economic transformations of the post-1845 years seem to have undermined paternalistic relations and released smallholders from onerous labor obligations vis-à-vis larger landowners as patrons. The topic of patron-client networks in the hinterlands of the Northeast needs further empirical research, especially in light of the findings presented in this chapter regarding changes in the land tenure structure, since latifundia have been considered for so long as the main material basis for the clientelistic power of large landowners. Nevertheless, a few existing studies suggest that the rise of a sizable stratum of independent agricultural workers and farmers, the entrance of new cash crops in the repertoire available for smallholders—especially the cotton boom—and the recruitment of poor men as soldiers to fight in the Paraguayan War (1864–70) contributed to the erosion of the power and influence of large landowners over free poor populations in the backlands. In Roger Cunniff's words, this broad social change explains why by 1877, on the eve of the Great Drought, the "patriarchal clan" was "no longer the powerful social institution it had been."[64]

Yet, for foreign and Brazilian observers, the small farmers and ranchers' autonomy and their assertive resistance to providing full-time and year-round wage labor for others was only one more example of the "indomitable," "unruly," and "independent" spirit that, in their view, characterized sertanejos. For example, foreign travelers noted that backlanders enjoyed "lazy" lives and that no matter how poor they were they refused to engage in full-time and permanent wage labor, "even when they were freed blacks." These commentators further emphasized that poor Cearense men were "indolent, inconstant in their employment, and generally hostile to labor."[65] Such accusations which, in all likelihood, originated in information provided by large landowners, reveal the extent to which contemporary observers from elite groups failed to recognize that access to frontier lands allowed poor Cearense families a measure of independence. This discourse also obscures the fact that poor male smallholders, as household heads and providers, came to enjoy a margin of flexibility in their decision to work for others for wages. Instead, the large landowners and authorities saw the sertanejos' yearning for and celebration of their autonomy as part and parcel of their independent and "rebellious" masculinities and their penchant for vagrancy.

The concern with the "vagrancy" and, consequently, the defective masculinity of the free poor men from Ceará led local elites and provincial authorities to propose several projects designed to force rural men to work for others for wages. According to these plans, the state would be the organ in charge of enforcing sharecropping contracts between free workers and large landowners, coercing poor sertanejos to meet other labor obligations to fazendeiros, and imposing conditions on the morador relationship between landowners and squatters. Indeed, in 1857 the Provincial Assembly approved the creation of a "Companhia de Trabalhadores do Ceará," or a Company of Laborers, that was to follow a military organization. Even though research is still needed to determine the tangible results produced by the company, its duties included recruiting men from the "vagrant classes" who did not "obtain their sustenance through decent means" to become laborers; controlling the physical mobility of recruits through the requisition of licenses from the local captain to travel to other districts; and mediating the relationship between employers, mainly large landholders involved in agriculture, and recruits. Some landowners took upon themselves the task of solving their own labor problems, by filing civil suits against unreliable poor farmers when they did not meet the labor requirements that had been specified in verbal contracts.[66]

As recent research in other regions of Brazil has shown, *vadiagem*, or vagrancy, and "laziness" were hardly unique to the sertanejos. From the mid-nineteenth century until the abolition of slavery in 1888, municipal authorities, provincial elites, and landowners in locations ranging from rural townships in Minas Gerais to the city of Porto Alegre bitterly complained about the offensive ability of "vagrants" to roam freely without subjecting themselves to labor. This elite "ideology of vagrancy," as historians have called it, revealed anxieties on the part of large landowners and other employers about solving the labor shortages that many feared would result from the dwindling number of slaves that would inevitably follow the 1850 end of the transatlantic slave trade. Just like the elites and provincial authorities from Ceará, those from elsewhere in Brazil expressed this concern by disparaging of the moral fiber and potential for labor of the free poor.[67] But crucially, as Roger Kittelson argues in his recent study of political culture in Porto Alegre, the ideology of vagrancy also articulated the elite perception that those who resisted relations of dependence with their social superiors were, in fact, challenging the place of subordination and deference in the seigniorial hierarchy of the empire that they expected of the poor.[68]

In the province of Ceará, allegations of vadiagem and apprehension over the challenges to hierarchy that independent sertanejos represented carried a racial component, as men of color constituted the majority of the free poor population. Thus, local and provincial elites—who considered themselves white—sought to assert domination and dependence on wage labor over men of color who, because of their access to land, could obtain their sustenance without having to permanently work in lands belonging to others. This is clearly visible in an article published in the newspaper *Araripe*, in which the author denounced the refusal of poor men of color to work for others by arguing that "the vagrants judge themselves at liberty since they cannot be coerced into service or employment of their natural faculties, without offending their freedom."[69] Likewise, as late as 1878, Cearense fazendeiros who attended the Agricultural Congress in Recife complained of the resistance, particularly of the caboclo population, to work in a disciplined manner and pointed this rejection of labor as one of the main obstacles that the province needed to overcome if it was to reach progress and civilization.[70]

Thus, while a stratum of free poor sertanejos were able to achieve a degree of autonomy and even prosperity during the post-1845 years, their subordinate positions in the racial and class hierarchies of their communities made their social-economic position paradoxical and unstable. The most fortunate of the small farmers and ranchers had become slaveholders and, therefore, were able to exercise authority over others. Yet, their economic independence was construed by their social superiors as a challenge to traditional forms of class domination. Even more, within a context of competition for labor, smallholders guarded their autonomy as rural producers, as it signified their ability to work for themselves and not for others.

Conclusions

Extreme privation, submission, and dependence on large landowners loom large in the scholarship as the unchanging lot of free poor peoples in the Northeastern backlands for much of its colonial and nineteenth-century history. A careful examination of land registries and postmortem inventories, however, demonstrates that the emergence of a land tenure pattern based on smallholdings and the rapid transformations in the provincial economy during the years after 1845 allowed a stratum of rural Cearense families to develop more or less independent livelihoods. As the traditionally cattle-ranching province of Ceará experienced the marked expansion of its commercial agriculture—both for internal markets and for export—poor sertanejos who gained access to small parcels of land attained a measure of security and some, even a degree of prosperity. They eked out their sustenance primarily from the cultivation of subsistence and commercial crops and from the raising of small herds of animals in smallholdings. The most successful among the poor farmers and ranchers were even able to purchase one or two slaves to help their families in the performance of agricultural and ranching tasks, or in domestic activities. As a result, they often enjoyed the freedom to choose *when* and *whether* to hire themselves out to fazendeiros as laborers. In this way, poor sertanejos were able to retain the autonomy that they, like many of the rural poor in the rest of Imperial Brazil, dearly valued, and even to step out of onerous clientelistic relations with large landowners as patrons. Nevertheless, in reaching a measure of control over their own labor power, these small farmers and ranchers came into conflict with the interests of local notables, who required hired labor for their own agrarian activities, within the context of the decline of slavery at the provincial level.

The next chapter will demonstrate that the brief moment of prosperity of the free poor Cearenses was tainted: men and women from this group occupied a precarious social position within the hierarchical relations that characterized their society. Facing limited citizenship rights and a weak legal standing within the political order of the empire, sertanejo men relied on their honorable reputations as strategic resources to retain autonomy, personal freedom, and even a measure of dignity within a rigid hierarchy that ranked their masculinities as dishonorable, vagrant, and criminal. As we will see, smallholders attempted to bolster these claims to status by flaunting their achievement of a measure of economic security and independence as symbols of masculine honor and respectability.

Chapter 2

Unruly Soldiers and Honorable Providers: Paradoxes of Masculinity and State Formation in the Backlands, 1840s–89

On the night of June 24, 1874, the illiterate farmer Francisco Angelino de Sousa attended a St. John's party in the house of João Pereira, located in the estate Barra do Felipe in the municipality of Jucás. The celebrations unfolded uneventfully, with the guests singing to the rhythms of a *viola* (small guitar, typical of the Northeastern backlands) and drinking the sugarcane brandy called *cachaça* until late in the night. However, unexpectedly, a fight erupted between Francisco Angelino and Antônio Rodrigues de Sousa. According to eyewitnesses, Francisco Angelino stabbed Antônio's leg with his knife after he had "offended" Francisco Angelino's reputation. In the midst of this commotion, one of the party guests performed an *in flagrante* arrest, taking an indignant Francisco Angelino to jail, while he clamored at the top of his lungs that he "was not afraid of any man, or even of being jailed, because he had a bull, a horse, lands and money" to defend himself.[1]

The narrative presented in this court case neatly encapsulates the points of contradiction and paradox that surrounded the expansion of the political-legal institutions of the Imperial state into the backlands during the second half of the nineteenth century. As this chapter will demonstrate, distance did not shield free poor Cearenses from the growth of the police and criminal justice systems that accompanied the centralization of a state power bent on imposing order in every corner of the empire and on disciplining its "insubordinate" free poor masculine population. Nevertheless, just as in the case of Francisco Angelino's apprehension, where a party guest arrested a drunk and disorderly reveler, the growing state presence in the frontierlike conditions of the hinterlands relied on the manpower of common sertanejos to execute the official functions of repressing and controlling other rural men. As it will become apparent below, the regulative capacity of the expanding Imperial state was extremely weak. Moreover, the police and army soldiers and civilian auxiliaries who became representatives of the state were untrained, poorly paid, unsupervised, and often undisciplined. Within this context, the spreading police and criminal justice institutions of the centralized state failed to deliver the order that Imperial and provincial elites had hoped for. Instead, as this chapter will reveal, the inept state structure that spread into the interior generated interpersonal masculine violence as it disrupted power relations among men and created controversies over the exercise of authority and the legitimate use of masculine violence.

One of the goals of this chapter is to explore the gendered dimensions of state formation practices in the backlands and the ways in which they nourished specific types of masculinity among free poor Cearense men. As scholars of masculinity in modern Europe and the United States have noted, the exclusion of women and femininity from politics, war, and service as state agents has produced an explicitly gendered discussion, whereas the presence of men in these fields is assumed as so self-evident that it requires no confirmation. Likewise, until very recently, the relationship between the realm of politics and manhood has been taken for granted as a given, so much so that any analysis of the historical nature of that relationship appeared redundant.[2] Yet, as John Horne has argued, war, politics, and the construction of political legitimacy "turn on issues of power and force. They concern the foundation and maintenance of systems of dominance.... They also involve the cultural representation of dominance—power expressed as authority." Therefore, as he explains, the world of politics has been filled by "predominantly masculine voices that construed men in different ways as the source and subject of power and authority."[3] Such constructions are gendered, not just because they included men and excluded women, but because, as Joan Scott has shown, they involved power relations among men and the legitimation of domination, central authority, and power as masculine.[4] Inspired by this scholarship, it is my hope to illuminate at least some aspects of the political history of Ceará by paying close attention to the contests for power and authority that involved free poor sertanejos and that were unleashed by the paradoxical manner in which the Imperial state expanded into the interior during the second half of the nineteenth century.

This chapter will also explore some of the ways in which free poor sertanejos who came into contact with the growing presence of inept police and criminal justice institutions in their lives responded to such intrusions.

Francisco Angelino's drunken boast that he had animals, lands, and money to defend himself as depicted above is emblematic of the strategy that some fortunate farmers and ranchers who had access to material resources deployed in such circumstances. As we will see below, these sertanejos were able to reproduce seigniorial understandings of masculine honor, according to which their precedence, derived from their wealth—even if very small—and reputation, ensured privileged treatment from others, including the representatives of the state. These responses also put in evidence the paradoxical nature of the process of state formation during the Imperial period: in spite of the liberal language that characterized some of the legislation adopted since the attainment of Brazilian independence, the practice of politics was permeated by patronage and paternalism, and was influenced by a hierarchy that was as much socially and racially based as it was gendered.

Imperial State Building: Liberalism, Patronage, and Order

In order to understand the practice at the local level of Imperial state building and its effects on constructs of honor and masculinity among free poor Cearenses, it is necessary to describe the ideology and structures of the monarchical political system that emerged in Brazil after independence, and the process of centralization it experienced beginning in the 1840s. Upon separation from Portugal in 1822, male ruling elites made up of planters and merchants adopted constitutional monarchy as the form of government that they hoped would ensure the continuation of the cornerstones of the colonial social-economic structure—namely, slavery, the plantation system, and the agriculturally based export economy in Brazil.[5] As a strategy to help them achieve these goals, the dominant elites also imported and adapted European liberal principles. The Constitution of 1824, modeled after the 1789 French Declaration of the Rights of Man, defined freedom and equality as inalienable rights of men, established a division of powers between the executive, legislative, and judicial branches, and the "moderating power" of the emperor, and extended the vote to "the mass of active citizens"—that is, free men twenty-five years of age and older, a category that also included freedmen and illiterate men. The constitution also protected the right of property, and sanctioned competition and the pursuit of profit.[6] Nevertheless, as several scholars have noted, Brazilian liberalism, like the one practiced in other Latin American countries and the United States at the time, was internally contradictory. For all its emphasis on equality of all men before the law, the Constitution of 1824 did not mention how that gender-abstract principle applied to slaves, nor did it include slaves or women in the category of active citizens. Likewise, even though voting laws incorporated a broad segment of the free male population, property requirements circumscribed the exercise of active citizenship.[7]

The first decades of consolidation of this liberal political system were marred by disputes over the meanings of independence, the limits of liberalism, and the power of the central government vis-à-vis provincial and local autonomy. These upheavals also reflected the strong regional identities and lack of integration that threatened the territorial unity of the newly created empire.[8] Following Dom Pedro I's abdication of the throne in favor of his five-year-old son in 1831, a three-man Regency was appointed to govern until Pedro II reached his majority. The faction of the political elite that came to exercise power during the Regency (1831–40) was made up of Brazilian liberals, called *moderados* (moderates), to differentiate themselves from the more radical *exaltados* or *farroupilhas*. The moderados advocated decentralizing reforms (some even pressed for federalism) as a vehicle to a more meaningful form of liberalism. In addition, some of the legislation they supported was designed as an attack on the power of magistrates and judges (normally Portuguese-born) to act arbitrarily, and provided for more democratic instruments to select judges and juries.[9] The Regency also created the National Guard as a substitute for the colonial militias and a new counterbalance to the power of the Imperial army established by Brazil's first emperor, Pedro I. Service in the Guard, either in high office or in the rank and file, was affected by social class, which turned the institution into an instrument of clientelistic politics. High-ranking officers, who were elected before 1850 and appointed after that date, had to prove a minimum income of Rs. 200$000 in the countryside to obtain those posts. Appointment to these positions symbolized masculine prestige and, in practice, served as a venue to further local potentates' political purposes, since they nominated their clients to Guard posts. Guard officers vouched for their clients' meeting the annual minimum income of Rs. 100$000 in rural areas to enlist as National Guardsmen, which, in turn, granted enlistees immunity from army recruitment. This minimum income also made the clients eligible to vote.[10]

The Regency's decentralizing reforms and military reorganization had the paradoxical effect of fueling regional tensions, which led to a series of armed revolts, particularly in the Northeast and the far South. Ideologically, the insurrections and riots expressed federalist, liberal, nativist, or restorationist agendas. Yet a common thread among them was the escalation of power struggles among landowners, military men, and educated men into broad-based and even mass movements. Indeed, one of the most significant aspects of these uprisings is that they drew wide involvement from free poor men (some of them in uniform) and in some cases even from slaves, who saw the conflicts as an opportunity to press their own agendas. Moreover, in some provinces, such as Bahia and Pernambuco, slave flight and slave rebellions created anxieties among planters and ruling elites from across Brazil not only about public order but more importantly, about their security as slaveowners and about the continued viability of the slave regime.[11]

This serious instability swayed the male oligarchy in Rio de Janeiro to support the creation of a strong, central government. Both Liberals and Conservatives, who began organizing themselves in parties from the late 1830s on, supported the coronation of the young Pedro II before he reached his majority as a measure to maintain territorial and political unity. But very soon after he assumed the throne in 1840, the Conservatives—self-identified as the "Party of Order"—gained control of the cabinet and the parliament. As Jeffrey Needell has demonstrated, the Party of Order which is credited with initiating what is commonly called the *regresso*, or the trend toward recentralization of political power, endorsed generally liberal principles, including a commitment to the Constitution and to the viability of an elected parliament. Moreover, by the 1840s, a consensus among all political elites favored a centralized political system in order to contain the threat to the slave-based export economy and the hierarchical character of social relations that had been unleashed by the decentralizing reforms of the 1830s.[12] In this sense, the practice of liberalism that emerged victorious out of the early political struggles of state-formation in Brazil was, as Roger Kittelson aptly calls it, a "seigniorial" liberalism that allowed the planter and merchant ruling elite to effectively defend and advance their own class and race interests.[13]

One of the main reforms of the conservative regresso was the 1841 reformulation of the Procedural Code, which strengthened the central government by establishing an extensive and centralized police administration and judicial bureaucracy. The law created the office of the provincial chief of police—appointed by the emperor—and granted this official the power to select *delegados* and *subdelegados* (police commissioners and deputies) at the municipal level. The law also vested these police authorities with judicial powers to arrest, press chargers against, and convict suspects in a series of lesser offenses. In addition, the reform of the Code abolished the police functions of the justice of the peace and provided for the appointment of municipal judges, district judges, and local prosecutors by the central government. The centralizing trend also included the restoration of the moderating power created under the Constitution of 1824 but suspended during the Regency.[14]

By 1850, these and other measures had created a highly centralized Imperial state which, despite its liberal underpinnings, was exclusionary and elitist. This state functioned through a complex machinery of patronage that linked local notables to provincial elites and then to representatives of the central government in Rio de Janeiro. In this system, municipal elites played a crucial role, as they delivered the votes and electors from local communities for politicians at the provincial and Imperial levels to reach high office. These men, in turn, returned those deeds with local appointments in favor of political bosses and the dispersal of much needed resources for provinces and localities. Just as important, the state that emerged out of the political-administrative experimentation of the 1830s and that relied on centralization of the police and criminal justice systems had succeeded in maintaining unity among the various regions and safeguarding slavery. Once unity had been achieved, preserving order became the central concern for the planter class that constituted the ruling elite. The notion of order, however, did not denote just the absence of rebellion. Rather, it designated a concern with the perpetuation of the social order that the centralizing reforms had been able to maintain: a hierarchical society based on slaveholding and racial inequality, and the promotion and protection of the export economy of agricultural products, with the use of slaves, or other forms of cheap and disciplined labor. With the purpose of maintaining this order, ruling elites—who saw themselves as liberal—pushed the expansion of a centralized state into every corner of the empire.[15]

The hierarchical order that Brazilian elites defended through the discourse and practice of seigniorial liberalism had gender as one of its central components. The broad base of voters allowed by the Constitution of 1824 (until the electoral reform of 1881) did not facilitate the relations of equality among all men, not even free males, that the more radically liberal principle of universal male citizenship in theory would have promised. Instead, political legitimacy in Brazil was grounded on paternalism, the ideology of the seigniorial class that, according to Sidney Chalhoub, "based its power on the institution of slavery and the production of personal dependence." It was, of course, paternalism that justified the exclusion of women from the political sphere, the continued authorization in Brazilian civil law of the patriarchal power of male household heads over their wives and children, and the legal authority of masters over slaves. But paternalism as an elite ideology also included a ranking of masculinities according to class, color, connections, and political power. Men from the ruling elite who belonged to the "class of respectable persons," "propertied groups," and "influential citizens" and who were often also slaveholders claimed honor and status superior to all others and conferred the patronage necessary to verify whether free poor men qualified as voters or National Guard officers. In contrast, those "less favored by fortune"—that is, free poor men who were mostly racially mixed and of African descent—found it necessary to enter into paternalist relationships of subordination and deference with elite men in order to exercise their political rights as citizens.[16] Within this context, it could be argued that the seigniorial code of manhood focused on hierarchy, honor, wealth, and the production of dependence was hegemonic. As John Tosh defines it, hegemonic masculinity includes "the masculine norms and practices which are most valued by the politically dominant class and which help to maintain its authority."[17]

The integration of men into the military during the Imperial period did not erode the hierarchical nature of the relationships between men in Brazilian society either. Despite Pedro I's promise to create an "army of disciplined citizens" that incarnated "civic virtue," enlistment did not extend full rights of citizenship to poor men. According to the 1822 instructions for recruitment, in effect until 1875, "single white and also freed mulatto men" between the ages of eighteen and thirty-five were subject to recruitment. But by providing exemptions to those who were economically active and engaged in professions, as well as sons of farmers, the instructions safeguarded young men from the upper classes from having to serve in the army.[18] Just as important, during peacetime, those among the poor who had powerful patrons to help them claim exempted status were protected from recruitment. In practice, those men who were subject to impressment (or forced recruitment) were the under- or unemployed unskilled laborers who remained outside of clientelistic relationships, and who by virtue of such characteristics were often accused of embodying the deficient masculinities of "vagrants" and "criminals." In fact, as Peter Beattie has demonstrated, military impressment served to reinforce masculine distinctions between honorable and dishonorable poor, free and slave, and law-abiding and criminal. Furthermore, the army played a central role as an institution of discipline for poor men during the nineteenth century.[19] Clearly, the political order of the empire included and excluded different categories of men according to race, class, and their place in the seigniorial hierarchy upheld by the elites. Even more, as the Imperial state consolidated its power after the mid-nineteenth century, male ruling elites used political institutions to enhance their own conception of masculinity and maintain their class, gender, and racial dominance.[20]

Institutions of Social Control Expand into the Backlands of Ceará

During the first half of the nineteenth century, the consolidation of the postcolonial state in Ceará involved, above all else, an effort to curb the private power that large fazendeiros had retained throughout most of the colonial period and their capacity to sponsor violence. During the late seventeenth century and through much of the eighteenth century, large potentates who received royal nominations as officers in the militia performed state functions such as arresting criminals, expelling undesirables from a community, and informing the governor of the captaincy about happenings in the interior. The power of the fazendeiros was large indeed, as they lived in the isolation of backlands towns and ranches, where representatives of the Crown only occasionally appeared. Moreover, potentates commanded militia units or, conversely, their own private armies made up of *vaqueiros* (cowboys), farmers, and artisans, who often were their dependants and with whom they established social bonds of patronage. These large landowners in effect ruled the sertões, and as they competed for lands, power, or other resources with rival family clans and their armies, they regularly resorted to violence, which resulted in low-level warfare in the region.[21]

During the late colonial period, officials of the captaincy progressively exercised authority over potentates of the interior. Yet families of large landowners retained much influence in their communities through control of the municipal councils, their continued positions as high officers of the militias, and their capacity to inspire fear and exercise violence. Thus, after independence, and until about the 1840s, Imperial authorities deployed to the province showed a steadfast resolve to subordinate the large fazendeiros, as they attempted to consolidate the power of the state and to preserve the unity of the nascent empire. After all, some of the most threatening secessionist movements and restorationist rebellions of the First Reign and the Regency had been initiated by large fazendeiros from the Northeast in their struggles for power against their rivals.[22]

The first concerted campaign to end what contemporaries called the "climate of lawlessness" that reigned in Ceará came in the mid-1830s, under the leadership of the politician-priest and moderate liberal José Martiniano de Alencar. As provincial president of Ceará between 1834 and 1837 and again between 1840 and 1841, Alencar enacted a series of laws and policies designed to pacify and disarm the interior. For example, in 1835 and in accord with legislation of 1831, he created a provincial police corps which he charged with the function of arresting and punishing *criminosos prepotentes e de séquito*—that is, domineering criminals who had "toughs" at their service. President Alencar also established bonuses for police agents and even civilians who apprehended these offenders or killed them if they resisted the authorities. Nevertheless, great difficulties in terms of budget and human capacity to patrol the vast interior, which was only scantily populated, undermined the ability of the police corps to accomplish the mission of ridding the backlands of tough fazendeiros and their armed gangs. Moreover, between 1835 and 1837 most of the police soldiers from Ceará remained in Pará, where they had been deployed to assist in the suppression of the Cabanagem rebellion and thus had to neglect their duties in Ceará.[23] The paradox of the expansion of policing institutions that despite their enlarged reach were weak and insufficient in subordinating rebellious backlands populations was not limited to the initial decades of consolidation of Imperial power. Instead, as we will see below, this became a recurrent theme in the process of state formation in the interior during the nineteenth century.[24]

From 1840 onward, and as a result of the conservative reaction that established an expanding and centralized police administration as one of the main tenets of government, Imperial and provincial authorities launched a greater effort to deploy a stronger and more efficient state presence in the countryside. Increased provincial revenues that resulted from the growth of Cearense agricultural and livestock exports since the 1850s aided the provincial authorities in this task, as they could assign larger budgets to the police and other state institutions. For ruling groups in Imperial Brazil during the late 1840s and 1850s, a larger, more effective, and centralized state presence in the backlands of Ceará, as well as in the interiors of the other provinces, was necessary to maintain order. As we have seen, order denoted above all a concern with the preservation of a hierarchical social and gender order and the agrarian basis of the export economy, with its need for disciplined labor, whether slave or free. Thus, during the second half of the nineteenth century, state repressive functions in Ceará ceased to aim primarily at taming the private power of large fazendeiros. As local notables organized themselves in political parties and understood that their authority and prestige came to depend, to a large extent, on the resources—in the form of votes—that they were able to mobilize on behalf of provincial and national politicians, police and criminal justice work focused more squarely on the subordination of the rural poor, and particularly, free poor men.[25]

The few scholars that have analyzed the political history of Ceará during the Imperial period have argued that partisan politics shaped the functioning of the police and criminal justice systems in interior municipalities. According to Abelardo Montenegro, the political faction to which the provincial president belonged counted on the police apparatus, including the local police commissioners, to affect the outcome of elections, as these authorities could order arrests and criminal proceedings against their political opponents or their clients. Likewise, the party in power could use the criminal justice system either to prosecute or to dispense judicial favors to voters, including free poor men, according to their political leanings. It is for this reason that men from influential families coveted nominations to municipal and district judgeships and even service on jury boards.[26] Nevertheless, although local notables as office holders with definite party loyalties influenced much of the practice of state formation, it is highly likely that not all facets of state action in the interior involved chiefly the exercise of elite partisan politics. And even in the cases when they did, it is my contention that the work of the police and criminal justice institutions unleashed contests for power and domination not only between elite men, or elite and subordinate males, but also *among* free poor men—an aspect that will be of central interest throughout much of this chapter.

In making free poor men one of the focal subjects of police and criminal justice power, provincial and municipal police authorities granted attention to the arrest and punishment of public-order violations, especially vagrancy and public drunkenness, that led to disorder. For these officials, repression of vadiagem was necessary to instill work habits on "indomitable" free poor masculine populations and to prevent the incidence of violent crime.[27] In fact, authorities saw police repressive action as part of a broader civilizing project of reforming the deficient masculinities of backlands men by "taming their customs" and inculcating in them a "moral consciousness" that would allow them to recognize good from evil, and to become hardworking individuals. This disciplining of male sertanejos became even more necessary from the perspective of a provincial elite composed predominantly of fazendeiros and merchants because, as Chapter 1 has demonstrated, access to land allowed the free poor a degree of independence from wage labor and a measure of social-economic agency. But the criminalization of vagrancy was not limited to the province of Ceará. Instead, after the end of the transatlantic slave trade in 1850, and as the country experienced its transition from slavery to free wage labor, ruling elites throughout Brazil increasingly expressed concern regarding the capacity of Brazilian workers to become dependable laborers. They, in fact, elaborated what Lúcio Kowarick calls an "ideology of vagrancy" that emphasized the "inherent" aversion to work and "preference for idleness" of the free poor populations of Brazil. The repressive action of a centralized and strong police was thus needed to transform *vadios*, or vagrants, into disciplined workers.[28]

Concern with disciplining poor men in Ceará also gained significance since a series of broad social and economic transformations precipitated far-reaching conflict and dislocation, especially from the mid-1860s onward. As Chapter 6, below, will demonstrate, that social change also contributed to the reproduction of interpersonal masculine violence, as well as the flaring up of banditry, and even some small-scale rebellions among the poor. Local and provincial authorities also saw police action focused on lower-class men as a vehicle to curb the incidence of violent crime (murders, assaults, and fights) in the countryside. In their view, the "ignorant" customs of the male sertanejos, including their "habits" of drinking and seeking revenge for any offense to their honor through violence, led to widespread criminality. Thus, in an attempt to restrain poor men's capacity to exercise violence in rebellions, bandit gangs, and fights, and acknowledging that the easy availability of rifles, daggers, knives, and machetes hindered any effort to bring order to the sertão, police officials made the confiscation of weapons a component of social control efforts.[29]

The endeavor of subordinating free poor sertanejos and transforming them into reliable laborers and moral individuals required at least a minimum state presence—embodied in the police corps—in all interior localities. During the course of the second half of the nineteenth century, the size of the police force—organized in the fashion of a military institution—varied. In 1851, a total of 196 *praças* (soldiers or privates) served in the police corps. During the late 1870s, in an attempt to deal with banditry, the number of praças rose to 600. By 1887, 300 enlisted privates served in the corps.[30] Clearly, the diminutive size of the police corps was insufficient to effectively control and discipline the provincial population that by the mid-nineteenth century amounted to more than half a million people. Indeed, provincial authorities regularly complained that the police force did not possess enough praças to patrol the interior adequately. The Cearense sertão, with its inhabitants spread out in villages, fazendas, and small sítios, represented a serious challenge for what amounted to a severely undersized police corps. Consequently, most small towns did not have even a minimum permanent police presence. Instead, police detachments were deployed to different locations as needs arose, and very often, these units were made up of only a handful of praças. For instance, according to a certificate by the Tamboril police commissioner, issued in April of 1875, "[T]he police detachment in this village consists of one praça who has not been active since June of last year due to illness, as well as three privates who are suspended because they are responding to criminal charges for facilitating prisoner escape." The delegado added that "currently, there is only one available praça, given that the others are performing official proceedings in the capital."[31]

Because of the insufficient number of police troops, army personnel and particularly army privates (also called praças) were in charge of a variety of police functions, including making arrests, breaking up fights and other violent encounters, transporting prisoners, as well as manning jails. At the request of police delegados and subdelegados, army detachments were deployed to backlands towns to assist with immediate public order needs. Nonetheless, provincial authorities regularly complained that even with the assistance of the army praças, the personnel available for policing functions were simply in short supply.[32]

The expanding structure of the centralized police administration was more clearly visible in the gradual increase of police jurisdictions such as *delegacias* and *subdelegacias* and their corresponding commissioners and deputies. As towns and villages grew in size and many became seats of independent municipalities, more police officials were needed, especially between 1841 and 1871, when delegados and subdelegados had wide police and judicial powers that included issuing search warrants, preparing written cases, hearing witnesses, and judging offenders on a variety of misdemeanor cases. Until 1871 these officials were the sole authorities responsible for accusing, pressing charges, judging, and sentencing those who committed public order violations such as vagrancy and begging, or possessed and used illegal weapons.[33] Thus, by 1865 there were 32 delegacia districts and 105 subdelegacia jurisdictions in Ceará. In 1877, there were 50 jurisdictions of delegacia and 138 of subdelegacia. And by 1887 there were 57 delegacias and 175 districts of subdelegacia.[34]

Notwithstanding the increase in the number of delegados and subdelegados, police jurisdictions were not adequately staffed to patrol the vast interior and to effectively repress public order offenders or violent criminals. Instead, *inspeitores de quarteirão,* or ward inspectors, who were unpaid civilian auxiliaries of the delegados and subdelegados, *oficiais de justiça,* or paid lower-ranking court officials, and men from the general populace who witnessed criminal or threatening acts were the ones in charge of arresting those who upset the public order. These men often lacked legitimacy in their functions among both the wealthy and the poor, which in some cases led to disorderly apprehensions. For instance, according to witness testimony in an *inquérito policial,* or police investigation, of a homicide allegedly committed by a Tamboril ward inspector named Manoel Rodrigues Furtado, João Francisco da Fonseca—a white single man who lived in Piauí—and his four *cabras*[35] had been whipping a man named Antônio Carlos in the grazing fields of the Fazenda Conceição, on July 2, 1843. Antônio Carlos's wife had called Manoel Rodrigues to help her husband, and he immediately rounded up twenty civilian men to assist in the capture of João Francisco and his men. But when the ward inspector arrived and attempted to put these men under arrest, João Francisco responded that "he would go to prison only if Manoel presented him with a written order from the Subdelegado." He also noted that "of course he [the ward inspector] did not have an order because neither he nor his cabras were criminals." This exchange degenerated into violence as the cabra Francisco *de tal* [36] and Manoel Rodrigues began fighting with knives. Likewise, other men from João Francisco's group and those rounded up by the ward inspector also used their weapons against each other. Eventually, according to several witnesses, Manoel Rodrigues fired a shot with his shotgun that killed João Francisco. [37]

This case is interesting because it illustrates how men who were required to submit to the control and repression exercised by a representative of the state questioned the authority of a ward inspector. Furthermore, because this case dates from before 1850, we have information on the racial background of the men involved. [38] João Francisco was white, and even though we do not know his profession, it is clear that he had some economic means, as he had four "cabras" traveling with him through Tamboril. Manoel Rodrigues was pardo (or brown), which in all likelihood also contributed to his perceived lack of legitimacy as a law enforcement agent, especially in relationship to a white man of property. But the document makes clear that João Francisco's cabras did not respect Manoel Rodrigues's authority either. Witness testimony indicates that the cabra Francisco de tal ran into a house in the fazenda to get the knife that he used to fight Manoel Rodrigues. Other criminal cases demonstrate that illiterate men also questioned the authority of ward inspectors, which made their execution of official functions ineffective. [39]

The criminal justice structure also expanded during these years. By 1861 the province was divided into fourteen *comarcas,* or judicial districts, and all of them were staffed with district judges and public prosecutors. The comarcas were divided into twenty-nine judicial subdivisions called *termos* with their own municipal judges and substitutes and jury tribunals. In 1874 a High Court, or *Relação,* was established in Fortaleza in order to expedite appeals and other judicial processes that were previously sent to Pernambuco. By 1887, there were twenty-eight comarcas in the interior with their own district judges and public prosecutors, thirty-one subdistricts, each with its municipal judges and substitutes, and fifty-six jury tribunals. The increase in the number of municipal judgeships took on an added significance after the judicial reform of 1871 limited the judicial powers of police delegados and subdelegados to arbitrate decisions in cases of public order offenses and transferred these functions to the municipal and district judges. Police officials were still in charge of conducting criminal investigations, but they were required to draw up reports and deliver them to judges and prosecutors for final decision. [40]

Nevertheless, serious problems undermined the administration of criminal justice by this expanding judicial structure. Droughts or inclement weather slowed down the regularity with which juries met to decide criminal cases at the municipal level. Judges and public prosecutors also abandoned the countryside when epidemics or droughts threatened the lives of its inhabitants. According to provincial presidents, the lack of familiarity with the law by judges, who were not always formally trained in jurisprudence, and by jurors, undermined their capacity to exercise justice, especially when wealthy defendants hired knowledgeable lawyers who manipulated the presentation of evidence in criminal proceedings. Moreover, despite their growing number, the comarcas covered enormous territories. The comarca district judges were required to supervise and approve every legal procedure in municipal courts in two or three termos, a task that, given the difficulties of transportation and communication, significantly delayed decision-making or resolution of criminal cases.[41]

According to provincial presidents, the influence of patronage and political loyalties in rulings on criminal cases by jurors and judges was the "cancer" that beset the administration of criminal justice in the backlands. Jurors routinely absolved criminals from influential families or promised absolution in favor of local notables' dependants as they enacted their part in relations of reciprocity with powerful patrons. Judges promised *despronúncias,* or dismissal of charges, of indicted offenders in exchange for assurances of votes for their political party. In fact, at least in the eyes of José Júlio de Albuquerque Barros, provincial president of Ceará in 1880, despronúncia and acquittal resulting from influence of local notables were the rule in the criminal process, and not the exception. These problems, according to the provincial presidents, tended to invalidate the practice of the criminal justice institutions. But they also demonstrated that the expansion of the centralized judicial system did not succeed at suppressing the private power of large landowners. Instead, local notables interacted in various ways with the public power of the state and continued exercising considerable influence in their regions.[42]

Another facet of the expansion of state presence was the construction and repair of prisons. As authorities emphasized the punishment of public order offenses, along with major violent crimes, they saw a need for increasing the number of jails in the province. In 1848, a provincial law authorized the building of a penitentiary in Fortaleza, designed according to the Auburn system of individual cells and common spaces for workshop labor during the day. By 1858, the Fortaleza prison served as a provincial center of detention. The number of *cadeias,* or jails, in the backlands also increased during the period between 1850 and 1881. In 1851, there were only three proper cadeias in interior towns, and a few rented houses served as jails in several other municipalities. But by 1881, and as a result of the addition of forty-three cadeias built with the labor of *retirantes*, or refugees, during the Great Drought of 1877–79, most cities and towns in the countryside had detention quarters.[43]

Still, provincial authorities noted that many of these jails were not secure, and that prisoner flight was common. According to the police commissioner of Tamboril, the village jail housed ten criminals in 1875, and "did not offer any security whatsoever." These conditions forced authorities to rely on a system of transporting detainees and indicted criminals from the small, crowded, and unhealthful dungeons in the villages to the larger jails located in principal towns. But the system proved challenging because it employed police and army praças from the already insufficient battalions to escort the criminals. Moreover, it was precisely during these trips that detainees and indicted criminals fled, often with the covert or overt assent of their escorts.[44]

The ineffective, disorganized, and corrupt manner in which the police and criminal justice system expanded in the hinterlands touched the lives of sertanejo men when they committed crimes or became targets of social control efforts, and left the poorest and least protected of them with very limited options to defend themselves from incarceration or criminal prosecution. For instance, detentions, particularly those performed in flagrante, often took place in a chaotic manner, which caused the long imprisonment of free poor men whose crimes were not even recorded in police reports.[45] A circular letter from the provincial chief of police to delegados includes several recommendations that in fact illustrate how these problems initiated. The police chief advised that after an in flagrante detention, the delegado should interrogate the prisoner regarding the reasons or motivations given by the "conductor" (which was often a civilian who had observed the crime) and other witnesses, and then should draw up a report. In addition, he mentioned that in cases of detentions for disorder and disturbances of the peace, the "ruffians" should not remain in jail without the delegado—in whose name the arrest was performed—learning the motives of the detention from the detainee directly. Yet ward inspectors, subdelegados, and delegados often neglected to draw up the report on this type of arrest. Consequently, there was no record that legalized these arrests, and detainees could sit in jail for an indeterminate time without an official indictment.[46]

Free poor men who ended up in jail for police investigation when they were accused of a crime and who did not have connections with wealthier patrons experienced serious difficulties in hiring lawyers, whose fees were prohibitive. Moreover, the great expanses that judicial authorities had to cover and their lack of interest in judicial matters that involved the poor meant that any appeal to a public prosecutor could take months to draw up.[47] Thus, the jails in interior towns as well as in Fortaleza were full of a mix of inmates, mostly male, including petty offenders, hardened criminals, vagrants, habitual drunkards, and recruits, whose records were often nonexistent. The provincial chief of police complained in 1887 that even in the Fortaleza prison there was almost no documentation on prisoners from the interior and that information about the crimes they committed and how long their sentences were was lacking. He also mentioned that the records that existed were of such a confusing nature that they contained contradictory information.[48]

In sum, the regulatory capacity of the Imperial state apparatus expanded into the Cearense backlands during the second half of the nineteenth century. Reflecting the political elites' goal of bringing order into every corner of the empire, a centralized police and criminal justice administration reached isolated and small communities in the interior. Moreover, in an attempt to subordinate male backlanders and transform them into reliable laborers for the growing agricultural and ranching economies of the province, authorities focused their efforts, or at least their rhetoric, on controlling the poor and reshaping their defective masculinities. Nevertheless, this state apparatus, with its proliferating policing functions, was not strong. The police corps was understaffed and completely unable to patrol the vast hinterlands. The insufficient number of delegados and subdelegados created a situation in which they could not fulfill their function of maintaining public order in all towns, villages, and ranches; and, therefore, they left police matters in the hands of civilian auxiliaries, who lacked legitimacy in their actions. The Imperial state also failed to curb the private power of large landowners. Instead, local notables swayed criminal justice decisions through structures of patronage and in this way maintained a measure of influence in their localities. For those free poor men who were caught in the widening net of arrests and criminal prosecution, and who remained outside of clientelistic relationships, the avenues for recourse were minimal indeed. Thus, even though the Imperial state had reached many areas of the interior, the functioning and structure of this state was faulty and deficient.[49] As we will see below, a measure of the weakness of the growing police and criminal justice institutions was their reliance on common sertanejos, as army and police soldiers and civilian auxiliaries, to enforce law and order. Moreover, because these state representatives lacked the authority and social recognition necessary to uphold such power, they often used violence as they fulfilled their repressive functions, which injected a measure of disorder into the process of state formation in the backlands.

Police Soldiers, Army Praças, and Disorder

Throughout the nineteenth century, the police corps in Ceará, as well as those created in other areas of Brazil, drew their rank-and-file members from the same lower classes that were significant targets of social control. At least in principle, the police was organized as a military institution that followed strict standards of discipline and a hierarchical order. As Thomas Holloway has demonstrated in the case of Rio de Janeiro, the rationale behind the military organization of the police during the empire implied that discipline and hierarchy would control and systematize the use of force by all members of the police, and direct it only at the specific targets of repression. The belief in the efficiency of a military organization coupled with the difficulties in staffing the low-paid positions of police privates and corporals resulted in the extensive use of forced recruitment of men from the lower classes to work in these positions in Ceará. Moreover, according to provincial authorities, the police recruits generally were men who had committed petty crimes, participated in bandit gangs, or were vagrants. Clearly, authorities saw the recruitment of these men as a way to channel the sertanejos' unsanctioned use of violence or their offensive ability to roam the sertão into service for state institutions, which, in turn, would spread and enforce order. Some poor sertanejos volunteered to serve in the police. But police officials at the provincial level also noted that the very low salary and almost no benefits that police soldiers received when they retired attracted men full of "vices" as volunteers into the corps, and that those who were "lost" in lives of crime often sought careers in the police as a way to guarantee their safety.[50]

The police corps was not the only state institution with social control functions that relied on poor men as soldiers. The army also played a crucial role in enforcing the law. Moreover, as Beattie has shown, the army had the double duty of punishing and disciplining the minor criminals, vagrants, and unprotected men who were forcefully recruited into service. According to his study of the army in Imperial Brazil, during the last third of the nineteenth century, at least half of the praças that were recruited had committed some form of criminal offense.[51] In the backlands, both authorities and the populace regarded the army as a repository for thieves, vagrants, and other threats to both the wealthy and the poor. And it was these poor men—who often had a violent and shady past, and who did not command much respect among the population—that were granted the power to temporarily direct and control the behavior of other sertanejos as they performed arrests, transported prisoners, or engaged in other law enforcement tasks.[52] The popular poet Sinfrônio expressed this paradox and the connection between this form of law enforcement and violence by narrating in verse the mythical life-story of the criminal Vilela—a bandit who "lived" in the backlands of Pernambuco during the nineteenth century. According to the poem, the police delegado and provincial police chief had sent arresting squads of ten, forty, and sixty police and army praças to capture Vilela, but because of his bravery, he always defeated them. After six months of unsuccessful attempts to detain him, the police commandant ordered a larger contingent of army soldiers to surround Vilela's house, and said the following words as he commanded him to surrender:

. . . *Eu trago a tropa da linha*	I am bringing troops
Do Monarca-Imperadô . . .	From the monarch emperor…
. . . *Trago cento e oitenta praça*	I bring 180 soldiers
Negro nascido em baruio,	Blacks who were born in disorder
Criado em meio de desgraça . . .	Raised in the midst of misfortune…
Pra te mandá pro outro mundo	Just to send you to the next world
Nem eu nem ninguém se embaraça.	I don't need to give myself trouble.[53]

As these verses suggest, the authority and power of the praças to subordinate other men was not contingent on their rank or their belonging to a disciplined Imperial army. Instead, it was related to their physicality and proven capacity to exercise a boisterous form of violence.

Criminal records from Tamboril, Jucás, and Itapagé demonstrate that some police and army soldiers performed their functions in a disorderly manner and also used violence in their interactions with civilians when they did not submit to their commands. For example, according to witnesses who testified in an assault trial against the police privates Luís Pacheco Amaro, José Antônio de Almeida, Antônio Jatobá, and Antônio Mendes, on October 31, 1875, the cowboy Fortunato Alves da Fortuna was on his way from Tamboril to the Fazenda Olho d'agua on horseback, at around five in the afternoon. The soldiers Amaro and Almeida showed up and, without issuing an order for his arrest, began threatening to beat Fortunato. As the witnesses noted, the two soldiers, in fact, thrashed the vaqueiro Fortuna, and when the soldiers Jatobá and Mendes arrived, they helped in the beating, since Fortunato was resisting his capture. In fact, as the record shows, the four praças continued thrashing the cowboy all through the streets of Tamboril until they arrived at the jail.[54] It is true that as agents of the state, praças had the power and even the function of exerting physical force over noncompliant and wayward subjects of the empire. Nevertheless, the disorganized practice of physical intimidation of suspects and the excessive use of force against detainees did not have any legal foundation. In fact, instructions from the central government prohibited the "mistreatment" of prisoners, unless they resisted arrest or attempted to flee, but even in that case, the directives did not sanction police brutality. In addition, at least once, a police chief from Ceará forcefully exhorted the delegados not to assent to the use of violence and mistreatment of detainees by the agents of public force.[55]

What is more, despite their hierarchical organization, the police corps and the army did not have sufficient resources or even authority to subordinate the undisciplined praças and channel what authorities saw as their "criminal instincts" solely toward the exercise of state-sponsored violence. The tasks of patrolling the sertão, arresting bandits or vagrants, or deploying detachments to areas where elections, drought, or other factors caused upheavals were seen as so urgent that the police corps regularly sent recent recruits who had no training, no weapons, and sometimes even no uniforms into local communities. Foreign travelers even remarked on the spectacle of army and police praças who had no shoes, and were armed with clubs, like bandits in the backlands.[56]

Consequently, the deployment of poorly trained, nonuniformed, and often unsupervised army and police detachments caused a measure of disorder and violence. For example, judicial authorities from the municipality of Tamboril complained that an army unit deployed to the town of Telha in 1876 had brought veritable terror to the population. In particular, the authorities described the actions of one praça who whipped several townspeople and desecrated the church. Apparently this private was so uncontrollable that the police commandant "did not know what to do with him." During the Great Drought, some army units deployed to interior towns to defend them from bandit attacks performed beatings on townsmen and even insulted police officials.[57] In addition, praças's neglectful performance of their official tasks undermined some police work and brought into question the efficacy of state institutions. This is particularly evident in cases where police and army praças transported prisoners between interior villages and larger towns and they either collaborated with detainees or neglected their duties and allowed the arrested men to escape. For instance, according to the declarations by one police soldier who was criminally charged, along with two others, for facilitating the escape of two prisoners, this small contingent was transporting João da Costa Vieira, who was sentenced to life in prison, and José Joaquim de Sousa, who was indicted for assault, from the town of Ipu to Tamboril on May 27, 1874. As they made their way through the caatinga, two of the soldiers stayed behind to buy eggs and a pot to prepare their lunch. When they joined the other soldier, they found that he was sleeping and the prisoners had escaped.[58]

Some police and army praças were not only inept in carrying out official functions but also disobeyed their superiors' orders. For example, a group of police soldiers attacked and beat two men in the streets of Tamboril. When the police commandant ordered them to end their attack, they replied that "no delegado could stop them." In one instance in Tamboril, a police soldier who had resisted arrest because of his participation in an incident of prisoner flight from a transporting squad responded that the reason he did not respond to the call for his detention was that "he did not want to."[59] These examples suggest that even those free poor Cearense men who were charged with performing arrests and other official functions questioned the authority of their superiors, and consequently of the state they were made to represent. Indeed, it seems clear that Imperial institutions such as the army and the police corps failed to provide the discipline necessary to transform petty criminals and conscripted poor men into effective sources of state power and law enforcement.

The unsanctioned use of violence by some police and army praças also became evident in their involvement in crimes of various types. Police chief reports presented examples of army and police privates who killed or wounded prostitutes, lovers, other service men, or civilians in violent displays of anger, and often with the use of state weapons while off-duty. Authorities often remarked on the "immorality" of privates who took sexual advantage of young and unprotected women. While some police authorities at the municipal and provincial levels demonized the criminality of praças by calling them "veritable cannibals" or "barbarians," others more soberly noted that army and police privates failed to be examples for the society they were trying to reform.[60]

Despite this outcry, contradictions inherent in the functioning of the police and criminal justice systems let off praças who committed crimes against civilians, neglected their duties, or engaged in police brutality, virtually scot-free, even when they were accused and brought to trial for their offenses. Criminal cases featuring police and army privates accused of a variety of crimes in the municipalities of Tamboril and Jucás reveal that jurors treated praça offenses with the same degree of permissiveness that they did other offenders. From a total of 27 police and army privates accused of various crimes, 21 were acquitted, while only 2 were condemned. The remaining 4 cases were dismissed after initial investigations. In four instances of acquittal, district judges appealed the decisions and ordered the reinstallment of the cases. The crimes for which praças were tried included attempted murder, rape, severe injuries, disobedience, and laxity leading to the escape of prisoners.

Provincial police reports confirm the leniency of the criminal courts at least with privates of the police corps. According to the police commandant of Ceará, during the year 1869, 8 praças were incarcerated and awaiting jury decisions in several cities from the interior. Most of them, in fact, expected the decisions of second jury sessions, since the first one—invariably an acquittal—had been appealed by district judges. The crimes for which they had been tried included allowing prisoners to escape, releasing a convict from prison, and physical assault. By contrast, praças who had been tried in military courts for the crimes of desertion, threats, and assault to a superior were all convicted and serving sentences in local jails. The provincial president report of 1870 presents a similar situation. Of 18 police praças serving sentences in local jails throughout the province, 17 had been tried for military crimes, and only 1 for a civil crime.[61]

This official neglect of army and police soldiers' irresponsibility in professional matters and their use of violence against civilians reflects another one of the paradoxes of state formation in the interior. While police delegados and subdelegados insisted on tougher social control, jury members were typically lenient in their decisions. District judges sometimes exercised their right to overturn verdicts when they found them faulty, but usually political partisanship meddled in these decisions. Moreover, as Hendrik Kraay has argued in the case of the Bahian army during the first half of the nineteenth century, judges and juries as members of the upper classes did not much care about displays of soldier violence, as long as they did not affect them.[62] By absolving praças who committed crimes, got involved in fights, and were neglectful of their functions, and by disregarding their actions, judges and juries, and not only praças, contributed to the disorder often observed in the hinterlands. Moreover, the judicial inattention to praças' aggressions became another factor in the failure of state power to impose its discipline over police and army soldiers and to clearly systematize their authority and the use of violence.

Sertanejos, Weapons, and Social (Dis)control

A concern for provincial and local authorities who sought to discipline rebellious backlanders and transform them into hard-working men was to curtail their access to knives, rifles, and other arms by confiscating them and arresting those among the poor caught using illegal weapons. From a legal perspective, the impounding of weapons or arrest of those who bore them was not a class-specific measure. The Criminal Code made illegal and subject to punishment the unlicensed use of guns, rifles, knives, daggers, and other puncturing instruments. Nevertheless, notable citizens, by virtue of their high-ranking positions in the National Guard with authorization to

carry and use weapons or by possessing licenses to bear arms, were effectively excluded from arrest for carrying weapons. By contrast, some free poor
men and slaves who, according to their own depositions, customarily carried
knives and rifles to protect themselves as well as to kill destructive animals,
skin cattle, or cut hides, became targets of the coercive arm of the state for
offenses related to the possession and use of illegal weapons. Authorities even
prohibited what they called the "vulgar use among the lower classes of wear-
ing untucked shirts on top of the pants," in order to foment "decency" and
prevent the concealment of weapons.[63]

In spite of the emphasis of delegados and police chiefs on arresting and
prosecuting those among the poor who possessed illegal arms, local authorities in Ceará did not have enough resources or even authority to rid the
sertão of weapons. For instance, in an incident that took place in 1870, the
second substitute of the subdelegado of Quixará failed to arrest four men
who were armed with illegal weapons because he confessed that he was
afraid of being "insulted, offended and physically assaulted" by them.[64] Even
more important, the serious staffing problems that the police corps experienced forced authorities to rely heavily on unpaid volunteers from among
the poor, who were "invited" to perform everyday police work, such as
confiscating illegal weapons, as well as apprehending criminals and accom-
panying detainees to jails in larger towns. These unpaid volunteers—usually
illiterate cowboys, farmers, and day laborers—in turn, were not only allowed
to carry weapons but also provided with arms, if they did not possess them.
Even the instructions from the central government on the duties of police
delegados and subdelegados allowed the police as an institution to "grant"
the use of offensive weapons to "trustworthy" persons, while prohibiting the
use of them to "everyone else."[65]

Competition between criminal justice officers and police authorities in
the performance of police functions also resulted in the arming of poor
civilian men, as the following incident that took place in the town of Jucás
in 1872 illustrates. National Guard lieutenant João Leite de Sousa Sobrinho,
who occupied the post of justice of the peace in the district of Jucás, and
several civilian men who formed an arresting squad armed with knives and
clubs attempted to apprehend Francisco da Penha from the house of the
police delegado of the municipality, an initiative that culminated in a fight.
According to the lieutenant, he had decided to arrest Francisco da Penha
because there was an order from the provincial chief of police for his capture,
and also because he "moved around the streets of the town with a formi-
dable dagger." Sousa Sobrinho, as justice of the peace, did not have police
functions. Moreover, the criminal case reveals that rivalry with the delegado,

whom he implied protected da Penha, motivated the attempted arrest on the part of Sousa Sobrinho. Nonetheless, he armed poor civilian men who did not even know who the legitimate authority was, which later led to their arrest and criminal prosecution. One of them, Manoel Pinheiro de Sousa, a twenty-six-year-old illiterate farmer who lived in the town of Pajaú, declared in criminal proceedings how he became involved in the situation. He had arrived in Jucás with another man one afternoon when he encountered the lieutenant and João, an old acquaintance. João invited them to have some alcoholic drinks and then took them to Sousa Sobrinho's house. There, the lieutenant supplied the two men along with "two mulattoes and one black man" with knives and a pistol and told them to go with him to undertake a *diligência,* or official proceeding. Manoel added in his testimony that he thought that "the lieutenant was delegado" and that he was "taking part in a squad" to apprehend a criminal.[66]

The reliance on civilian helpers to assist in police duties did not merely undermine the goal of dispossessing poor sertanejos of their weapons, and more broadly, of bringing order to the province. In fact, it caused a measure of disorder and interpersonal violence. As the following case describing a fight that ensued after a ward inspector attempted to arrest a man for making threats with a knife will demonstrate, violence arose when those sertanejos who were subject to apprehension because of their illegal possession or use of weapons failed to accept the authority of local *civilians* to exercise that power over them. According to his deposition as a defendant in an assault trial, the ironsmith Antônio Saraiva da Silva, who served as ward inspector in the village of São Francisco, Itapagé, had summoned thirteen civilian men (most of whom were illiterate farmers) to assist in the capture of Severino de tal on May 24, 1873. Antônio explained his decision to arrest Severino de tal by narrating how, on May 20, Severino had confronted him when he unsuccessfully tried to impound his knife, and said that "either today or tomorrow there will be a dead body." In an attempt "to avoid a problem with more lamentable consequences," and knowing that Severino had the protection of a man named Francisco Miguel, the ward inspector assembled the thirteen-man arresting squad to capture Severino. When this group descended upon Francisco Miguel's house on May 24, Antônio verbally issued the order for Severino's arrest, "in the name of the police commissioner." Yet, "[T]his order was not obeyed, a fact that resulted in a fight." Crucially, after being questioned by the judge, Antônio mentioned that he had not obtained a written order from the delegado for Severino's imprisonment, and that on May 24, when Severino and Francisco Miguel heard his command, "they asked to see the signature." This case also demonstrates that when free poor sertanejos were summoned to help in the performance of official functions, they became involved in violent confrontations that did not have much to do with them, and that often led to concussions or other physical injuries and to being charged as defendants in criminal assault trials. Indeed, Venâncio das Chagas Freitas, an illiterate farmer who was part of the squad of civilian men deployed to arrest Severino, mentioned in his deposition as a defendant that, as a result of the fight, he, Joaquim Chagas, and Jõao Moreira were wounded.[67]

Another case from Tamboril illustrates that rural men also found the police soldiers' authority to confiscate their weapons wanting or illegitimate, which led praças or others to call upon free poor men to reinforce their positions, and to the consequent use of violence by these civilian men in their attempts to help in these arrests. Here, the police commissioner of Tamboril had ordered the impounding of a dagger that the farmer Manoel Francelino de Almeida allegedly carried with him. A squad manned by a police soldier and a civilian court officer had been deployed to confiscate this weapon on February 17, 1860. According to one of the witnesses, when the police soldier and court officer arrived in Manoel Francelino's house, instead of relinquishing his weapon, he began fighting with the police soldier. At that point, the court officer asked several civilian men, including the farmer Eufrásio Alves Feitosa and the stonemason José Leandro Alves, to "help" them apprehend Manoel. As they did, they became involved in a fight, and Eufrásio ended up with a contusion on his left arm and a wound in the face.[68]

To be sure, attempts at expanding the reach of repressive state institutions that did not possess sufficient personnel determined the arming of poor civilians to perform police duties, a practice that, in turn, led to some disorderly arrests and aggression. Thus, instead of exercising effective social control over the poor by dispossessing them of their weapons, the weakness of the Imperial state apparatus generated a measure of social (dis)control. Indeed, under such conditions, the offensive "custom" by poor men of carrying weapons—both to defend themselves or to attack others in fights—could not be stamped out. In addition to the brawls that armed sertanejos fought for their own reasons, the process of state formation determined the engagement in violent disputes by some, as they fulfilled their responsibilities to the authorities, and by others, as they resisted the coercion of a state presence that they saw as unsanctioned and personally biased. In either case, the police and judicial institutions' attempt at ending the sertanejo "habit" of possessing weapons only made it necessary for free poor men to carry such arms in order to navigate the uncertainty and violence affecting their lives.

Paraguayan War Abroad and Violence at Home

The onset of the Paraguayan War and the massive mobilization effort required to staff the Brazilian army during its duration (1864–70) put in evidence the weaknesses and contradictions inherent in the processes of state formation both in the Brazilian Empire as a whole and in the province of Ceará. At the outset of the war the Paraguayan army consisted of 70,000 well-armed and trained soldiers, a figure that by far outnumbered the military capabilities of the Argentine, Uruguayan, and Brazilian armies combined. Even though Brazil was the largest and wealthiest of the countries that constituted the Triple Alliance, its military did not possess sufficient weapons, resources, or manpower.[69] In particular, the forced recruitment of free poor men, which was the main method that the Imperial army utilized to staff its rank and file, proved largely ineffective in obtaining an ever-increasing number of soldiers to deploy to the front. As Beattie has shown, notwithstanding the fact that during the early days of combat some men voluntarily responded to the call to arms to defend the nation, most of those who fought had to be coerced to serve in the war. In fact, an expanding crusade of impressment swept Brazilian cities and the countryside, especially during the period between 1866 and 1868, that sent many men fleeing and created a great deal of conflict. The interior of the province of Ceará was not an exception to this campaign of impressment. In effect, the Paraguayan War accelerated the process of expansion of the Imperial state into the hinterlands, especially of the Northeastern provinces, since 48 percent of all the soldiers sent to the front during the war hailed from the Northeast.[70]

The province of Ceará sent an estimated 5,769 troops to the front lines, a number that included designated National Guardsmen, volunteers, recruits, and navy apprentices who were minors.[71] Brazil's initial declaration of war sparked a wave of mobilization that led thousands of men, and even some women, from all over the country, including Ceará, to volunteer to take up arms in service to the nation. Indeed, in January of 1865, the government created the *Voluntários da Pátria*, or Volunteers of the Fatherland, an elite corps that offered an enlistment bonus, better salaries than those paid to the regulars, and land grants as incentives for men to join the war effort. These terms were later extended to National Guardsmen called into service.[72] In Ceará, the creation of the Volunteers led to a brief reprieve in the practice of pressing poor and unprotected young men into service. By October 1865, nine months after the creation of the Volunteers corps, 489 men had enlisted voluntarily, although there is evidence that at least some of them had, in fact, been coerced into serving against their will. Furthermore, even with the patriotic fervor that inundated the country, Ceará was unable to meet the minimum number of 1,060 volunteer soldiers required from the province by the Imperial government.[73] By late in 1866, as the defeat at Curupayty sent signals that the Brazilian mobilization efforts were not enough to fill the ranks, impressment resumed and intensified, even to the point where wealthy patrons were unable to shield their clients from being dragooned to the front lines.[74] Even more, National Guardsmen, who were normally exempted from service in the army, were forcefully recruited into the war effort.

This wave of violent impressment, which intensified at the national level between 1866 and 1868, generated disorder in the Cearense interior. Recruiters and army officers organized raids into backlands towns and fazendas to catch men for the war and to dragoon designated National Guardsmen. This far-reaching effort, in turn, led to violence and "insubordination" on the part of sertanejos who resisted the Imperial orders with all their might. For instance, police records for these years report violent clashes that often led to murders between recruits, *designados,* or designated National Guardsmen, and often their protectors, on one side, and press gangs, made up predominantly by poor sertanejos, and army and police praças, on the other. Fathers and brothers defended their sons and siblings from recruiters and press gangs, and engaged in bitter knife fights as these surrounded their houses. National Guard lieutenants and colonels armed cowboys, moradores, and others among the free poor to fight with recruiting squads or soldiers guarding jails where recruits were deposited in order to prevent their transportation or to release them. Angry mobs commanded by local notables ranging in numbers from 50, to 400, and even to 1,000 men attacked jails, threatening to set them on fire and release recruits. On the other side, recruiters reportedly beat designados and recruits into submission, and thus contributed to create a climate of confusion and violence. One police soldier in Granja tied and beat an elderly man who attempted to protect his son, while a recruiter flogged a pregnant woman with a knife after she attacked him in order to prevent her consensual partner's recruitment in Tamboril.[75]

Political partisanship and local elections often intersected with the disorganized process of impressment, which led to aggression among free poor men. The elite practice of threatening to recruit or causing the recruitment of qualified voters as a way to control elections and gain political appointments from the central government was well established before the war. Indeed, recruitment and exemption served local elites as tools to pressure free poor men to vote for either the Liberal or Conservative factions, according to their designs. But arbitrary impressment and release of well-connected recruits or designados by authorities who maintained relations of patronage with local notables took place in a larger scale during the most intense years of impressment for the war. For instance, according to the conservative newspaper *Constituição,* the police subdelegado from Coité, João Leite, who became general recruiter for the municipality of Milagres in 1865, had publicly sworn that he would "end with the township's *saquarema* or Conservative faction" and therefore proceeded to press for the war effort free poor men who had voted for the Conservative Party in a previous election, even when those men possessed legal exemptions. The newspaper denounced the case of Manoel Antônio Figueiredo Sabra, only son of a widow and hardworking father who supported two young daughters, and João Gonçalves Dantas Grade, who sustained with his work a paralyzed old father and several small children—two men who, despite their exemptions, were forcefully recruited by Leite because of their Conservative voting record and their association with municipal elites from that party.[76]

While it is true that the *Constituição*—a conservative newspaper—only censured the cases in which Liberal local authorities, such as Leite, committed abuses in recruitment procedures, the liberal newspaper *O Cearense* accomplished the same function with regard to arbitrary impressment by Conservative officials. Moreover, police records confirm that these practices took place across party lines. For example, according to an 1868 police report from Jardim, a delegado sought to strike an alliance with the army recruiter deployed in the municipality by confiding in him his attempts to organize political action for elections and his need to release recruits that were protected by a few powerful townsmen whose support he was courting. Facing a negative answer from the recruiter, the delegado, along with a National Guard colonel, a ward inspector, and others forcefully released one man from the squad that was transporting recruits to the Crato jail, an action that culminated in a fight.[77] In addition, according to Chandler, the 1868 political turnover, or Conservative ascendance at the national level after four years of Liberal control, intensified violent recruitment of political opponents of the newly appointed Conservative officials in several hinterlands municipalities of Ceará.[78]

In sum, a measure of disorder enveloped the Cearense backlands during the most intense period of recruitment for the Paraguayan War. Clearly, geographic remoteness did not insulate free poor men from being dragooned to fight a war in the far-away Southwestern border with Paraguay. Likewise, the press gangs that were deployed to forcefully submit poor young men into recruitment were also constituted by common sertanejos. The influence of political factionalism in struggles associated with impressment and the chaotic empowerment of poor rural men to impose aggression upon potential recruits places in evidence the manner in which the exercise of personalized masculine violence intersected with the public functions of the state during these conflictive years.

Aggression, Law Enforcement, Resistance, and Masculinity

As we have seen, police and army praças did not enjoy a great deal of legitimacy as authority figures among the rest of the population, which often resulted in their use of aggression as the means to assert their power over other men when they performed law enforcement tasks. This lack of public regard or respect was related both to their low rank in the army and police corps and their lack of weapons, discipline, and even uniforms. Nevertheless, the fact that police and army praças were mostly racially mixed men of meager means, and therefore, characterized as members of the dishonorable poor, in all likelihood, also accounted for their lack of legitimacy. Personal data of police soldiers briefly serving in the municipalities of Jucás and Tamboril who figured in criminal cases demonstrates that all the privates in the sample were illiterate, which immediately locates them in the lower orders of society. The ages of police soldiers varied between nineteen and forty, with the majority, or 74 percent, of the men ranging between nineteen and twenty-four years of age.[79] The profile of army praças detached to the municipalities of Jucás and Tamboril and who appear in criminal proceedings was very similar to the one of police soldiers.[80] They were overwhelmingly illiterate and young, ranging in age between twenty and thirty years old. While the criminal cases do not include information on the racial makeup of army soldiers, Kraay's studies of army soldiers in Bahia, and Beattie's work on the Brazilian army as a whole, indicate that most praças during the Imperial period were either black, Indian, or of mixed race. Considering that 61 percent of the free masculine population of Ceará by 1872 consisted of blacks, pardos, and caboclos, and that the proportion of free poor men of color in all likelihood was even higher, it is safe to assume that the majority of enlisted men serving in the army in Ceará belonged to these racial groupings.[81]

Facing a marginal social standing, it appears as if some police and army recruits used their position as low-level state agents, and their capacity to use violence, as a way to establish a measure of status and masculine respectability. For instance, according to a criminal accusation, on a January day in 1876 the army private Antônio Tomás da Silva apparently gratuitously whipped a young slave when he was making his way from Tamboril to Telha. To this attack, the slave responded by throwing a rock at the face of the private, fracturing his nose. Kraay has noted that race and status were important parts of soldiers' identities in Bahia even before 1837, when recruitment practices largely discriminated against black men and soldiers often competed with civilians in violent ways over points of honor. Thus, it is plausible that during the second half of the nineteenth century, when more blacks constituted the army rank and file, and within the context of the gradual decline of slavery, soldiers in Ceará used violence against slaves as a way to assert honor or masculine respectability. This violent search for honor and status, in turn, speaks of the contradictory positions of army and police privates in Brazilian society throughout the Imperial period. As Kraay has argued, privates, who were often men of color, were put in a position of authority not only over slaves or other men of color but also over the honorable poor, and even over notable white members of society.[82]

Free poor men as civilian auxiliaries of police delegados and subdelegados also made claims to social superiority through the violent performance of official state functions against slaves. For instance, because of a lack of police praças and ward inspectors, the court officer Gonçalo Francisco de Carvalho had been charged with patrolling the town of Tamboril on Christmas Eve, 1875. As the slave Cipriano declared in a criminal assault trial in which he and the slave Gregório featured as defendants, they had been singing and dancing in a *samba* (dance party) on December 24, when the court officer arrived and ordered the party to end by saying, "[T]onight the blacks are going to pay for their sins." Cipriano mentioned that at that particular moment he asked "who had issued that order," and Gonçalo Francisco replied that "he himself was the one who issued that command." After this exchange, the court officer struck Cipriano on the head. The legal complaint presented Gonçalo Francisco's version of the events. According to this narrative, he had ordered the end of the party "because the slaves were fighting among themselves," and then they attacked him with clubs. He also noted that "those slaves were constantly armed in the town." Here, it appears as if Gonçalo Francisco was asserting his racial superiority over the slaves as well as his authority to terminate their party. But crucially, the slave's statements show that even for a slave, the authority of a lowly paid, probably racially mixed, court officer was questionable. Furthermore, through this case we can observe that on account of the precarious conditions in which efforts at social control, arrests, and jailings took place, the exercise of state functions could become a contested process focused on the violent assertion of masculine power. Regardless of whose version of the events was true, the result of this encounter was a fight in which several men wounded each other with clubs.[83]

Indeed, police reports and criminal records unambiguously demonstrate

that free poor men contested the attempts to capture them, forcefully recruit them, or jail them through the use of violence. Within a context in
which being caught by the police or criminal justice agents often meant
indeterminate time in jail, enlistment into the army, or becoming a victim
of aggression, it is not surprising that free poor men resorted to violence as
a means of resistance. Thus for instance, the illiterate farmer Ladislau Capistrano apparently was being "turbulent" and insulting another man when
a ward inspector first attempted to "pacify the situation" and later to detain
Ladislau in Jucás. To this, Ladislau responded by shooting the inspector with
a shotgun. Violent confrontations also occurred when privates and others
arrested drunks who were being disorderly and transported them to prison.
For example, the friends of an inebriated man got into a fight with a police
soldier and some civilian auxiliaries when they were taking him to the jail
in Acarape.[84] Poor sertanejos who had been jailed also resorted to violence
against army and police praças and jailers who guarded the small dungeons as
they attempted to escape. Parties of relatives and friends of incarcerated men
armed themselves with clubs, knives, and shotguns to break into the jails and
liberate the inmates.[85] The threat of being caught as recruits or designados
during the most intense years of recruitment for the Paraguayan War also
encouraged men to arm themselves with daggers, knives, and rifles and to
carry their weapons even to work in the fields or while traveling. Moreover,
sertanejos highlighted their possession of weapons and what they saw as their
superior force, in an attempt to warn those sent to apprehend them. For
instance, according to the delegado of Sobral, in February of 1868 a group
of nineteen armed men, which included one designated Guardsman and
eighteen army recruits, had taken refuge in the Lugar Barro, and threatened
the ward inspector, by showing their weapons and telling him that "they
were waiting and were ready for any troops" that would dare show up at that
location.[86]

It is this quality of precariousness in law enforcement activities in the
Cearense sertão, where state agents did not have legitimacy and where at
least some sertanejos violently resisted efforts to repress them, that often
rendered the practice of state functions into a contest in which the stron-
gest man, or the one with the better weapon, achieved the objective of
dominating his opponent. This masculine competition is observable in the
language that sertanejos, both as sources and subjects of state power, used to
address their adversaries in their violent struggles. Police and army praças,
ward inspectors, court officers, and other civilian "aids" reportedly issued
arrest orders that sometimes invoked the authority of police delegados, but
that often conjured up images of violent subordination of other men. For

instance, according to his deposition in a criminal case initiated by the court officer Francisco Gonçalves Nogueira against the ward inspector of Quixará Liberalino Duartes Brandão, the ward inspector ordered a squad of civilian men to arrest him by saying "stick the clubs in that Nogueira and imprison him." In a similar case, a group of four army soldiers from Tamboril gave a beating to João Sampaio on August 11, 1867, as they arrested him. According to witnesses, the soldiers shouted "João Sampaio is a nobody, he is a nothing," as they publicly struck him with clubs and shotguns in a town street. Those sertanejos who were targets of violent state intervention and who had recourse to aggression as their only viable means of resistance also pulled out knives and guns and said that "whoever came close will die," that they were "not about to surrender," that they were "not afraid of any men," or that "nobody will imprison anybody here."[87] In 1851, the cowboy Pedro Ferreira Sampaio from the Fazenda Vítor in Tamboril resisted a squad that came to arrest him for the crime of carrying an illegal weapon, and said that "he was not afraid of the authorities" because "they are just a few men." Evidently, he had confidence that his expertise in the manipulation of weapons and that of his friends were greater than those of the squad sent to apprehend him, and that their superior physical power would keep him free from state domination, and consequently, from imprisonment.[88]

Thus, as the previous sections have shown, the increasing, and paradoxically inadequate, presence of political-legal and military institutions of the Imperial state in the backlands generated tensions regarding the exercise of masculine authority and the legitimate use of violence at the local level. Moreover, state representatives failed to resolve this conflict and to impose themselves as the privileged sources of authority to control and direct the behavior of other men. Racially mixed sertanejos as law enforcement agents who lacked uniforms, insignias, proper weaponry, and most important, legitimacy among the populace often relied on violence to perform the functions of arresting, recruiting, and transporting other sertanejos to jail. As Connell has argued, even though violence is an important component of systems of domination, "a thoroughly legitimate hierarchy would have less need to intimidate."[89] Clearly, the reproduction of violence by sertanejos as low-level law enforcement agents with questionable claims to authority was not a product of their inherent, naturally vile, instincts, or their strange adherence to anachronistic violent ideals. Instead, this form of violence resulted from the paradoxical efforts by a ruling elite to discipline and reform what they saw as the rowdy masculinities of free poor men through the deployment of weak state institutions that relied on these same men for law enforcement tasks—without providing them with the superior sanction, regulation, and even the material accoutrements needed to become effective state representatives. Within that context, the exercise of state repressive functions by sertanejos resembled more personalized, violent assertions of superior masculine power than the effective and dutiful fulfillment of law enforcement commands. On the other end of the spectrum, those free poor men who got caught in the expanding web of arrest, criminal prosecution, and recruitment, and who did not have other recourse to obtain their freedom or dispute criminal accusations, engaged in violent acts as a way to resist state intrusion into their lives.

Honorable Providers Face Officials of the State

The encounters that free poor sertanejos sustained with state institutions either as a result of social control efforts or their involvement in legal disputes forced some of them to rely on patron-client relations with local elites as a way to defend themselves from such incursions, or achieve positive judicial outcomes, in a nonviolent manner. For instance, according to a legal complaint for livestock theft against the illiterate farmer José Bernardo da Silva, he had stolen a horse that displayed Francisco Rodrigues Xavier's brand from the grazing fields of the Fazenda Morro Agudo in May 1869. After being taken into custody and jailed, "he was released, thanks to the Lieutenant Colonel Lemos Braga's perseverant efforts." In several cases, wealthier men entered the courtroom as patrons who paid bail for free poor men who had committed crimes and had been indicted. For instance, the farmer Antônio Alves Bezerra, indicted for stealing a steer from the Fazenda Cajazeiras in 1877, requested bail "and presented as his bondsman the well-to-do citizen and inhabitant of the village of São Mateus, Inácio da Silva Pereira Costa Leal." The farmer Canuto Marques de Sousa, who had been charged with cattle theft in Tamboril in 1878, offered as bondsmen Rochael Cavalcante de Albuquerque and Jôao Gomes de Rego, "two well-off proprietors who reside in this town." In both cases, the bond requests were granted.[90]

Nevertheless, while patrons' protection was necessary for free poor men to navigate the police and criminal justice system, it appears as if the social and economic transformations of the post-1845 years actually undermined those paternalistic relations. As Chapter 1 demonstrated, small farmers and ranchers who had access to plots of land, in fact, competed with larger fazendeiros and other landowners for control over their own labor, as both wealthy and poor attempted to take advantage of the prosperity brought about by the expansion of the commercial agriculture and ranching industries. Furthermore, the accelerated recruitment for the Paraguayan War, which left many patrons unable to protect their clients from impressment, the cotton boom, and the Great Drought seem to have weakened ties of patronage between free poor and elites.[91] Within that context, for those sertanejos who did not have powerful patrons, or for whom violence was not an option, a tool to engage the institutions of the state and to establish minimum claims to citizenship appears to have been the display of their honorable masculine reputations. As we shall see, these men held to versions of the seigniorial code of honor and used the language of the dominant culture to wield their own influence over a political culture permeated by hierarchy and patronage.

Free poor Cearense men who had gained a small measure of economic success during the post-1845 years sought to contend with the police and criminal justice system by basing their claims to honor on property ownership and access to material wealth. This can be seen in the remark by the illiterate farmer Francisco Angelino de Sousa, presented in the introduction to this chapter, according to which he could easily vindicate himself in a criminal assault trial because he had land, livestock, and money. That assertion could indicate that in his own view, Francisco Angelino's honor, predicated on his material possessions, would ensure special treatment from local police and judicial authorities. Alternatively, that declaration could denote the illiterate farmer's pride in his ability to pay bail. A similar assessment of an illiterate farmer's capacity—based on access to material prosperity—to positively reach an advantageous outcome from a criminal court was demonstrated in 1867 by Francisco Antônio Diaz, from the municipality of Itapagé. A witness in a criminal suit against Francisco Antônio's seventeen-year-old son, João Antônio Diaz, had heard him boast that "he had the Rs. 300$000 or Rs. 400$000 necessary to free his son" after João Antônio had been indicted for the murder of their neighbor Benedito Coelho Moraes.[92] The cases of both Francisco Angelino and Francisco Antônio demonstrate that these free poor men saw themselves as honorable members of their society, whose economic independence secured them privileged status, at least within the boundaries of the court room and police station. As Chapter 3, below, will show, some small farmers and ranchers deployed an honorable reputation reliant on their status as proprietors and *senhores* (landlords) as a bargaining chip when they faced legal conflict with other male community members for access to land, animals, and other resources.

Official documents pertaining to army recruitment confirm that some small farmers and ranchers did reproduce seigniorial ideals of masculine honor as they pursued their own goals when they came into contact with state institutions. Just like candidates who sought political appointments at the highest level of the Imperial court, free poor sertanejos associated their masculine honor with their ability to provide for and protect their families, or their recognized qualities as *bons pais de família,* or good family men.[93] For example, in his official petition for release from forced recruitment to the police commissioner of the town of São Francisco, the illiterate farmer Inocêncio Francisco dos Santos affirmed that he was married, and that he "administered all the necessities to his wife" from the work that he performed in "his own agriculture." Three character witnesses asserted that they indeed knew that the petitioner sustained his wife from "his own agriculture." Inocêncio's exemption was granted, as these sworn declarations proved that he belonged to the ranks of the honorable poor. This document's stress on Inocêncio's masculine reputation could be seen as derived exclusively from the fact that being married and actively employed, as well as having good behavior, were required to enjoy immunity from impressment. Yet this affirmation of diligence as a family man reveals the peculiarities of this historical moment as it tied this poor man's capacity to provide for his wife to the small-scale, and autonomous, agricultural work that he performed on his plot of land.[94]

Popular poems by backlands bards reveal that the performance of the role of effective providers, or at least its public recognition, was an important measure of honorable manhood for poor *sertanejos,* even outside the presence of police officers, judges, and scribes. In the poetic challenges in which they participated, popular poets buttressed their masculine reputations by deploying the language of effective provision for wife and children. For instance, the following verses from the popular poet Pedro Nonato da Cunha—born in Itapipoca, Ceará, in the 1840s—articulate a popular version of the concept of the bom pai de família.

Me dizem que eu não trabaio,	They say that I don't work,
Que eu não sustento o meu brio . . .	That I don't maintain my dignity . . .
Assim mesmo preguiçoso,	But lazy as they say I am,
Sustento muié e fio!	I still provide for my wife and children!
No ano que eu não trabaio,	In the year that I do not work,
Planto dez quarta de mio,	I plant ten *quartas* [800 liters] of corn,
Quando acaba inda hai quem diga,	When those are finished, still some say,
Que o nego veio é vadio,	That the old black man is a loafer,
Mas eu sou é trem de ferro:	But I am like an iron train:
Só corro atrás dos meus trio . . .	I only run on my own rails . . .[95]

In these verses, Pedro Nonato informed his listeners that he planted eight hundred liters of corn, which implies that he enjoyed access to arable land, as well as presumably sufficient access to the water sources needed to grow the crop. The connections between landholding as the means to provide economic security and masculine honor are clearly spelled out when Pedro

Nonato asserted that he maintained his dignity by providing for his family from the work he did on his land.

But Nonato's emphasis on his hardworking abilities suggests that the verbalization of stereotypical notions of masculine honor could be affected by the vulnerable standing of free poor men in the hierarchical social relations that surrounded their lives. In particular, Nonato's emphasis on his status as a dignified man, and not a "loafer," could be read as a rhetorical strategy to confront the disparagement of lower-class masculinities that larger landowners, authorities, and municipal elites expressed through the constant accusations of "vagrancy" labeled against those free poor men who refused to work for wages.[96] In fact, Nonato's verses illustrate the importance of honorable masculinities in a milieu where racial constructs derived from a slave-holding society included the expected normative condition of servility for those of African descent. Confronting those expectations, Nonato, a former slave, explained how he maintained his dignity as a free man of color, while he also established one of the measures of manhood—capacity to work for himself and not for others—that he believed defined his male identity as a member of the honorable poor when he asserted "But I am like an iron train: I only run on my own rails."[97]

The importance of honorable masculine reputations as a tool for free poor men to negotiate the political culture of the Imperial period is also evident in the cases of patronless small farmers and ranchers who were accused of cattle rustling and who attempted to use their reputation for trustworthiness as livestock managers as a way to effect a positive conclusion to their legal trials. As Chapter 3 will demonstrate, sertanejos employed unwritten conventions that required reliance on the recognized honesty of ranchers and cowboys to guarantee the ownership of highly mobile cattle that pastured in the open range. Thus, when the farmer and cowboy João Ferreira Lima was accused of stealing a head of cattle from the grazing fields of Captain Vicente Ferreira Marques's fazenda in 1868, he noted in his defense that "he is not accustomed to stealing other people's cattle." This statement indicated not only that he had not stolen this particular head of cattle, but that he was an honest man who transacted honorably with livestock. João Ferreira, in all likelihood, hoped that this line of defense, reliant on the public recognition of his honor, would be sufficient to free him of the charges he was facing. In fact, it seems as if a man's honorable reputation centered on trustworthiness did play a role in the assessment of cattle theft cases, since witnesses in several of these trials were asked whether those defendants were accustomed to taking other people's cattle or not.[98]

The task of determining to what extent judicial authorities responded to these proclamations of male honorability with favorable rulings on behalf of free poor male defendants is very difficult to accomplish, as many discrete considerations influenced judges' and juries' decisions. Nevertheless, various pieces of evidence from criminal cases demonstrate that at least on some occasions, members of the elite acknowledged the honorable reputation of free poor sertanejos who derived their status from ownership of small landed properties and provision for family members. For instance, after being indicted for the physical assault of Antônio Rodrigues de Sousa at a party, Francisco Angelino's request for bail was granted. In the words of the district judge of São Mateus, "[T]he defendant is not vagrant, and therefore, I believe it is fair to concede him bail and do him justice." This statement refers to criminal procedure regulations, according to which vagrants were not to be granted bail even in less severe crimes in which it was not required for a suspect to remain in prison during the criminal trial. As the regulations stated, a vagrant was a person "without fixed residence, without habitual profession or trade, and without income." Clearly, even though Francisco Angelino was an illiterate farmer, he was not considered a vagrant, and therefore not a member of the dishonorable poor, and his ranking as above vagrant, in turn, was bolstered by the same quality that Francisco Angelino had bragged about when he got arrested: his possession of material wealth.[99]

It is possible to observe this recognition of free poor men's claims to honor on occasions in which they served as witnesses in criminal proceedings that judged others, and therefore exposed their good name to assessment by the courts. Even though the Code of Criminal Procedure did not rank the credibility of witnesses' testimony, as it only requested that judges take note of kinship, enmity, or dependency relationships between witnesses and plaintiffs and defendants, in practice, judicial officials, lawyers, and other court participants regarded some witnesses' declarations as more credible than others.[100] In particular, attributes that tainted a man's ability to present impartial testimony appeared to have been poverty, and its consequent dependency from relations of subordination to either one of the parties involved, and a reputation for dishonesty. In fact, according to Pedro Honorato de Araújo Chaves, a notable citizen of Campo Grande, Ipu, who was indicted and sentenced for the homicide of Raimundo Gaia, "[H]onorable men should have been called to be witnesses in this trial." Instead, he called into question the testimony that had been offered by three court officers, the pardos Antônio dos Santos Bizerra, Francisco Rosa, and José Luís de Oliveira, who in his view were "not credible witnesses due to the severity of their misery." A similar assessment was presented by Captain Laurenio Dias Martins, who after being indicted for assault against the merchant Benvindo Cavalcante de Albuquerque, argued that many irregularities had characterized his indictment. Among them, the court had accepted as valid the testimony of the court officer João Luís do Nascimento, a witness that he deemed "defective" because "despite his employment, he lives wrestling with misery." By contrast, the merchant Joaquim José Pereira de Sousa from the town of Jucás declared in a criminal suit against José Luís dos Santos that the illiterate farmer Manoel Ferreira "was not a miserable person," and obviously not dishonorable, "since he worked and had a roça" and he "maintained his family"—qualifications that in Pereira de Sousa's view made his testimony acceptable. The difference in the assessment of these witnesses' worth lay in the fact that because of their poverty, and in all likelihood also their race, the court officers' partiality and, therefore their honor, were called into question, whereas Manoel Ferreira's economic autonomy (even if derived from agricultural work in a roça) ensured his independent judgment and honorable reputation.[101]

Clearly, free poor men from the Cearense interior articulated hegemonic understandings of honor—particularly, the link between economic independence, property ownership, provision for family, and masculine reputation, that resonated with and sometimes were accepted by elite society. However, these claims to honor did not constitute merely acts of imitation of official ideologies by sertanejos, nor did they represent their adherence to an unchanging cultural complex. Instead, as responses to the incursions by the state into their lives and as attempts to advance their interests in criminal courts, these assertions represented strategic resources used by unprotected rural men to negotiate their precarious legal positions within the political order of the empire. Therefore, it appears as if free poor sertanejos, just like those poor men that Brodwyn Fischer studied in twentieth-century Rio de Janeiro, regarded the ability to credibly sustain honorable masculine reputations "as crucial to the successful navigation of most public and private systems of punishment, reward and patronage."[102] The credibility of such claims, in turn, could be bolstered by the fact that the structural transformations affecting the province of Ceará during the nineteenth century had made it possible for some among the rural poor to achieve a degree of prosperity and even autonomy, based on agricultural and ranching work performed in smallholdings.

Conclusions

By the mid-nineteenth century, a centralized state had emerged out of the social-political conflict and administrative experimentation that enveloped the nascent Brazilian Empire during the first half of the nineteenth century. For the planter class that constituted the ruling elite, a larger, effective, and

centralized bureaucracy that controlled police administration and the criminal justice system figured prominently in the imposition and maintenance
of order throughout the country. Order signified the efforts to safeguard the
social, racial, and gender hierarchy in place in Brazil and the agrarian basis of
the export economy, with its need for disciplined labor, whether slave or free.
Thus, as the Imperial political-legal institutions became consolidated, their
reach progressively expanded even in isolated areas, such as the backlands of
the province of Ceará. It is true that the imposition of state power coexisted
with the traditional exercise of authority through private hierarchies, most
notably, patronage and slavery, during the Imperial period. Yet it is undeniable that at least some Brazilian institutions of government underwent a
process of modernization that included efforts—albeit incomplete and contradictory—to rationalize the relationship between the population and the
authority of the state, even if this was to serve elite interests.[103]

The implementation of this new type of political legitimacy impinged
directly on the social organization of gender, and especially on the practices
of masculinity and the power of real men. Policies and institutions designed
to promote law and order in the interior of Ceará expanded the repertoire
of masculine authority, even to include poor sertanejos as sources of state
power. Paradoxically, as the bureaucratic capacities of the state grew, provincial and municipal elites concerned with the need to discipline the "insubordinate" sertanejos and transform them into dependable laborers focused the
attention of repressive institutions on poor men. In particular, in an attempt
to "reform" what they saw as the entrenched "bad habits" and "rebellious"
masculinities of the backlanders, provincial authorities directed at least some
social control efforts to arresting and punishing those who committed public
order offenses, especially habitual drunkenness, possession of illegal weapons,
and vagrancy.

As Judy Bieber has argued, the extent of political change in Imperial Brazil becomes more clearly visible through an examination of the periphery
instead of only the center.[104] The regulative capacity of this growing state
presence in the Cearense countryside was extremely weak, as the police
corps and the army, which was regularly charged with assisting in police duties, suffered from chronic understaffing problems. Police jurisdictions were
not manned with sufficient delegados and subdelegados and consequently
relied on the help of local civilian auxiliaries. The criminal justice system,
subject to the influence of patronage and political partisanship, did not enjoy
the autonomous power necessary to effectively punish criminality. These
weaknesses resulted in a lack of success on the part of the centralized state
in meeting its objectives of social control and imposition of order. In fact,

seen from the periphery, the consolidation of Imperial state power in Brazil was anything but a process that brought order; instead, it generated conflict, disorder, and interpersonal violence.

The violent conflict that resulted from some of the practices of state politics in the interior was related to the controversies over the exercise of authority and the legitimate use of masculine violence that were unleashed, and remained unresolved, by this haphazard process of state formation. The police corps and the army relied on the assimilation of free poor men and petty criminals—considered dishonorable because of their race and social position—to staff its poorly paid rank and file. These institutions of social control, however, did not have enough resources to train, uniform, supervise, or discipline poor praças, and to transform their use of violence into systematic practice. Moreover, poor and racially mixed sertanejos were critical to the everyday functioning of the state apparatus as civilian auxiliaries to delegados and subdelegados. Yet, these impromptu agents of the state, just like police and army praças, did not embody legitimacy as state representatives and, therefore, relied on acts of violence to direct the behavior of those who were subjected to state action. Furthermore, poor male backlanders who did not have patrons that could help negotiate this chaotic and corrupt system, and who had violated public order, resisted impressment, or committed crimes, resorted to violence as a way to oppose or evade the attempts at domination exercised by government agents. Viewed from this perspective, the performance of violence by poor Cearense males as sources and subjects of a state power that failed to monopolize legitimate aggression cannot be explained by invoking the "natural aggression" that supposedly has characterized sertanejos since time immemorial. Instead, this form of violence constituted a strategy by rural men with minimum influence and limited claims to citizenship to establish the physical superiority that ultimately sustained the authority of those who represented the state and the capacity to resist of those who were subject to that power. As such, these violent acts can be seen as practices through which free poor men, even if located in positions of subordination vis-à-vis the elites, articulated hegemonic masculinities that affirmed—if only through violence—hierarchies of superiority and inferiority between men.

Nevertheless, sertanejos did not only use violence as a means to assert a hegemonic position when they navigated the vagaries of the disorganized and corrupt practice of arrest, criminal prosecution, and punishment in the backlands. Those free poor men who could credibly claim to possess at least some of the yardsticks of honorable masculinity sought to influence the police and criminal justice systems by proving that they belonged to the ranks of the honorable poor, even if they did not have powerful patrons to bolster their position. Instead, grounding their proclamations of masculine honor on the ability to provide for their families and the demonstrable degree of wealth that some had gained as small farmers and ranchers, these sertanejos endeavored to obtain favorable rulings and establish the citizenship rights that were denied to the poor and unprotected. Paradoxically, in using this strategy to tackle the formal politics of exclusion of the hierarchical order of the empire, these free poor men reaffirmed the seigniorial code of manhood, according to which only propertied, economically independent, and honorable men would enjoy equality of citizenship rights.[105]

Chapter 3

Poor but Respectable: Community, Family, and the Gendered Negotiation of Daily Life, 1845–89

Venha cá, Seu Secundino,	Come here Mr. Secundino,
Dance no samba daqui,	Dance in this party,
Que estes caboco são pobe,	That these caboclos are poor,
Mais têm honra consigo.	But they have honor in themselves.
Mas têm honra consigo,	But they have honor in themselves,
E toitiço no cupim,	And good judgment in their curly heads,
Só não são da cor de leite	Only they are not the color of milk
E nem da cor de alfenim . . .	Nor of white sugar dough . . . [1]

Popular poets living in the Northeastern backlands during the late-nineteenth and early twentieth centuries expressed a profound concern with the assertion and defense of masculine honor. In their verses, cantadores celebrated the social prestige of men who, through different deeds, attitudes, and postures, earned respect and esteem from other inhabitants of the sertão. Likewise, in the poetic contests with rival poets, they boasted of their own honor by asserting that, even though they were poor and of racially mixed backgrounds, they were respectable.[2] Although elite-based racial hierarchies often denied free poor men of color broad recognition of their claims to honor, cantadores, who belonged to this group,[3] proudly claimed honorable reputations.

Outsiders traveling in the sertão, provincial authorities, and other observers also ascribed to poor sertanejos an almost obsessive preoccupation with establishing male reputation and respect. According to these commentators, sertanejos were "revengeful" and more than ready to settle a variety of offenses to their honor through the use of violence. In particular, these representations depict backlanders as possessors of a legendary jealousy and an extraordinary readiness to kill those who sullied the family's honor by violating the sexual chastity of female kin.[4] Too often, students of folklore and sometimes even historians of the sertão have explained these extreme behaviors by asserting that, in constantly emphasizing masculine reputation and respect, sertanejos were, in fact, enacting the dictates of an unchanging culture that placed excessive importance on personal honor.[5]

This chapter challenges this widely accepted interpretation by analyzing another facet of life for the rural poor—the struggle to preserve access to land, water, and animals in a drought-prone region—that gave the code of honor and the preoccupation with masculine status a specific meaning and purpose during the post-1845 years. Here, I argue that pressures in the material foundations of community and family life, including fragility in access to the productive resources needed to survive from agriculture and ranching, go a long way in explaining why small farmers and ranchers felt compelled to persistently assert their masculine honor. Ironically, the strengthened presence of an Imperial state that was incapable of regulating property boundaries and usufruct of land did nothing to decrease the need for personalized claims to masculine respectability, as these remained pivotal in the smallholders' daily negotiations for access to badly demarcated and often communally owned resources. Furthermore, reliance on cooperation between male family and joint landholding members, in a context of fierce competition for land, animals, and water, and continuous subdivision of family landed patrimonies, also helps elucidate the sertanejos' preoccupation with female chastity and their subscription to an ideology that regarded women as repositories of family honor. In addition to these concerns, the emphasis on defense of landed patrimony and provision for family members as signifiers of masculine honor allowed small farmers and ranchers to claim patriarchal authority over female kin. Thus, this chapter demonstrates that instead of symbolizing the sertanejos' attachment to an anachronistic cultural legacy, defense of masculine honor and reputation represented a rational strategy—elaborated within the cultural idiom of honor—to ensure access to material resources in a highly conflictive and competitive milieu. Likewise, the following pages illustrate how the lived experience of insecurity of survival gave specific meanings to the social organization of gender, including attempts at masculine domination over family women, within sertanejo households.

Competition for Scarce Resources

A discussion of the relationship between material life and masculinity in the backlands requires us to first sketch out the serious difficulties that families of poor farmers and ranchers faced in order to retain or expand their access to productive resources during the second half of the nineteenth century. The increasing demand for arable lands, grazing fields, water, and woods that paralleled the growth of the Cearense economy after 1845 and the environmental calamity of the late 1870s, brought consequences such as the overgrazing of the range and devastation of forested areas. Moreover, fierce competition for shrinking resources, especially during periods of drought and scarcity, pitted neighbors against each other, as all of them sought to use every bit of available land to guarantee their survival, or increase their income. These struggles reveal the limitations of an agricultural and ranching expansion that came about in a context of small landholdings. But even more fundamentally, these conflicts demonstrate the highly competitive association between agriculture and ranching in the semiarid backlands of Ceará, where agriculture never displaced cattle grazing, and where both activities coexisted and expanded through the use of the same insufficient resources.

In their attempt to raise and commercialize increasing numbers of livestock, many small ranchers overgrazed their smallholdings. Municipal ordinances and local custom established that the equivalent of at least ten hectares of land were necessary to graze one head of cattle in the sertão. Small-scale *criadores* who lacked sufficient land to graze their animals, in some cases, engaged in informal arrangements with other landowners, for access to land; in other cases, as heirs, they relied on pastures in jointly held properties.[6]

But obviously, such options were not open to all small-scale ranchers, who as a result found themselves forced to engage in overgrazing. As provincial president José Júlio de Albuquerque Barros remarked in his 1878 report, too often "speculators raise their livestock in the open fields" and in this manner "frustrate the calculations of provident ranchers, who find it impossible to stop the invasion of other people's cattle in grazing fields."[7] Indeed, the analysis of land registries presented in Chapter 1 clearly indicates that many small proprietors lacked sufficient land to graze their livestock. The evidence from postmortem inventories from the municipality of Jucás points in the same direction. For instance, when Antônio de Sousa Bezerra died in 1867, his family declared ownership of 78 braças of land in the Sítio da Mutrica in Jucás. A multiplication of this frontage size by one league (the largest depth noted in land registries) gives an equivalent of 113.2 hectares of land, not enough space to graze the twenty head of cattle that the family kept, along with eleven goats and two horses.[8]

The rapid decrease in the amount of land available for open-range grazing and the multiplication of small ranches not only translated into abusive pasturing but also led to the grazing of animals beyond areas designated for that purpose. Since the mid-nineteenth century, municipal councils attempted to regulate zones for ranching and agriculture. Generally, municipal ordinances established that the lands on the tops or slopes of hills and mountains or in the valleys between certain low mountain chains should be used exclusively for agriculture. Often, the ordinances allowed draft animals in these regions only under supervision, or in corrals. Municipal laws sometimes gave farmers the right to compensation when service animals not adequately kept or loose pigs, goats, and sheep invaded their fields. In some localities, the laws required leaving a clearing of about two leagues between the edge of planting lands on the slopes of a hill and the areas for open-range grazing in the neighboring sertões. In primarily ranching areas, or zones designated for both ranching and agriculture, farmers were required to build fences in order to protect their crops from roaming animals.[9] Yet, the evidence from criminal cases and other sources indicates that animals often invaded the planted fields of neighboring farms.[10] Moreover, during the summer months and during droughts, such as the one affecting some regions of Ceará in the mid-1860s, and the Great Drought of 1877–79, cattle raisers moved their animals to the fresh serras or elevated areas within each municipality and consequently destroyed planted fields.[11]

The unfettered expansion of agriculture also came into conflict with the pastoral activities of the sertão and caused destruction of forested lands with reserves of wood. The slash-and-burn agriculture that sertanejos practiced with ever-growing intensity during these years endangered pasturelands and devastated the reserves of timber available in mountain slopes. As agriculture continued spreading into the hillsides, forests were destroyed with great rapidity. With that destruction came the loss of the scrubland trees and bushes that Cearenses used to feed cattle, especially during the long summer months and droughts.[12] Municipal laws once again attempted to slow the effects of deforestation, by prohibiting or imposing fines on the cutting of trees located along springs and creeks. Ordinances also required farmers to plant trees near sources of water.[13] However, the laws were not enough to slow the damaging effects of the reckless advance of agriculture in the sertão. The system of slash-and-burn agriculture and other voracious farming methods practiced in the smallholdings resulted in the reduction of soil productivity over time. In this context, free poor Cearenses faced great difficulties in attaining the increasing access to arable lands that they needed, as well as to woods. Consequently, they competed bitterly for these resources.[14]

Access to water was another matter of severe contention in the interior of Ceará, a drought-prone province where rivers and streams flowed only during the rainy season, and availability of permanent water was restricted to mountaintops. Sertanejos from all racial and class groups faced enormous difficulties in irrigating their roças and in providing water for themselves and their animals. Moreover, some appropriated natural water sources, as in the case of the residents of Crato, who according to an observer "believed they needed one spring for themselves," which resulted in continuous tension.[15] Municipal legislation makes it abundantly clear that it was customary in some places to divert streams and small rivers and that some landholders used branches, woods, or fences to impede the free flow of water. Ordinances from many municipalities required farmers who built small reservoirs, or *açudes*, in elevated areas to let water run downward during specific periods so that enough water flow would reach the lower river and streambeds. Ordinances that required ranchers to dig and preserve wells, or *cacimbas*, in the streambeds on their fazendas prohibited building fences around the wells or requiring payments for their use.[16] Nevertheless, landowners such as *Dona*[17] Francisca Gonçalves de Moura, from the municipality of Souré, kept fences around the cacimbas in order to restrict the use of those waters by the "general populace" of their localities.[18]

The accelerated competition for resources brought about by the growing agricultural and ranching economies that developed in a context of scarce natural resources operated as a disintegrating force of backlands society. Intra-community conflict among neighbors and coproprietors in joint landhold-ings arose as people competed for productive resources. Verbal and sometimes physical fights broke out between neighbors when loose animals damaged roças. In some cases, angry neighbors killed invading cows or goats. Livestock owners, in turn, accused their neighbors of keeping roças without fences and therefore refused to pay reparations.[19] Moreover, the ability of some landhold-ers to restrict water use seems to have generated grave tensions. For instance, during the dry winter of 1859, in the municipality of Baturité, a group of armed men destroyed the walls of a large reservoir that belonged to Lieu-tenant Colonel Hermenegildo Furtado de Mendonça.[20] Smallholders also challenged each other's claims to possession of certain lands and encroached on plots that others declared as their own. Thus they set afire or axed down fences, fruit trees, houses, and planted fields on land that belonged to their neighbors or to other co-owners of joint landholdings.[21]

Community, Masculine Honor, and
the Negotiation of Land, Water, and Animals

In this context, the ability of free poor Cearense families to maintain ac-cess to their small plots of land, to effectively use them to derive their suste-

nance, and to keep them long enough to be able to bequeath them to their
children relied, in large part, on the deployment of masculinities, centered
on the concept of honor, and on the performance of the role of defenders
of patrimony, by men as family heads. The designation of the husband as the
head of the household and of his functions within the family was a matter
of law as well as practice. The *Ordenações Filipinas* explicitly established that
the husband was the *cabeça do casal*, or legal head of household. One of the
aspects that defined the role of household heads was their juridical right to
administer both the couple's community property and his wife's property. In
the Cearense interior, gender ideals shared by both the wealthy and the poor,
posited that men, as *donos de casa* (literally, owners of the house, or household
heads), were in charge of the family's economic decisions and of defending
its patrimony, even with violence if necessary.[22]

The land registries completed in the 1850s help to illustrate the masculine prerogative of being household heads and administrators of the family's
property. For instance, of a total of 420 individuals who appear as registrants
of landholdings in the surviving portion of the cadastre from the township
of Ipu, only 52, or 12.3 percent, were women. These women were, for the
most part, widows, as was the case of Lourença Maria de Morais, widow of
Pedro Alves de Araújo, who recorded her possession of three plots of land
that she claimed she inherited from her husband. Single adult women who,
in all likelihood, did not have any male relatives living nearby were the only
other category of women that appeared as land claimants in the register. For
instance, Maria Rodrigues de Oliveira and Rita Duartes de Azevedo were
single and each registered one piece of land in the Sítio Boa Vista. All the rest
of the entries were listed by men, who either as husbands, fathers, or brothers of siblings who were minors, fulfilled their role of managers of landed
patrimony by recording their families' properties with the local priest.[23]

Yet, the masculine defense and administration of landed patrimony of
poor families did not require only the registration of smallholdings, or the
signing of contracts of purchase or rent. Instead, as we will see below, because
of the ambiguities in the landholding structure in Imperial Brazil and the
accelerated competition for pasturing and agricultural lands affecting the
province, poor sertanejos depended on the assertion of respectable masculinities as one of the main strategies to defend family landed patrimonies and
to negotiate the use of productive resources.

Several factors account for the fragility and ambiguity in land tenure
practices in Ceará during these years. First, since the colonial period, the
limits of most sesmarias, or royal land grants, had not been properly established through judicial surveys. Thus, as the subdivision of sesmarias took

place through inheritance and sales, boundaries between the increasingly smaller plots became even more uncertain.[24] During the nineteenth century, legal demarcation of lands remained an expensive civil process that involved requesting an initial survey, measurement of the lands, and placement of markers from the municipal judge. This judicial procedure also required the presentation of titles and the summoning of immediate neighbors to all the proceedings as defendants, so that they could expound their cases. While setting legally ruled land markers did not necessarily involve a legal quarrel, contested claims over the same lands and questions regarding the validity of each party's titles could lead to lengthy litigations.[25] Most small farmers and ranchers who had inherited or purchased lands derived from sesmarias could not afford such procedures or lacked the contacts or property titles necessary to pursue legal demarcation of their lands.

Second, the practice of joint landholding seems to have been in widespread use in the backlands. According to two anthropological studies of peasant communities in backlands districts of Bahia and Piauí, beginning in the first half of the nineteenth century, large families of subsistence farmers collectively owned or occupied landholdings, such as fazendas or larger sítios. Individuals and nuclear families that belonged to the larger family units that claimed possession of these landholdings independently used small plots within them to raise cattle and to grow subsistence crops. The studies further point out that these communities resulted from both the geographic conditions and the landholding patterns of the sertão.[26] In Ceará, joint landholding helped to provide free poor families with access to productive resources. Moreover, heirs who inherited increasingly smaller and unmarked plots of land that had constituted a sesmaria or a large fazenda, used coproprietorship as a strategy to avoid the continuing division of lands and to collaborate to survive from agricultural and ranching activities. For example, according to the land registry of Santa Quitéria, the widow Eugênia Peres Nunes, her adult children Manoel Ferreira de Sousa, Ana Francisca de Sousa, Luís Ferreira de Sousa, Francisco Ferreira de Sousa, Joaquim Peres Nunes Brito, Vicente Ferreira de Sousa, Antônio Francisco de Sousa, and Elena Ferreira de Sousa, and her sons-in-law João de Paiva Dias Timbo and Florêncio Pereira da Costa were coproprietors of the Fazenda Cajazeiras. The widow Eugênia and each of the heirs claimed ownership over one or two of the seventeen unmarked plots of land that constituted the Fazenda, and that had resulted from its subdivision at the time of death of Eugenia's husband, João Ferreira de Sousa.[27]

Coproprietorship was not limited to family members or heirs of larger fazendas, however. As land became an increasingly important resource in the agriculture and ranching economies of the province, outsiders and even migrants who could afford to purchase only one smallholding often did so in estates belonging to several coproprietors. In this way, they acquired access not only to planting lands but also to grazing fields and water sources, which were shared by all members of a joint landholding. For example, Manoel Dourado de Oliveira declared in the land registry of Santa Quitéria that he had purchased one plot of grazing land, whose exact limits he did not know, from the heirs of Silvestre Afonso Barroso and Clara Maria dos Santos, who were coproprietors of the Fazenda Santa Luzia. The neighboring entries also made clear that the original heirs and coproprietors had sold other pieces of this Fazenda to several people, who then became co-owners of the Fazenda; among them were Raimundo Ferreira Santiago, Alexandrino Rodrigues da Costa, Joana de Barros Bezerra, Joana Ferreira Passos, Manoel Martins Pereira, Antônio Pereira dos Reis, and Joaquim Pereira dos Reis.[28]

A quantitative examination of the land registry from the township of Ipu indicates that joint landholding was a significant land tenure arrangement.[29] For instance, of a total of 856 landholdings listed in the surviving portion of the land registry, 327, or 38 percent, were held in common. The entries describe these landholdings variously as *terras incorporadas* or *englobadas* (incorporated lands), *terras unidas com outros do mesmo sítio* (joint landholding with others in the farm), or *terras envolvidas* (lands involved with those of others). It is necessary to stress that the entries in the land registries make clear that delimitation of internal boundaries within these jointly owned landholdings was nonexistent.

All importantly, forms of joint ownership and shared use of land were not exclusive of coproprietors who inherited, purchased, or even occupied lands in a fazenda or sítio.[30] Other means of more or less stable access to arable and grazing lands incorporated joint use of resources. For example, foreiros in Jucás and Tamboril paid for access to lands in the patrimônio of Nossa Senhora do Carmo and Santo Anastácio, respectively. But the actual usufruct of such lands, whether for ranching or agriculture, was sanctioned by communal regulations, since foreiros shared land tenure with others in the patrimônios. Likewise, rendeiros signed contracts that established different lengths of tenure on rented lands. However, they often rented plots of land in larger fazendas owned or rented by several other families. For example, between 1853 and 1854, the illiterate farmer João Alves da Cruz and his wife rented a plot of land, a house, corrals, and a cacimba, in the Fazenda Lugar Mulungú, in the municipality of Itapagé, for Rs. 49$000 per year. The landlady, Dona Joana Ferreira Chaves, resided in the mountainous district of Maranguape. Among those who also lived in the Lugar Mulungú were Dona

Joana's nephew João de Oliveira, the vaqueiros Luís Gomes and Luduvico, and their families.[31]

Third, as Chapter 1 has shown, after 1822, the formal end of the distribution of sesmarias brought about a process of occupation of public lands without legal demarcation of boundaries, or the requirement of land titles. The lack of land legislation between the years 1822 and 1850 implied the continuation of "effective occupation" as the most common method to sanction rights to land posses and their usufruct throughout Brazil.[32] Under the posse regime, the fact of occupation—the ultimate proof of which relied on cultivation or use of land—engendered subsequent rights to control, as well as to sell, buy, and bequeath posses. These transactions were then recorded in documents such as deeds of purchase and *partilhas* (the documents attached to postmortem inventories that detail the legal subdivision of assets), though descriptions of posse boundaries were typically vague. What is most significant about this landholding regime is that because it originated in effective occupation, it required neighbors' acknowledgment and recognition of one's claims to specific plots of land, planted fields, and land improvements in order to function and to generate land titles and other legal documents.[33]

Fourth, after the enactment of the 1850 Land Law, neighbors' recognition of claims to plots of land and planted fields remained central to guarantee land usufruct and property rights in Ceará. The law required that landholders register their properties and revalidate them with the state, which, in principle, delegitimized the customary relations that formed the basis of the posse regime. Nevertheless, several of the law's stipulations continued to give sanction to the principle that cultivation effectively legitimated posse. These included the regulation that "the sesmarias and peaceful posses by the first occupants would be revalidated if they were cultivated" and that "posses acquired through peaceful occupation would be legitimated if they were cultivated, or represented the habitual residence of the *posseiro* (occupant, or technically a squatter)." In addition, because "peaceful occupation" was defined as the occupation to which "no one had posed obstacle," in practice, the Land Law of 1850 did not abolish the public's reliance on neighbors' acknowledgment of the limits to a person's posse and the exact location of his or her *cultivos* (plantings). What is more, since the obligatory registration of landholdings in the parish registers did not require the presentation of any supporting evidence to back up a land claim, the law did not end the validity of effective occupation, with all its uncertainties, as an organizing principle of rural land tenure.[34]

In a milieu in which land boundaries were, for nearly all practical purposes, nonexistent, joint-ownership and shared use of land was common, and the recognition by neighbors and others was necessary to guarantee a family's right to occupy and use landholdings, interpersonal relationships were the main medium through which men, as family heads, negotiated land use.[35] They relied on consensus to organize these matters, as neighbors, fellow renters, and coproprietors mutually recognized a specific stream, hill, or even a tree as a boundary to their possessions. Landholders expected acknowledgment of what they saw as their "traditional" rights to specific areas when they and their forebears had been established in there for generations. The construction or destruction of land improvements, such as corrals, fences, houses, roças, water reservoirs, and sugar mills required informal permission from coproprietors, when they were located on shared properties, and from neighbors when they were situated on or around the presumed boundaries between properties.[36] In estates whose owners engaged in both grazing and planting, co-owners were expected to seek neighbors' approval to plant or graze in particular locations whose ownership was unclear.[37]

These arrangements were necessarily unstable, as they were contingent on the changing fortunes, designs on land utilization, and relative power of men to negotiate with neighbors and coproprietors. Other factors, such as the frequent absenteeism of wealthy landholders, the continued subdivision of lands, and increasing land sales contributed to make this system of allocation of resources increasingly fragile. Criminal cases from the municipalities of Jucás, Tamboril, and Itapagé illustrate the veritable state of confusion in which matters of land use remained during these years. For instance, in July of 1870, the illiterate farmer Manoel de Sousa Bezerra accused his neighbors José Raimundo Ferreira, Bernabé Ferreira Marques, João Diniz Maciel, João Ferreira Marques, João Diniz de Moraes, and Bento Ferreira Marques of invading a section of what he considered his land in the Sítio Canabrava, municipality of Jucás, and of burning his fences and corrals, repeatedly, since the end of 1868. According to the plaintiff's legal complaint, he possessed the plot of land adjacent to that of the defendants since the legal subdivision of his father's property took place after his death. What is interesting about Manoel de Sousa Bezerra's grievance is that it reveals how rapid changes in land ownership undermined old conventions between neighbors, and how, in a context of urgency to put to use every available space for small-scale agriculture and ranching, it became increasingly difficult to renegotiate them. Manoel de Sousa noted that "the limits between the two landholdings were always recognized by all his ancestors and [previous] neighbors." Yet the defendants "have distanced themselves from the path of their ancestors, and have invaded those lands, and attempted to take possession of them, by opening roças, and engaging in other acts of possession."[38]

As the sertanejos' needs for arable lands, grazing fields, water, and wood increased with the expansion of commercial agriculture and ranching, small-holders attempted to negotiate access to these natural resources through the constant assertion of property rights over them, and the backing up of such claims by honorable masculine reputations. Criminal trial transcripts of *dano* (property damage) featuring land disputes between smallholders and larger or more established landowners help to illustrate these points. Here, we can begin with an 1866 case in which Francisco de Abreu Barros, a major in the National Guard and notary public in the town of Saboeiro, accused the farmers José Rodrigues de Macedo, Bartolomeu Rodrigues, Antônio Ro-drigues de Macedo, and several of their respective sons, of physically harming his property. The information presented by both the plaintiff and defendants makes clear that all these men, except for Antônio Rodrigues and his son, lived in the Fazenda Cajazeiras, and therefore were coproprietors and neigh-bors. The accusation stated that the defendants had "disturbed" Francisco de Abreu's "tranquility" when "they began to open up fields and demol-ish fences, under the pretence of being *senhores* of those lands." The choice of the term *senhores* is significant, because according to nineteenth-century dictionary definitions, the word *senhor* denoted a series of meanings that had clear associations with honor. To be a senhor meant not only "to be owner and absolute proprietor of something" but also, in the masculine gender, "a man who exercises power, domination and influence," or "someone who receives respectable treatment from others." Indeed, *senhor* was defined as "an honorific title conferred on distinguished individuals either because of their position or the dignity invested on them."[39] It is clear that the small-holders who entered into conflict with Francisco de Abreu were not nobles. They were illiterate men "who lived off agriculture."Yet, at least according to the accusation, they had claimed the honorific title of senhores to exercise power, authority, and, consequently, property rights over lands that they had come to consider theirs and begun using them as they saw fit.[40]

Obviously, one needs to be careful not to interpret what appears to be an annoyed local notable's declaration in a criminal court that his illiter-ate neighbors had appropriated the title of senhores as direct evidence that smallholders aspired to obtain such honorific recognitions. Nevertheless, an-other dano case, this time from the municipality of Tamboril, confirms that smallholders in conflict with their social superiors for access to land tied their claims to property rights to honorable status. In this case, Antônio Ricardo Albuquerque Cavalcante, a priest in charge of the parish of Independência, Piauí, accused his illiterate neighbor, the smallholder and rancher José dos Santos Marinho, of illicitly logging a great quantity of wood, including carnaúba trees, from his lands in the Fazenda Riacho dos Bois, in Tamboril. In his 1872 legal complaint, Albuquerque Cavalcante noted that Marinho had begun logging in 1870, when he commenced work on his house, corral, and fences, and that since then "he complained and even admonished Marinho" who "routinely ignored him, due to the fact that he was, as he calls himself, a *proprietário* (proprietor)."[41] Crucially, in his defense during the judicial investigation, Marinho did not offer any documents to prove how he came to possess the landholding next to Albuquerque Cavalcante's, and he simply argued that he was "proprietor of the lands in question in the Fazenda Riacho dos Bois," and that "the plaintiff did not know to whom the land where the woods had been cut belonged to." According to a nineteenth-century dictionary, the word *proprietário* denoted the objective "possessor of property," but also "the individual who retained legal possession especially of urban or rural real estate."[42] This seems to indicate that in Marinho's view, the rhetorical assertion of the title of proprietor, both in the fields and in the courtroom, conferred upon him the legal, and therefore socially sanctioned, right to utilize certain landed resources according to his own designs and to demand respect from his neighbors for his usufruct of landed property. The paradox of these assertions, of course, is that in a context where the principle of effective occupation continued to sanction property rights and where clear boundaries between posses were nonexistent, it was nearly impossible to verify what exactly constituted "legal" possession of land. But it is telling that according to the information presented in the document, Marinho constantly depicted himself as a proprietário, therefore a socially sanctioned landholder, not a squatter or even a *possuidor*—somebody who possessed something *as* property—as the latter two terms did not, on their own, denote a link between authority, respectability, and property rights.[43]

These two examples suggest that at least some small farmers and ranchers made use of seigniorial understandings of honor, by claiming the titles of senhores and proprietários, as a way to assert a privileged and publicly recognized authority to use certain landholdings. In doing so, they were emulating the strategies of their social superiors, who often did not possess titles to their lands either.[44] As we shall see through the trial transcript detailing the land dispute between Dona Joana Ferreira Chaves and two of her former rendeiros, local notables also relied on honorable status and the public recognition of honor to justify their occupation and even ownership of land. Dona Joana belonged to a wealthy family, who possessed landholdings in several municipalities. In fact, one of her legal representatives was Tomás Pompeu de Sousa Brasil, a leading Cearense political figure, who was elected imperial senator in 1864 and who subsequently became head of the

Liberal Party of Ceará.[45] In 1861 Dona Joana filed a criminal suit against the illiterate farmer João Alves and his wife, accusing them of illegally occupying a plot in her lands in the Lugar Mulungú, in Itapagé, since 1854, when they were her tenants. She argued that the couple had paid the agreed-upon annual rent of Rs. 49$000 for only one year, between 1853 and 1854, and then ceased to make payments. As a consequence of this, she requested "the reintegration of her posse of rented lands, the eviction of João Alves and his wife, and the payment of the amount equivalent to seven years of past rent that had been unpaid." Through their attorney, the defendants maintained that they stopped paying rent in 1854 because "they bought a parcel of land that was adjacent to the one referred to by the plaintiff, and that was, in fact, divided from it." Therefore, they argued that "they lived in their lands" and did not owe any money to the plaintiff for past rent. Crucially, despite all her influence and connections, Dona Joana did not possess any written title that certified her land tenure or specified its boundaries. Therefore, her case was entirely dependent on witness testimony.[46]

The rhetoric employed by the plaintiff's witnesses reveals the function that honor and gendered symbolism could play in the validation of a party's claim to possession of landed resources. A typical deposition by these witnesses is the one by João Roberto de Sousa, who maintained that "he knows because he has seen and witnessed (*por ver e presenciar*) during at least twenty years that the plaintiff is *senhora e possuidora* (landlady and possessor) of the Mulungú lands." Moreover, he knows that "she has exercised dominion over those lands by placing vaqueiros in them," and that "they have lived there, raising their cattle and treating a cacimba."[47] João Roberto's references to ver e presenciar, the exercise of dominion over land, the placing of vaqueiros, and the work they have performed in the sítio were in accordance to the legal specifications of the posse regime and the 1850 Land Law discussed above. Under that legal system, de facto occupation of a landholding could be legitimated by proving that it had been cultivated or utilized in some other fashion. Witness testimony was critical in this process because it established the public recognition of the usufruct of land that validated effective occupation. Yet, the references to Dona Joana as senhora e possuidora are also significant because they helped to differentiate the land claims by an elite woman from those by a common squatter. In the context of a seigniorial and patriarchal society such as Imperial Brazil, to assert that someone was senhor e possuidor implied that the claimant of such title had a privileged position in society and, consequently, his or her effective occupation deserved deference and respect. Furthermore, these declarations denoted that, even though Dona Joana was a woman, she exercised some of the masculine prerogatives of honor, by independently administrating and controlling her landholding, which also contributed to her high status.

Clearly, the validity of effective occupation as a landholding regime and the continued reliance on public acknowledgment of possession and occupation as a legal requisite to authorize land tenure influenced the assertion of honorable status among wealthy and poor as a way to uphold a presumed privilege to particular landed resources. It could be argued, then, that the smallholders' flaunting of masculine honor as a strategy to maintain access to land as discussed so far is only a by-product of the legal framework behind property damage cases and the fact that they featured smallholders in land disputes with more established landowners. According to Articles 266 and 267 of the Criminal Code, the demolition of someone else's property and the destruction of the means to delimit properties constituted crimes of dano. In lieu of payment of indemnities for the losses, the Criminal Code stipulated incarceration of the guilty parties as sentences.[48] During dano trial proceedings the court had to determine the culpability of the defendant, by examining the injured property, and then establish the amount that needed to be paid as reparation. But because of the uncertainty surrounding land tenure, the court also had to verify which party was the legitimate owner of the property in question. Thus, plaintiffs and defendants sought to persuade the judicial authorities of the legality of their land tenure by presenting documents, if possible, and by bringing witness testimony. Legal arguments centered on what constituted legitimate or illegitimate occupation, who had the right to possession, and who had used a landholding and for how long. These questions, in turn, required the public corroboration of neighbors and witnesses, a form of validation that was subject to the influence of family status and honorable reputation.[49]

Yet, trial transcripts for the crime of assault show that smallholders attempted to use attitudes and words that denoted masculine respectability in an effort to uphold their claims to property rights in extralegal struggles for landed resources. For example, according to witness testimony, in July of 1873, the illiterate farmer Joaquim Jerônimo da Silva was at work collecting *maniçobas* (wild tubers of the manioc family) in the Lugar Conceição, in the municipality of Itapagé, when his neighbor and coproprietor, the illiterate rancher Raimundo José Ferreira Nunes, "asked him under whose orders he was working." He responded by saying that "he did not need anybody's authorization to collect the maniçobas because those lands belonged to him." In his answers to the legal questioning, Joaquim Jerônimo also asserted that there was already an agreement between his father and Raimundo José regarding the use of that specific parcel of land.

In an 1876 case from Tamboril, the semiliterate farmer Antônio Francisco Ribeiro declared "that he was working in his roça" in the Lugar Ferreiros, when "the old man Antônio Alves appeared and told him that he could not continue his labor because he did not have any lands there." To this, he had replied by saying that "he knew his rights [to those lands] and he would keep working there."[50] Evidently, these smallholders expected that their authoritative claims to dominion or right over a particular landholding would be enough to earn deference and respect from their neighbors and, consequently, ensure the achievement of their designs on those lands.

If claims to masculine honor and respectability served the practical purpose of enforcing and maintaining property rights over contested natural resources, then it is not surprising that smallholders should display an intense sensitivity to insults that questioned their honor. For, according to this logic, a poor farmer or rancher's loss of his claim to honor, and therefore to a form of social authority, could entail the loss of what he considered to be his or his family's landed patrimony. One place to see how the sertanejos' much commented-upon touchiness regarding their honorable reputations was linked to the defense of property rights over land, animals, or land improvements is in the response by some of them to being called "thieves"—an insult that challenged a man's credibility and honor, and that could incite violent fights, or accusations of slander (*injúrias verbais*) in criminal courts. For instance, in 1853 the illiterate farmer Francisco Antônio de Oliveira, who lived in the Lugar Bebedor in the municipality of Jucás, accused his neighbor Mateus Francisco Leite, from the Lugar Cara Queimada, of insulting him by calling him a "thief" and beating his son, the minor João Lucas. The plaintiff's and witnesses' depositions permit us to reconstruct, in part, the events that had led to this incident, at least from Francisco Antônio's perspective. According to the plaintiff's legal complaint, on October 10, 1853, João Lucas was walking near Mateus Francisco's house, when he suddenly attacked the young boy and insulted him, calling him "little thief" and "wretch," and saying, "[Y]ou and your father are all thieves." The witnesses elaborated that Mateus Francisco also accused João Lucas of letting dogs loose on his goats, although some of them mentioned that those goats were actually pasturing in Francisco Antônio's lands. These depositions demonstrate the problems created by a lack of clear boundaries between plots of land and the undermining of neighborly relations that resulted from those tensions. But this case also reveals perceptions that sertanejos had regarding the importance of maintaining an honorable masculine reputation for the defense and management of landed patrimony. According to the witness Joaquim Alves da Silva, "[It] was publicly known [*público e notório*]" that Mateus Francisco "absolutely wanted to *se apossar* (take possession) of a small house and lands that belonged to Francisco Antônio's father, and that Francisco Antônio rented on his behalf [...], while he was sick and bed-ridden," and this was the motive for the attack on both father and son. Another witness, Vicente Ferreira de Sousa, clarified that Mateus Francisco "wanted to live in the lands that the defendant's father had rented, and since the defendant did not allow him to live there, he instigated this scuffle." It appears as if, from this perspective, dishonoring a man by calling him a thief did not constitute only an insult to his reputation but also an attempt to publicly discredit his dominion or authority over a particular landholding or land improvement as a way to establish a contested claim over the same property.[51]

The link between attacks on a man's honor through charges of dishonesty and thievery and attempts by neighbors or coproprietors to assert competing property rights over the same natural resources or land improvements is further elucidated in the following slander case that focuses on conflicts for the management and ownership of water sources within joint landholdings. In 1852, the illiterate farmer Francisco Félix da Cunha from the Sítio São Matias, in Itapagé, filed a criminal suit against his neighbor and coproprietor João Florêncio da Cunha and his wife, Feliciana de tal, for insulting him by calling him "thief" and "dishonest." According to Francisco Félix's accusation, he and his brother José Alves da Cunha, who was also a co-owner in the same sítio, had built a cacimba. He had also prohibited João Francisco and his family from using the well's water to wash and tend animals. One morning in October, a son of João Francisco's was taking a horse to drink from the cacimba when Francisco Félix stopped him. To this action, Feliciana de tal responded by shouting that Francisco Félix was a "thief" and "dishonest." The shouts, according to Francisco Félix, were so loud that many people from the neighborhood heard them and descended upon the place, prompting him to initiate the criminal procedure against João Florêncio, as the legitimate husband and household head of Feliciana de tal, in order to avenge his reputation. It is significant that in his answers to the judicial inquest, Francisco Félix argued that "the defendants directed [him] that name [thief] as a result of their desire to illegally appropriate themselves (*em consequência de querer esbulhar-lhe*) of the cacimba that he owned in common with his brother." Even though embellished by the legal conventions required by the nature of this document, this assertion illustrates that Francisco Félix's preoccupation with being called a "thief" betrayed his apprehension that through this insult on his masculine honor, the offenders were both calling into question his claims to ownership of the water well and establishing a counterclaim of authority and dominion over the same resource.[52]

This case illustrates, as well, that when competition for scarce productive resources became fiercer, the notion that conventions should regulate their use by all members of joint properties lost currency, at least among some of the parties involved, who claimed private property rights—sanctioned by honor—over them. Thus, as stated in Francisco Félix's legal complaint, "[T]he cacimba in question had been built at the expense of the plaintiff, who has also maintained the water clean and drinkable." A witness also declared that "it was public knowledge that Francisco Félix had impeded João Florêncio da Cunha from using *his* cacimba's water to tend animals, because it was quickly drying" [my emphasis].[53] According to this line of reasoning, the well was Francisco Félix's (and his brother's) private property because he had paid for its construction and preservation. As a consequence, it was his prerogative to manage the use of the cacimba's water as he saw fit. Yet, when Feliciana de tal called Francisco Félix a "thief" because of his prohibition to use the cacimba's water, she deployed an understanding, common among sertanejos, that water sources were communal property, regardless of who built or owned them, and that mutually agreed upon conventions regulated their use in joint landholdings.[54] In this competing view, by controlling the well's use, Francisco Félix was "stealing" the water that should be regarded as common property. Thus, it appears as if insulting a man's honor by calling him a thief achieved the function of contesting his claim to private or personal ownership and management of resources that customarily were considered communal.

The conflicts between private and communal property rights over water and the ways in which smallholders used attacks on the honorable reputations of their neighbors as a strategy to attempt to impose their designs on its usufruct can be seen in another injúrias case. In 1867, the farmer Mateus Bezerra de Oliveira accused his coproprietor, João Lucas de Oliveira, of verbally insulting him, by calling him a "thief." In his legal complaint, the plaintiff stated that "he has an açude in lands that belong to him in the Sítio das Bezerras. During the month of March, the reservoir filled up to excess and the plaintiff found himself in the necessity of taking down its walls because the water was destroying his plantings." The accusation continues by saying that "the defendant, then, claiming for himself an incompetent domain over the lands where the açude is located, began deprecating the plaintiff . . . and saying that whoever had taken down the reservoir's walls was a thief." Through the legal language of the accusation, Mateus Bezerra expressed the views articulated by Francisco Félix in his complaint that whoever built and owned a water source, in this case an açude, should be able to decide, on his own, how to manage it, and use its water to take care of the needs of his cattle and plantings first, as it is done with private property. He also betrayed a similar anxiety to that of Francisco Félix's that a man who insulted his honor by labeling him a thief was in reality attempting to establish a competing claim of authority and property rights over a water source. On the opposite side, João Lucas de Oliveira's response to the judicial inquest demonstrates that his counterclaim to have a say over the use of the reservoir's water was based on the customarily accepted notion that water sources were to be administered communally. In his defense, he explained that "when he said that whoever had taken down the walls of the açude was a thief he did not know that the plaintiff had done it." Instead, "[He] had thought that only a thief, and therefore an outsider, could do such action in a secretive manner in a property with so many heirs." Invoking the same understandings of Feliciana de tal's about the necessity of those who lived in joint landholdings to look out for each other's needs, he implied that the man who destroyed the reservoir's walls was, in fact, "stealing" water from the community to which it rightfully belonged.[55]

Access to the open range for pasturing, allocation of grazing areas, and management of cattle also required mutual understandings between members of joint landholdings and neighbors, which were mediated by honorable masculine reputations. The frequent movement of animals for watering, feeding, treating, and marketing, coupled with the open range system, and the confusing land delimitation practices of the backlands, generated uncertainty and anxiety regarding the state of ownership of livestock. While provincial and municipal legislation established regulations intended to clear confusions regarding ownership of livestock, ranchers, both large and small, often relied on personal relations with neighbors, vaqueiros, and others to guarantee their possession of highly mobile cattle.[56] According to backlands custom, vaqueiros and ranchers memorized the shapes of their neighbors' brands in order to return animals to their rightful owners, when they had trespassed into their fields. The convention also held that, if an unmarked head of cattle, or one with an unknown mark, appeared in somebody's grazing areas, the criador or vaqueiro was to retain the animal in his fields until somebody claimed it. If nobody did, the animal was to remain under that rancher's care until its death, and was not to be sold.[57] Collaboration among neighbors and fellow ranchers was central even to certain aspects of cattle treatment, such as the yearly roundups, or the tracing and catching of head of cattle gone astray.[58] A reputation for trustworthiness and male respectability was necessary in all these face-to-face dealings regarding the management of cattle, an exclusively masculine occupation.

A slander trial transcript featuring a dispute between two established cattle ranchers from the municipality of Tamboril puts in evidence how pre-occupations with masculine reputation and a defensive watchfulness against the accusation of being called a "thief" were linked to men's attempts to establish ownership over highly mobile cattle. According to a legal accusation by the rancher Manoel Martins Sampaio, who lived in the fazenda Pastos Bons and was member of an influential local family, he had sold on credit several cows to Manoel Batista dos Santos, from the Fazenda Cajueiro. In the first week of June of 1865, Martins Sampaio went to the Fazenda Cajueiro to collect the payment for the cows. In response, Batista dos Santos accused Martins Sampaio of being a "thief" and of having stolen one of his cows, which had been spotted by several people in Martins Sampaio's fields, even though the cow in question displayed Batista dos Santos's brand. Moreover, the defendant refused to pay for the cows that, according to Martins Sampaio, he had sold to Batista dos Santos. In an attempt to avenge this offense, Martins Sampaio initiated a slander suit against Batista dos Santos, arguing that "until the present time, he had enjoyed the good judgment of public society, and that his reputation had been sullied in this occasion, for the first time." While this case clearly reveals a cattle raiser's defensiveness with regard to verbal affronts to his character, it also demonstrates that an accusation of thievery represented an effort to discredit his reputation by implying that he violated one of the unwritten conventions that regulated management of cattle and took possession of someone else's livestock. Not only that, this particular insult called into question Martins Sampaio's claim to legitimate ownership over the animals that he had already sold on credit, and this opened the possibility for Batista to attempt to appropriate himself of them, without payment.[59]

As a general rule, most poor sertanejos did not have the economic means or connections necessary to criminally pursue those who offended their reputation by calling them thieves. *Calúnia* and injúria (defamation and insult, or slander), which were defined in the Criminal Code as offenses against honor, were considered private crimes, whose punishment was of concern to only one party, as opposed to the social body as a whole. Therefore, the victim had to initiate and pay the costs associated with the investigation and criminal prosecution.[60] It is not surprising, then, that small farmers and ranchers who sought to safeguard their reputation for honesty and credibility insisted on saying that their "word" was "harder than iron," and that they were men of "strong words."[61] The surviving verses that complete the popular poem at the start of this chapter also underscore that, regardless of color and poverty, cantadores saw themselves as honorable because they knew how to keep their word.

Venha cá, Seu Secundino,	Come here Mr. Secundino,
Dance no samba daqui,	Dance in this party,
Que estes caboco são pobe,	That these caboclos are poor,
Mais têm honra consigo.	But they have honor in themselves.
Mas têm honra consigo,	But they have honor in themselves,
E toitiço no cupim,	And good judgment in their curly heads,
Só não são da cor de leite	Only they are not the color of milk
E nem da cor de alfenim:	Nor of white sugar dough:
Quando dizem: Não! tá dito,	But when they say: No! that's their last word,
Não trocam não, pelo Sim,	They will not change their mind,
Nem mesmo cabra chamurro	Not even if they are simple half-castes
Nem mesmo caboco ruim.	Not even if they are damned caboclos.[62]

As these verses suggest, for popular poets, who belonged to the ranks of the poor, masculine respectability—centered on their honesty and the solidity of their "word"—outranked the inferior place assigned to those of mixed race and to the poor in the seigniorial order of Imperial Brazil, and elevated them to the status of those of the "color of milk." Yet, as this section has shown, the preoccupation with honor demonstrated by small farmers and ranchers in Ceará during the post-1845 years did not represent an empty concern with social prestige or a simple emulation of seigniorial honorable postures. Instead, honorable masculine reputations conveyed a form of social authority that served as the leverage with which sertanejos attempted to sway different kinds of negotiations to their own benefit in face-to-face masculine exchanges with elites and peers over issues of landed property, water, and livestock. The precarious legal structure under which public acknowledgment of land tenure continued to serve as the final proof to sanction property rights contributed to the smallholders' reliance on honor as the assurance of the validity, strength, and superiority of their claims to the occupation and usufruct of land. Just as important, in a context of fierce competition for increasingly scarce natural resources the defense and attack on honorable masculine reputations served to establish claims and counterclaims over water wells, land improvements, and livestock, and to attempt to enforce different visions of communal versus private property rights over the same resources. It was, then, in a environment that pitted a small degree of prosperity against fragility in access to economic resources, individual or family needs against those of a larger community, and private authority against a weak state, that sertanejos placed such a premium on cultural markers of masculine honor—the status, respectability, and honesty that they hoped would ensure their survival and that of their families.

Family, Patriarchy, and Honor

If the increasing pressures in the material foundations of life in the drought-prone interior of Ceará demanded a watchful concern with maintaining honorable reputations and a constant assertion of respectable status among free poor men, the same stresses contributed to their preoccupation with another dimension of masculine honor—the vigilant control over family women's sexual propriety. As we will see below, a strategy that sertanejo men used to cope with fierce competition for communal resources, poorly delimited land boundaries, and partible inheritance—forces that threatened to disintegrate communities and to place men from the same families against each other—was to build male solidarity through the public revenge of sexual offenses against the honor of family women. Furthermore, anxieties regarding the continued subdivision of small landholdings and other family patrimony appear to have affected the poor men's attempts to regulate women's sexuality and their reproductive power in accordance to their interests as household heads. Thus, this section will demonstrate that sertanejo men exercised patriarchal authority over family women and articulated such power through the gendered language of honor that is familiar to students of Latin American and Mediterranean cultures.[63] Yet, these behaviors did not constitute simply the enactment of normative cultural scripts. Rather, they represented rational responses, elaborated within the cultural idiom of honor, to the particular material configurations affecting their everyday lives and their positions of dominance within their families and communities.

Historical studies on constructions of honor in Brazil and elsewhere in Latin America have reached a consensus regarding notable families' need to defend family honor—centered on control of women's sexuality—as a strategy to ensure legitimacy and convenient marriage alliances. According to the historiography, defense of family honor served to preserve those families' economic wealth, especially in the form of landed property, as well as political power, and racial hierarchies during the colonial period and the nineteenth century.[64] More problematic for the existing scholarship has been the assessment of the importance of women's sexual purity for the construction of notions of honor among subordinate men, especially the rural poor. In particular, since the literature as a whole focuses on poor men and women's claims to honor as reliant on conduct and merit, and rarely investigates their actual economic status and access to material wealth, these studies have overlooked the possible interconnections between lower-class men's assertions of honor, possession of property, and issues of succession. Consequently, while the scholarship has historicized the political dimensions of plebeian men's affirmations of honor and the ways in which honor mediated hierarchical relationships among the poor, the male preoccupation with the sexual control of family women has often been portrayed as either the result of inflexible cultural prescriptions, or as a simple and desperate attempt to establish masculine authority within their households.[65]

Yet, as this work has demonstrated, free poor families in Ceará had landed patrimonies, although small and poorly delimited, as well as other inheritable assets, such as livestock and even slaves. Thus, it is highly possible that these families were anxious about issues of inheritance and division of property. A concern with succession among the rural poor in Ceará makes sense within the Luso-Brazilian system of dividing inheritances, which worked to fragment family property, and civil laws that allowed even some illegitimate children to easily inherit their parents' wealth. In direct opposition to the Anglo-American tradition, Portuguese inheritance laws, valid in Brazil until 1916, established *ab intestato* (intestate) succession—that is, devolution without a will, among all members of the blood kindred, independent of age and sex. The laws specified a ranked order of "necessary heirs," beginning with all recognized children, who received equal shares of their parents' wealth. In case of deceased children, the law called the next direct descendants as heirs. In absence of descendants, ascendants, then collateral heirs (the decedent's relatives as distant as the tenth degree of collateral kinship), the surviving spouse, or the royal treasury were called to inherit. Equally important, Portuguese civil legislation granted "natural" children (offspring of unmarried parents that were legally able to marry at the time of the child's birth) the same ab intestato succession rights as children born within legally sanctioned marriages. The Luso-Brazilian inheritance system, which substantially differed from its Anglo-American counterpart in this regard, distinguished between natural and "spurious" offspring, even though both were illegitimate because they were born outside of wedlock. Natural children, if appropriately recognized, enjoyed a status as coequal with legitimate children in terms of inheritance, whereas spurious children, or those born of "punishable" sexual unions (incestuous, adulterine, and sacrilegious) were barred from intestate succession to a parent's estate. In fact, in cases when they were the only offspring of an otherwise marriageable couple that had not consecrated their union, natural children were the exclusive heirs in succession, as long as they were recognized by their parents at baptism or later.[66]

Because of a lack of primary source information on marriage practices in the backlands, a place to begin an analysis of family constitution and preoccupations with matters of inheritance among the free poor is an examination of illegitimacy rates. Here, the available evidence based on baptismal records indicates that, although illegitimacy was a significant feature of backlands society, legally constituted marriages were not all that uncommon in Ceará. The proportion of illegitimate births in the municipality of Jucás between 1857 and 1860 was 25 percent. According to Sousa Brasil's calculations based on baptismal records from thirty-three interior parishes and Fortaleza during the same time period, the provincial rate of illegitimacy was even lower: just under 20 percent.[67]

The rates of illegitimacy found in Ceará are consistent with proportions found in agricultural areas of the Brazilian Southeast during the eighteenth and early nineteenth centuries. The scholarship has found illegitimacy rates ranging between 20 and 35 percent of the total number of registered births in various locations of that region.[68] These rates sharply contrast with the 45, 55 and even 60 percent of illegitimate births in urban and mining districts of the Southeast.[69] As Sheila de Castro Faria has noted for the colonial period, the lower rates of illegitimacy in rural agricultural areas seem to have been related to individuals' need to establish familial and matrimonial bonds as a way to ensure their continued control over rural properties and the reproduction of households.[70] Thus, it is probable that, under similar circumstances, free poor Cearenses living during the second half of the nineteenth century strove to create legal family units as a way to guarantee the succession of property as well as the provision of labor.

Nevertheless, attaining a legal marriage presented financial and other practical difficulties in the interior. Above and beyond the payment of fees to priests, a problem that free poor Cearenses might have found with more regularity when trying to obtain the legal consecration of their unions was the shortage of priests. Several authors have noted that sertanejos rarely encountered members of the clergy to perform basic Catholic rites, and that often, visiting priests performed marriages and baptisms on those occasions when they visited fazendas and interior locations. Thus, it is possible that in Ceará, consensual unions and marriage existed in a fluid relationship to one another, as Elizabeth Kuznesof has suggested for other regions. Under such an understanding, individuals might have seen concubinage as a step toward obtaining a formal marriage when that became a possibility.[71]

In any case, the central issue regarding succession of family patrimony, even among the poor, is that the peculiarities of the Brazilian inheritance system worked to divide family property rapidly, regardless of legal marriage. As Chapter 1 has shown, the system of partible inheritance was one of the major factors that contributed to the transformation of landholding patterns from the large sesmarias of the colonial period to the majority of small-holdings observed by the mid-nineteenth century. But inheritance practices continued fragmenting the smallholdings of free poor Cearenses after 1850. In 1858, an editorialist for the *Araripe* newspaper demanded government measures to stop the subdivision of landed properties in the Cariri area. He argued that sítios "had been transformed into hundreds of small *prédios* (land parcels)" and that if this practice continued, smallholdings were going to "end up reduced to the size of *capoeiras* (small enclosures for keeping domestic animals)." Foreign travelers and other observers noted the same practices of land subdivision in the dry areas of the interior.[72] If outsiders anxiously remarked on this pattern, there is no reason to believe that male sertanejos as managers of patrimony were not concerned with the division of property, especially in a context in which high mortality rates and epidemics placed large numbers of grandchildren and even great grandchildren in the category of heirs early on in a family's life cycle.[73]

The land registries compiled during the 1850s provide a glimpse of how the process of land subdivision related to inheritance affected the landholding capacity of poor rural families. For instance, several entries in the land registry of Icó show that the Sítio Cachoeira, located in the Riacho do Canto, came to be divided into eleven different plots by the time of death of its owner, Manoel Mendes Leal. The eleven heirs that included three adult sons, two single adult daughters, and six sons-in-law (who administered the inheritance of their wives, or Manoel Mendes Leal's married daughters), each registered one parcel of land worth Rs. 45$000 in an individual entry, claiming that they had inherited the plot from their father or father-in-law. These plots of land were, no doubt, very small, as they measured either 45 or 90 braças of frontage (approximately 65 or 131 hectares). In all probability, in order to compensate for their small size, four of the heirs (perhaps the most prosperous ones) had each purchased an additional plot of land in the same sítio. The value of each one of these plots was Rs. 78$000, which indicates possible measurements of 78 or 156 braças of frontage (approximately 113 or 226 hectares).[74]

Partilhas reveal the effects of partible inheritance on the rapid fragmentation of landed properties as late as the 1880s. For instance, the partilha of the assets of Francisco Chaves Martins from Jucás indicates that the number of legal heirs for his estate was eleven. This number included his two surviving adult children, seven grandchildren (who represented two deceased daughters) ranging in ages from twenty-nine to thirty-four years old, and two great grandchildren who were minors, and who represented two deceased grandchildren. The 1889 inventory of Francisco's estate declared that he and his wife, Maria Teresa de Jesus, owned, among other assets, one landholding in the Sítio Estreito Riacho, appraised by the court judges at Rs. 125$000.

The partilha established the division of this landholding in the following manner: the widow received a portion worth Rs. 17$500, as part of the payment of the *meia*, or half of the joint estate that was due to her as the wife of the deceased. The surviving son Manoel Joaquim Pessoa, and the surviving daughter, represented by her husband, Antônio Pinheiro Torres, each received portions worth Rs. 30$812 on the same lands. Teresa, granddaughter of Francisco's, Mariano Gonçalves, who represented his wife, the deceased granddaughter Maria, and Frederica, daughter of Manoel, a deceased son of Francisco's, each received portions worth Rs. 10$270 on the same land, since the three of them shared the portion that was the legal inheritance of Francisco's deceased daughter Francisca. Finally, the six surviving children and one grandchild of Rosalina, the youngest daughter of Francisco's, who was also deceased, each received portions worth Rs. 5$135 on the same landholding in the Sítio Estreito Riacho.[75] Indeed, as Chapter 4 will demonstrate, partially as a result of inheritance laws, and in combination with other factors, families of poor sertanejos increasingly lost access to their smallholdings, beginning in the 1860s.

The system of dividing inheritances did not break up only landholdings but also other forms of productive property, including slaves. This is observable through the partilha of the assets owned by Antônio da Costa Villar and his wife, Ana Desideria de Menezes. Upon Ana Desideria's death in 1855, the couple had five heirs: the oldest daughter, Cândida, who was married to Raimundo José de Brito, the second daughter Isabel Francelina, who was fifteen, Vitorino, aged ten, Maria, seven, and Antônio, four. Antônio da Costa and his wife did not own any landholdings. Instead, most of their very modest wealth, which totaled Rs. 767$500, was made up of livestock (ten head of cattle and four horses), and one twenty-eight-year-old female slave named Ana, whose value was estimated at Rs. 500$000. When the authorities divided up the property in the partilha, the widower received the following assets as payment of his meia: a few pieces of furniture, two horses, and one portion, worth Rs. 246$750, of the slave's total value. Per the division of the assets by the court judges, each of the three daughters' portion of the maternal wealth included one pair of earrings, two cows, and one portion worth Rs. 49$250 on Ana's total value. The two sons, Vitorino and Antônio, received two cows and one part of the total value of the slave Ana, worth Rs. 52$750, each. What this division signified was that Antônio da Costa and the heirs were legally required to share ownership of the slave. This matter would not have been too difficult to manage if all the heirs were minors and lived in the same household. But since Cândida was married, and perhaps had established her own household with Raimundo José, it is probable that

Antônio da Costa had to enter into some sort of arrangement with his son-in-law for custody and shared use of the services provided by the slave.[76]

This trend toward fragmentation of smallholdings and other property generated conflict and antagonism among male relatives who competed for the same shrinking resources necessary for the well-being and subsistence of their own individual families. For example, in 1861, the father of Francisco Rodrigues da Costa—a twenty-two-year-old illiterate young man from Tamboril—flogged him with a leather whip because he insisted on building a separate house for himself and his wife in the same lands where the entire family lived. Along the same lines, the author of the *Araripe* editorial that called for change of the partible system of succession also remarked that the small landholders who inherited increasingly subdivided plots often fought for water and wood.[77]

In this context, it is conceivable that men, as household heads or as those in charge of economic decisions, attempted to devise strategies to reintegrate the family patrimony and facilitate male collaboration for its communal use. Jane Schneider has argued that this is the case among some contemporary Mediterranean societies of pastoralists and agriculturalists that share characteristics, including equal inheritance, with the interior of Ceará of the mid-nineteenth century. The author notes that those strategies are especially necessary to prevent the disintegration not only of landholdings but also of entire families, since competition for fragmented resources within the family can cause rivalries and feuds between fathers and sons as well as between brothers. According to Schneider, a common interest in, and regulation of, the sexual comportment of women by fathers, brothers, and other male family members in these communities is one of the main strategies to unify men and to maintain family patrimony. Thus, the ideology of honor, with its focus on women as repositories of family honor, "helps shore up the identity of a group (a family or a lineage), and commit to it the loyalties of otherwise doubtful members."[78]

Indeed, the case of Ceará suggests that control of the sexuality of unmarried female dependants as a symbol of honor provided free poor men, who were relatives or members of joint landholdings, with an incentive to overcome their differences and unite in the common defense of family honor. This type of male solidarity was often observed in the rescuing of kidnapped women. *Rapto* (kidnapping of young women or bride abduction) seems to have been a fairly common practice in the interior not only of Ceará but also in other regions of Brazil. It included a promise of marriage and entailed removing, usually on horseback, the young woman from her parents' house and then placing her in the care of friends or relatives. Then, the young couple engaged in sexual relations and, if possible, established their own household. Kidnapping thus accomplished the objective of publicly consummating a consensual union or forcing a marriage.[79] Despite the regularity with which rapto occurred, the Criminal Code prescribed the kidnapping of women (virgins or not) with "libidinous objectives" as an honor crime punishable by jailing and obligation to pay a dowry to the offended woman. Yet, as Linda Lewin has argued, the meaning of rapto could also suggest elopement, which entailed the idea of female agency.[80] In any event, a sample of criminal proceedings for rapto illustrates the implications of women's sexuality on relations among male members of families and joint landholdings.

In some cases, poor fathers, brothers, and other male relatives, in "agreement" with the kidnapper "allowed" the flight of their daughters. The young women could also consent to their kidnapping.[81] But when these unions did not meet the approval of the woman's family, the males took it upon themselves to return the kidnapped woman to the parental house. This endeavor entailed a highly theatrical display of masculine prowess and male solidarity. Cousins, brothers, uncles, and other male residents in joint landholdings worked as one in the removal, usually on horseback, of the young woman from the house where she had been placed.[82] Criminal proceedings also provide evidence that the killing of a kidnapper could generate solidarity among family males. For example, Bernardo José Pinheiro, an eighteen-year-old illiterate farmer from Jucás, murdered João Vieira de Sousa two days after he had kidnapped his sister Maria Teresa de Jesus. The black farmer Antônio Joaquim da Lima, who was the head of the household and Maria Teresa's stepfather, upon learning about her kidnapping, exclaimed that "this can only be avenged with death," thus, showing his approval of his stepson's action.[83] Literary works and travelers' accounts also indicate that fathers and brothers worked together in the pursuit and killing of men who had kidnapped family women with the intention of marrying them or engaging in sexual relations against family wishes.[84]

In his study of family and gender relations in the Cearense sertão during the first half of the nineteenth century, A. Otaviano Vieira Jr. examines a judicial indictment of two offenders who committed a crime in defense of honor against a forty-year-old farmer named Bernardino Gomes de Vasconcelos. This case is useful to illustrate the centrality of a militant vigilance of female honor in the construction of solidarity ties among male relatives in a situation other than rapto. According to Bernardino's deposition, two pardo men, Francisco Gomes and João Batista, beat and wounded him in the road between the Canindé River and the village of São Francisco, and left him prostrate and with his testicles crushed. During the beating, the aggressors informed

Bernardino that Manoel Gomes, who was Francisco's father, had commanded them to perform the thrashing because his daughter Joana had become pregnant, and Bernardino—who was the presumptive father of the child—had refused to marry her. As Vieira Jr. argues, this case clearly demonstrates how father and son built an alliance when they found out about Joana's pregnancy, in order to avenge the affront that Bernardino had committed against the family's and Joana's honor—an offense that he refused to repair by marrying her.[85] Moreover, the attack on Bernardino's genitalia was a clear assertion of superior masculinities, and the symbolic subordination, through violence, of the most palpable emblem of Bernardino's masculine power.

The timing of the attack on Bernardino Gomes illustrates that the conception of offspring from unsanctioned sexual encounters with female relatives appeared as a public symbol of men's failure to effectively protect the chastity of family women. Obviously, Bernardino's and Francisco's sister's sexual encounters must have occurred at least a few weeks before the pregnancy became evident, yet the confrontation took place after it became known that she was pregnant, and that Bernardino did not want to marry her. Criminal trial transcripts detailing offenses such as rape and murder also demonstrate that male kin sought judicial reparation of their daughters' or sisters' wounded honor or performed violent acts against these women's partners or offenders, exactly after pregnancies occurred or when the offspring that resulted from those sexual relationships were born. For instance, in 1871 the farmer Ildefonso Atunes Pereira killed Manoel Francisco Gomes de Mattos in the Lugar Canga, in Jucás. According to the witnesses' and Ildefonso's declarations, the defendant had murdered Manoel Francisco "in defense of the honor of his sister, and consequently of the honor of his family." Manoel Gomes had kidnapped Quitéria, Ildefonso's sister, who was widowed, and had placed her in the house of a woman named Januária. There, Manoel and Quitéria had maintained "illicit relations" for a long time, and Quitéria had borne a son. It was at this point in the relationship that Ildefonso decided to confront the offense to the honor of his family by killing Manoel.[86]

The fact that these acts in defense of family honor took place after women became pregnant or after the birth of offspring from unsanctioned unions also suggests that in addition to unifying family men, male regulation of women's sexuality could be a way to channel women's childbearing capacities to advance family interests. On the one hand, as it will become evident below, sertanejo families relied on the labor of a large number of children for reproduction and production activities in their smallholdings. Under such conditions, an additional child could be advantageous, as he or she could provide additional help in agricultural and ranching tasks. But on the other hand, the birth of a child that resulted from a relationship that was not approved by male household heads potentially could undermine the strategies that they designed for the future succession of family patrimony. As mentioned above, the Luso-Brazilian inheritance system established ab intestato succession for legitimate heirs *and* for natural children, or those born of unmarried parents that did not have any legal impediments to marry. Consequently, natural offspring were legal heirs and capable of inheriting equally, and without the requirement of a will, with their legitimate siblings. In a context in which families had many children, where epidemics and droughts meant high mortality rates, even among adults, and where grandchildren and great grandchildren inherited in absence of children, it is not completely inconceivable that the birth of a child from a union that was unsanctified by family interests could be seen as a threat to men's designs on the inheritance of land and other family property—especially as male household heads were often disputing access to and control of productive resources with other men.

In sum, the concern with maintaining male solidarity within a context of severe competition for landed resources and the preoccupation with protecting family patrimonies from the disintegration that resulted from partible inheritance go far in explaining free poor men's emphasis on the defense of family honor, centered on the sexual propriety of female kin. Male family and joint-landholding members collaborated in the rituals and exchanges through which families avenged their sullied honor in cases of bride abduction or other unsanctioned sexual relations with female relatives. The common pursuit of offenders to the family's honor served as an integrating force that counterbalanced the discord created by accelerated conflict for scarce resources among family men. Likewise, male attempts to manage women's reproductive power according to the family's interests appear to have been another tactic to protect their small patrimonies from further subdivision. In turn, the performance of the roles of guardians of family honor allowed men to exercise patriarchal authority in their households, as they endeavored to monitor women's physical mobility and regulate their sexual behavior. Under these conditions, a cultural ideal of male dominance and control of family women's sexuality was buttressed by preoccupations with the management of household and community economic resources.

Provision, Family Labor, and Masculine Reputation

As Chapter 2 demonstrated, a significant strategy that free poor men used to negotiate citizenship rights within the seigniorial order of the empire was the stress on their fulfillment of the role of family providers, which func-

tioned as an emblem of masculine honor. The following verses recited by
the popular poet Anselmo, born in Ipueiras in 1867, also expressed a cultural
exaltation of the ability of a sertanejo man to materially sustain his family:

Uma vez, havia um home	Once upon a time
Que êle até vivia bem,	There was a man who lived well,
Não era rico demais,	He was not very rich,
Possuía algum vintém,	But had a few cents,
Vivia criando os filho	He sustained his children
Sem ser pesado a ninguém.	Without being a burden to anyone.[87]

As these verses suggest, public recognition of the autonomous capacity to
sustain his children symbolized the elevated status that distinguished a man,
even if not rich, from others who did not "live well." Yet, the emphasis on
provision for wife and children as a signifier of an honorable masculinity
obscures the fact that families of small farmers and ranchers relied, to a very
large extent, on the labor of women as well as that of their large number
of children for the performance of agricultural and ranching tasks. In fact,
as this section will illustrate, these claims to masculine honor not only concealed the hard work of women and children within sertanejo households
but also helped men to establish the material basis for the exercise of patriarchal authority over wives and consensual wives.

The reliance by sertanejo families on the labor of all household members
was, in large part, conditioned by the smallholding pattern of land tenure
observable in Ceará. Poor rural Cearenses employed family labor not only in
activities related to household reproduction, but also in those associated with
production in small parcels of land. As we will see below, these included field
work and processing of agricultural goods; feeding, grazing, gathering, and
providing health care for animals; and transporting and marketing harvest,
animal products, and livestock. For this reason, sertanejos put a premium
on large families. According to Freire Alemão, the huts and houses of the
poor caboclos who, in his analysis, constituted the majority of the free poor
population of Ceará, were always "full of children," with an average of ten
per family.[88] Postmortem inventories from the municipality of Jucás reveal
that the average number of surviving children per family in the 1850s was
seven.[89] Thus, it can be argued that for smallholders who directly participated
in the agricultural and ranching economy of Ceará, as for those from other
regions of Brazil, the constitution of families was a precondition for the
prosperity they could derive from their land.[90]

It is important to consider, however, that a sexual and generational division of labor underpinned the performance of reproduction and production activities in agrarian Cearense households. While both men and women

worked in the roças, men's tasks were usually performed standing up, and in positions of leadership, whereas women's and children's activities were associated with bending, and following men's lead. In addition, a technical division of labor determined that men used tools, especially larger ones, such as hoes, hatchets, and axes, while women and small children more often worked with their hands or with small instruments.[91] For instance, the preparation of the soil for planting beans, corn, and manioc—the staples of the family diet—was done by men, normally in the month of November, when they burned off the dry stalks that remained from the proceeding season. In January or February, after the first rains of the year had fallen, women and children followed men in the sowing of manioc and corn. During the months of April or May smallholding families sowed beans in the same manner. Women and children harvested manioc, manually uprooting the tubers, six months to a year after it had been planted. Bean plants—both the string beans (*feijão de corda*) and black beans that were most common in the backlands—have a two- to three-month growing cycle. Women and young children picked the bean pods by hand, when they had ripened, usually in June, shortly before the maize harvest.[92]

The sexual, generational, and technical division of labor was also observable in the cultivation, harvest, and preparation of cotton. During planting season, from December to March, older sons and fathers dug out four-inch-deep holes, about five feet apart, with their hoes. Women and small children, following closely behind, sowed the cotton seeds into each groove. When the seedlings began growing, women and children weeded around them and pulled up the scrawnier stalks in order to leave only the more wholesome ones on the ground. Cotton harvests began seven to eight months after planting, and they extended from July until December. Normally, women and children picked cotton from family roças, and they also prepared the crop for sale by drying it and removing the seeds by hand. But during the peak years of the cotton boom, the most successful small farmers were able to accumulate enough income, through the use of family labor, to hire, periodically, wage laborers, and in some cases, even to buy a few slaves. For example, Rodolpho Theophilo noted in his *História da secca do Ceará* that small cotton farmers paid Rs. 1$280 a day to workers during clearing, planting, and especially harvesting seasons and that they preferred to use the labor of their few slaves in subsistence activities.[93]

The labor-intensive process of scraping and transforming poisonous manioc roots into edible and long-lasting farinha necessitated the assistance of nonhousehold members and neighbors; but even in that case, a sexual and technical division of labor determined activities for men and women. Not all smallholding families owned the equipment necessary to produce farinha, especially the grating wheel, or *roda de ralar,* that was used to grind manioc. Thus, men as household heads negotiated with the owners of *casas de farinha* (small sheds attached to a farmer's house with *aviamento,* or equipment to make flour, including the roda de ralar) in order to grind the manioc for their own consumption or for sale in local markets. For example, they agreed on making the labor of their entire families available to the communal work of the *farinhada* (the process of making farinha for various families) and some-times also on paying to the aviamento's owner a portion of their share of the farinha. The preparation of flour began very early in the morning when women gathered together to peel the roots with blunt knives. Following that, the roots were shredded or grated on the roda de ralar. The roda was placed in a frame that possessed two handles, one on each side. Two men turned the wheel at great speed, while the manioc roots were forced into it. Once ground, the manioc fell into the trough underneath, from where it was placed into a press that squeezed out the poisonous juices. Next, the pressed manioc was sifted, and then heated, or more properly toasted, in a stove made up of a huge stone slab. Those in charge of toasting the manioc had to regularly rake it, so as to avoid burning. Another sifting divided the coarser from the finer quality flour. Once placed in sacks, the farinha was now ready for consumption, storage, or sale.[94]

Activities related to the care of animals also followed a sexual division of labor. Men and older boys grazed, fed, and rounded up cattle, goats, and sheep. Their work was associated with managing herds of animals and facing the uncertainties of the open range. Women's work was more often confined to the care of smaller animals such as pigs and chickens or livestock that re-mained enclosed in corrals or near the houses. In addition, the marketing of agricultural crops, livestock, and small animals was organized along a pattern of sexual division of labor. Men negotiated the prices of commercial crops such as cotton and tobacco, and they typically traveled the longer distances to regional fairs to sell cattle, large animals such as horses, and produce. By contrast, women sold the chickens, goats, and pigs raised in the capoeiras in their own houses and commercialized surpluses of agricultural crops in local weekly feiras.[95]

A significant consequence of the sexual, generational, and technical divi-sion of labor was the undervaluing of the labor of women and children, not only in reproduction but also in production tasks. This is possible to observe in the conceptualization, by sertanejo men and women alike, that women's work in the fields constituted simply "helping out." It is noteworthy that poor married women, or those in consensual unions, and single daughters, who appeared as plaintiffs, defendants, and witnesses in the entire collection of criminal cases analyzed for this work almost never declared "farming," "fieldwork," or "ranching" as their occupation. Indeed, the social concealment of family women's work in agrarian activities is evident in the fact that no occupation for them was registered in the criminal records, except for a few married women who were characterized as "living off the work of her husband" or "helping her husband out in agricultural work." Clearly, these women were considered dependent on their husbands or other male providers. By contrast, women who were single or widowed, and who did not live with male relatives, declared their occupations, but these included only those jobs performed outside agriculture, such as the trades of seamstresses, domestic workers, laundresses, and ironing women. Only in a few occasions independent women appeared as "living by farming." Thus, in these myriad ways, free poor Cearenses constructed a relationship between dependence and femininity, regardless of the actual labor performed by women in production and reproduction tasks.

In addition, because women and children did not often use tools in their agricultural labors, these were regarded as less important, as they were seen as "easy" to do or less strenuous. Likewise, other production activities that women and children undertook, even when they brought income to the family, were understood as mere supplements to the more important ways of deriving a household sustenance, which were performed by men. This was the case particularly in the perception, by both men and women, that the female labors of spinning and weaving cotton to make garments and hammocks for sale, and producing *rendas,* or bobbin lace, to sell in markets or peddle in town streets, were simply ancillary to the masculine tasks of household production.[96]

The undervaluing and socially constructed concealment of women's and children's labor went hand in hand with the display among small farmers and ranchers of their ability to provide for their families as a prerogative of masculinity. In addition, free poor men saw their material support of women and children as the fulfillment of their part in pacts of mutual obligations with their wives or consensual partners. As various historians have noted, explicit understandings regarding men's and women's rights, privileges, and mutual responsibilities regulated both consensual unions and marriages in various regions of Latin America.[97] In the gendered pacts that were established in the sertão, a man acquired the responsibility of *amparar,* or to support and protect, a woman when he married or entered into a consensual union with her.[98] The following verses by Anselmo, who disparaged what he saw as women's habit of demanding the immediate satisfaction of their wants and needs, illustrate the idea that women were dependent on male providers and that they did not hesitate in commanding their husbands or consensual partners to constantly discharge those duties.

A muié, assim que casa,	As soon as a woman gets married,
Tudo pede e tudo qué:	She wants and demands everything:
Qué a carne e a farinha,	She wants meat and farinha
Qué o doce e o café,	She wants sweets and coffee
Qué a saia e a camisa,	She wants skirts and shirts
Qué a chinela pro o pé . . .	And sandals for her feet . . .
. . . Coitadinho dos marido	Poor are the men
Que se vê nas amarela!	Who are in those situations![99]

According to the information presented in criminal cases, it also appears as if in the Cearense context of poverty and scarcity, a concern for women was men's fulfillment of the role of providers, especially for their offspring, even when they held their own remunerated employment or actively participated in household production tasks in other ways. For example, Vivência Tomasa de Andrade, a single domestic worker from Tamboril, was in a consensual union with the army corporal named Mandaú, and together they had a baby girl. Vivência clearly expected the corporal to contribute to providing for the baby's sustenance. Thus, on a day when he left the town of Tamboril in an official proceeding without "leaving money to buy food for their daughter," she ran after the corporal, and confronted him, an action that ended up in a fight.[100]

Fulfilling the role of effective providers for their families, in turn, served as a basis for men to bolster their control over the sexuality of wives and *amásias* (consensual wives) and to structure relationships of patriarchal authority with women at home. The following case analyzed by Vieira Jr., even though from an earlier period, offers an illustration of a poor man's conceptualization of his relation with his wife as an exchange between economic provision and sexual possession. According to his own narrative in 1808, Luís, who lived by means of agrarian activities outside of the city of Fortaleza, had traveled away from his home to sell livestock in another location. During his absence, his wife had sustained "illicit sexual relations" with another man. Demonstrating his indignation over his wife's unfaithfulness, Luís sought judicial retribution by filing an official accusation against her for adultery. In his deposition, he remarked on his fulfillment of a marital pact, by asserting that he "provided for all the necessities of his home and his wife." Based on this characterization of himself as an effective provider, he requested the condemnation of his wife, since in his view, her sexual encounter with another man constituted a breach on the terms of that pact.[101] A criminal case from

Tamboril demonstrates that even in cases of consensual unions, there were social expectations regarding men's provision for the women with whom they established sexual relationships. As stated in an 1873 legal complaint, the stonemason Francisco Pereira dos Santos allegedly killed Antônio Joaquim Brasileiro because he had sustained an adulterous relationship with his wife during several months. Yet, several witnesses declared that Antônio Joaquim provided for the expenses of Francisco Pereira's wife, especially since Pereira dos Santos often traveled to fazendas in other municipios for reasons of work.[102]

As part of these reciprocal pacts, husbands and *amásios* (male consensual partners) expected to exercise control over their wives' and consensual partners' physical mobility, even if they had to use violence to do it. For instance, a police soldier from Barbalha stabbed his amásia because she insisted on visiting her girlfriend in another town.[103] Yet, poor sertanejos did not tolerate a comparable restriction on their own movement and their own sexual freedom by their wives or amásias. When women attempted to impose such restrictions, they were accused of jealousy by their partners and often faced violent attacks at home. For example, the illiterate farmer José Borges de Oliveira from Jucás declared in a criminal case in which he was accused of killing his *mulher*[104] that he did not kill her and that "he never really mistreated her, except for a few small beatings he gave to her, because she deserved them since she was extremely jealous."[105]

The idea that men enjoyed patriarchal authority to dominate, beat, and whip women when they expressed feelings of jealousy is also present in popular poetry from the late nineteenth and early twentieth centuries. For instance, the black cantador Severino, who lived much of his life in Quixadá, mentioned that

Há quarto coisa no mundo	There are four things in this world
Que afragela um cristão:	That can scare a Christian:
É uma muié ciumenta,	One, is a jealous woman,
É um menino chorão,	Another one is a crying baby,
É uma casa que goteja,	Another one is a leaky roof
É um burro topão.	And yet another one is a burro that stumbles a lot.
O menino se acalenta,	The baby can be warmed
A casa a gente retêia,	The roof can be repaired
O burro se apara os casco,	A trimming of the hoof can help the burro,
Tudo isso se arremideia:	Everything can be fixed:
Mas o diabo da muié	But the devil of a jealous woman
Só se indo com ela à peia.	Can be fixed only with a whipping.[106]

Thus, even though women participated actively in the activities that contributed to the entire family's sustenance, and contracts regulated mutual obligations between married and consensual partners, men and women did not enjoy the same power in those relations. With the assistance of physical force, marital pacts reproduced a hierarchical order in which rural men exercised unequal authority over women at home.

Nonetheless, women did not passively accept male domination or even violence without contestation. Criminal cases demonstrate that poor women often left abusive relationships, as was the case of Ana Maria do Espírito Santo, who "abandoned" her former amásio João José da Costa because of the "bad treatment" that she received from him. In fact, when because of this abandonment João José threatened to flog Ana Maria, she sought refuge in Antônio Joaquim de Sousa's house, where she spent several nights. Likewise, Mariana Francisca de Maria, wife of the illiterate farmer Brasilino José de Monteiro, from the town of Santa Cruz, had lived at least five years separated from her husband because he very often beat her in a brutal manner and several times he threatened to kill her. In fact, according to the farmer Francisco Chaves de Araújo, Mariana had gone to his house a few times to tell him about her predicament. It is true that these strategies by battered wives or amásias did not necessarily result in an end to the whippings that they suffered at the hands of their spouses, since even legal precepts recognized the rights of men as household heads to physically castigate their dependents. Yet, these attempts at escaping their situation demonstrate that the ideal of violent male subordination of women did not exist without opposition.[107] These examples also suggest that husbands and amásios saw recourse to domestic violence as a way to sustain their often-challenged attempts at dominance and exercise of power over female kin.

Conclusions

Without a doubt, free poor Cearense men who derived their sustenance from small-scale agriculture and ranching during the post-1845 years subscribed to a cultural ideology of honor. Like their wealthier and even poor counterparts throughout the rest of Latin America, these men based their masculine claims to honor on their status as proprietors, family providers, honest members of their communities, and effective guardians of the sexuality of female kin. Yet, this emphasis on honor did not amount to the simple enactment of cultural prescriptions. Instead, it constituted a strategic resource that smallholders used to contend with the intense and sustained conflict for productive resources that characterized life in the interior during these years. These tensions originated in the accelerated competition for land and water, and the failure of the Imperial state to arbitrate their possession and usufruct through systematic, depersonalized means. Moreover, as smallholding families faced the continuous legal significance of public recognition of land claims and the fragmentation of their patrimony because of the effects of partible inheritance, free poor men enacted what Bourdieu has called "the punctilious watchfulness of the point of honor."[108] The active vigilance of honor, predicated on respectable reputations for men, served male household heads in their attempts to establish the social authority that was necessary to sway personal negotiations with coproprietors and neighbors to their benefit and to enforce the fulfillment of agreements that regulated the use of communal resources. Poor men's militant watchfulness of honor, as dependent on the sexual purity of family women, constituted a tactic to strengthen bonds and cooperation between male members of families and joint landholdings, who competed against each other to satisfy their particularized productive needs from the same plots of land. Male control of women's sexuality also had the practical effect of attempting to channel women's reproductive capacities to bear children only as sanctioned by family interests, in a move that sought to avoid the disintegration of smallholdings and other patrimony that could result from the system of dividing inheritances.

In all the personal interactions required to materially or symbolically organize the use of productive resources and retain possession of them, sertanejos reproduced a series of cultural exchanges—asserting their respectability as proprietors, defending themselves from charges of thievery, or riding horses to rescue kidnapped women—that manifested a hegemonic masculinity centered on the concept of honor. This type of manhood was hegemonic because through their social relations with men who vied with them for resources and with family women, small farmers and ranchers attempted to establish authority and dominance. But if gender and honor were the main interactional strategies for poor smallholders to maintain their claims of ownership or authority over land, water, and animals, the enactment of these respectable masculinities also had consequences for the organization of power relations within the family. As Connell has argued, the reproduction of a particular type of hegemonic masculinity makes sense because it "pays dividends" for men in their social relations with others.[109] In this case, besides the material benefits that honorable masculinities paid to sertanejos in terms of continued access to fragile productive resources and control of the labor of women and young children, patriarchal authority over female kin constituted a "dividend" paid to men for the vigilance of family honor. Likewise, free poor men's emphasis on their ability to provide for wife and children helped in the constitution of unequal power relations with women within the household. The social concealment of women's and children's labor in smallholdings, which bolstered the idea that women were dependent, and the use of male physical force, especially in the form of whippings of wives and amásias, also contributed to the construction of the asymmetrical basis of patriarchal power among sertanejo families.

Chapter 4

A Changing World: Deprivation, Dislocation, and the Disruption of Honorable Masculinity, 1865–89

"It was a sad picture indeed," was the beginning of Rodolpho Theophilo's description of the flocks of *retirantes* (drought refugees) from the backlands that began arriving in Fortaleza as early as June 1877. By that month it had become clear that no rains would fall, and a drought dawned again in the interior. Theophilo continued his harrowing narrative of the trials of seemingly countless victims during the Great Drought of 1877–79 with the following words:

> True live skeletons, with the skin stuck to the bones and darkened by the dust of the roads. They stretched their bony hands to whomever they saw, and begged for alms. Their sight made you pity them. The wretched fathers sacrificed themselves carrying on their backs two, three and even four little children, who, defeated by heat exhaustion and hunger, emaciated and skeletal, represented a vivid picture of despair. The unfortunate women, the wretched mothers, overcoming the fragility of their sex, like heroines, carried bundles of clothes, the only symbols of past fortunes, along with one and even two small children, innocent victims of such terrible calamity.[1]

The Great Drought was indeed a disaster of enormous proportions that plagued most of the province and caused widespread dislocation and misery, as well as great mortality, especially among the poor. Nevertheless, this catastrophic event in the history of Ceará, and the Northeast more broadly, was not the sole cause of far-reaching hardship during the late nineteenth century. Instead, a series of economic, political, and social transformations affecting the sertão from the mid-1860s on began disrupting the lives of backlanders, especially those who lived by means of small-scale agriculture and cattle grazing. These changes progressively undermined the livelihoods of smallholders and caused the gradual loss of their meager resources, leaving them extremely vulnerable to any form of calamity. In fact, the period between 1865 and 1889 represents the end of the brief moment of prosperity that a sizable group of free poor Cearenses had come to enjoy since 1845. When the disastrous drought struck in 1877, families of sertanejos already suffering impoverishment and social displacement were reduced to the condition of nomads, refugees who migrated to the coastal cities and even to other provinces in search of work, food, and charity. As Linda Lewin has argued, widespread social change precipitated deep economic and social disorientation in much of the Northeast during the last decades of the nineteenth century.[2]

In this chapter I seek to demonstrate that free poor sertanejos lived this period of intense economic, physical, and social dislocation as a true "state of emergency" in the sense that Walter Benjamin applied the term in his last reflections on the eve of World War II. "The tradition of the oppressed teaches us that the 'state of emergency' in which we live is not the exception, but the rule," wrote Benjamin. He added, "We must attain to a conception of history that is in keeping with this insight."[3] While this approach has often been used to illuminate the generalized terror caused by state institutions in societies facing repressive military dictatorships or other forms of terrorism,[4] I see its value in helping to demonstrate the everyday hardship that marked the lives of poor sertanejo families during the last decades of the nineteenth century. Moreover, Benjamin's understanding of a "state of emergency" as a rule for the "oppressed," instead of the exception, seems useful in my attempt to make sense of the continuous state of hopelessness and despair that accompanied the sertanejos' everyday lives as they navigated these difficult years.

In tracing the trials and tribulations affecting smallholding families, the groups that were most vulnerable to hardship, and the strategies that they developed to contend with destitution, I also seek to illuminate the effects of broad social change on the male sertanejos' ability to attain the culturally accepted signifiers of honor. As the previous chapters have shown, measures of honorable manhood, including display of property ownership, provision of family members, and effective guardianship of the sexual propriety of female kin had served free poor men to navigate their positions in the political order of the empire and to negotiate access to scarce productive resources. Yet, as we will see below, the late-nineteenth-century alteration in the fortunes of smallholding families undermined free poor men's capacities to enjoy the material advantages that upheld these notions of honor. Even more, these rapid transformations eroded the social-economic foundations that sustained free poor men's claims to hegemonic positions within their households and communities. Under such conditions, impoverished and destitute sertanejos faced the underlying contradiction between culturally sanctioned and strategically useful ideals of honorable manhood and the lived reality of hardship, dislocation, and despair.

A Changing World

Between late 1864 and 1870, Brazil was involved in the Paraguayan War, the longest and most exhausting international military conflict in its history. As noted in Chapter 2, the province of Ceará sent an estimated 5,769 troops to the front lines, most of whom had been coerced into service against their will. Moreover, between 1866 and 1868, the most intense period of impressment for the war, many poor young men who were potential recruits, as well as designated National Guardsmen, fled to mountains, caves, and fields. Fleeing represented one of the strategies that poor young men used to resist their capture by press gangs, police soldiers, and local authorities who sought to fill the provincial quota of enlisted troops to deploy to the border with Paraguay.

These conditions effectively disrupted the livelihoods of at least some smallholding families. As autonomous but small-scale participants in the expanding agricultural and cattle-grazing economies that emerged out of the 1845 drought, these families were also extremely vulnerable to any change that would disrupt their ability to survive. Thus, when military service (whether voluntary or coerced, as was more often the case) removed young men from smallholding families that relied on the labor of all able-bodied household members, they became unable to meet their labor needs. Consequently, they quickly lost animals and other resources. According to the *Constituição*, a conservative newspaper, poor older ranchers began losing cattle because they could not count on the assistance of their impressed sons to treat and feed their small herds. Typically, young men performed the work of manually feeding the branches of *juazeiro* trees (a type of tree that remains green during the dry season) to cattle during droughts. A regional drought that affected some areas of the interior in 1865 and 1866 thus exacerbated this problem and the losses of poor families. The flight of young men from their households and fazendas also disrupted the male capacity to work in agrarian activities. For instance, the liberal newspaper *Cearense* reported that, in Aquiraz and Maraguape, it was impossible to find "even one individual of the masculine sex, except for some old men, and perhaps a boy, because all the other ones had emigrated or fled." Editorials published in *Constituição* and *Pedro II*, another conservative paper, also noted that the flight and recruitment of young men interrupted the provision of labor in coffee, cotton, and sugar harvests.[5]

It is true that political partisanship and local elections intensified the problem of arbitrary impressment, and that the main provincial newspapers, such as *Cearense, Pedro II*, and *Constituição* were induced to exaggerate the dislocations created by forced recruitment as a way to denounce the abuses committed by the opposite party. Nevertheless, other sources confirm that impressment for the Paraguayan War did disorganize the survival strategies of some poor rural families. In her study of army recruitment in Ceará, Xislei Araújo Ramos analyzes correspondence between National Guard commanders from interior municipalities and the provincial president, and finds evidence that recruitment disrupted the provision of labor by poor sertanejos, both for themselves and for others. In a letter written in 1867 by the National Guard detachment commander of Sobral, he noted that "this is a very inconvenient time to recruit farmers and day laborers, who are indispensable for the harvests of cotton and coffee. In addition, they resist any effort to recruit them and prefer to die rather than serve in the war." Contemporary observers also noted the challenges that free poor families faced to feed themselves when young men were recruited. For instance, in his trips to the interior of Ceará, Juvenal Galeno met an old man who derived his sustenance mainly from the labor his young son performed at their small farm. When recruiters took away his son, the old man, no longer able to work, was forced to become a beggar in a small town. Galeno also met a recruit who had been the main source of sustenance for his old and widowed mother before impressment. According to the author, as the recruit waited for his deployment, he wondered about the fate that might befall his mother and whether she would be subjected to wretched poverty because of his absence.[6]

The mobilization of young men for the Paraguayan War effort coincided with the onset of the end of the cotton boom, which further contributed to the hardship that free poor Cearenses endured during these years. With the end of the U.S. Civil War in 1865 and the gradual return of American cotton to the international market, British buyers began to reject the lower-quality product from Brazil.[7] In fact, as early as 1868, Cearense merchants found out that thousands of bales of Brazilian cotton lay unsold in British warehouses. By the late 1860s, cotton acreage in Ceará, as well as other Northeastern provinces, began to diminish. Cotton cultivation gradually disappeared from the more remote municipalities, such as Ipu, where costly overland transport, coupled with declining cotton prices, made cultivation of the crop increasingly unprofitable. During the early 1870s, cotton prices fell precipitously, reaching Rs. $416 per kilo (about U.S. $0.20) in 1875, which was less than half of what they had been in 1865.[8] Consequently, exports of cotton—a crop produced largely by small farmers—began to fall from the peak they had reached in the year 1871–72.

Yet, the drop in cotton production in Ceará was not absolute. For most of the 1870s, and until the Great Drought, the province of Ceará continued exporting cotton in quantities that largely exceeded those of the years before the boom. Even more important, with the persistent downward trend in cotton prices, Cearense farmers sought to make up for their losses by cultivating additional cotton trees and opening up new plots. They increasingly neglected the cultivation of manioc and beans in order to transform whatever was left of their smallholdings into cotton fields.[9] Thus, it is not surprising that, despite falling prices, the province exported 7,253,893 kilos of cotton in 1870–71 and 8,324,258 kilos in 1871–72—more than double the cotton exports of 1867–68 and 1868–69. (See Table 1.4.)

Declining prices on the Liverpool cotton exchange resulted in heavy borrowing and eventually dispossession of their meager properties among the poor cotton farmers who had enjoyed a degree of prosperity during the boom years. According to Theophilo, large and small producers became indebted to merchants and other money lenders, as they tried to remain afloat and counterweight decreasing cotton prices.[10] But the credit system of the rural backlands worked largely against the cash-starved and often illiterate small farmers. The mostly literate merchant-lenders from towns such as Aracati, Baturité, Icó, and Fortaleza furnished farmers with cash advances for crop production and increasingly for subsistence goods on credit at interest rates ranging from 12 to 24 percent per annum.[11] In turn, the farmers handed over their entire cotton harvests at decreasing prices to cover these advances, but still remained unable to repay the expensive money they had borrowed.[12] As their debts mounted and cotton prices continued dropping, small cotton farmers became more and more vulnerable to the pressures of wealthier merchants, who often sued them in civil courts for payment of debts. Unable to pay for lawyers to defend them, a number of poor farmers lost their lands, few animals, and slaves, when they had them, during these years.[13]

If the early 1870s were marked by adversity and difficulties for poor farmers and ranchers, the onslaught of the Great Drought only deepened their misery and provoked widespread dispossession and death. Geographical location and climatic patterns have made periodic drought a persistent problem for the inhabitants of the sertão in all of recorded history.[14] Yet, the length and severity of the Great Drought, combined with the changing social and economic conditions in the backlands before the calamity, and the woefully inadequate and self-centered Imperial, provincial, and municipal responses to the crisis, contributed to make it the greatest disaster in Brazilian history.[15]

An 1878 report by the provincial president of Ceará claimed that small landholders, subsistence peasants, and wage laborers were the groups most severely affected by the drought.[16] Having very little land on which to raise subsistence crops, smallholders quickly consumed the supplies of corn and beans that they customarily kept for survival during the dry summer months.[17] Without any crops to harvest, and too poor to buy subsistence items, which were scarce or sold at exorbitant prices, many of these formerly prosperous farmers and ranchers became retirantes who migrated to mountain lands, the coast, and even other provinces, in a desperate search of work for wages or relief help.[18]

In his study of the impact of the Great Drought, Roger Cunniff notes that in areas such as the Uruburetama hills, where the end of the cotton boom had left "a particularly disjointed society," smallholders anxiously requested support from the provincial government to migrate to the Amazon, once it became clear that the rains would not arrive. He further notes that in other areas in the interior, where smallholders had been able to produce commercial crops during the prosperous years, ties of patronage between small farmers and larger landowners had loosened or had become permanently severed. In his analysis, this partly explains the extreme susceptibility of smallholders and subsistence peasants to climatic disaster, as well as the inability of reciprocal relations between wealthier fazendeiros and small farmers and ranchers to guarantee the welfare of the rural poor during the drought.[19] The heavy borrowing in which many sertanejos had engaged as the cotton boom drew to a close also accounted for the vulnerability to dispossession that small farmers and ranchers experienced during the drought. According to the *Cearense*, as small farmers and ranchers struggled simply to survive during the first dry months, merchant-lenders quickly moved to discharge their debts. Thus, creditors took away the sertanejos' last few goats, sheep, oxen, or even jewels, in forceful acts of foreclosure, and left them empty-handed, and thus more determined to migrate.[20]

A class-based accessibility to water from the largest and deepest reservoirs capable of holding enough water to withstand the crisis also played an important role in worsening conditions for the rural poor. For many sertanejos, those conditions resulted in desperate migrations or even death during the Great Drought. As Chapter 3 revealed, backlanders regarded water sources as communal property and negotiated conventions for the use of water from the small reservoirs and cacimbas that were built in joint landholdings. Nevertheless, only wealthier fazendeiros, with the help of provincial funding, had been able to build large açudes since the early part of the nineteenth century. Ever since the enactment of the 1832 provincial law that established subsidies to cattle ranchers and farmers who built açudes in their lands, a total of sixty-seven private reservoirs were built throughout the province.[21] The construction of reservoirs intensified as the expanding agricultural and livestock economies of the second half of the nineteenth century required ever-increasing amounts of water to flourish. But only wealthier families had the means to build dams, either on their own or with the help of provincial subsidies.[22] Moreover, landowners restricted access to the reservoirs and even used them as tools to attempt to fix highly mobile sertanejos on their land as laborers, even though the açude law specified that use of reservoir water was to remain public.[23]

During the Great Drought, wealthier families counted on the dams as a resource to sustain themselves, and even profit from the lack of rains, while poorer sertanejos had access only to public or communal açudes, which in many cases were small and did not hold enough water for longer than a year.[24] Theophilo, in his vivid description of the horrors of the drought, pointed out that families of fazendeiros who possessed large dams were able to irrigate some adjacent plots and grow fruits, such as melons and watermelons, as well as beans and manioc, which they sold at substantially inflated prices. He also observed that, when these fazendeiros were able to keep thieves away, they enjoyed a large supply of fish to help them go through the famines associated with droughts.[25] An 1877 report from a committee that investigated the drought also stated that the bigger and better-built açudes had been instrumental in saving most of the cattle and some of the plantings of their owners. Commenting on the opposite trend, the presidential report of 1878 noted that peasants and day laborers were ill equipped to deal with the crisis, and consequently, they quickly lost their few animals and small roça plantings.[26]

The relief programs undertaken during the Great Drought largely used Imperial and provincial funds to pay wages to the masses of wretched refugees for the construction of public projects, including water reservoirs. Those programs further reinforced the control that wealthier landowners exercised over water.[27] Retirantes built at least seventy-three açudes and thirty-one wells throughout the interior between 1877 and 1879. While these water projects were to be located in public areas and open for the general use, the opposite was often true. The *Cearense* pointed out that some of the açudes built with retirante labor benefited only the owners of the estates where they were located and not the population of the neighboring areas at large.[28]

As Cunniff has demonstrated, small farmers and ranchers, subsistence peasants, squatters, and day laborers were the greatest victims of the drought. Through a series of calculations, the author estimates that the total number of drought-related deaths in Ceará between 1877 and 1879 was 127,243. For the Northeast as a whole, Cunniff calculates a total of 220,725 drought deaths. The interaction of the drought with the increasing control over water sources by wealthier backlanders, and the greater vulnerability to sudden crisis that independent, but extremely poor, farmers and ranchers had come to experience since the prosperous years, helped set in place an enduring pattern of out-migration from the interior. During the Great Drought, Cearenses not only migrated from the backlands to the mountaintops or the coast. They also represented the largest proportion of interprovincial migrants. The main destinations were the provinces of Piauí, Maranhão, Espírito Santo, Rio de Janeiro, and particularly Pará. According to Cunniff's estimates, almost 83,000 people from Ceará migrated by foot and by sea to other provinces in 1877 and 1878.[29] The migration to the Amazon basin—and, specifically, the provinces of Pará, Amazonas, and Maranhão—continued during the 1880s, as a rubber boom blossomed with the large-scale participation of Cearenses as laborers.

Downward Mobility

The disruption of livelihoods caused by changing social, political, and economic conditions in the sertão, coupled with the disaster brought by the Great Drought, translated into downward mobility for a growing stratum of free poor Cearenses. Nowhere is this trend more apparent than in the increasing inability of poorer sertanejos to retain the slaves that they had been able to acquire during the prosperous years. A decline in the slave population in the interior of Ceará, and in the Northeast in general during the second half of the nineteenth century, played a key role in bringing about economic difficulties to poor farmers and ranchers. In 1850, the transatlantic slave trade that had furnished Brazilian planters, ranchers, and other slaveowners with a steady supply of African slaves came to an end, largely as a result of British pressure. An internal slave trade that delivered slaves acquired in the Northeast to the coffee plantations of the Southeast grew quickly.[30] Between 1864 and 1874, the number of slaves in the Northeast declined from 774,000 (or 45 percent of all Brazilian slaves) to 435,687 (28 percent). Meanwhile, the coffee regions of the Southeast increased their slave population from 645,000 (43 percent) to 809,575 (56 percent) during the same years.[31] In Ceará, gradual manumissions facilitated by the establishment of an emancipation fund in 1868 further contributed to the overall declining rates of slaves in the interior. By 1854, slaves represented 8 percent of the total population of the province. In four years, that proportion had already been reduced to 7 percent. Between 1860 and 1872, the slave population of the province decreased by 3,528 slaves, which represented 4 percent of the total population of the province as listed in the 1872 census.[32]

Postmortem inventories from Jucás demonstrate that the decreasing slave population diminished the capacity of poorer slaveowners to acquire slaves, and even to hold on to their captives. Slave prices rose rapidly from Rs. 500$000 in the 1850s to Rs. 900$000 in the late 1870s for a prime working-age slave.[33] Consequently, as the estate inventories show, the families of smaller means lost their ability to purchase and retain slaves sooner than better-off families. Slaveowners located in the poorer half of all inventoried estates in the sample, approximately Rs. 1:000$000, represent 32 percent of all slaveholders in the 1860s, 23 percent in the 1870s, and 0 percent in the 1880s. These numbers in fact exaggerate the real slaveholding capabilities of individuals in this group because the calculations include increasing proportions of "parts" in the value of slaves that some heirs shared with others. Conversely, as a group, those families of slaveowners located in the wealthier 50 percent of all inventoried estates were comparatively better able to retain their slaves until abolition, despite the overall decline of slavery in the region. Thus, these families represent 68 percent of all slaveholders in the 1860s, 77 percent in the 1870s, and 100 percent in the 1880s.[34]

Robert Slenes's analysis of the demography and economics of the internal slave trade further sustains the hypothesis that small cotton farmers and other free poor families in the interior of Ceará were the first to lose their ability to hold on to their captives during the late nineteenth century. According to his study, the volume of the internal trade in slaves from the North and Northeastern provinces to the Southeast increased dramatically during the 1870s. Slenes argues that the decline of the cotton economy in the Northeast—practiced largely by poor farmers—explains, in part, the high levels of slave sales to the Southeast. His calculations demonstrate that the provinces that exported the greatest proportionate number of captives between 1873 and 1881 were the cotton-producing ones, especially Rio Grande do Norte, Ceará, Paraíba, and Piauí. A second and, according to the author, more significant factor that explains the high out-migration of slaves from the four provinces was the impact of the Great Drought, which hit these very same areas harder than others of the Northeast. It is worth mentioning that the Great Drought also claimed the highest losses in lives and property among the humble populations of the interior. Consequently, between 1873 and 1881 Ceará lost 11,622 slaves of the 30,905 bondsmen and bondswomen registered in 1873, or 37.6 percent of its slave population. By contrast, Pernambuco and Bahia—provinces with larger and more diverse agricultural economies less affected by the end of the cotton boom and the Great Drought—lost only 8.0 and 8.2 percent, respectively, of the slave population registered in 1873.[35]

The loss of slaves among the poorer populations and the trend toward concentration in slaveownership among the wealthiest segments of the inventoried population roughly parallels a concentration of landholding capabilities among the better-off population of wealthholders during the same years. Postmortem inventories from Jucás indicate that the percentage of families with one landholding decreased from 43 percent to 27 percent between the 1860s and the 1880s, whereas the number of families that held six or more pieces of land increased from 4 percent to 24 percent during the same years. Moreover, families claiming two holdings or more represented an increasing share of the sample, ranging from 57 percent in the 1860s, 64 percent in the 1870s, to 73 percent in the 1880s. These figures contrast markedly with the 41 percent of families with two or more holdings in the 1830s.[36]

Chapter 3 has already established that competition for scarce agricultural and grazing lands was a feature of everyday life for families of small farmers and ranchers, beginning in the late 1840s. Likewise, even the smallholdings that the rural poor held continued a trend of rapid fragmentation, as a result of the partible inheritance system, during the latter half of the nineteenth century. In addition, Chapter 6 will provide evidence to show that because of the general dislocation and movement of populations precipitated by the upheavals of these years, the old conventions that regulated land use completely gave way, and neighbors often fought in order to retain or increase possession over the plots of land that were claimed by others. Thus, through practices that included loss of landholdings that became so small as to be uneconomical, outright invasion and violent encroachment on neighbors' or coproprietors' lands, alienation of lands of poor farmers in lieu of debts, and occupation of lands abandoned by *retirantes*, a new landholding pattern began to emerge in the last quarter of the nineteenth century.[37] In this more concentrated pattern of agrarian organization, prosperous proprietors progressively held more and more of the small- and medium-size plots of land, while the owners of one plot were unable to retain their smallholdings. Postmortem inventories show that during the late nineteenth century, wealthier families owned considerable numbers of holdings, as many as seventeen, twenty-five, and even forty-five plots, frequently in separate rather than contiguous locations. On those lands, prosperous families kept large herds of cattle, grew commercial crops, installed engenhocas or farinha houses, built water reservoirs, and often raised draft animals to use in larger-scale transportation businesses.[38]

The sweeping changes of the last four decades of the nineteenth century not only brought loss of slaves and land to the poorer sertanejos who had enjoyed an ephemeral, if small, degree of success since the late 1840s. Probate records demonstrate that these transformations brought measurable downward mobility and decreasing economic capacity for the poorest segments of the wealthholding population. A comparison of postmortem inventories from Jucás for the 1860s, 1870s, and 1880s shows that mean and median wealth per inventoried family was lower in the 1860s than it had been in the 1850s. Mean wealth fell from Rs. 2:108$313 in the 1850s to 909$134 in the 1860s. While the values of mean and median wealth increased slightly during the 1870s, and decreased slightly again in the 1880s, the proportion of all inventories with a gross value of less than Rs. 250$000 shows an increasing trend over time. Thus, wealthholders with appraised estates worth Rs. 250$000 and less represent 27 percent of the total number of inventories consulted for the 1860s, 29 percent of those for the 1870s, and 31 percent of those for the 1880s. Therefore, these figures demonstrate a trend of decline in wealthholding capacity of the poorest decedents, despite high levels of inflation, especially between 1850 and 1870.[39]

The privation of the poor farmers and ranchers during these years can also be illustrated by a quick examination of the types of assets that the poorest wealthholders had been able to retain until the time of their death. For instance, the total estate of João Ferreira Marques, worth Rs. 153$000 in 1857, included a landholding measuring 108 braças, a house on the same land, four cows, six sheep, a small share in the value of an old slave named Inácia, and a pair of earrings. The estate of Isabel Maria da Conceição included only four cows and one pair of earrings, appraised at Rs. 66$000 by the time of her death in 1868. The estate of the poorest wealthholder in the sample, Joaquim Alves Ferreira, included only two goats, two hoes, one scythe, an old shotgun, and a large bottle, worth a total of Rs. 7$440 in 1875.[40]

The data reveal that the far-reaching social change of these years hit hardest the poorer segments of the free population and undermined their ability to hold on to household resources, especially land, slaves, and animals. Pressured by debts, falling cotton prices, and drought, free poor farmers and ranchers were no longer able to benefit from the smallholding pattern characteristic of the interior. Moreover, without access to slaves as a more dependable form of labor, free poor Cearenses began to lose the autonomy they had enjoyed during the prosperous years by growing their own foodstuffs and some commercial crops. Furthermore, the loss of the small herds of livestock that poor sertanejos routinely kept, and other meager possessions, signaled their complete dispossession and precipitated their migration. Under those circumstances, the problems of livelihood became urgent, leading to much distress and to the development of new strategies of survival.

The Plight of the Young

It is clear that, in last four decades of the nineteenth century, achieving economic security, and even survival, in the Cearense sertão was precarious for most among the rural poor. Yet, for one particular group more than any other, the end of the ephemeral affluence of the period between the late 1840s and mid-1860s signified the loss of the faintest hopes of achieving success, and even honor, and respectability. Analysis of estate inventories demonstrates that, between the mid-1860s and 1889, young families experienced even greater difficulties than older families in acquiring and retaining the material resources necessary for survival, and a degree of prosperity as farmers and ranchers. It is true that studies of wealthholding in other locations point out that older individuals and families hold more wealth than younger ones, as a result of the passage of time and lifecycle, and the consequent ability of older individuals to accumulate more assets.[41] But what the probate records from Jucás demonstrate is that, over time, poor younger families were increasingly unable to acquire the assets necessary to subsist and to prosper in their rural economic activities.

Because postmortem inventories generally do not provide the age of the decedent wealthholder, this study relies on the age of the oldest surviving child listed as a proxy for the age, or relative youth, of the decedent's family. Thus, the sample indicates that between the 1850s and the 1880s, younger families with an oldest surviving child aged fifteen or younger were consistently located at the lower end of the wealthholding population.[42] Figures 4.1 through 4.4 indicate that the vast majority of families with an oldest surviving child under the age of fifteen were located in the 50 percent below the mean of roughly Rs. 1:000$000 during the period between 1850 and 1890. In fact, younger families with appraised estates worth less than Rs. 1:000$000 represent 65 percent of all the inventories of young families in the 1850s, 93 percent of those for the 1860s, and 91 percent of those for the 1870s, as well as for the 1880s.

Even more important, the sample indicates an overall trend by which, over time, proportionally more and more of the younger families were located at the lowest end of the wealth range. Younger families with appraised estates worth less than Rs. 500$000 represent 57 percent of all the inventories of young families in the 1850s, 75 percent in the 1860s, 72 percent in the 1870s, and 82 percent in the 1880s. By contrast, the majority of families with an oldest surviving child older than fifteen years old and often with a number of grandchildren were located on the top of the wealth range, especially during the 1850s (older families with appraised estates worth Rs. 1:000$000 and more represent 70 percent of all the older families during this decade). The inventories further indicate that wealthier and older families were also vulnerable to the hardship that affected the backlands since the late 1860s. Nonetheless, these families as a group were better able to reach the highest wealthholding levels during the trying 1860s, 1870s, and 1880s. (See figures 4.1 through 4.4.)

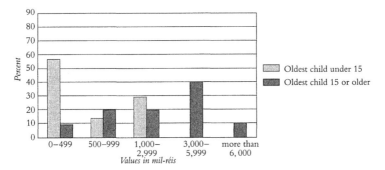

Fig. 4.1. Total Gross Value of Appraised Assets According to the Age of the Oldest Surviving Child. Jucás, 1850–59. Sources: Thirty postmortem inventories from Jucás from the period between 1850 and 1859.

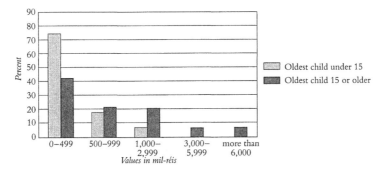

Fig. 4.2. Total Gross Value of Appraised Assets According to the Age of the Oldest Surviving Child. Jucás, 1860–69. Sources: Sixty postmortem inventories from the municipality of Jucás from the period between 1860 and 1869.

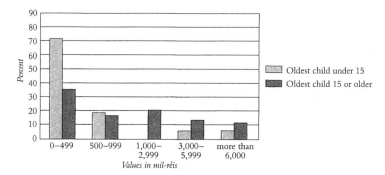

Fig. 4.3. Total Gross Value of Appraised Assets According to the Age of the Oldest Surviving Child. Jucás, 1870–79. Sources: Sixty postmortem inventories from Jucás from the period between 1870 and 1879.

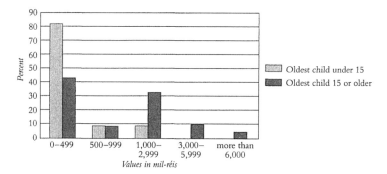

Fig. 4.4. Total Gross Value of Appraised Assets According to the Age of the Oldest Surviving Child. Jucás, 1880–89. Sources: Thirty-five postmortem inventories from Jucás from the period between 1880 and 1889.

This analysis of postmortem inventories from Jucás confirms the importance of the constitution of families for the establishment and success of farming-and-ranching households. Profiles of young men who appear as defendants, plaintiffs, and witnesses in criminal cases demonstrate that farmers and ranchers were married or engaged in stable consensual relations as early as the age of twenty-one.[43] But, for many young families, the obstacles that they needed to overcome in order to reach a degree of economic security seem to have become insurmountable, especially during the 1860s, 1870s, and 1880s. With slave prices rising, and a mobile labor force, poor families had to rely more heavily on family labor. Broader pressures, such as recruitment for the Paraguayan War, disrupted the ability of young men from poor families to provide labor in family fields and ranches. Impressment practices singled out young poor men between the ages of eighteen and twenty-one. Recruiters impressed married men along with single males, under the excuse of detaining men with "bad behavior," even though the recruitment laws provided exemptions to married men.[44]

Moreover, it is likely that the severe epidemics and droughts that assailed the backlands population during the second half of the nineteenth century diminished the labor force available for peasant households, by decreasing the adult population, and reducing the survival rate of children. Until about the late 1850s, observers had noted the general healthiness of the sertão, and the good fortune of the Cearenses, who had not been afflicted by a smallpox epidemic since the 1825 drought. But beginning in the early 1860s, a wave of infectious diseases viciously attacked many localities in the interior, causing crippling illness and death. In 1862 a cholera epidemic reached "horrendous proportions," especially in the municipalities located along the Jaguaribe River, as well as several of the mountainous areas such as Pacatuba, Maranguape, and the fertile Crato valley. The epidemic wiped out entire families and claimed the lives of at least 11,000 Cearenses, most of them from the interior.[45] A new cholera outbreak took place in 1864, affecting especially the Southeastern and South central areas of the province and infecting almost 7,000 people, of whom about 900 perished.[46] Malaria, typhus, and other "intermittent fevers" also reached epidemic proportions in the interior during the 1870s and 1880s. According to provincial presidential reports, these fevers attacked mostly "the indigent" and quickly brought famine and greater poverty to their households.[47] During these years, beriberi, a multiple-deficiency disease that caused crippling effects to its sufferers, began to spread into the Cearense sertão. According to Cunniff, nutritional deficiencies in the progressively insufficient food supplies available to the sertanejos explain the proliferation of this disease, as well as the rapid spread of contagious illnesses.[48]

The greatest epidemic of the nineteenth century was the outbreak of smallpox in 1878. During the Great Drought, smallpox spread like wildfire among the rapidly moving, concentrated, and undernourished population of retirantes. The disease first struck the port cities of Aracati and Fortaleza and then spread to the refugee camps in coastal and mountain towns. Furthermore, as those refugees who continued hoping for rainfall returned to the interior in January of 1879, they carried the infection deep into the backlands and into the Crato valley. An estimated 100,000 deaths associated with the Great Drought were most likely caused by smallpox in Ceará.[49]

It is conceivable that this rash of infectious disease, coupled with the implacable effects of the drought, affected young children in particular, increasing infant mortality rates and thus contributing to greater economic in-security among young families. Infant mortality rates were high throughout Brazil during the nineteenth century, not only in the backlands but in other regions as well.[50] Yet, it is very likely that these rates were especially high in Ceará during epidemic and drought years. Documents from drought relief commissions demonstrate that children were the first and perhaps most common victims of death from exposure during the Great Drought. For instance, of the nineteen people buried in the cemetery from the town of Jucás in the month of October 1877, seventeen were children between the ages of three months and ten years.[51] Likewise, the medical doctor Barão de Studart expressed feelings of sorrow after observing a refugee camp in Maranguape, where mainly children were affected with smallpox and other infectious diseases during the Great Drought. According to Marco Antonio Villa, travelers commented on the poisoning especially of desperately hungry children from the ingestion of toxic plants, such as the *mucunã* (a poisonous root).[52]

The absence of infant mortality estimates for the interior makes it difficult to calculate exactly how many children died during the Great Drought and the years of widespread epidemic disease. But a comparison of the number of children's deaths registered in Fortaleza in 1899, a year when another drought assailed the province causing dislocation and impoverishment, with those registered in the years following the drought offers some insights into differential infant mortality rates related to natural calamity. In 1899, 1,059 children ten years of age or younger died in Fortaleza. In 1900 the number was 1,037, and decreased to 393 only in 1,902.[53] These data suggest that drought, or other hardships such as epidemic disease that claimed the lives of children in proportions even higher than during regular years, added to the economic insecurity and impoverishment of young families. During the years of natural calamity and epidemics, these families were increasingly unable to see their children survive at least until the first years of adolescence, a time when they could become significant contributors of labor for the household economy.

Another factor that helps explain the inability of young poor families to establish themselves during these years is their decreasing capacity to inherit assets from their impoverished parents, which, in turn, kept them from obtaining the minimum resources necessary for their survival. Because of the heavy indebtedness confronting many Cearense families, poorer parents had no valuable assets to bequeath to their young children. Legal procedure required the payment of debts of the deceased before the division of the estate among all heirs in the *partilhas*, and that left little to distribute.[54] For example, José Gonçalves de Melo and his wife Josefa Maria dos Santos from

Jucás had accumulated an estate worth Rs. 599$000, including two landhold-ings, one engenhoca, one aviamento to make farinha, and three and a half sugarcane tarefas. They also had a total of Rs. 458$000 worth of debts to several wealthier men from the municipality. After José's death in 1869, the judges set aside the most valuable assets, such as the better located landhold-ing, the sugar and farinha-making equipment, and the sugarcane plantings, for the payment of debts. By contrast, the widow and her three boys, ages two to fourteen, inherited only the smaller landholding and a house worth Rs. 10$000.[55] In cases in which the debts surpassed the total estate of a fam-ily at the time of one of the spouses' death, the offspring could become truly dispossessed. For example, the total inheritable wealth of Maria José da Con-ceição and Manoel Leandro Correia from Jucás was Rs. 612$000, while their debt with just one merchant from Icó amounted to Rs. 750$720 at the time of Maria José's death in 1867. After assigning to the merchant the planted roça (worth Rs. 300$000), the old house (appraised at Rs. 12$000), and Rs. 300$000 on the proportion of the value of a slave that they owned, there was nothing left for the spouse and the offspring to inherit. Consequently, when the merchant collected the payments, Manoel Leandro and his three young sons, Antônio (who was twenty years old), Raimundo (sixteen years old), and Cipriano (thirteen years old) became completely destitute.[56]

Consequently, young Cearense families experienced serious difficulties in setting up and retaining viable and autonomous households for them-selves during the calamitous years. They initiated family life without any or with few resources in the form of land, slaves, or animals to help sustain the household at a time when competition for land increased and food prices soared. Moreover, they were increasingly unable to raise their small children to the age at which they could become effective providers of labor in family plots on account of the periodic attack of epidemic disease and drought. It is difficult to imagine how, with the loss of the labor and protection of the young men who fled to the mountains to avoid recruitment or those who were in fact pressed into military service, these families escaped the abject poverty and dislocation of the 1870s and the years that followed the Great Drought. Within this context, young men as heads of new families were, in all likelihood, increasingly unable to constitute honorable masculine identi-ties on the basis of their capacity to sustain their wives and children. Without material resources, young men as a group were also deprived of their role of defenders of landed patrimony, and as they came to experience poverty and sustained deprivation, became vulnerable to dishonor and shame.

Diversification of Survival Strategies

As small farmers and ranchers began losing their meager resources, various members of rural households sought paid employment in a number of different activities. In doing so, they began joining the ranks of those that they saw as dishonorable: people who depended exclusively on wages for their livelihood, and who had no material resources to uphold claims to honorable masculinity. The low wages paid for agricultural and other types of work in Ceará aggravated the situation of hardship of those backlanders who could no longer rely primarily on small-scale agriculture and ranching to survive. According to Sousa Brasil, the labor force in the province was abundant and therefore salaries were minimal, as compared to those paid in other provinces of the empire, including Pernambuco, Amazonas, and Pará.[57] Average pay for day laborers (*jornaleiros*) ranged from Rs. $400 (U.S. $0.20) to Rs. $600 (U.S. $0.30) by the 1860s, according to region and season in the agricultural cycle. Laborers in coffee and cotton harvests could make up to one mil-réis (U.S. $0.50) a day, in addition to meals, while children in agricultural work, field hands, and men in other occupations made Rs. $320 (U.S. $ 0.16) for a day's labor. Wages for men who worked as cowboys or ranch hands in cattle ranches reportedly were even lower than those paid to agricultural workers.[58] In some agricultural establishments, particularly in the coffee-producing regions such as Maranguape and Pacatuba, laborers worked under the *empreitada* system—a piecework form of labor contract by which they received one mil-réis and meals for picking coffee from the plants cultivated in 100 braças of land.[59] The decline of the cotton economy decreased wages for workers employed in cotton harvests. According to Theophilo, cotton laborers' daily wages plummeted from the Rs. 1$280 paid at the peak of the boom in the 1860s, to Rs. $500 at the end of the cotton boom in the 1870s.[60]

What is striking about the living conditions in the interior is that overall wages remained stable from the late 1850s to the late 1880s,[61] even though prices of basic foods increased steadily during the same years.[62] A series of articles published in the *Cearense* indicate that increasing demand for cattle in neighboring provinces as well as in Ceará, and the escalating cultivation of cash crops for export at the expense of subsistence items in many municipalities, began to drive food costs up as early as the late 1850s.[63] The 1860s and 1870s witnessed a continued crisis in the supply of subsistence products within Ceará, with a parallel inflation of their prices. According to some authors, these trends demonstrated that the food shortage experienced in the province had reached the state of famine even before the onslaught of the Great Drought in 1877.[64] By 1876, a kilogram of fresh meat with bone sold for Rs. $560 in Fortaleza, more than half a day's wage of the better paid agricultural workers. During the catastrophic years of the Great Drought, contemporary daily wages were insufficient to feed a single person, let alone provide clothes and other necessities to a family. By August of 1877, a bowl of farinha sold for a whole day's salary, Rs. $400 (U.S. $0.20), a rapadura cake for Rs. $320 (U.S. $0.16), and a pound of meat for Rs. $200 (U.S. $0.10) when available in Jucás.[65]

Because a single person's wages, even in combination with domestic farming, were insufficient to guarantee a family's survival, adult household members were forced to perform a variety of occupational roles. Men, in particular, employed themselves in activities that required high degrees of physical mobility and absence, often for prolonged periods of time, from their homes. Farmers worked in their own roças, but also sought employment as vaqueiros and ranch hands on larger estates. Laborers, who worked in agriculture, also employed themselves in public projects, such as road building and, beginning in 1870, railroad construction in Maranguape and Baturité.[66] Farmers and vaqueiros assisted comboieiros and merchants as *cargueiros* (loaders) in the transportation of cotton, coffee, rapaduras, and other products, in exchange for daily wages. Jornaleiros or others "without certain occupation" traveled to other locations, even to neighboring provinces, when they were inspecting cattle that they intended to buy for themselves or for resale.[67]

Seasonal labor in agriculture also required mobility. The coffee harvests that drew large numbers of workers to larger establishments in the mountainous areas of Baturité, Maranguape, and Pacatuba began in August and extended only until November or December. Likewise, cotton, with its short cycle, did not require the attention of paid laborers year round. Clearing and preparation of roças took place between July and December, and planting was performed in January. Cotton harvests during the months of May and June attracted migrant workers to the Uruburetama hills, where larger-scale cotton establishments sought paid laborers. Work in sugarcane cultivation and harvesting and in making cachaça drew seasonal laborers to the Cariri area, as well as Baturité, Maranguape, and Pacatuba.[68] Thus, Freire Alemão commented on what he saw as the remarkable mobility of Cearense men as related to the work they performed: "I have noticed that most of the men here possess a more or less adequate knowledge of their province and even of the neighboring ones," he said. "They all have visited this or that far-away location in the sertão. They speak about one place, and when asked how far it is, they confidently reply that it is located within sixty to one hundred leagues and even more."[69]

Women also undertook paid employment in agricultural and other economic activities in order to meet household needs. For instance, visitors from the coast and popular poets observed married and single women doing field-work for wages along with men and children, especially in coffee-picking activities in Baturité and other mountainous regions.[70] In fact, according to the 1872 census, women represented a sizable proportion of all agricultural workers: they were 16 percent of all the "servants and day laborers" listed in the census.[71] The census category "servants and day laborers" is, to be sure, somewhat ambiguous. Nevertheless, the fact that census takers assigned work in textiles, arts and crafts, manufacturing, commerce, and domestic service to other classifications indicates that this term defined agricultural workers. The census did not indicate whether these women were heads of household or members of households headed by their husbands, consensual partners, fathers, or other male relatives. Considering the fact that sertanejos classified women's work in family plots of land merely as "help" to male providers, it is highly likely that women who appeared as day laborers in the census were independent or heads of their own household. But in any case, the figures do show women's significant participation in the agricultural labor force. This type of work varied according to municipality. In Baturité and Pacatuba, two mostly farming regions famous for their production of coffee, sugar, and other crops, women accounted for 17 percent of the agricultural labor force. By contrast, in Quixeramobim, a mainly cattle-producing municipality, women were only 4 percent of all servants and day-laborers.[72]

Women found other ways to earn some regular cash income by employing themselves in domestic service and related activities. Opportunities in this area of paid female employment undoubtedly rose as a result of the economic expansion, the demographic growth of interior towns and villages, and the gradual decline of slavery during the second half of the nineteenth century. According to the 1872 census, over 50 percent of all the women in Ceará with a recorded occupation worked in domestic service; 19 percent were seamstresses, and 9 percent were laborers in clothes-making industries.[73]

For poor families who were losing their resources and struggling to survive in a province where wages were low and food prices were on the rise, the possibility of migrating to neighboring provinces, and in particular to the promising Amazon basin, might have seemed a hopeful solution. Beginning in the 1860s, and continuing during the early twentieth century, a rubber boom in the provinces of Amazonas and Pará enticed impoverished Northeasterners, and especially Cearenses, to make the trek northward and westward and become *seringueiros* (rubber tappers). Rubber wages were high in comparison to those paid in Ceará, about one dollar a day in the Amazon. An estimated 255,526 Cearenses emigrated to the Amazon between 1869 and 1900, even though the sources generally acknowledge that the greatest movement to the region was a result of the Great Drought.[74]

The available information indicates that at least until the Great Drought, men often migrated to the Amazon on their own, leaving their wives and families behind. For instance, in 1869, 1,676 migrants from the Northeast, most of whom were Cearenses, arrived in Manaus. Of this total, 1,348 were men and 328 were women. According to Samuel Benchimol, single and married Cearense men left their brides and wives with promises to return.[75] Robin Anderson argues that substantially more men than women migrated into the upriver province, and later state of Amazonas, to become rubber tappers. Her calculations of the changes in percentages of males and females in the total population of Pará between 1856 and 1872 also point to a trend of male immigration to that province. In 1856, males represented 49.6 percent of the total population, whereas by 1872 the proportion of males had increased to 51.7 percent.[76] Anderson also notes that a number of Cearense families migrated to and settled in Pará as a result of official colonization programs. During the late 1870s, 1880s, and 1890s, provincial authorities from Pará devised subsidized immigration programs that sought to attract Northeastern families not only to rubber but also to the production of subsistence crops in the region.[77] But as Barbara Weinstein has suggested, this subsidized migration probably represented a tiny proportion of the overall migration to the Amazon from the Northeast.[78]

Male out-migration to the Amazon was one of the strategies that impoverished families used to cope with the distressing transformations of this period. Cearenses sought to "make their fortune" and escape poverty by moving to the Amazon and often remitting part of their earnings to the families left behind in Ceará.[79] A poem written by Juvenal Galeno in the 1860s does indeed suggest that out-migration to the Amazon was often one way that men tried to fulfill their role of providers for their families in the midst of hardship.

Vou deixar a minha terra,	I am leaving my homeland
Vou para os matos d'além . . .	I am going to the forests beyond . . .
Que aqui não acho serviço	Here I cannot find any work
Para ganhar meu vintém! . . .	To earn my bread! . . .
Mas, que fazer? Se os filinhos	But what can I do? If my little children
Precisam roupa . . . estão nus . . .	Need clothes . . . They are naked . . .
Se a mulher pede um vestido . . .	If my wife wants a dress . . .
Se vejo a fome, ó Jesus? . . .	If all I see is hunger, oh Jesus? . . .
Que espere, me dizem todos,	Everyone tells me to wait,
Que passem tempos tão maus:	That these bad times will go away
De que me servem conselhos...	But what is this advice good for . . .
E do futuro os mingaus?	And what is only porridge in the future good for?
Aqui não prospera o pobre...	This is not a place for a poor man to prosper . . .
Me empurro para Manaus.	I am going to Manaus.[80]

A significant outcome of this type of migration was the separation of sertanejo families, whether temporarily or permanently. But other factors forced estrangement and perhaps even the disintegration of rural families during these years as well. Besides the recruitment of young men for the Paraguayan War and the flight of male household members to mountains and caves, banditry—an activity that proliferated during the 1870s—removed able-bodied men from their homes.[81] Moreover, as Chapter 5 will demonstrate, the widespread migration and dislocation occasioned by the Great Drought also caused the separation of family members and forced women to face the time of adversity on their own.

In sum, increased hardship led to diverse survival strategies among the growing population of free poor sertanejos whose fortunes and subsistence could no longer rest directly on land and animals. Free poor Cearense men and women adopted wage labor as a means to supplement the increasing void of agricultural production in their household income. Families resorted to alternative modes of survival that often required men to be absent from home. This, in turn, resulted in their separation from their wives and children. Moreover, the rise of the rubber boom in the Amazonian region attracted a large population of impoverished Cearense men who tried to escape poverty and achieve the opulence that rubber tapping seemed to promise.

Honorable Masculinities Disrupted

In sketching patterns of change and impoverishment, this chapter has emphasized the strong connections between land and livelihood for free poor Cearenses and the ways in which they responded to the loss of access to productive resources during the last four decades of the nineteenth century. In this section, I will argue that these distressing transformations were accompanied by an erosion of the ability of free poor men to establish hegemonic honorable masculinities. As the previous chapters have revealed, male sertanejos had relied on the proud display of the outer manifestations of masculine honor, including access to property ownership, effective provision for family members, and guardianship over the sexuality of female kin, as a strategy to deal with conflict for land, water, and animals, and to establish claims to citizenship within the seigniorial order of the empire. Yet, under the new conditions of dislocation, downward mobility and for some, even destitution, access to the material foundations that sustained these emblems of honor and provided a social legitimization for patriarchy and masculine authority had practically vanished. Indeed, economic upheaval and hardship challenged the terms through which those sertanejos who had achieved a measure of success earlier in the nineteenth century had constructed hegemonic honorable masculinities. Connell's elaboration of the concept of "crisis tendency of a gender order" is helpful to analyze how models or "configurations" of masculinity can come to clash with rapid social, economic, and political change. According to Connell, a "crisis tendency" is made up of historical factors that lead to the disruption of the practices, symbols, and attributes that are culturally assigned as masculine and that contribute to the hegemonic position of men within a system of gender relations.[82] As we will see below, the "state of emergency" that engulfed free poor Cearense families produced a disjuncture between the cultural ideal of male dominance bolstered by social authority and economic power and the reality of dislocation, despair, and calamity that they faced during these years. This disjuncture, in turn, appears to have been experienced by male sertanejos as a source of masculine dishonor and shame.

While archival sources that bear witness to the sertanejos' perceptions of the "state of emergency" are few and far between, popular poetry and other literary sources can help us appreciate the probable gendered meanings of the experiences of destitution and social and geographical displacement. Chapter 2 demonstrated that sertanejo men wielded their capacity to work for themselves and not for others as signifiers of honor. But, during this period of extreme economic difficulty, when many were forced to look for outside employment as the main form of family sustenance, dependence on wage labor destabilized that notion. Indeed, it appears as if working for others for wages symbolized a sense of humiliation and dishonor because it publicly laid bare the demise of small farmers and ranchers, their loss of autonomy, and their inability to adequately provide for their families. Anselmo, a popular poet born in Ipu in 1867, articulated the sense of masculine shame that laboring for wages represented by relating the fate of a fictional sertanejo after he lost his resources.

Ficou o home em misera,	The man ended up in misery
Ao redô dos seus vizim,	Among all his neighbors
Foi trabaiá alugado	He hired himself out as laborer
Pra sustentá dois fiim,	To sustain his two small children
Só não morrero de fome	They did not die
Por Jesus sê seu Padrim!	But only because Jesus was their Godfather!
Foi trabaiá alugado	He hired himself out
Aos conhecido e aos estranho;	To both acquaintances and strangers;
Sua muié coitadinha,	His poor wife,
Lavava roupa de ganho,	She took in washing,
As vergonha para ele	The humiliations for him
Eram de todo tamanho! . . .	Came in all sizes! . . . [83]

The fictional sertanejo's sense of dishonor in this poem not only derived from having to hire himself out as a laborer but also from the fact that his wife had to take in washing, which publicly demonstrated his failure to fulfill the expected masculine role as provider for his family. The poem also reveals that ties of fictive kinship with wealthier landowners had either loosened or were ineffective in guaranteeing the survival of downwardly mobile small farmers and ranchers during times of hardship.

The increasing participation of women in wage labor and women's greater visibility outside of the household that resulted from the broad changes of this period represented a contradiction to the ideal of patriarchal authority at home—an aspect that was central to the constitution of hegemonic masculinities centered on honor. In this context, it is conceivable that men saw themselves as facing greater difficulties in effectively controlling the sexuality of increasingly mobile female kin. For example, the following verses that Leonardo Mota collected in the coffee-producing municipality of Baturité in the 1910s, illustrate the public perception that fathers faced serious problems in preventing their daughters' sexual activity, once they left home to work for wages in agricultural activities:

Quem tivé sua fía virge	Whoever has a virgin daughter
Não mande apanhá café:	Don't send her to pick coffee
Se fô menina – vem moça,	If she is a little girl she will return pubescent
Se fô moça – vem muié . . .	If she is a pubescent, she will return trans- formed into a woman . . .[84]

Men's absences from their homes or towns of normal residence in combination with women's movement to work in fields or other forms of employment could also contribute to weakening the ties between consensual partners. These separations, in turn, diminished the ability on the part of men to effectively control the movements and sexuality of women. For example, a woman whom the stonemason Antônio Pereira claimed was his mulher had become amásia of Antônio Joaquim Brasileiro during a trip that Antônio Pereira had made to the Fazenda Espírito Santo. It seems likely that Pereira's neglect of his economic obligations to his family largely motivated this decision, since, in his own testimony, he mentioned that Antônio Joaquim provided sustenance for his wife and paid other expenses incurred by the Pereira household during his absence.[85] In addition, as this example suggests, women could use men's absence due to out-migration, work, recruitment, or drought to end relationships that they considered no longer tenable for a variety of reasons. They could also cement such separations, or enlist the support of another man for themselves and their children, by engaging in new consensual unions.[86]

In turn, sertanejo men who faced challenges to their honorable manhood in various ways, in all likelihood, perceived the change of heart of their amásias as a public source of dishonor and, obviously, of pain. For instance, after his return from the Amazon, the region he had migrated to, Joaquim Ferreira da Silva had gone to see his amásia in Baturité and found that she was already engaged in another consensual relationship. He then attempted suicide.[87] In some cases, when amásias terminated their liaisons, the offended men sought revenge against them or their lovers with acts of violence designed to repair their wounded honor. Thus, the amorous triangle mentioned above ended when Antônio Pereira killed Antônio Joaquim, arguing that he was defending his honor. In other cases, when women ended the relationship, amásios sought to punish them with violent attacks, which, in turn, illustrates their perception that women's actions constituted a form of defiance to their masculine honor and their prerogative in making decisions regarding consensual unions. For instance, the police soldier Antônio Rodrigues de Oliveira shot his amásia with his police gun because she had "abandoned" him.[88] In another case from Paracuru, Liberato Barroso stabbed his amásia three times because she, "unable to tolerate the disorderly life he led," had returned to her parent's house.[89] But women's "betrayals" were not the only public symbols of the inability of impoverished men to establish credible claims to honor.

The forced migration that resulted from economic hardship and destitution was clearly out of synch with cultural notions of honor under which men demonstrated their status by claiming to be effective providers and protectors of their families. Throughout the nineteenth century, sertanejos had faced periodic droughts, epidemics, search for land, and seasonal labor and, therefore, they had learned to coexist with a degree of physical mobility. Moreover, during times of family crisis, sertanejos moved to other locations in search of assistance from friends and relatives.[90] Nevertheless, when poor Cearenses came into contact with migration as the result of impoverishment and destitution, they most likely experienced feelings of humiliation. An early 1860s poem from Galeno demonstrates an impoverished man's perception that moving away could be seen as a shameful act of acknowledgment of one's failure as a father and provider.

Maria, vamos, Maria	Let's go Maria
Por esses mundos d'além,	Out into those worlds that lie beyond,
Que nos persegue a desgraça . . .	For disgrace is hunting us . . .
Ferinas dores também!	And savage pain as well!
Vamos, vamos esconder-nos,	Let's go, let's go to hide,
Onde não saiba ninguém . . .	Where nobody will know . . .

—Nova terra, nova sorte . . .	—New land, new luck . . .
Acharemos a ventura;	We might find good fortune;
Com estes nove filinhos	With our nine little children
Fujamos em noite escura . . .	Let's flee in the dark of night . . . [91]

Contemporary novels also provide an opportunity to observe how a context of drought and impoverishment could leave men powerless to publicly project the outer manifestations of honor that were so closely associated with possession of economic fortune, even if very small. In his novel *Dona Guidinha do Poço*, Oliveira Paiva depicted a family of retirantes from Rio Grande do Norte, who, after having lost their few animals and land, arrived at the Fazenda Poço da Moita, along the Jaguaribe River, looking for shelter during the 1845 drought. Upon recognizing that the owner of the fazenda was an old acquaintance, Toinho, the head of the family of retirantes, hesitantly approached him requesting assistance. Toinho expressed his shame to his wife, saying, "*Naufragado* (sunk) as I am, I don't want to introduce myself to an acquaintance; I would do it only if he was a stranger." As this family of retirantes described their journey, they expressed the extent of their shame: "Ah, because of the drought. It would be better to be an animal than a baptized Christian. . . . You don't know what these eyes have seen. . . . We were all like slaves. No, even worse, like dogs without owners, like bandits roaming in this land of God."[92] The statements suggest that, for dispossessed Cearense men, becoming retirantes was the ultimate culmination of their loss of honorable status, a form of recognition that in other times had served to separate them from slaves, beggars, and bandits. As drought refugees, they were only part of an undifferentiated lower class of desperate people in search of the most basic necessities, such as food, water, and shelter.

The need to rely on the handouts that others were willing to give as charitable acts contrasts sharply with the celebrated resourcefulness and autonomy that once had defined the honor of successful small farmers and ranchers. In the eyes of others, the drought refugees could be "tamed, resigned, and unpretentious." Their humiliation showed in their worn-out walk and their *cabisbaixo* (head bowed) demeanor—the antithesis of the proud posture of honorable men. Retirantes were sertanejos that had become weak and were dirty and naked.[93] As the crisis drew out and retirantes turned to petty thievery of basic foodstuffs—corn, manioc, or mucunãs—to avoid death from exposure, they became subject to violent punishment designed to debase them; in some cases, they were even killed.[94] For instance, after a group of twenty men, including some slaves, were found stealing mucunãs from lands belonging to the wealthy fazendeiro Manoel Leite da Silva in Jucás, they were tied down and transported to the fazenda's main house. At this location, and under the orders of the army detachment commander, the retirantes were punished with twenty lashes each and their dogs were shot.[95] These punishments dishonored male refugees, since whippings equated the status of free people to that of slaves. For, since the passing of the 1824 Constitution, slaves were the only social category that was legally subject to punishment by whipping.[96] The public whipping of male retirantes by fazendeiros or representatives of the police also constituted a feminization of previously honorable small farmers and ranchers who, as Chapter 3 has shown, saw in the flogging of wives and amásias a sanctioned masculine means to correct them.

The social-economic and environmental conditions of the last third of the nineteenth century, coupled with the hardship represented by the Great Drought, forced some sertanejos to steal cattle out of sheer desperation and hunger. The recognition that they had committed such acts could not be farther removed from the ostentation of success as household providers and the active vigilance of a reputation for honesty that constituted some of the measures of sertanejo honorable manhood. For instance, the farmer Manoel Francisco de Prado from Jucás confessed that he had stolen a cow from the grazing fields of the Fazenda Boa Vista in June of 1877. Moreover, he admitted that he "stole only to feed his family," since his children "could no longer resist their hunger." When asked why he did not buy meat instead of stealing, he answered that "the cattle owners no longer sold livestock and refused to give meat away to the poor."[97] These actions demonstrate that those men who had lost everything to drought, debts, or other hardships were no longer able to construct themselves as respectable and honest proprietors, senhores, or ranchers. Instead, men like Manoel Francisco had been reduced to the condition of thieves and beggars to sustain their families. Furthermore, they had lost their autonomy and independence as providers and now had to wait for charitable donations "for the poor." Enraged ranchers, frustrated with animal theft, and facing a more inefficient police and judicial system than usual, took matters into their own hands and gave exemplary beatings to cattle thieves in the town's square, or even murdered them. Such violent punishments undoubtedly increased the sense of shame felt by dispossessed and hungry sertanejos.[98]

One of Galeno's poems also captured the despair of young families, who could not get ahead in life, despite their best attempts, in a context of low wages, epidemics, and serious hardship. In the following verses, a *fiandeira* (spinner), who lived in a hut with her husband or consensual partner, who was a day laborer, and their six young children, attempted to comfort him after he learned of their youngest daughter's death.

—*Sempre a dor segue à alegria*	Always pain follows happiness
Eis a vida. . . Oh, que destino!	That is life . . . Oh, what a fate!
—*Não te maldigas, Antônio. . .*	—Don't curse yourself, Antônio . . .
Foi vontade do Divino!	It was God's will![99]

These verses powerfully contrast with the hopeful prospects and pride that roça owners boasted when they had experienced prosperity. They also demonstrate that, when poor sertanejo families looked into the future, they did not see evidence of improvement or a return to the brief moment of success, at least while they stayed in Ceará. Clearly, the "state of emergency" was a time not only of dishonor but also of despair and hopelessness.

Despite the official claims that the Paraguayan War was necessary to restore the collective honor of Brazil, for young men who were pressed to serve in the front lines their forced recruitment did not bring public recognition of honorable status. Instead, recruitment was seen as a shameful act, capable of destroying a man's reputation, prospects, and future. In fact, forced recruitment equated the status of poor young men, who might have been successful cowboys, farmers, or ranchers, to that of slaves and criminals. Press gangs forcefully removed young men from their families and took them to local jails where they shared their living spaces with criminals until their deployment.[100] According to Galeno's description of a town's jail, recruits were shackled and tied down with ropes. A recruit thus lamented:

E ora vou como um escravo,	And now, like a slave, I am going
Em breve jurar bandeira . . .	Very soon to pledge my allegiance to the flag . . .
. . . Ora preso e torturado	. . . Now, arrested and tortured
Qual se fora um delinquente,	As if I were a criminal
Qual rola fraca e tremente	Like a weak and shaky sparrow
Nas unhas do gavião . . .	In the clutches of a hawk.[101]

Clearly, impressment stripped young sertanejo men of their autonomy, their freedom, and their honor, and made them, in Galeno's words, mere "prey" of the police.

Conclusions

An emerging trend in the historical scholarship on the Northeastern backlands has paid increasing attention to the ways in which discourses and practices by political and economic elites from the region have contributed to shape certain stereotypical understandings about the history of the sertão. In particular, these studies have begun demonstrating how and why local elites, provincial politicians, intellectuals, and folklorists have created a discourse that characterizes the backlands as fated to poverty and misery because of recurrent drought. Several of these works, centered especially on the Great Drought of 1877–79, have attempted to denaturalize the association between drought and poverty that for many years had been so central in discussions about the region and its inhabitants. Other studies have demonstrated that the catastrophic effects of the Great Drought on the lives of ordinary sertanejos were not the result of scarcity of water alone. Instead, they were caused by structural inequalities that allowed the emergence of a "drought industry," through which municipal, provincial, and urban elites derived untold economic benefits for their own particular projects, while retirantes perished in large numbers.[102] Surprisingly, however, little attention has been paid to the transformations in landholding patterns and social-economic structure in the sertão, or the political pressures on the everyday lives of the rural poor, that predated and interacted with the Great Drought, and that brought about the levels of impoverishment and misery observed during the last third of the nineteenth century.

Certainly, from the mid-1860s on, the forced recruitment of free poor young men to fight in the Paraguayan War, the end of cotton boom that had accounted for the prosperity of many small farmers, the gradual decline of slavery, the continuous subdivision of smallholdings caused by partible inheritance, in addition to the ruinous three-year drought of 1877–79, put enormous pressures on the fragile system of survival of small farmers and ranchers. These processes disrupted the livelihoods of free poor Cearenses and gradually brought about indebtedness, downward mobility, dispossession, geographic dislocation, separation of families, and even death. Attempting to diversify their survival strategies, sertanejos sought paid employment; men migrated in large numbers to the rubber estates of the Amazon River basin, while women remained behind in Ceará; others became retirantes, and moved alone or with their families to Fortaleza, to other cities in the littoral, or to the Brazilian South. Thus, a series of complex factors, and not the workings of a drought industry alone, were responsible for the transformation of poor sertanejos into refugees, beggars, and migrants.

Material destitution and social dislocation, in turn, had important consequences on the male sertanejos' ability to achieve honorable status and to dominate women at home. Their new lives as day laborers, retirantes, vagrants, bandits, and men permanently separated from their families no longer sustained a hegemonic honorable masculinity that was contingent on the possession of resources such as land, animals, and slaves, or on the militant defense of such patrimony. These years also witnessed the growing disjuncture between the social ideal of male dominance over women and the reality of men's increasing incapacity to monitor the sexuality of female kin and to credibly claim to maintain their wives and families from the work performed in smallholdings. Moreover, the mounting difficulties that ser-tanejos faced in drawing a livelihood from small-scale farming and ranching undermined especially young men's efforts to establish viable agrarian-based households and consequently their attainment of honorable masculinities. Without secure access to land and other resources, as indebted parents could not bequeath anything to their children, and besieged by drought and epi-demics that claimed the lives of young children first—important sources of labor in family farming and ranching—young men systematically failed in their efforts to provide for their families. Clearly, the material foundations for the defense of patriarchy within the household and for the small farmers' and ranchers' claims of social superiority and authority over other men had been unsettled. In fact, the "state of emergency" brought with it a "crisis tendency" in the gender order of the backlands and in the practices that sertanejos had used to constitute hegemonic masculinities.

Chapter 5

Masculinity Challenged and Affirmed: Autonomous Women, Men, and Violent Patriarchy, 1865–89

Some time in the late nineteenth century, a memorable poetic contest between the Cearense cantador Jerônimo do Junqueiro and the renowned *cantadora* (female popular poet) Zefinha do Chabocão took place in the backlands of Ceará. Many of the better known popular poets, including Romano do Teixeira, attended the event, which had been organized as a poetic challenge initiated by Zefinha.[1] In the following verses, later repeated by the poet Cego Sinfrônio, Jerônimo expressed his first feelings upon meeting Zefinha and his apprehensions about the contest.

Me assentei perante o povo,	I sat down in front of everyone
(Parecia uma sessão)	(It looked more like an assembly)
Quando me saiu Zefinha	When Zefinha came out
Com grande preparação:	All made up:
Era baixa, grossa e alva,	She was short, plump and fair
Bonita até de feição . . .	With a beautiful countenance . . .
. . . Vinha tão perfeitazinha,	. . . She had made herself up,
Bonitinha como o cão!	And looked pretty as the devil!
Para confeito da obra:	To complete the picture:
Uma viola na mão.	She carried a guitar [*viola*] in her hand.[2]
Aí chamaro pra janta,	Then, they called everyone for dinner,
Eu fui pra comparecê:	I presented myself at the table.
Levava o bocado à boca	I put the food in my mouth
Mas não podia descê	But it would not go down my throat

153

Maginando na vergonha	Just from thinking of the shame
Que eu havéra de sofrê	That I would suffer,
Andando na terra aléia	If I walked along in other people's land
E uma muié me vencê . . .	And everyone knew a woman had
	prevailed over me.[3]

As soon as dinner was over, Zefinha initiated the dispute by inquiring as to the whereabouts of her challenger. An exchange of rhythmical improvisations, through which the poets measured their rhetorical abilities, immediately followed. But in the end, at least according to oral tradition, Jerônimo defeated Zefinha by asking her a question to which she did not know the answer. As a result, Jerônimo's reputation remained intact; a woman had not publicly defeated him, and therefore he had no reason to feel shame.

The poetic contest between Jerônimo and Zefinha can serve as a metaphor to illustrate the ways in which the profound social-economic transformations of the last third of the nineteenth century strained the gender order that was socially sanctioned in backlands communities. Zefinha's prominent presence as a famous cantadora (an occupation dominated by men) symbolizes the greater visibility of women as wage earners and the increased female physical mobility that accompanied the separation and hardship endured by sertanejo families during these years. In fact, as I will argue below, the social disorganization that marked this period forced free poor women to become the main source of sustenance for their families and to navigate public spaces without the support and protection of family patriarchs. The fact that Zefinha dared Jerônimo to a poetic competition and that he feared the loss of his honor if defeated by a woman is emblematic of another of the themes of this chapter: the challenge that women who lived outside familial patriarchy represented to men and to a society that upheld patriarchal values. By working for wages or self-managing petty businesses, by living apart from men, and by heading their own households, these women exercised a degree of initiative and freedom that subverted the social ideal that family men controlled women's sexuality, physical mobility, and labor. But, while Jerônimo was able to defeat Zefinha in poetic improvisations and in this manner maintain his reputation, many free poor Cearense men did not have an equivalent symbolic opportunity to establish masculine authority and prestige. Chapter 4 demonstrated that the disruptions of the last third of the nineteenth century divested formerly successful, if still poor, sertanejos of the material basis that gave credibility to their claims to masculine honor and that justified patriarchal rule within households. As this chapter will show, within a context of fragile patriarchy, some men resorted to violence as a way to solve their gender-rooted disputes with unprotected women who, through defiant attitudes, lack of verbal deference or sexual modesty, had contested these men's claims to authority. But this form of aggression was not a simple reaction to worsening economic conditions or to the "crisis tendency" in the gender order of the sertão. Instead, violence against unprotected women represented a form of cultural coercion, enforced mainly by men, to set constraints on autonomous women's behavior and actions, and to ensure the continuation of a patriarchal order, even in the face of rapid social changes that called into question its relevance and legitimacy.

Autonomous Women Confront a Changing World

Writing the social history of free poor women from the Northeastern backlands constitutes a challenging task. This group of women, unless single or widowed, do not often feature in official correspondence from municipal authorities, land registries, and documents from civil courts. Furthermore, in the absence of household censuses and other demographic data from interior townships, it is difficult to establish for certain the living conditions, household composition, and even marital status of sertanejo women in different locales and time periods. Nevertheless, through analysis of a series of scattered primary and secondary sources it is possible to observe that the rapid social-economic transformations that swept the Cearense hinterlands during the last third of the nineteenth century tore free poor families apart and drove many sertanejas into living unattached to domestic patriarchs. According to a coastal writer who visited the sertão during the 1860s, young women, many of whom were orphaned or abandoned by their husbands or other relatives, wandered in towns and fazendas in search of work, housing, and other forms of assistance. Ralph Della Cava's study on a popular religious movement in Ceará in the early twentieth century also provides evidence of a visible population of poor women who did not have familial support. According to Della Cava, Father José Maria Ibiapina founded four charity houses—institutions that constituted a mix of orphanage, school for the daughters of wealthy landowners, and convent—in the Cariri valley, and another eighteen elsewhere in the arid Northeast, during the 1860s. While Ibiapina had hoped the houses would attract some elite women, most of the women who entered and who in effect became *beatas* (female mystics who dedicated their life to prayer) were poor.[4]

The widespread migration and dislocation occasioned by the Great Drought, which disrupted the ability of a segment of the sertanejo population to maintain their families together, appears to have forced free poor women to confront the horrors of this calamity and its aftermath on their own. Contemporary commentators remarked on the disproportionate number of women who arrived and remained alone in refugee camps in Fortaleza and other coastal cities, citing begging and prostitution as a common fate.[5] Roger Cunniff's examination of lists of refugees aided by relief commissions from Ceará and other Northeastern provinces indicates that the same disproportion also prevailed in backlands towns, where large groups of retirantes congregated. The most telling figures presented in his study come from the town of Palmares in Pernambuco. There, of 1,795 family heads that received aid on June 5, 1878, 436 were wives without spouses and 688 were widows; only 671 were married men. Cunniff also argues that the official policy of removing men from the camps, relocating them to public works sites, and providing them with food only if they worked contributed to men's lower representation in refugee camps and to the disintegration of families.[6]

Another factor that helps explain the disparity of men and women in the distribution of refugees in camps in Ceará and Piauí is the excess of widows in relation to widowers among them. Cunniff's analysis of the marital status of refugees aged eighteen and older in relief colonies in Piauí in 1878 reveals 79 widows and 38 widowers. He also demonstrates that these figures are not so unusual because widows in Piauí, according to the 1872 national census, outnumbered widowers 5,187 to 3,705. The widowed population in Ceará was also elevated. According to the same census, widows there outnumbered widowers 14,597 to 9,299.[7] It is difficult to determine whether the excess population of widows in the documentation demonstrates actual high rates of women who outlived their husbands. Indeed, it is highly likely that, given the social constructs according to which women needed the protection and sustenance provided by a husband to be considered honorable, separated or abandoned women simply called themselves widows.[8] Nevertheless, the data clearly show that, increasingly, women in the backlands lacked marital or quasi-marital networks of support—a situation that, in practice, contributed to loosen the protective vigilance of some family patriarchs over a segment of sertanejo women.

The military recruitment of retirante men in Fortaleza and other coastal cities also helps to account for the relative absence of men from family circles and refugee camps in Ceará during the Great Drought. According to Beattie, Ceará's provincial president secured special permission from the minister of war in 1877 to recruit drought victims beyond quota levels and enacted this policy as a drought-relief measure. Indeed, enlistment into the army provided male refugees with an opportunity to escape disaster. Thus, according to the provincial president, every day about sixty civilians "volunteered" for army service, hoping to stay in their native province. Nevertheless, as Beattie notes, drought victims who enlisted were most likely transferred to distant garrisons and were unable to remain close to their families, as they had hoped.[9]

As a substantial number of women became separated from their husbands or other male relatives, they enacted a variety of survival strategies to cope with hardship and misery, and to provide for their children on their own. In order to analyze these strategies, the conditions in which these women lived and their position in backlands society, this chapter classifies adult orphaned, unmarried, widowed, and separated women who were apart from their fathers, husbands, consensual partners, or other male relatives for longer or shorter periods of time under the single category of "women alone." In doing so, this work applies Maura Palazzi's conceptualization derived from the Italian *donna sola* to the study of women's lives in Ceará during the late nineteenth century. For Palazzi, "women alone" is a category that includes women in different conditions, whose "solitude" is not a function of marital status but rather the consequence of a suspension of normative gender roles that result from periods of living apart from men.[10]

In the case of the Cearense backlands, "women alone" took on the role of providers, and in all probability, the sole or main earners of their own sustenance and that of their children or other dependents. As a consequence, it is likely that these women became heads of their own households. Researchers have, so far, not located household censuses that would allow for detailed analysis of household composition and headship in the interior of Ceará. Nevertheless, studies of family organization and household structure in various regions during the late eighteenth century and early nineteenth century demonstrate that female-headed households were not uncommon in Brazil. Those studies show that female household heads constituted between 10 and 40 percent of all heads in rural areas of the Southeast as well as in two parishes of the Recôncavo of the Northeastern province of Bahia during the early nineteenth century.[11] There is no reason to believe that the backlands of Ceará, or of other Northeastern provinces, were any exception to this pattern. Indeed, census data from Piauí point to the fact that female-headed households existed in that cattle-grazing province during the late eighteenth century. For instance, 28.8 percent of all households listed in a 1762 manuscript census of the backlands town of Oeiras were headed by women.[12] Therefore, it would be surprising if a similar proportion did not characterize the interior of Ceará. And even more surprising, if in the wake of the broad and far-reaching transformations that overtook the Cearense interior, the proportion of female-headed households did not increase in the second half of the nineteenth century. A piece of evidence pointing in this direction comes from the 1887 manuscript census of Fortaleza, consulted by Eni de Mesquita Samara and José Weyne de Freitas Sousa. According to these researchers, 36 percent of all the households in that coastal location were headed by women. This figure reflects the high proportion of "women alone," especially widows, who had arrived in massive numbers from the interior with their children in tow, since the Great Drought.[13]

As household heads, women performed a variety of occupations to sustain themselves and their families. Furthermore, the separation that accompanied the hardship and dislocation of free poor families appears to have created a situation in which unattached females and their labor remained beyond the control that fathers, husbands, brothers, or other male relatives exercised over them under more normal circumstances. These features of late-nineteenth-century sertanejo society are observable in a series of poems that Juvenal Galeno wrote in the 1860s that depict the lives of seamstresses, laundresses, and in one case, an ironing woman. These sertanejas are characterized as residing in rural towns and deriving their livelihood from sewing and tending clothes for the families of wealthier fazendeiros, state officials, and elite members of the National Guard. Through the use of the first person, the seamstress, who is the subject matter of "A costureira," narrated her life story. She declared herself to be an abandoned woman who found herself without bread or clothes, until she acquired skills in sewing and repairing dresses.[14] Likewise, the laundress featured in the poem "A lavandeira" points out in the following verses that she managed her petty business on her own, since, presumably, she is unattached.

Já devo à dona, já devo,	I owe money to the lady,
Se não me engano um tostão,	A penny, if I am not incorrect,
Que por conta da lavagem	That I took when I needed
Eu tomei na precisão.	As a cash advance for the washing.[15]

This poem also provides evidence that "women alone" often counted on female, rather than male, networks of support to perform the labor that sustained them. For instance, after she finished washing and folding a load of clothes, the laundress said:

Entrouxei contando tudo . . .	I organized and counted everything . . .
Três patacas e um vintêm;	Three silver coins and one copper coin;
Vou levar a roupa . . . Agora	I am going to take the clothes . . . But now
Quem me ajuda? A Rita vem.	Who will help me? There, Rita comes.[16]

The variety of occupations that allowed unattached sertanejas to earn independent income streams also becomes evident through an examination of criminal cases. For example, only 11 percent of the total of free poor women whose profiles appear in criminal cases from Tamboril and Jucás between 1865 and 1889 claimed to "live by the labor of their husbands" or to "live in their parents' company," a phrase used in the case of minors who did not have specific occupations of their own. The other 89 percent was comprised of poor women who were laundresses, seamstresses, ironing women, spinsters, midwives, *quitandeiras* (small-scale fruit and vegetable vendors), and domestic servants.[17] Domestic occupations and petty businesses as pathways for female livelihood among the free poor in all likelihood expanded as the decline of slavery in interior townships eliminated the service of female slaves in those areas.

But farming also provided an opportunity for those female household heads who were able to retain access to land and labor to support themselves and their families. The 1872 census indicates that 19.5 percent of all *lavradores*, or farmers, in Ceará were women. The census figures do not provide information about the proportion of female farmers who could be classified as poor; nor do they indicate how many of those women were the main source of sustenance for their dependants. Yet, if we consider that customarily sertanejos subsumed female labor in family plots under the occupation of male providers, it is likely that the women who appeared in the census as farmers were alone and heads of their own households. Other sources indicate that women earned their livelihoods and those of their families through farming. For instance, Rodolpho Theophilo noted that poor women were often engaged in cotton farming in the late 1860s and early 1870s. Criminal cases corroborate that information. For example, Maria Rosa, a free poor single woman, had access to land as a moradora on a property belonging to Gonçalo Martins Chaves, where she cultivated cotton.[18] Postmortem inventories also provide a glimpse into the lives of poor widows who did not remarry and single women who relied on farming as a survival strategy. An example of this is provided by the widow Teresa Maria de Jesus, who, in all likelihood, cultivated the one thousand manioc *covas*, or small mounds where manioc roots were planted, in her family's field with the help of her children. These included the first-born daughter Florinda; who was twenty-three years old; José, the second child, who was nineteen years old; Joaquina, who was fourteen years old; and Luís, who was eleven years old, by the time of their mother's death in 1868.[19]

The fact that Rosa Maria and Teresa Maria de Jesus appear in the documentation as cotton and manioc farmers in itself might be of special significance. Cotton and food crops, such as beans, manioc, and corn, could be planted in smallholdings and harvested and processed with the help of children, other family members, or when available, a couple of slaves. The cultivation of other crops that required larger investments in land, labor, and equipment was in all likelihood beyond the means of poor "women alone."[20] Those more fortunate autonomous women who retained access to comparatively larger landholdings and could count on the labor of their children or slaves could also be small ranchers. The 1872 census indicates that women were 7.2 percent of all criadores at the provincial level, although, as in the case of the farmers, these data do not specify the number of free poor women who were ranchers.[21]

When smallholding families became destitute or their members separated, women performed a variety of roles normally associated with male household heads. The 1903 naturalist novel *Luzia-Homem*, written by the Cearense author Domingos Olímpio, illustrates the strategies that sertanejas employed to confront family life disruptions—strategies that opened opportunities for female initiative and independence, even within the very precarious conditions that surrounded them. Inspired by observations of squalor and despair in his native town of Sobral during the Great Drought, Olímpio's novel also illustrates how women's adaptations to hardship could be characterized as inversions of prevalent gender roles in their communities. The main character, Luzia, a young retirante woman, had earned the nickname of "Luzia-Homen" or "Luzia-man" since her early years as a youngster in the small fazenda where she lived with her father, a vaqueiro, and her mother, an infirm and aging woman. According to her life story, as told to a public prosecutor, as a girl Luzia performed traditionally masculine work, such as pasturing cattle, digging cacimbas, and clearing land for cultivation, in order to help her father, who did not have any sons. When her father died, a time that coincided with the Great Drought and the decline of the small fortune of her family, Luzia performed other masculine activities. For instance, she sold the family's livestock and house in an attempt to gain sustenance for her and her mother for a few more months. At that stage, Luzia was eighteen years old. Once they became completely dispossessed, Luzia and her mother, whose rheumatic condition worsened, made the trek from their former fazenda in Ipu to Sobral. In that town Luzia once again took on a masculine role by working on the construction of the local jail—a public-works project designed to use male retirante labor—as she desperately sought means to keep herself and her mother alive. According to Olímpio's narrative, Luzia's performance of predominantly male occupations and her strong "masculine" appearance made her the butt of jokes and the subject of humiliation by townspeople. Apparently, her inversion of normative gender roles made Luzia into a *homem*, or a man, and therefore an image of deviance.[22]

Archival sources pertaining to the drought of 1888–89, another period when unattached sertanejas and their children concentrated in coastal cities and other towns, confirm the reversal of traditional gender roles that resulted from drought-related dislocation. In such situations, women made decisions with regard to the location where the family group of retirantes would migrate, and protected their families while traveling. For instance, according to a letter in which the widow Maria Joaquina do Bomfim asked for public assistance to migrate from the province of Ceará to Pará, she and her four young children had traveled on their own from the South-Central municipality of Tauá to Fortaleza during the month of June of 1889, as they sought to escape the effects of the drought. Once in the city, she requested a grant from the provincial government to cover her passage, and those of her children, to Pará.[23]

While rural "women alone" could turn to a variety of strategies to maintain their families, it is clear that the absence of husbands, boyfriends, fathers, brothers, or other male relatives meant additional hardship and further economic and physical insecurity. That women feared such outcomes is evident in a series of incidents that took place in Tamboril and a few other municipalities in 1876. According to a provincial presidential report, some women, including "mothers, wives, daughters and sisters, terrified by the new Recruitment Law [of 1874] . . . , invaded the locations where enrollment boards functioned in Tamboril, União, Santa Quitéria, and Acarape, and destroyed enrollment records."[24] The Recruitment Law of 1874 established a draft lottery by which Brazilian men from all social classes could be drafted so that the burden of military service would not fall exclusively on the poor. Even more important, the law did away with marriage as an exemption for military service. The protests demonstrate that sertanejo women saw the law as jeopardizing the already precarious existence of free poor families, by threatening to press into service male family providers. Indeed, as Beattie has shown, the draft of a male family member to a six-year, low-paying contract could mean severe hardship to impoverished households and even dislocation if families decided to uproot themselves to accompany draftees.[25] As this chapter will further elaborate below, for women, the loss of their husbands or male family members also meant additional vulnerability to violence from unrelated men and other forms of humiliation. Consequently, women who would have to take up the responsibility of their households on their own feared such outcomes and protested against the law.

The difficulties that female providers faced as they adapted to the new conditions of hardship and deprivation, on their own, are also made evident in the letter that the widow Maria Joaquina submitted requesting assistance to migrate away from Ceará during the drought of 1888. According to the letter, she had four young children who were her dependants: Cesáreo, who was sixteen years old; Cândida, who was fourteen years old; Raimundo, who was four years old; and José, the youngest, who was three years old. She mentioned that the family needed to emigrate because "in this province she can no longer survive, due to her poverty." Moreover, she noted that her relatives in Pará were "calling on her, in order to provide her sustenance." In some cases, poor women from the interior who could not secure passage to other provinces and remained behind with their children in Fortaleza or other coastal towns survived by means of domestic employment, or selling sweets and cakes in the streets. But many could not get by in this manner and therefore were forced to beg for alms or even steal.[26]

Extreme precariousness and economic deprivation could drive unattached women and young girls to prostitution or part-time prostitution as an alternative to earn money. Contemporary observers, usually elite men from coastal cities or from the Brazilian Southeast, remarked on what they perceived to be a pervasive practice of prostitution in sertanejo communities by the 1840s, then again during the 1860s, and even more so during the Great Drought.[27] In particular, observers of the calamities associated with the Great Drought commented on the fate of prostitution that befell many retirante women during their travels of penury in the interior and once they arrived in coastal towns. According to their narratives, mothers of small children who became separated from their male relatives during the trip, widows, and orphan girls engaged in prostitution in exchange for food and shelter.[28] The poet Galeno also noted that the *tutorias,* or guardianship system,[29] neither protected property nor guaranteed the well-being of the large pool of orphan girls who roamed around in the interior. Instead, powerful men or even poorer relatives of female orphans who became their guardians at the time of their fathers' death often took sexual advantage of them. Tainted by the stigma of being "lost" when they reached legal emancipation from their tutors, these female orphans did not receive any stipend and often turned to prostitution as a means to survive.[30]

It is difficult to establish to what extent these narratives demonstrate the reality of a widespread practice of prostitution among sertanejas. As several scholars have shown, official depictions of poor female household heads and other women who moved about in public in Brazil often employed a deprecating language that called into question their "honesty" and the propriety of their sexual behavior.[31] Thus, it is plausible that the authors' remarks on the inevitability of prostitution for women who lost their male relatives during the drought or for young girls who were sexually abused by their tutors reveals more about their elite notions of female honor than about the reality of the sertão. Interestingly, however, such characterizations expose the elite observers' fears that women who headed their families or women who traveled alone inverted the social ideal according to which men controlled the mobility and sexuality of women—an ideal that, as we have seen, the Cearense poor also subscribed to. It is also likely that this type of representation of prostitution among sertanejas constitutes what Steve Stern described in a different context as "an exaggerated characterization for women who supplemented other means of support with occasional sexual visitations by two or three male clients or friends."[32]

Another type of source, this time the 1887 manuscript census of Fortaleza consulted by Samara, can help illustrate the extent of the practice of prostitution among poor women, even when they had some form of remunerated employment. It is necessary to note that the census as a historical document is also not an unproblematic source to portray prostitution, as we do not have any information on how the census takers decided who qualified as a prostitute. Yet, we can gain a partial, if still blurry, perspective on prostitution in this coastal town. According to the data, 10.3 percent of all 1,984 women without property listed prostitution as their main occupation, while 14 other women were seamstresses, domestic workers, ironing women, weavers as well as part-time prostitutes. Full-time and part-time prostitution in the interior was in all likelihood less prominent than in Fortaleza, since backlands towns were smaller and presumably did not have the same proportion of male clientele. It is also likely that this census reflects an increased proportion of prostitutes in Fortaleza as a result of the dislocating effects of the Great Drought.[33]

To summarize, the rapid social-economic transformations that swept the interior during the last third of the nineteenth century tore families apart and drove women into living unattached to domestic patriarchs, becoming household heads, and earning their livelihood, and that of their children, on their own. Free poor women worked for wages in domestic service and in a variety of self-managed petty businesses. Women from this group also grew cotton and manioc when they were able to retain some form of access to land and could count on the labor of family members or a few slaves. Through these various activities, women attempted to keep their families afloat in the midst of destitution. Yet, the public performance of these roles, the physical mobility that they required, and the sertanejas' self-management of income streams laid bare the weakened grip of male control over female kin and the disruption of the social ideal of female dependence on male providers.

Unattached Sertanejas, Violent Patriarchy, and Masculine Honor

What effects did the apparent rise in female-headed households and the increased visibility, autonomy, and mobility of unattached sertanejas have in patriarchal relations in the Cearense backlands? Did conceptualizations of the position of men and women in rural society change as a result of the broad social transformations of the period between 1865 and 1889, which forced many women to live apart from men and to become the main providers for their families? In order to answer these questions, it is first necessary to dialogue with the extensive historiography on the family and patriarchy in Brazil during the late colonial period and the nineteenth century.

An enduring trend in the scholarship, dating back to the early 1930s, maintained that the most significant family type in colonial and nineteenth-century Brazil was the patriarchal extended family. According to this perspective, derived largely from Gilberto Freyre's 1933 seminal work *Casa-grande & senzala*,[34] from research by other scholars, and from more current interpretations of Freyre's work, sugar planters and other large landowners retained absolute authority and control over all members of their families and households. These families included the planters' wives, children, mistresses, illegitimate children as well as all the slaves, dependents, and other inhabitants of their extensive landholdings.[35] Since the late 1960s, a large body of revisionist studies has challenged this view. Drawing on household census materials from the Southeast, this scholarship has identified a diversity of family and household arrangements and has shown that chief among them was the nuclear family, both among elite and lower-class groups. In addition, several scholars have found high rates of female-headed households and matrifocal families in many locales.[36] Nevertheless, if the revisionist scholarship has succeeded in defying the idea that the extended family household was the norm at least in the Southeast of Brazil, it has been less successful at demonstrating the significance of its findings to understanding the functioning of patriarchy. The authors of these studies seek to challenge the idea that the extended-family patriarchs enjoyed absolute power over women by showing high rates of female household heads, thus conflating female independent living and work with freedom from patriarchy.[37]

An examination of the victimization of "women alone" in the interior of Ceará during the period between 1865 and 1889 as revealed in criminal proceedings and other sources will demonstrate that patriarchal values did not diminish as a result of the separation of family members and the visibility of women as household heads. Instead, as free poor women escaped familial patriarchal vigilance, earned their livelihoods independently of men, and moved about the backlands on their own, a form of public patriarchy worked to defend the hegemonic position of men in society and to establish limits to female autonomy and initiative. As scholars who study patriarchal systems have noted, when women's independence strain a patriarchal gender order, cultural sanctions or institutional repression, acting as substitutes for, or in conjunction with, familial patriarchal controls, serve to restrain women's behaviors and power.[38] As we will see below, men—including free poor sertanejos—enforced patriarchal claims and authority over unattached women, even if they were not family members or fictive-kin relatives. These men claimed a social sanction to act as the guardians of a gender order in which unsupervised women were to be kept subordinated and restrained as a way to ensure the continuation of at least some form of male precedence in backlands society. Thus, the conditions that determined an expansion in the number of female headed households within a society where patriarchal values were upheld, in fact, subjected women who found themselves alone and unprotected to forms of humiliation and even violence enacted to ensure the continued validity of patriarchy.

A first place to see the stigmatization of unattached women is in the treatment of a female popular poet by her male peers. In his 1921 anthology of Northeastern popular poetry, Leonardo Mota indicates that Rita Medeiros, a cantadora from the northwest of Ceará, was extremely popular, especially among the black population of the area during the late nineteenth century. Yet, male cantadores composed a series of "obscene parodies" of her own poetry that they repeated to male-only audiences. Some of these verses reveal that male cantadores rhetorically scorned Rita Medeiros. In the following lines, the cantador Anselmo expressed this masculine disdain for a woman who did not fit accepted patterns of feminine behavior.

Vá-se embora, esgalopada	Go away, gluttonous woman
Que não tem quem lhe agüente,	For nobody can bear you,
Vá-se embora pros inferno	Go to hell now
Que não tem quem lhe sustente!	For you have no one to maintain you![39]

Here, Anselmo's poetry criticized Rita for not having a male provider. According to predominant patriarchal constructions, a woman needed a husband, lover, or other masculine figure of authority to sustain and protect her. Another portion of the poem reveals that Rita in fact lived off the money she earned as a cantadora and also worked in cart drives that transported goods. Therefore, Anselmo was correct in pointing out that Rita did not have a male provider, since she seems to have been economically independent. Still, from the perspective of men who defined their masculinity and honor in terms of provision for wife and children, the presence of an autonomous woman appeared as a challenge to masculine roles and privileges. Moreover, the absence of a male protector in Rita's life subjected her to impertinent remarks about her sexual propriety. The verses reproduced above describe Rita as "gluttonous," a term that could denote obesity or an insatiable sexual appetite. If the first interpretation holds water, this insult would render Rita unattractive. If the second one does, it would imply that Rita was a sexually transgressive woman and, therefore, immoral. This interpretation seems plausible, since Anselmo mentioned in different sections of the poem that Rita *é muié do Vicente*, "is Vicente's woman," "claims to be a virgin," and "wants to marry him."[40] All of these qualifications, of course, amount to a discursive construction of Rita as a dishonorable woman who lacked sexual modesty. According to prevalent understandings of honor and patriarchy, a woman's honor lay tied to her sexual purity. Thus, these verses present a series of associations that construct an independent and economically successful woman as deviant and dishonorable and, therefore, the deserving object of insults and humiliation that warned of the danger she posed to the moral order.

The condemnation of Rita's reputation as revealed in the poem could be considered extreme and perhaps unrepresentative. Most working women in the interior were not cantadoras, who moved in a predominantly masculine world and competed against men in public, verbal improvisations. Instead, they performed work that was considered suitable for females.[41] Nevertheless, the questioning of the reputation of unattached females as centered on their sexual propriety also becomes explicit in criminal cases that offer details on the lives of some of these women. For example, a notable male citizen of Tamboril challenged the validity of two single women workers' declarations in a criminal case by saying that they were "immoral" and "accustomed to exchanging their desires for money," implying that they were prostitutes.[42] The fact that, because of the precariousness of their lives despite their work, some of these women engaged in part-time prostitution, or at times accepted help from men in exchange for sexual favors, undoubtedly exacerbated the perception that they were immoral.[43] Clearly, the disruption of family life that forced free poor women into heading their own households, into poverty, and even into prostitution subjected them to public humiliation, which often centered on accusations of sexual impropriety. But, as Rita Medeiro's case makes clear, regardless of whether they actually engaged in prostitution, autonomous women could earn a dishonorable reputation because of the absence of male figures in their lives and their subversion of normative gender roles.[44]

An examination of criminal cases from Jucás, Tamboril, and Itapagé reveals that unprotected women were also subject to violence from men who were not their relatives, husbands, or consensual partners. Unattached women were the most common victims of reported incidents of male violence against females in the three municipalities. Of a total of forty-five examined court cases detailing various episodes of violent aggression against women, 71.1 percent, or thirty-two cases, involved *surras,* or floggings, beatings, or other violent attacks, on poor, single, or widowed females as well as women who obviously did not have male relatives to protect them. Undoubtedly, a great deal of domestic violence went unreported in Ceará. As Chapter 3 showed, the practice of wife-beating was a socially sanctioned means to establish patriarchal authority within the household. These understandings about gender power could have influenced women's unwillingness to report domestic abuse to the authorities, as they probably feared that they would not receive a favorable ruling. Likewise, the visibility of violent crime against unprotected sertanejas might be related to the growing availability of criminal courts in the backlands, which allowed them an opportunity to initiate judicial proceedings against their offenders. Yet, it is noteworthy that the proportion of reported violent crime against women observed in the sample from Ceará sharply contrasts with Susan Socolow's findings in her analysis of crime in the province of Buenos Aires during the second half of the eighteenth century. The author indicates that the overwhelming majority of reported incidents of physical abuse against females in Buenos Aires involved acts of aggression perpetrated by their husbands and consensual partners.[45] It is difficult to establish whether the high proportion of unattached sertanejas as victims of male violence in the sample from Ceará represents a new or unusual pattern of gendered aggression that operated as a substitute for intrafamilial means of establishing patriarchal claims. Nevertheless, it is undeniable that the female vulnerability to male assault that emerges out of these cases was affected by the conditions that sustained gender relations, both within and outside households, during these very difficult years. As scholars of gender have argued, masculinity and the practices in defense of patriarchy are constructed within specific fields of power relations, even though they are also informed by cultural referents.[46]

Unattached women who feature in criminal cases as victims of male floggings are almost always described in the court records as "living in a state of poverty." In a good number of cases, the victims of male surras were impoverished widows. Yet, while these women clearly were poor and even defenseless, they had publicly asserted some form of power vis-à-vis a man of their acquaintance in the days prior to the attacks, or were perceived in the community as having a particular form of power.[47] For example, in 1875 Apolônia de tal, from Jucás, allegedly had performed witchcraft against the illiterate farmer Francisco Américo, which according to him and his friends had, in fact, provoked an illness. In the same year, Ana Morena, an old, black, and poor woman who worked tending clothes in Tamboril, angered the illiterate farmer Estêvão da Mota Silveira by refusing to leave a meeting with friends in order to return his clothes and break larger currency into change. In 1865, Maria José de Carvalho, who "lived off her own work" in the Fazenda Sipó in Tamboril, had attempted to defend her mother, whom she lived with, from the farmer Tomé Alves da Cruz's attacks, and in the fight had called him "drunk." And in 1868, Senhorinha Ferreira de Carvalho, who performed agricultural work in the Fazenda Mutuca, of Jucás, allegedly had refused the sexual advances of the illiterate farmer André.[48] In other cases, women "had spoken" of some men's character or questionable actions, or of the sexual purity of their wives, and in this way tainted their reputation.[49]

According to the male offenders' descriptions of the beatings, their victims' actions or words constituted "provocations" and required the performance of violence in retribution. A close reading of the cases shows that these women's public assertions of power became "provocations" because they came at the expense of the reputation of a particular man, and they were performed by women whose way of life was already suspect as a result of their independence from patriarchal control. According to Estêvão da Mota Silveira, who beat the old Ana Morena in the head with a live coal, she had "incited" his anger because she had been "impudent" when she told him to find someone else to get his clothes, in front of a large group of people. The fifteen-year-old domestic worker Maria Martins from Tamboril had offended Elias de tal by refusing his sexual advances, and by spitting in his direction once when he passed her in a town street.[50] In the case of Apolônia de tal, her magical powers publicly challenged, even if temporarily, a man's activity and freedom of movement. Using Ruth Behar's words, Apolônia "turn[ed] the world upside down" and exercised control over a vital aspect of a man's life, by causing him an illness.[51] The other women also subverted the patriarchal social structure when they publicly challenged men's perceived right to sexually seize women at their discretion, or to fight and be aggressive. Insulted by these women's actions or words, poor men typically enacted a violent form of revenge and often rounded up the help of other, normally younger, illiterate men, ambushed their victims, and flogged them with leather whips, tree trunks with thorns, or beat them with clubs. In some cases, men entered into these women's houses and attacked and wounded them with knives.

It is true that this type of aggression was inserted in a cultural context in which male violence against women was common in a variety of situations.[52] Yet, the beatings of unattached sertanejas during the period between 1865 and 1889 speak to the defense of the hegemonic position of men in a context in which familial patriarchal authority was weak. On the one hand, the difficult conditions of the late nineteenth century effectively divested free poor Cearense men of the material symbols of masculine honor and social status, as well as of their ability to effectively supervise and control female kin. On the other hand, women's increasing visibility as household heads and providers for their children and dependents placed them in prominent public positions, but without the backing of men who could protect them and vouchsafe for their honor. This disjuncture resulted in gendered forms of humiliation designed to warn of the dangers that unattached women represented to the moral order. But, just as important, in a milieu where the basis that upheld the poor backlanders' sense of dominant masculinity had become undermined, these women's visibility called into question a patriarchal order in which men effectively controlled female sexuality, mobility, and labor. Thus, bold actions or words from autonomous women may have appeared as powerful symbols of the disruption in gendered power relations and of the crisis of legitimacy of patriarchy that affected interior communities in a state of flux.

The words the male assailants directed to their victims during or after the attacks reveal that verbal abuse and violence against unattached females constituted attempts to reaffirm masculine precedence. Indeed, male batterers deployed a language of legitimacy and authority in correcting unmanageable women when they flogged them. For example, according to his own deposition, Estêvão da Mota said to Ana Morena that he was beating her because she had "refused to obey him." Gonçalo Gabriel told Imaria Alves, according to witnesses, that he stabbed her so that she would "learn not to interfere in men's fights," since she had defended a man in a confrontation he had with Gabriel. After Elias de tal gave a beating to Maria Martins, he had shouted that "he would give a whipping anytime to teach some women not to demean a man (*fazer pouco de homem*)."[53] Words such as these bear witness to men's use of violence as a way to teach those unprotected women they saw as insolent a lesson regarding their place in a patriarchal hierarchy and the boundaries to the behavior that would be acceptable of autonomous females.

Some of the men who committed acts of violence against unattached sertanejas framed their actions as responses to the damage to their honor that these women's words and gossip had caused. The farmer João Ferreira de Sousa, from the Lugar Baixa Grande, Itapagé, publicly threatened the spinner Joana Maria da Conceição with a flogging because she was "insulting and provoking." In his own words, she "disregarded all notions of honor and insulted him and his family," and she had "very bad behavior." A farmer from Jucás began beating Matilde Maria da Conceição and asked her, "[W]hat have you been saying about me, bitch?"[54] Apparently, through the use of aggression and verbal abuse men who were unrelated to these autonomous females also sought to impose the patriarchal control that family men normally enforced over women's ability to talk. The English traveler Henry Koster noted that, in the early part of the nineteenth century, sertanejas very seldom took part in conversations when their husbands were present, and when the men were talking, women stood or squatted down, merely listening.[55]

Clearly, these women did not have any male protectors. Otherwise, unrelated men would not have dared to attack them and instead would have attempted to defend their honor by fighting with the women's husbands, fathers, or brothers. Moreover, the criminal cases make clear that other men, such as neighbors or acquaintances, often refused to intervene in gendered forms of violence that sought to re-establish masculine authority and honor. For instance, the court official João Gomes de Mattos noted in his deposition as a witness of Maria Martins's whipping by Elias de tal that he was in a house located next to the one where Maria was spending the night in Tamboril, and he saw Elias de Tal entering there with a whip. He described that he heard Maria's screams asking for rescue, and her saying, "Senhor Elias, please do not beat me more." Yet, he did nothing. The tailor Raimundo José Bezerra lived next door to Micaela Maria da Conceição and confessed that he had heard her screaming, but he did not help her because, by the time he had put on his pants (he had been undressed) and run to her house, the "executor" of the thrashing had left.[56] Without any male defense or protection, these women suffered severe injuries at the hands of their assailants as they learned a lesson in public patriarchy. In a few instances, the victims either died or miscarried as a result of the brutality of the whippings. In two of the incidents where women had refused men's sexual advances, the flogging was accompanied by violent rape that left their sexual organs bleeding and swollen.[57]

This highly theatrical form of humiliation centered on women's bodies, since the body is, as Michel Foucault argues, a privileged site for the inscription of meanings of power and, in short, for forcing submission. These surras were clear attempts on the part of men to inscribe forcefully on unattached women's bodies the meanings of a patriarchal order that demanded female respect for men or, at least, the appearance of acknowledgment of the privileges of patriarchy. This form of gendered violence differed sharply from fights between men, even though they also constituted embodied attempts to restore men's wounded honor. Masculine fights were contests, in which the action of winning allowed the ultimate encoding of submission on the body of the loser. By contrast, the flogging of a woman was not a contest but a simple and brutal assertion of power.[58]

The act of flogging and its symbolic association with humiliation and subjection had a gender-specific meaning, since backlands communities regarded women and the feminine as dependent, and therefore as rightful objects of domination and discipline—activities that were construed as masculine. The practice of discipline included whipping, a feminizing form of punishment that also equated the status of punished free women and men to that of slaves. The gendered symbolism of whipping as a form of punishment is demonstrated in the following verses, recited by the popular poet Azulão, which recalled a desafio between the Paraiban cantadora Chica Barrosa and the Cearense poet Neco Martins, from Paracuru. In the opening of the desafio, Chica Barrosa established her credentials as a cantadora by embodying violent masculinity and saying:

A Barrosa se zangando	If Barrosa gets angry
Lhe dá uma grande pisa,	She will give you a good beating
Daquelas de engrossá couro . . .	One that will leave your skin swollen . . .
Veja lá, que ela lhe avisa!	Consider yourself warned!

Neco Martins responded to the warning by arguing that nobody had been able to whip him yet, and, in this way, asserting his untainted masculinity:

Inda que o diabo lhe atente,	Even if the devil attempts to
Nem assim isso acontece,	This will never happen
Porque de peia no lombo	Because I have not found anybody
Eu nunca achei quem me desse.	Who could whip me in my back.

Chica Barrosa's reply shows both the symbolic associations between whipping and subordination that derived from the use of this form of punishment against slaves and her own elevation over the status of dominated people:

Não me ameace de peia	Don't threaten me with a whip
Que me faz ficá danada;	That you make me really angry;
Eu não sou sua cativa	I am not your slave
Nem também sua criada.	Neither am I your servant.[59]

Violent attacks on unattached females did not only function as a way to maintain a patriarchal order by teaching wayward women to keep their place and to remain socially subordinate. This form of aggression, in fact, contributed to the constitution of hegemonic masculinities through the execution of violence in service of the assertion of male dominance over women's bodies. This gendered performance of violence took place in public, and often in the presence of other men, thus making the event a shared bodily experience among males. For instance, the thirty-year-old illiterate farmer Teodoro Ferreira de Oliveira and the twenty-year-old illiterate farmer Clemente Alves de Oliveira from the São Bartolomeo district of Jucás whipped the forty-year-old widow Joaquina Alves de Oliveira, in March of 1874, because she "had made ill remarks" about Teodoro. The flogging of Apolônia de tal, which eventually caused her death, was performed by Rufino Rodrigues de Oliveira, a twenty-two-year-old illiterate farmer from the Fazenda Santo Agostinho, in Jucás, and the brothers Fructuoso Ferreira de Oliveira, a twenty-eight-year-old illiterate farmer, and Gabriel Ferreira de Oliveira, a twenty-two-year-old illiterate farmer, both from the same fazenda.[60]

The male sociability created through the shared bodily performance of violence factored in the social construction of the unprotected female body, or those men deemed feminine or weak, as dominated objects of righteous violence from men. This can be exemplified in the case of the flogging of Senhorinha Ferreira da Conceição. According to João Evangelista—a sixty-year-old farmer who was picking beans with Senhorinha in a roça located in the Lugar Mutuca—Rogério Luís dos Santos (a thirty-year-old illiterate farmer), André Pereira da Silva, Antônio Pereira and José Pereira physically assaulted her. In his testimony during the criminal proceedings, he narrated that the attackers appeared next to Senhorinha, grabbed her by the neck and took her to a creek with running water, where they buried her face, while Rogério whipped her. This attack did not only achieve the intimidation of Senhorinha, who allegedly had refused Rogério's sexual advances, but also the humiliation of the elderly João Evangelista, who attempted to stand up for her during this assault. He was unable to do so because Rogério pushed him to the ground, dispossessed him of a small knife, and shouted for him not to move, while Antônio kept vigil. Moreover, even though João Evangelista never mentioned this in his testimony, since Rogério and the other three men were charged for assaulting Senhorinha, he had been forced to witness the raping of Senhorinha. The physical examination, or *corpo de delito,* performed in Senhorinha during the criminal investigation showed that her hips and legs were bruised and "appeared black and purple," and her sexual organs were swollen and bleeding. The cornering of the weak and elderly João Evangelista, in turn, constituted a feminization, as he was forced to observe, without being able to do anything, the whipping and raping of Senhorinha.[61]

In addition, these violent acts constituted a platform for the assertion of masculine reputation built on the violent domination of unprotected women. For instance, according to witnesses, after beating Maria Pereira, the illiterate farmer Antônio Lindo da Silva had taken his knife out of its casing and said that he "wanted to know who was manly enough to dare defend Maria Pereira." Along the same lines, Estêvão da Mota Silveira, after whipping Matilde Maria da Conceição, asked the farmer AntônioVicente da Silva to bring him a bottle of brandy, and to have a few drinks with him.[62]

While most of the examined cases of violence against unattached sertanejas reveal that they became victims of physical and verbal abuse as a result of gender-rooted disputes with their male assailants, some of them demonstrate that these women were also vulnerable to male violence at the orders of other females. This was particularly true in cases of haircutting accompanied by other aggressions. For instance, on the night of May 31, 1864, several men flogged Micaela Maria da Conceição in her house. According to one of the witnesses, after the offenders left Micaela Maria's house, he saw that her body was bloody, and that her hair had been cut with a knife. This witness also mentioned that while he was not entirely sure who performed the beating, "[It] was known in the village of São Mateus," that Josefa, wife of Senhor Barbosa, had "intrigues" with Micaela, because of jealousy. In this way he hinted that Josefa had commanded Micaela's flogging.[63] In other cases, witnesses and plaintiffs pointed to women who ordered mainly young men to whip unprotected females, because they suspected that these women were having affairs with their husbands, although those who presumably commanded the beatings were never brought to trial. A different case details how a widow, Alexandrina Maria Paulina do Espírito Santo "had been insolent" in her dealings with another woman, and because of this was beaten by the sixteen-year-old farmer Raimundo Ximenes, at the orders of his grandmother, Maria Prenda Rica.[64] Taken together, these cases suggest that violent repression against unattached sertanejas received cultural sanction not only among men but also among women. Through the performance of aggression against unprotected women, various members of backlands communities sought to exercise the familial patriarchy that in normal circumstances would restrain their sexuality and enforce their verbal deference.

Another criminal case from the municipality of Itapagé demonstrates how various community members, even when they were not related to the married men who allegedly had illicit sexual relations with unattached women, or their wives, flogged them with the goal of instilling moral discipline. According to a legal complaint detailing the assault of the twenty-two-year-old seamstress Francisca Ferreira Barbosa, the farmer José Felicio Primo had whipped her in her house, one day in May 1873. In July of the same year, Joaquina de tal, who was married, and the single Filadelfa de tal invited Francisca to eat *cajás* (hog plums) with them, in Joaquina's house, located in the

Lugar Espírito Santo. But as soon as they arrived, the two women proceeded to whip Francisca and cut her hair. According to Francisca's deposition, Joaquina had told her after the attack that "she would send her braid to Bento's wife."[65] Clearly, some women, typically married and older, exercised power over unattached females and policed their moral behavior. Moreover, repression of unprotected women by both males and females appears to have been a socially sanctioned mechanism to define the boundaries of independent women' sexual behavior. Nevertheless, since in most of the examined cases, those who performed these acts of violence on their own accord, or on orders from others, were men, it is clear that various groups in rural communities approved the performance of masculine violence as a tool to discipline "women alone."

In sum, autonomous women in the backlands of Ceará were subject to violent patriarchy even as they lived unattached from men, headed their own households, and self-managed petty businesses during the period between 1865 and 1880. Thus, these findings indicate the usefulness of looking beyond household composition and headship as a way to understand the functioning of patriarchy in Brazil. Because unattached sertanejas in Ceará remained free from the supervision by family patriarchs for shorter or longer periods of time, a culturally sanctioned violent coercion, enforced by unrelated men, operated to establish the boundaries of acceptable independent female comportment and to guarantee the continuation of a patriarchal order in the interior. Given the erosion of the material basis for the constitution of honorable masculinities, and the weakened grip of men over female kin that accompanied the years of hardship, the autonomy and initiative of "women alone" appeared as a challenge to patriarchal power and to the hegemonic position of men in society. Under these conditions, acts of aggression constituted attempts by free poor men who did not have other venues to claim social authority to dominate unattached women who had asserted a form of power in their interpersonal relations with them. Likewise, cultural coercion of autonomous females (focused on insults, humiliations, and violent acts committed by men, but also by other women) functioned as a countervailing force to the social-economic transformations that had brought in their wake a visible population of autonomous women.

Autonomous Women, Masculine Honor, and the Practice of Criminal Justice

On May 24, 1865, Antônia Maria da Anunciação, a poor single woman who lived in the Lugar Casão, Tamboril, informed the public prosecutor of her district that she had been whipped by Joaquim de tal and Antônio de tal, and lodged a formal criminal complaint against them. The police investigation, based on the deposition of nine witnesses and the physical examination of the plaintiff, revealed that she had multiple wounds and contusions, and that her sexual organs were inflamed and bleeding. The two defendants were indicted and subsequently tried for assaulting Antônia Maria. Nevertheless, almost a year after the attack, the municipal jury acquitted the defendants, arguing that the wounds sustained by the victim were not "serious" as the initial accusation stated, but rather *leves*, or minor.[66]

For free poor women like Antônia Maria, who were illiterate, and who did not have familial networks of men to defend them, the courts constituted a resource to which they could turn in their attempts to obtain judicial retribution, or even a form of security against future attacks. In reporting these acts, unprotected women further defied gender power relations, especially with their male offenders, and sometimes even put themselves at risk of additional beatings. For instance, Maria Paulina de Oliveira, a forty-year-old woman from the town of Tamboril, was a witness in the criminal trial against the police soldier Joaquim Manoel, who allegedly assaulted the eighteen-year-old domestic worker Marcelina Maria da Conceição. In her deposition, Maria Paulina declared that she found Marcelina in the street after the *espancamento*, or thrashing, and saw her body and dress covered in blood. Moreover, Marcelina told her that Joaquim Manoel had beaten her and that, precisely at the time of their encounter in the street, she was walking to the public prosecutor's house to file a legal complaint. A few moments later, Joaquim Manoel appeared next to the two women and asked Marcelina if she had already lodged her accusation. When she replied that she had not, his answer, according to Maria Paulina, was: "I am sorry that you have not done it, because if you had, I would beat you even more, right here."[67] Nevertheless, at least for some of these women, no doubt, the court represented an avenue, perhaps the only one, to contest their social subordination, or, at minimum, the use of brutal aggression in its service. Of the total of thirty-two criminal proceedings that feature acts of violence against unprotected sertanejas, twenty-four, or 75 percent, were initiated at the request of the aggrieved women, while eight, or 25 percent, began as a result of complaints by police or other local authorities.

The criminal investigation and legal prosecution of men who offended unattached women by whipping, beating, or raping them was possible under regulations provided in the 1830 Imperial Criminal Code and the 1832 Code of Criminal Procedure. This body of criminal law—like much of the legal system adopted in Brazil after independence—was based on liberal legal principles that included individual equality before the law, proportionate punishment, and moral responsibility.[68] Thus, the Imperial criminal laws and procedures contained certain implicit promises to guarantee the civil liberties and bodily integrity of all free peoples, including women, whether wealthy or poor, married or unprotected. For example, Title II of the Criminal Code specified all the different crimes against individual security and their sentences. Section IV of this title established that causing physical injuries, cuts, and wounds on the body of another person, with the objective of insulting and hurting, were crimes against the security of life and of personhood, punishable by incarceration for one month to eight years, depending on the severity of the wounds produced and on aggravating or extenuating circumstances.[69] According to legal stipulations from 1854, the crime of assault was subject to public or official prosecution, which meant that authorities such as the public prosecutor had the obligation to legally denounce and initiate the investigation of these offenses, regardless of the ability of the victim to pay for the costs normally associated with a private lawsuit.[70] Section VI of Title II established that invading somebody's home (*casa*) without permission of its owner, constituted a crime punishable by incarceration for a period of two to six months.[71] This offense was considered a "private crime" whose punishment was of concern only to one party (as opposed to the social body as a whole, or the state) and therefore required a private accusation, or *queixa,* to initiate a lawsuit, as well as the payment of all fees by the plaintiff. Yet, even in the case of private crimes, criminal procedure established that when plaintiffs were impoverished and unable to afford the cost of an accusation and of pursuing a lawsuit, the legal action became public or official, and therefore an obligation of the judicial authorities.[72] These specifications provided the legal foundations even for unprotected women to attain judicial retribution when they suffered violent attacks at the hands of unrelated men. What is more, the Code established that "superiority in sex, force, and weapons" was an aggravating circumstance to be considered in the judging of all crimes.

Given the Imperial, provincial, and local elites' concern with the punishment of crime and the upholding of order during the second half of the nineteenth century, public prosecutors from interior locations did take some measures to put on trial and punish men who had assaulted unprotected females. The narratives of the actual attacks and of the character of the injured parties, provided by the plaintiffs and filtered through the interrogation of the public prosecutors, constitute a rich source material to understand some of the strategies that these women used to attain legal protection. While the motives for these offenses and other details varied, the narratives tended to follow a set pattern, especially in the representation of the victimized women as passive and, despite their material poverty, as respectable. Typical of this characterization is the legal complaint of the beating of Raimunda Maria de Jesus by the blacksmith Antônio Gordo, which reads in this manner:

> On the night of the first of this month, in the village of São Francisco, the plaintiff Raimunda Maria de Jesus was sleeping in her house at about 10:00 at night, when she was awoken by someone pounding at her door, who eventually knocked it down. A person entered her room, whom the plaintiff recognized as the blacksmith Antônio Gordo, and invited her to have carnal copulation with him. Because she refused, she was offered the amount of Rs. 5$000 for the same purpose, but since she refused again [Antônio] said that he would make noise. To this, she replied that he could make as much noise as he wished, but she did not want to [have sexual relations with him]. When the defendant heard this answer, he grabbed a club with which he gave a trashing to the plaintiff, and not happy with this, he also banged her with his feet, resulting in the wounds and contusions that are described in the physical examination.[73]

According to Eileen Findlay's analysis of rapto and rape suits in nineteenth-century Puerto Rico, participants in criminal cases, including magistrates, plaintiffs, defendants, and witnesses built their depositions on dominant scripts that were shaped by the legal definitions of crimes, the juridical procedure, as well as culturally accepted conceptualizations of masculinity and femininity and of gender power relations.[74] Indeed, the Cearense assault suits featuring unprotected women as victims demonstrate that they deployed a legal script focused on their respectability, passivity, and domesticity as they reached for a form of vindication against their offenders from the representatives of the state. Considered dishonorable because of their lack of male protection, women like Raimunda Maria, along with public prosecutors, often emphasized that they were in their houses at the moment of the attacks. The house or home served as the ideal signifier of honor, a space where honorable women were *recolhidas*, or secluded from the dangers of the outside world, which, according to the classic Brazilian metaphor, was symbolized by the street. Even though normative gender concepts defined men as the protectors and defenders of the home, the reference to the unprotected women's location at home or in their houses at the moment of the attack served to affirm their honor, and their respect for the spatial geography of gender.[75] This respectability, in turn, established these women as worthy of defense and protection, even if only from the state. It is interesting that in this discourse unattached sertanejas did not often reveal the causes of the beating, if they knew them, as they tried to represent themselves as completely passive. In the few cases where the legal complaints mentioned the reasons for the attack, as in Raimunda Maria's case, they alluded only to men's attempts to have illicit sexual relations with them, which as respectable women, they had rejected, and not to other assertions of power in their past interactions with their offenders.

Judicial procedures also helped shape the legal script on the domesticity of autonomous females. The Criminal Code established that entering into the victim's home with the explicit intent of committing a crime and performing criminal acts at night were aggravating circumstances to be considered in deciding sentences for all crimes. This helped reinforce a dominant script focused on the centrality of the house as a place that had been violated, in addition to the women's bodies, and the specification that the attacks took place at night.[76]

Furthermore, legal descriptions influenced the production of a legal script that, in fact, hid sexual offenses against unattached sertanejas when they occurred. Sexual violence against these women was not tried under the legal category of *estupro*, or statutory rape. This had to do with the official definition of estupro as the "deflowering of a virgin woman, younger than seventeen years old," or the "violent copulation with" or "seduction" of an "honest woman." The references to honesty in the legal conceptualization of rape refer to women's honor, centered on their sexual purity as protected by family men.[77] "Women alone" who were neither virgins, nor honorable because of their lack of male protection, could not prosecute their rapists under this crime. Consequently, in their depositions, they did not mention the sexual abuse, which became obvious only after the physical examinations established which organs and body parts had been injured. Apparently, for the Criminal Code, public prosecutors, and other judicial officials, violent sexual abuse of a nonvirgin woman with the clear intent of intimidating was not a crime.

The narratives of men as aggressors also followed a script that was both shaped by and expressed dominant ideas that sanctioned violence in defense of honor, even if against unprotected females. This script, like the one on the respectability of sheltered women, was not confined to the lower classes. Instead, it was shared by both poor sertanejos and elites. Furthermore, elements of this discourse reflected legal definitions contained in the Criminal Code, which, in contradiction to its liberal principles, effectively authorized the performance of aggression in vindication of honor.[78] This is evident in the deposition of the police soldier Joaquim Manoel, who according to Marcelina Maria da Conceicão and seven witnesses, had beaten Marcelina with a club, causing a deep wound in her face, and several contusions in her head. In his response to a formulaic question as to whether there were any facts that would justify his acts or would show his innocence, Joaquim Manoel replied, through the narrative of the court scribe: "He said that he does not have any [facts to prove his innocence] and that he confesses that he committed the crime to avenge the honor of his *mulher* that had been sullied by the plaintiff, who publicly spread the gossip that she was carrying on with an army corporal of the detachment stationed in town." In effect, several witnesses mentioned in their depositions that they either knew about or had heard Marcelina gossiping about a married woman named Maria Alvina de Sousa, although they never mentioned that she was Joaquim Manoel's *amásia*. Instead, witnesses declared that they had heard or knew that Maria Alvina had ordered the soldier, Joaquim Manoel, to perform the beating on Marcelina. Yet, Joaquim Manoel, perhaps at the counsel of his lawyer, or on his own, invoked culturally accepted notions according to which the cleansing of offended honor through violence was a justifiable masculine behavior, because they appealed to the sensitivities of male authorities and to judicial definitions. According to the Criminal Code, engaging in an act *em desafronta,* or vindication, of "an insult or dishonor against the delinquent, his or her ancestors, children, spouses, or siblings," constituted an extenuating circumstance in deciding the sentence of any crime. Moreover, the Criminal Code established, in an ambiguous manner, that "crimes committed in defense of a person and his or her rights," and "in defense of the delinquent's family," were justifiable, and therefore not punishable. For Joaquim Manoel, an appeal to male jury members on the basis that his actions were undertaken in vindication of his consensual wife's honor was potentially more advantageous than confessing that he had committed the crime for money, or because he had been having an affair with a married woman. Despite his confession, Maria Alvina in her own deposition declared that she was married, and had a husband and several sons who could defend her honor, and thus did not need to order someone whom she did not know well to beat Marcelina.[79]

The transcript of the criminal trial against Joaquim Manoel is incomplete, and thus it is impossible to know whether his moral justification of the violent act he practiced against Marcelina Maria worked in his favor. But other criminal suits demonstrate that municipal jurors, who were also participants and shapers of this dominant script, were indulgent in the treatment of these offenses and granted light sentences or acquittals to women batterers. It is true that the criminal justice system in the backlands was generally lenient, and that networks of patronage influenced favorable judicial decisions for the well connected. Yet, a closer look at some of these sentences reveals that juridical practice was influenced by local understandings regarding gender order, and by the legal precepts that sanctioned the use of male aggression in defense of honor. For instance, the jury of the village of Tamboril absolved

Elias de tal from the accusation of assaulting the fifteen-year-old Maria Martins, arguing that the depositions by the witnesses did not prove that he
indeed had committed the crime. This acquittal took place, even though all
of the six witnesses summoned in this case reported that they had heard or
seen Elias de tal beating Maria Martins one night in the house of the fifteen-
year-old Maria Joaquina. The district attorney appealed this decision to the
High Court in Fortaleza, arguing that the Tamboril jury clearly had ignored
that Elias de tal's actions were a violation of the security and personhood of
Maria Martins. Deploying social understandings regarding the sexual impu-
rity of unprotected women, the district attorney asserted that, even though
Maria Martins was a prostitute (none of the witnesses had referred to her as
a prostitute), the case against Elias was transparent. A second jury met in Tamboril in August of 1882. This jury found that Elias de tal was guilty, but there
were extenuating circumstances that warranted a reduced sentence. Citing
Article 18, paragraph 4 of the Criminal Code, the jury maintained that the
defendant had committed the crime in defense of his honor, which had been
insulted, or in their words "demeaned," through Maria's action of spitting in
his direction a day before the attack. Accordingly, he was condemned to six
months' incarceration in the Ipu prison.[80]

A criminal case from the town of São Francisco illustrates how local criminal courts, in fact, borrowed selectively from both the liberal principles contained in the legal codes and those that sanctioned hierarchy, in order to not
interfere in the perceived right of men to use violence to defend honor and
the privileges of patriarchy. In January of 1883, the farmer Bernardino Dias
do Nascimento was formally accused of physically injuring Maria Lucina, a
thirty-eight-year-old laundress, with a knife. According to the official complaint, Bernardino had come to the house where Maria Lucina was staying
one night in the Sítio São Miguel and tried to force her to go into another
room and engage in sexual relations with him. She resisted and got the help
of her sister Luzia to physically restrain Bernardino, at which point he bran-
dished a knife and wounded Maria Lucina. As witnesses noted, Maria Lucina
had said to Bernardino that he was "shameless" by trying to force her into a
sexual relation. The criminal investigation determined that Bernardino had
indeed assaulted Maria Lucina, through depositions from several witnesses,
the defendant, and the plaintiff, and through a physical examination. Yet the
jury absolved Bernardino, arguing that three extenuating circumstances that
were established in Article 18 of the Criminal Code applied in this case: first,
that the defendant had committed the crime in self-defense and in defense
of his rights. Through the deployment of this legal notion, the jury justified
Bernardino's violent act as one executed in vindication of his wounded

honor, a deed that, in turn, served to restitute his social precedence. After all, he had been called "shameless" in public. The second extenuating circumstance that applied in this case, according to the jury, was that the aggression had been initiated by the offended person, in this case Maria Lucina (this, despite the fact that, according to the records, neither Maria Lucina nor her sister threatened Bernardino with any weapon); the third indicated that the delinquent had been inebriated when he had committed the crime. Here, the jury from São Francisco invoked the principle of proportionate punishment to legitimize masculine aggression under the excuse of intoxication, while it subverted the Criminal Code's admonition that "superiority in sex, force, and weapons" had to be considered in sentencing any crime.[81]

By contrast, it appears as if the criminal courts did not readily judge violence as permissible, even if in defense of honor, if performed by women against men. While recognizing the distance between an accusation of assault, and one of homicide, the following example serves to demonstrate gendered understandings regarding the validity of the "vindication of honor" defense among judicial officers in local Cearense courts. According to the legal complaint, Maria Francisca do Nascimento, a married woman from the Lugar São Pedro, in Jucás, allegedly shot and killed Eufrásio Alves Pereira in August of 1876. In the answers to her interrogation, Maria Francisca declared that she had shot Eufrásio because, "for the last three years she had been pursued by the said Eufrásio, who wanted to perturb the peace and tranquility of her family, and to sully her reputation" by forcing her to have sexual relations with him. Moreover, according to her declarations, Eufrásio had once ambushed her in a roça and attempted to force her into a sexual encounter from which she had been "delivered" by her brother-in-law's intervention. On the day when she shot Eufrásio, as Maria Francisca continued, he had been making advances toward her, even though her husband was just outside the house. Therefore, she grabbed the shotgun and shot him, although "not with the intention of killing him, but only of expelling him from the house." These declarations followed a legal script in which Maria Francisca depicted herself as an honorable woman, whose main concern was to keep her sexual purity and reputation. In all likelihood, she even mentioned the episode in which her brother-in-law helped her to repel Eufrásio as a way to establish herself as a family woman who, under normal circumstances, deferred to men for the defense of her honor.

Nevertheless, the criminal court from Jucás found fault in Maria Francisca's actions and even in her representation of herself. In their questioning of the defendant, the judges and lawyers repeatedly asked Maria Francisca why she was afraid that Eufrásio would destroy her reputation if she was married and had a husband who could defend her. They even asked her why she did not tell her husband about these advances. She replied that since there was "enmity" between Eufrásio and her husband, she wanted to avoid a confrontation and, therefore, had not told him about Eufrásio's constant pursuit. The jury did not rule Maria Francisca's act of violence justifiable, even though she claimed that her honor was at stake, and even though the Criminal Code provided that certain crimes were excusable or less serious if committed in defense of honor. Consequently, she was condemned to seven years in prison. The significance of this case lies in the judges' and jurors' perplexity as to why Maria Francisca failed to allow her husband to defend her honor. This suggests that for judicial authorities in local courts a married woman's aggression in vindication of honor was inappropriate and unjustifiable because it constituted a subversion of patriarchal power and privileges and of normative gender roles under which men were in charge of performing these duties.[82]

The final resolution of these assault trials suggests that unprotected women's chances were not very good, to borrow a term from Findlay, against the "united front" between local elites and poor men, and against the selective application of contradictory legal precepts in defense of patriarchal prerogatives.[83] Of a total of twenty-one cases of physical injuries against women alone that ended with jury decisions from the three municipalities, five, or 23.8 percent, resulted in convictions; nine, or 42.8 percent, resulted in absolutions; six, or 28.5 percent, were dismissed; and one, or 4.7 percent, ended with the withdrawal of the legal complaint by the plaintiff. Some of the dismissals and acquittals, such as the case of the offenders of Antônia Maria mentioned above, hinged on technicalities in the judicial procedure that, more often than not, reveal unwillingness on the part of local judges and juries to effectively punish these crimes. Thus, even though the physical examination and witnesses demonstrated the severity of Antônia Maria's injuries, the jury contended that those wounds were superficial and, in accordance with Article 205 of the Criminal Code, they had not "caused inability to work for longer than a month." In coming to this decision, the jury clearly neglected Article 206 of the Criminal Code, which stated that "causing physical injuries with the only goal of insulting another person" already constituted a crime.[84] In other instances, municipal judges dismissed cases because the public prosecutors had failed to obtain from the victims the "certificates of poverty" that were needed to prove that a person was financially unable to pursue a criminal action without public assistance. However, this was a clear contravention of the criminal procedure regulations from 1854 which specified that assault was a crime subject to public or official prosecution.[85]

Transcripts of physical assault suits testify to the ways in which the practice of criminal justice produced effects of power that went beyond the acquittal or conviction of those men who beat unprotected women. For as Findlay has argued, the legal process and the dominant scripts circulated in them not only reflected, but also reinforced, dominant discourses about and practices of masculinity and femininity and cultural interpretations of sexuality and power.[86] It is evident that the Cearense courts not only helped normatize but also legitimized hegemonic masculinities predicated on violence against unprotected women. The public justification of masculine aggression as an acceptable means to subordinate "unruly" females or to cleanse sullied honor, within a largely male court environment that brought into contact men from different classes, made the courts another public arena for the performance and constitution of violent hegemonic masculinities. Moreover, this construct of masculinity was bolstered as courtroom stories, arguments, and verdicts recirculated common notions regarding the "natural" predisposition of men to commit acts of violence. This is visible in Joaquim Manoel's confession to the trashing of Marcelina Maria da Conceição, a statement in which he publicly constituted himself as a man who performed a violent act out of instinct. He noted, once again through the pen of the court scribe, that when he searched for Marcelina in order to confront her about the gossip regarding Maria Alvina, he did not intend to hit her, but "to counsel her to change her life system [of gossiping], but she became excited." According to the deposition, Marcelina "insulted him by pushing him, and telling him that she would not listen to him or that woman." Because of this, Joaquim Manoel noted, "he could not contain himself and punched Marcelina twice," and then he hit her with the wooden tip of a machete. Municipal juries added the legitimacy granted by legal codes to this discourse on the natural aggression of men. For instance, the criminal investigation, based on depositions by several witnesses, the plaintiff, and the defendant, and the physical examination of Raimunda Maria proved that Antônio Gordo had assaulted her on the night of January 1, 1873. Accordingly, that defendant was indicted for the crime. Yet, the jury absolved Antônio, arguing that there were extenuating circumstances in his favor, as spelled out in the first paragraph of Article 18 of the Criminal Code. According to this regulation, "[A] lack of direct intention to practice the crime, or lack of precise knowledge of the evil that would result from one's actions," needed to be considered as a factor in reducing a sentence. Thus, the jury from São Francisco disregarded the violence committed against Raimunda, by making it into an unconscious, and therefore meaningless, act, and, in turn, validated the idea that men were not responsible for their aggression.[87]

To be sure, the practice of criminal justice also reinforced domesticity, passivity, and bashfulness, or at least their appearance, as important values of normative sertanejo femininity, and as markers of the respectability that unattached females needed if they were to obtain the assistance of the state in their gender-rooted disputes with unrelated sertanejo men. Indeed, the juridical process appears to have contributed to recirculate normative precepts according to which women could not defend their honor or physical integrity on their own, and instead needed to rely on masculine mediation. Moreover, the courtrooms constituted themselves into a theater in which male subordination of unprotected sertanejas became re-enacted, amplified, and legitimated. For instance, even when women like Marcelina Maria found in the public prosecutor a friendly or compassionate ally, the judicial process placed them in a milieu in which their stories of victimization and their own battered bodies became subject to questioning and suspicion by male authorities and power figures, who often trivialized or dismissed their cases. The police investigation, initiated by the women's legal complaints, included not only the gathering of declarations by several witnesses but also the performance of a physical examination by "experts" who determined the severity of the physical injuries and the number of days of incapacitation caused by the wounds. These experts were male members of the local elite, usually large fazendeiros, wealthier farmers, town merchants, lawyers, and occasionally school teachers. In cases when sexual abuse was obvious or suspected, midwives were called to perform an examination of the sexual organs.[88] The experts then produced a written report that used scientific and juridical language in describing the physical injuries and their severity. However, the reports routinely minimized the violations performed on these women's bodies, since they often noted that the wounds were minor, and that the women were able to return to work in a few days. These assessments, in turn, became the basis for the dismissal of charges against several offenders.[89] Likewise, since the majority of the analyzed suits ended in an acquittal, a reduced sentence for the defendant, or the dismissal of the charges, despite the notorious pain and humiliation produced on these women, it is clear that the courts rendered men's need to defend their wounded honor and affirm their masculinity more powerful, credible, and significant than women's narratives of victimization, degradation, and pain.

Thus, despite the attempts by some district judges to prosecute and punish those men who attacked and flogged unprotected women, only a minority of them were ever indicted and convicted. Moreover, the practice of criminal justice by local judges and juries undermined the implicit promise of liberal legal codes to guarantee the security of women's physical person and home, regardless of class, race, or family condition. Instead, backlands male juries chose to invoke the paradoxical clauses of the Criminal Code that, in effect, ensured the continuation of a gender hierarchical order in which free men of all classes enjoyed a series of patriarchal privileges, including the right to violently control—or at least attempt to control—the sexuality, mobility, and even the speech of unattached females. The practice of prosecution of violent offenders of unprotected women, in turn, transformed the court system into another theater through which men constituted hegemonic masculinities centered on the perceived right to practice gendered violence as a means to assert superiority and dominance.

Conclusions

One of the most significant outcomes of the far-reaching economic, political, and environmental pressures affecting free poor Cearense families during the last third of the nineteenth century was the increasing visibility of a population of single women, widows, and other females who were temporarily or permanently separated from male family figures. The geographic and social dislocations of these years brought unattached sertanejas into the position of household heads, as they attempted to provide a livelihood for themselves and their families. Through a variety of self-managed occupations and activities, ranging from wage labor as laundresses and servants to small-scale farming, from petty trade to lace-making, from sewing to part-time prostitution, these women confronted the calamities of their time without the support of husbands, consensual partners, fathers, or other male kin.

The growing presence of autonomous women, related as it was to the separation of families and to the increasing incapacity of men to support them, or at least to credibly make such claims, disrupted the existing social organization of gender in sertanejo households. Moreover, the new avenues for female initiative and the seemingly unrestricted movement of "women alone" led to anxieties in backlands communities about the place of unprotected women in a patriarchal order, and about the functioning of patriarchy itself. Insults, jokes, obscene parodies, physical attacks, haircutting, and other forms of intimidation and humiliation, performed mostly by unrelated men, and also by a number of women, stigmatized these women as unrestrained and dishonorable, because of their lack of family male guardianship, and warned of their threat to the social order. But these forms of violence and verbal abuse achieved another function: in the absence of husbands, fathers, brothers, and other male kin who were regarded as the rightful custodians of the mobility, sexuality, labor, and even words of women, this public enforcement of patri-

archy partially filled that vacuum, as sertanejos who were not family members
flogged, beat, or insulted unattached females. Invoking a language of legitimate authority, men enacted violent patriarchy as a way to teach these women
a lesson in gender hierarchy and patriarchal power. Thus, violence became a
part of the system of gender domination of increasingly autonomous women,
but as Connell argues, also "a measure of its imperfection."[90]

Unprotected women did not passively accept the use of brutality in the
name of female subordination, for as Connell also maintains, "[T]he hegemonic position in a given pattern of gender relations" is "always contest-
able."[91] Battered women lodged official complaints with the public prosecutors and pursued legal actions against their attackers. Nevertheless, in a display
of solidarity among men from different classes, the local criminal courts in
most cases ruled against the plaintiffs, or dismissed their cases, and effectively
authorized the use of violence in defense of the privileges of patriarchy. Even
more, the invocation by judges and juries of contradictory principles contained in the Imperial Criminal Code contributed to normatize a discourse
by which sertanejos had the moral right to defend their honor with violence,
even if these assaults were to be performed against unprotected women. Just
as important, the courtrooms served as avenues for the reproduction of a discourse focused on the appropriate behavior of autonomous sertanejas. Combining several elements, including legal and judicial definitions and normative
understandings about gender, this discourse emphasized passivity and respectability, embodied in a type of domesticity, as important values of sertanejo
femininity. This discourse also prescribed that women defer the defense of
their honor to male patriarchs. Clearly out of place within a milieu of intense
dislocations, family separation, and even social disintegration, this discourse
allowed men and women alike to elude precisely the most distressing questions brought up by these rapid transformations, both for sertanejo families
and interior communities. Ultimately, however, the practice of criminal justice and the discourse associated with the prosecution of assault against unattached sertanejas served to reinforce the value of female passivity and the use
of male violence in an attempt to establish superiority and domination over
women during these difficult years.

Chapter 6

Of Courage and Manhood:
Masculine Spaces, Violence, and Honor, 1865–89

O nosso Zuza Tomás	Our Zuza Tomás
É homem de opinião . . .	Is a man of his word . . .
Não vejo neste sertão	I don't know any other in this sertão
Quem desfaça o que ele faz:	Who can undo what he does;
Apaga fogo com gás,	He puts out the fire with kerosene,
Rebate bala com a mão,	He repels bullets with his hand,
Tem mais força que Sansão!	He has more force than Samson!
Um dia, ele estando armado,	One day he was armed,
Apanhou de um aleijado	And was beaten by a disabled man
Mas deu num cego à traição!!! . . .	But he paid the treason by beating a blind man!!! . . .[1]

With these words, the late-nineteenth-century Cearense poet Luís Dantas Quesado described the defining characteristics of "a man of his word," a sertanejo who commanded the respect of those who knew him or came into contact with him. According to these verses, which used the metaphor of a physical fight to praise the honor of a popular bard, a man's worth was contingent on his capacity to exercise physical force, regardless of its objective. In turn, this aptitude for violence was defined in the poem as intrinsic, or essential, to the manly nature of a valiant sertanejo, in this case, the poet Zuza Tomás. The exaltation of manly courage contained in these verses also depicts one of the markers of the sertanejos' archetypal obsession with honor—the violent exercise of revenge against those who had affronted them.

Verses like Dantas Quesado's and other folkloric celebrations of the belligerency of sertanejos have been used in popular and scholarly forums as confirmations of the adherence to an unchanging culture of honor and the natural impulses toward violence supposedly displayed by male backlanders since time immemorial.[2] Nevertheless, such characterizations have ignored

that aggressive acts perpetrated in defense of honor and other forms of interpersonal masculine violence do not take place in a vacuum, and instead
emerge out of contextual, contingent conflicts and power relations that need
to be understood historically. Likewise, the widespread admiration or, conversely, the disparagement of the sertanejo macho as a figure conditioned to
violence by nature and culture, has obscured our understanding of how and
why specific actors, including common backlanders and popular poets, created, or at least propagated, this discourse, and what have been the effects of
such representations.[3]

This chapter examines some of the contexts for the reproduction of interpersonal violence, including acts of aggression in defense of honor, among
sertanejos during the period between 1865 and 1889. Here, I demonstrate
that in a milieu of rapid impoverishment, great geographic mobility, and
separation of families, free poor men, and especially young sertanejos, relied
on displays of courage and physical aggression as a way to prove and defend
personal honor. In addition, I illustrate how small farmers and ranchers who
managed to retain some of the productive resources necessary to survive
from agriculture and ranching turned to violence in their desperate attempts
to defend their patrimonies, as face-to-face negotiations became ineffective
in regulating property boundaries and usufruct of land. The chapter also
discusses how some downwardly mobile sertanejos, facing hunger and social
dislocation, came to depend on banditry as a means to derive their livelihood
and a form of masculine status. Even though these practices of violence were
shaped within a cultural language of honor that authorized certain acts of
aggression, they did not constitute empty reenactments of cultural scripts
and macho reflexes. After all, as previous chapters have shown, during more
prosperous times free poor men who had owned landed property, cattle, and
other resources and who could credibly provide for their families from their
own work established claims to honor based on their success and autonomy
as small farmers and ranchers. Instead, the following pages reveal that under the conditions of destitution and social displacement, when many poor
sertanejos no longer had access to material possessions as a basis for honor,
they could only count on violence as a strategic and culturally sanctioned
resource to establish masculine reputation and a form of respectability in
their communities.

Through analysis of the different ways in which sertanejos, local elites, and
popular poets explained, justified, belittled, or celebrated the performance of
violence in service of honor, this chapter also examines the representation of
sertanejos as "naturally" violent that surfaces out of the context of conflict
and hardship of the last third of the nineteenth century. Without claim-

ing that the legendary figure of the sertanejo macho originated during this particular time period, I seek to demonstrate how the rhetorical repetition of a discourse regarding the sertanejos' belligerent "nature" contributed to its diffusion and to shape the ways in which rural poor men were perceived by others and perhaps even understood themselves. As Stuart Hall has explained, discourse does not passively transmit meaning, but is productive, or constitutive of meaning. In the words of David Parker, discourse and figures of speech "when widely diffused" . . . "become culture."[4] Thus, I investigate some of the ways in which the discourse on the sertanejos' supposed inherent capacity to fight and "cleanse honor with blood" produced meanings such as the renewed cultural sanction and naturalization of the use of violence in service of masculine honor, which in turn, legitimized a violent form of masculine domination. In this way, it will be possible to observe that the culture of honor, far from being a timeless fixture, was, in fact, re-created through the everyday practice and discourses of sertanejos and other actors in the backlands of Ceará during these years.

Of Clubs and Whiskers: Young Men, Honor, and Violence

One October afternoon in 1883, the thirty-two-year-old and illiterate day laborer Alexandre Rodrigues and the twenty-five-year-old and illiterate farmer Luís Pereira de Sousa engaged in a fight at the residence of Anastácio Pontes, in the town of Santa Cruz, municipality of Itapagé. According to witnesses' depositions in an assault trial against Alexandre, he arrived in Anastácio's house armed with a machete and immediately began ridiculing Luís, and inviting him to a physical confrontation by saying that "Luís did not have any whiskers." Moreover, he referred to an old feud sustained by the two men as a result of their contested claim over a club and further taunted Luis with the words "Hadn't you been saying that you were going to take my club from me?" At this point, Luís and Alexandre went outside the house to exchange blows, for Luís, according to his declaration in the criminal proceedings, felt compelled "to defend his honor, as it was natural."[5]

This court case illustrates that some free poor men from the Cearense backlands, like their counterparts throughout Latin America, participated in face-to-face and ritualized exchanges of insult and provocation, which sometimes turned to violence, as a means to assert and defend manly honor. As the extensive body of scholarship on the topic has demonstrated, men from subordinated groups in different locales took offenses to their honor seriously, especially when they occurred in public. The apparent reliance of these men on face-to-face, and often violent, challenges and affirmations of honorable manhood has been explained in the literature by the structure of honor as a cultural complex and its interaction with subordinate men's social and class position. According to classic formulations, honor encompasses a man's evaluation of his own worth as well as the social validation of that estimation. Honor functions through an interplay between virtue (socially valued conduct) and precedence (a right to superiority or privileged power and social status). Because the social recognition of a claim to honor is pivotal in attaining honor, a man's honor is always insecure—as it can be contested—and requires constant renewal. These contests always occur in public, since public opinion serves as the ultimate tribunal that asserts or revokes a man's honor. Nevertheless, as the scholarship has noted, because plebeian men could not easily access the public forums that local male elites throughout the region used to settle their disputes of honor—namely, the print media and the courtroom—they were more likely to resort to violence, insult, and riposte as means to maintain and protect personal honor.[6]

As suggested by Steve Stern in his study of gender and honor in late-colonial Mexico, men from subordinated groups forged their manhood and ratified the connection between masculinity, honor, and power within public spheres of plebian male sociability. As he explains, "[In] this horizontal arena, men created cultural spaces to affirm their valor and competence, their honor and importance as men."[7] In the Cearense backlands, cultural spaces that provided opportunities for poor sertanejos to interact socially with men from the same color and class group, and to build what Stern calls the "status as a man among men," were parties, card games, markets, festivals, and the desafios in which popular poets asserted and questioned honor through verse.[8] Crucially, in all these forms of masculine socialization, the logic that publicly conferred this sense of honor was competition and the display of daring and physical prowess. For instance, card games—often accompanied by the consumption of alcohol—tested a man's boldness. The winners in these contests could publicly claim a momentary social superiority over other men. Free poor men also appear to have used betting as a way to measure daring. In several criminal cases, sertanejos declared that they had attended parties where they won items such as violas, clubs, and even dogs in their bets with other men. Even within the oral realm of the desafio, sertanejos demonstrated stamina and inventiveness—so as not to become entangled in complicated rhymes—but also bravery, as oral challenges could end in violence.[9]

The *vaquejadas* (cow-hunts) that took place during the months of June and July provided opportunities for cowboys to interact socially with other men and to perform feats of masculinity that put in evidence their courage. As Euclides da Cunha described, during the vaquejadas, cowboys from different ranches rounded up and then separated the cattle from various neighboring fazendas that pastured together in the open range. This task required one mounted cowboy to gallop into the caatinga and round up several head of cattle at a time, using strength and speed, until he could manage to herd them into a clearing, where the other cowboys encircled them. The same cowboy would repeat this action, going back into the scrub several more times. In the meantime, the vaqueiros in charge of the newly created herd would have to "plunge into the caatinga" to catch fugitive steers, pulling them by their tails while mounted and then quickly stopping them and immobilizing their legs with their fetters or leather blinkers. At the end of the vaquejada, the cowboys proudly recounted their exploits, exchanging "heroic impressions" among each other and using such adjectives as "courageous," "brave," and "audacious" to describe their performances. As da Cunha noted, the ostentatious retelling of the day's events continued when the vaqueiros returned to their homes and rested while drinking *umbusada*, a drink made from the fruit of the Brazilian plum tree called *umbú*.[10]

Yet, just as in other regions of Latin America, these forms of plebian gendered affirmation, reliant as they were on the principle of masculine competition and on the physical display of bravery, often led to violence, especially when a man publicly insulted another man's courage, his assertions of daring and fearlessness, or his masculine competency. Such challenges invited violent retribution because, as Ana Alonso has argued, in honor societies, the aspects of masculine honor that are constructed as "natural," such as virility, bravery, and valor, are also "considered to be the natural foundations for [male] power and honor-precedence." Within that context, not responding to words or acts of defiance would be tantamount to accepting one's weakness, powerlessness, and inability to exercise masculine dominance.[11] It is possible to observe the values and behaviors associated with the violent defense of honor through criminal trial records, especially of assaults, aggravated assaults, and homicides, which detail aggressive encounters between sertanejos and their peers. For instance, according to a legal complaint of assault against the thirty-year-old and illiterate farmer Francisco Alves Bezerra, he had used a hoe to wound two teenagers who had disputed his tale of valor during a *derrubada da vaca*, a contest that consisted of overturning cattle. As the complaint noted, the two youngsters had been questioning "whether he really had skills in handling cattle or he had enjoyed a streak of luck." Implicit in this violent response was the assumption that if Francisco Alves did not retaliate to the insult, he was conceding that he did not possess manly valor. According to another assault trial, on the night of July 29, 1874, the illiterate farmers Francisco Gonçalves da Silva, José Vicente da Silva, and José

Alexandre da Silva attended a samba at the house of the illiterate farmer Félix Pereira de Souza, in the Lugar São Tomé, municipality of Itapagé. According to eyewitnesses, a fight ensued after Francisco Gonçalves, a thirty-year-old man, began taunting and insulting José Vicente's competence as the lover of a woman named Ana. Under these circumstances, José Vicente, who was twenty-six years old, with the help of his brother José Alexandre, also in his twenties, confronted this taunt by getting out their knives and initiating a fight that resulted in the wounding of Francisco Gonçalves and the arrest of the three men.[12]

Criminal trial transcripts inevitably exaggerate the importance of physical aggression in the assertion and defense of honor and the gendered affirmation of free poor men among their peers. Yet, it is noteworthy that an examination of a sample of criminal cases featuring violent acts through which free poor Cearense men displayed strength in public contests, no doubt, for honorable status reveals that age was a factor in the reproduction of violence in service of masculine honor. The sample detailing these types of assault and homicides corresponds to the municipalities of Jucás and Tamboril and dates to the period between 1865 and 1889. From a total of forty-six men who appear as perpetrators and victims in twenty-eight criminal cases of this nature, 76 percent were illiterate and, therefore, most likely, poor. Moreover, the overwhelming majority of men featured in these cases were not only poor but also young. Males between the ages of sixteen and thirty constituted 74 percent of the perpetrators and victims in these cases while 26 percent were older than thirty. These numbers powerfully contrast with the age of those men involved in physical assaults related to disputes for landed property and other productive resources. Among forty-two men described in thirty-seven criminal cases of this type, 67 percent were older than thirty years old, while only 33 percent were between the ages of sixteen and thirty.

In his study of honor and violence among plebian men in late-colonial Buenos Aires, Lyman Johnson demonstrates that social and economic factors, including employment patterns, demographic makeup, and racial and class categories contributed to a more volatile culture of honor among young men in that city. He notes, for example, that many young men entered the labor force during their early teens and lived away from their families. As day laborers and apprentices in the artisan trades, these young men occupied the lowest ranks within workplace hierarchies marked by seniority, age, and strength. In addition, Buenos Aires's working class was highly fluid in nature, and many of the young men who made their way into the city were in transition to jobs in other towns or the agricultural frontier. In terms of race and ethnicity, this population of workers was not uniform. The labor market in

colonial Buenos Aires relied heavily on native workers, as well as large numbers of Portuguese and Italian immigrants, and also slaves. As Johnson shows,
because of these conditions, fewer older men could exercise a restraining
influence on the hotheaded passions of young men, while at the same time
young men were encouraged from their early years to "act like men."[13]

In looking at the Cearense hinterlands during the period after the mid-
1860s, several social-economic and demographic characteristics similar to
those pointed out by Johnson appear to have influenced the place of young
men within the masculine culture of challenge and riposte and their willingness to take physical risks as a way to establish masculine status and prestige.
Of course, most cities and towns in the interior of Ceará were not as large
or ethnically diverse as late-colonial Buenos Aires. Nevertheless, as Chapter
4 illustrated, many previously successful small farmers and ranchers were experiencing high degrees of physical mobility as they grappled with the new
conditions of downward mobility, social dislocation, and economic hardship
that affected their lives. Likewise, some sertanejo families developed strategies of survival that required men's geographic mobility, especially when they
labored for wages on public works projects, employed themselves seasonally
in agriculture or ranching, and migrated to other areas in search of better
opportunities. Many young men also spent time away from their families
when they hid from recruiters and press gangs during the most intense years
of recruitment for the Paraguayan War. Moreover, as we will see below, some
poor sertanejos lived outside family relationships for long stretches of time
when they turned to banditry, an activity that attracted mostly men. It is
also worth bearing in mind that social hierarchies in place in the backlands
classified those sertanejos who did not have economic autonomy, regular
employment, or powerful patrons as dishonorable, and ranked their masculinities as deficient, vagrant, and criminal. Given that the factors that brought
hardship to the rural poor during these very conflictive years targeted especially young families, and that young sertanejos were increasingly unable to
establish themselves or remain as independent small farmers and ranchers, it
is exceedingly likely that the category of free poor males that experienced
the highest degrees of physical mobility, degradation by their social superiors,
and poverty were young men.

Thus, it appears as if unconstrained by family obligations and facing itinerancy, humiliation, and impoverishment, some young sertanejos were comparatively more willing than their older counterparts to take risks and enact
violence in their competitive interactions with their peers. It is telling that
62 percent of the men involved in violent acts associated with honor in the
criminal cases from Jucás and Tamboril were not originally from the com-

munities in which they had engaged in fights and had been arrested. These acts of aggression, in turn, would serve to prove that even if poor, and therefore in lack of the material signifiers of honor, men possessed the "natural" attributes that guaranteed a form of masculine power and social dominance over a defeated rival, whether he was a newcomer or a more established male figure in the community. For example, Lourenço Alves Bezerra, a twenty-one-year-old and illiterate farmer from Jucás, allegedly attacked Antônio Francisco Gomes with a machete in a cane field in the Lugar Areias. According to a witness, Lourenço Alves arrived at a field one morning in August of 1875, whereupon he saw Antônio—who did not regularly work in the Lugar Areias—with an unconcealed knife ready to cut canes. He said that "he was not afraid of Antônio's knife," and that "he, Lourenço, was not afraid of any man." Lourenço then wounded Antônio in the head and hand.[14]

In the backlands and elsewhere in slaveholding Brazil, those who sought to belittle people of color used racial insults. Interacting in a slaveholding society in which African men and women and their descendants were held as human property and therefore as dishonorable, free people of color and whites alike used racial stereotypes to mark their presumed social superiority. Moreover, in the racial hierarchy of the sertão, nonslaves thought themselves entitled to ridiculing and committing acts of violence toward slaves and those constructed as such by virtue of their race or lowly status, without the expectation of retribution. After all, those who had no honor were not expected to defend it.[15] Thus, some young men used racial insults as a way to establish what they saw as their right to dominance over men of African descent. This, in turn, provoked violent conflict. For instance, in 1866 a young man from Tamboril boasted that he was "not afraid of insulting a man, and even less so of insulting a *negro* [black man or slave]." The insulted young man replied to this with an attack on his offender, and a fight ensued.[16]

Criminal cases demonstrate that during their fights, brawls, or other physical attacks, young men not only engaged in violence but also articulated a discourse that clearly defined courage as the means through which a man's superior manhood and status could be affirmed. This is observable in the fight between the twenty-one-year-old and illiterate day laborer José Francisco da Costa and the twenty-two-year-old farmer Trajino Gomes Guedes. According to a witness who testified in the assault trial against José Francisco, he (Francisco) had told Trajino to "stay away" from a woman named Inés— who allegedly had suffered a beating at the hands of Trajino—or, otherwise, "the one who would receive a beating would be him." To this remark Trajino had responded by holding his knife, saying that "no man is more macho, or brave, than another," and by daring José Francisco to a physical fight.[17] According to these understandings, the fight would determine who the bravest man was, and in consequence, the one whose orders would be obeyed, in spite of any other shortcomings in his life. Such assertions made sense within hierarchical communities in which class, color, economic autonomy, and connections with powerful patrons determined the rank of poor men as either honorable or dishonorable. Yet, they also reveal that some poor sertanejos interposed their claims to honor based on personal courage into the social ranking of masculinities and in that way asserted a form of power over others, especially among their peers.

In this discourse of masculinity, fear—as the opposite of courage—was shunned as an emotion that real men did not feel, and the performance of violence was required as the most visible sign of a man's lack of fear, or bravery. This is put in evidence in the 1871 case of the thirty-year-old and illiterate farmer José Ferino de Moraes, from the town of São Francisco, who exchanged blows with José Francisco de Sá. According to a witness, the fight started one afternoon because José Ferino had insulted José Francisco by asking him, "What are you running from, cabra. Are you afraid?" after gun shots that had been heard in the air had startled José Francisco.[18] The significance of José Merino's insinuation that José Francisco was a coward, or less than a man because he became startled, lies in the fact that it required an aggressive response in order for a man—even more a man of color—to stop the ridiculing of his character as passive, fearful, and obviously emasculated.

Clearly, some young men used violent assertions of masculine valor as a way to establish honor and reputation within relationships of power with their peers. Social-economic factors such as the itinerancy of poor young men, the fluidity in their employment arrangements, and the large numbers of men who lived outside family relationships injected a degree of danger and a sharp potential for physical aggression into the competitive culture of male sociability among young sertanejos. Moreover, because this culture of male interaction sanctioned risk-taking, rivalry, and physical daring as privileged avenues to demonstrate possession of the "natural" attributes of masculinity and honor, young sertanejos maintained that violent defense and protection of honor was a "natural" necessity.[19] Nevertheless, it was not only poor rural men, acting within a culture of honor that authorized violence, who construed their aggressive responses to insult as "natural," and therefore instinctive. Indeed, as we shall see, the practice of criminal justice played a part in strengthening the discourse according to which men, including those that were young and poor, enjoyed a gender-specific right to validate their honor through violence.

Because the expansion of the Imperial state translated into growing official preoccupation with the preservation of order and the punishment of crime, at least some young men who participated in drunken brawls and those who murdered other men for reasons of honor—actions that according to prosecutors and police authorities occurred as a result of "frivolous" motives—were arrested, indicted, and even put to trial. Yet, the workings of criminal courts in these cases, as in those of physical offenses against unattached women, were loaded with contradictions. For example, in several instances juries absolved young men who were indicted for physically assaulting other men in fights and sambas, in accordance with the extenuating circumstances established in the Criminal Code that justified the practice of certain acts in vindication of insults or other perceived attacks on honor. In these cases, the courts legitimized the practice of private vengeance among young men, and reinforced a discourse that justified masculine aggression in defense of honor.[20] This is visible through the case of the illiterate young brothers José Vicente and José Alexandre, from the Lugar São Tomé, Itapagé, who were absolved from a charge of aggravated assault, even after a police investigation based on witnesses' depositions and a physical exam established that the brothers had indeed assaulted and wounded the victim, Francisco Gonçalves da Silva. According to the jury, José Vicente and José Alexandre had committed the crime "in self-defense and in defense of their honor," which had been offended by Francisco Gonçalves's insinuations that José Vicente was impotent in his sexual relations with his lover Ana. The legal basis for this decision rested upon two extenuating circumstances established in the Criminal Code that allowed juries to sentence lesser punishments or even exonerate offenders when they could prove that they had perpetrated a crime in defense of honor.[21]

In addition, criminal courts contributed to recirculate shared assumptions regarding men's seeming innate tendencies to aggression and the inevitability and acceptability of violence in defense of honor. For instance, in his deposition in the aggravated assault trial of Alexandre Rodrigues, who had wounded Luís Pereira de Sousa in a fight, Alexandre emphasized that "it was natural" for him to defend himself violently from the insults launched by Luís, who attacked his honor by saying that he did not have any whiskers. This argumentation obviously achieved the goal of gaining the sympathies of male jury members in favor of Alexandre, as he was acquitted, despite the fact that the indictment, based on depositions by witnesses, had proven that Alexandre had committed the crime. Some of the rhetorical strategies that young sertanejos used to obtain exoneration or shorter sentences from jury tribunals included appeals to the idea that a "provocation" or insult launched against a man's honor necessitated a violent and automatic response. The thirty-year-old farmer Vicente Luís dos Santos, for instance, argued in his defense from charges of aggravated assault that the reason why he hit Manoel Alves with a club in the market of São Mateus was that "he had been provoked by Manoel, who was insulting and attacking him," and he "only wanted to defend himself." According to witnesses, Manoel Alves had violently shooed Vicente Luís's dog, an action that resulted in a fight during which Manoel Alves called Vicente Luís "a liar." The justification of his actions as in agreement with a code of honor worked effectively in Vicente Luís's case. Although in June of 1875 the municipal judge charged the defendant with aggravated assault and argued that "a disapproved motive compelled him to commit the crime," the jury sentenced Vicente Luís to a minimum prison term of six months because, in their view, "[He] did perpetrate the assault, but not due to a censured motivation."[22]

Clauses from the Criminal Code that were often invoked in the sentencing of these cases and that, in a paradoxical manner, excused drunken brawls also helped to perpetuate the discourse regarding men's inability to judge their capacity to inflict pain when they engaged in fights or other physical contests to prove personal honor. For instance, the twenty-four-year-old and illiterate farmer Felipe Gonçalves de Santiago was charged with the homicide of Francisco Benjamin, which took place in a samba in the municipality of Itapagé in June of 1874. According to the witnesses' declarations, a twenty-two-year-old man named Raimundo Vieira Venâncio was playing a viola in the samba when Felipe took it away from him and left the party. Benjamin got up and confronted Felipe, attempting to force him to return the viola so that the samba could continue. The witnesses noted that Benjamin attacked Felipe with a stick. Felipe then hit Benjamin with the viola, which ended up in pieces, and then wounded him with his knife. In his deposition during the proceedings, Felipe noted that "he did not know whether he was indeed the author of these wounds, since he was completely drunk on that occasion." In another section of the interrogation, the defendant explained that he did not remember much because "his judgment was totally impaired, as he was extremely inebriated." After testimony by several witnesses established that the defendant wounded Benjamin, the jury absolved him from the accusation, citing two extenuating circumstances stipulated in the Criminal Code. First, that "the delinquent committed the crime in response to another person's attack," and second, that "the delinquent perpetuated the crime in a state of intoxication."[23]

This type of judicial decision, in all probability, contributed to strengthen the notoriety of young men who not only used violence as a way to as-

sert masculine status but also got away with it, even if they were brought
to trial. Moreover, although only a minority of men who committed acts
of violence ever came under the radar of the criminal justice system, the
reputation of those who were exonerated most likely spread like wildfire in
backlands communities. As Domingos Olímpio described in his 1903 novel
Luzia-Homem, townspeople followed closely the developments in criminal
courts, and enthusiastically gossiped and embellished details of the depositions and results of criminal proceedings. Thus, in various ways, the criminal
justice system contributed to the diffusion of discourses that justified and
normatized the practice of violence in service of honor among young sertanejos.[24]

Popular poets also celebrated the violent deeds and daring of young men
in verse and, by traveling throughout the sertões and singing about courageous masculinities, contributed to the discursive exaltation of the reputation of tough men. For instance, the Cego Sinfrônio repeated the following
verses of the "Cantiga do Vilela," an Imperial-period popular poem that expressed exultation over the "bravery" of a violent man who established his
reputation by killing his own brother at a young age:

Com doze anos de idade,	When he was twelve years old,
Numa véspa de S. João,	In the night before the feast of Saint John
Vilela mais o seu mano	Vilela and his brother
Tivero uma altercação:	Had an altercation:
Só por causa dum cachimbo	Just because of a pipe
Vilela mata o irmão.	Vilela murdered his brother.[25]

By popularizing the courage of young sertanejo men, whether fictional or
real, cantadores played a part in conventionalizing the seemingly natural link
between a man's ability to exercise violence and honorable masculinities in
the backlands. This association, in turn, appealed to the needs of poor young
men who, in all likelihood, listened to and celebrated the verses of popular
poets. According to a foreign traveler who visited the backlands during the
first half of the nineteenth century, young men in particular congregated on
Sunday afternoons in cattle fazendas, where they entertained themselves by
joking around, drinking alcohol, and often singing and listening to the songs
and verses of popular poets.[26]

Ultimately, the discourse produced by young sertanejos, jury tribunals,
and popular poets who either exalted violent men or exonerated violent
deeds committed in the name of honor contributed to the representation
of the backlanders as "naturally" conditioned to violence and as obsessed
with honor. In turn, this discourse obscured the marginal positions of poor

sertanejos, especially young ones, within the social hierarchies of their communities and the forms of gendered denigration that accompanied their dislocation and the strategies they used to survive during the chaotic last third of the nineteenth century. Indeed, it was in a context of greater geographic mobility, family separation, and extreme subsistence insecurity in which some young sertanejos came to rely on a masculine culture of social interaction, shadowed by competition and physical risk, as a means to cultivate and defend their manhood and honor and their ability to exercise power over others, even if only for a moment.

Access to Resources, the Court System, and Violence

During the last third of the nineteenth century, poor sertanejos not only resorted to violence as a strategy to establish some claims to honor and respectability among their peers. As we will see, conflict over scarce natural resources such as land, water, and animals, which had a direct impact on the livelihood of the sertanejos, at times led to aggression, although the escalation to violence was not automatic. Chapter 3 has already established that face-to-face negotiations, mediated by honorable reputations, between men as household heads were of paramount importance in regulating land issues and resource utilization in the interior of Ceará, where land tenure structures were remarkably fragile, and land boundaries remained in a generalized state of confusion. We have also seen that fights tended to break out between neighbors and coproprietors in joint landholdings when accelerated competition for resources rendered honor-sanctioned conventions unworkable. Nevertheless, the precariousness and the proximity to ruin that resulted from environmental and social-economic factors during the late nineteenth century intensified tensions over land and resource utilization to the point that sertanejos were completely unable to share resources or reach compromises with their neighbors. For instance, during the Great Drought, José de Castro Torres stabbed his neighbor Delmiro Ferreira de Oliveira after Delmiro complained that José's removal of his horses from their joint capoeira had been harmful to his interests, since his animals were too thin and needed to be inside the enclosure. José de Castro claimed the horses were destroying what was left of his plantings in the capoeira.[27]

Moreover, as the disruption of livelihoods persisted over the years, and small ranchers and farmers persevered in their attempt to fully utilize resources, conflict and competition between neighbors and coproprietors became long-lasting and extremely urgent. Such conditions profoundly strained community and interpersonal relations, which, in turn, precipitated enduring rivalries. For instance, the farmer Raimundo Ferreira Saraiva, resident in the Lugar Olho d'Água, sustained a feud with José de Castro Silva for ten years, between 1866 and 1876. According to their neighbors, both of them "judged that they have rights over the lands where José's house was built in 1866."[28]

Evidently, the social relations that were crucial to guarantee access to scarce productive resources for poor families, and in particular to land and water, were fast eroding. Consequently, judicial demarcation of land or an alternative means of defining property boundaries became an urgent necessity. Yet, a series of conditions restricted the access of smallholders to the courts, despite the fact that judicial districts and municipal judgeships expanded during the second half of the nineteenth century. For instance, land delimitation through civil justice proceedings was out of reach for most poor farmers and ranchers because these processes required the presentation of deeds of sale, notarized copies of sesmaria grants, and less often, copies of partilhas, to prove the legitimacy of a family's claims to land. Small, mainly illiterate landowners often did not possess such documents, nor did they have enough resources to pay lawyers to prepare their cases. In addition, contested claims over the same lands and questions regarding the validity of each party's titles could lead to lengthy and costly litigations that were beyond the reach of the poor.[29]

Sertanejo men as household heads who disputed their neighbors' or co-proprietors' right to landed property or other resources typically could not defend their positions or settle their disagreements in civil courts because of the high cost of legal fees and attorneys. For instance, only two illiterate farmers and ranchers appeared as plaintiffs in the examined collection of civil proceedings related to land disputes (including citations for payment of indemnities, eviction actions, and suits for adjudication of lands) from the municipalities of Jucás and Tamboril.[30] The popular poet Dantas Quesado observed the class-based accessibility to the civil justice system and the inability of poor backlanders to access the courts to protect their interests and commented on that matter with these words:

Há quatro coisas no mundo,	There are four things in this world,
Que é difícil de se ver:	That are very difficult to encounter:
É pobre fazer ação,	The poor pursuing a suit,
Rico deixar de morrer,	The rich not dying,
Branco querer bem a negro,	White people caring for blacks,
Terra boa sem chover.	And good land without rains.[31]

Poor farmers and ranchers not only had great difficulties in gaining access to the civil justice apparatus. They also faced eviction and even confiscation of property as a result of their inability to defend themselves in legal suits against them for "squatting" on land they considered their own. Illiterate, without land titles, connections, or money with which to pay lawyers, people like the cotton farmers Manoel José de Sousa and his wife, Ana Alves de Brito, from Tamboril, and the manioc farmers Antônio Rodrigues Barreto and his wife, Germana Maria de Jesus, from Jucás, lost their access to land and their livelihoods as a result of eviction proceedings. By 1884, residents of the region of Ibiapaba decried larger and more powerful landowners' use of the civil courts as a means to deprive poorer neighbors of land by narrating a legend that told of the fate brought to the soul of a wealthy resident of São Bento. According to the legend, this greedy landowner who had dispossessed his poor neighbors of land through the use of civil courts, became a hairless dog after his death, and in a certain season of the year desperately ran barking through the entire mountain range, paying for his offense.[32]

Typically, smallholders could engage the mediation of civil courts in land delimitation disputes only when they were coproprietors or had ties of patronage with wealthier or more powerful landowners. For instance, illiterate and presumably poorer farmers and ranchers appeared as plaintiffs in land delimitation proceedings in Jucás only when they held lands jointly with wealthier individuals, such as Lieutenant Colonel Manoel da Silva Pereira Costa Leal, and Captain João da Silva Pereira, members of the very influential Silva Pereira family of this municipality.[33]

Poor farmers and ranchers who sought to use the criminal justice apparatus in their disputes for land or other productive resources also needed the assistance of wealthier landowners or local notables in order to criminally pursue neighbors or coproprietors who invaded or encroached on their lands through accusations of *dano*.[34] The criminal procedure established damage of property as a "private crime" whose punishment was of concern only to one party. Consequently, a *queixa* was necessary to initiate criminal proceedings. In principle, any offended person, regardless of class, could present a *queixa* to the municipal judge or police authorities in his absence. Certain conditions in the criminal procedure, however, limited the ability of poor, and often illiterate, farmers and ranchers to pursue these cases on their own. First, the accuser needed to sign the *queixa*, and if he or she did not know how to write, the court had to first sanction an acceptable *procurador*, or a person with power-of-attorney, as the one who could sign the document for the accuser. Second, because these criminal cases were private, the offended parties had to pay all the fees associated with the initial investigations. When the municipal judges or police authorities established that the accusers were "impoverished" and could not afford the cost of a lawsuit, the private accusations of these "miserable people" became public criminal investigations, headed by the district attorney.[35] Nevertheless, in order for the court to undertake such a case, it first had to establish the actual "state of misery" of a poor person, by demanding a letter from the local priest and other witnesses who attested to the "recognized" poverty of the accuser, as well as to his or her good name.

It is not surprising then that only those sertanejos who had connections with wealthier landowners or local notables could use the criminal courts to press for reparations when their property had been damaged, invaded, or encroached upon by land-hungry neighbors. For example, the illiterate farmer Joaquim Ferreira Diniz asserted that the also illiterate farmer Manoel Sousa had the support of an influential local notable and had enjoyed the assistance of the municipal judge and the public prosecutor in opening a criminal case against his family. The accusers sued Diniz and his family for payment of indemnities for the destruction of a property that Sousa considered his own.[36] Ties of patronage not only influenced the possibility of initiating these cases but also affected their outcome. Partial judges could order the arrest of those without powerful connections after indicting them for dano, without requesting land titles or surveying the landholdings in dispute. This was the experience of the cowboys Eufrásio Pereira da Silva and Estanislao de Oliveira Bastos from Jucás in 1864.[37]

Larger and more powerful landowners in competition for resources with smaller farmers and ranchers were comparatively more able to engage their neighbors in criminal courts. In fact, the majority of plaintiffs in a sample of criminal cases for dano from the municipalities of Jucás and Tamboril during the period between 1865 and 1889 were literate, and presumably wealthier. These prosecutions typically targeted poor and illiterate farmers and ranchers as defendants.[38] Moreover, larger and wealthier landholders could exercise influence not only over judges but also over police officials, who, in turn, further victimized unconnected farmers and ranchers and weakened their ability to hold on to landed resources. For instance, the semiliterate farmer Manoel Sousa Bezerra from Jucás declared that his literate coproprietor José Raimundo Ferreira along with a police detachment "despotically" removed him and his brothers from a property that they were clearing and that according to him belonged to his father.[39]

Small landowners who found themselves targeted by criminal proceedings for reparations faced additional hardship and a decreasing economic position as a result of arrests. In an attempt to pay bail, some of them mortgaged their properties, and if found guilty faced jail sentences of twenty days to four months. The prospect of such a bleak future undoubtedly forced some poor farmers and ranchers who found themselves involved in land disputes to seek help from influential patrons who could pay lawyers for their defense, thus minimizing the risks of reliance on public defenders who had no vested interest in their cases. They also appealed to wealthier patrons to finance their bails, as was the case of the illiterate farmer Antônio Ferreira de Lima, who got assistance from Pedro Alves de Oliveira and João Batista de Oliveira to pay his Rs. 5:000$000 bail in a property damage case.[40]

The limitations that poor sertanejos experienced in using the criminal and civil justice systems effectively barred them from judicially delimiting their landholdings or asserting their rights over landed property in a nonviolent manner. It was under these conditions that fights erupted in roças when one party attempted to keep the other from planting or harvesting, or from building fences or other land improvements. We can get a glimpse of these violent contests for resources in criminal cases of assault and unpremeditated homicide. For instance, in 1871, Pedro Antônio de Sousa and José Gomes da Mota murdered Antônio Batista in the Lugar Traição in Jucás, after Batista along with a group of armed men had attacked them with shotguns and accused them of taking the harvest that belonged to him. In some cases, sertanejos engaged the help of other men to perform assaults or armed attacks against those who had become their enemies because of competition for resources. For instance, in 1874 the farmer and rancher Antônio Rodrigues de Almeida sent a group of six men to attack Alexandre da Cunha Marreiro with knives and clubs. The group threw Alexandre on the ground and cut an ear and an arm to retaliate for his having cut some sugarcanes from lands that he considered his, but that Antônio regarded as his own.[41]

As they faced deadly competition for shrinking resources, an inability to reach consensus with neighbors and coproprietors, and the lack of access to a criminal and civil justice system that often victimized and dispossessed them, small farmers and ranchers also used bravado as the means to attempt to retain access to productive resources. For instance, the farmer Antônio Rodrigues de Almeida had said in front of a large group of people that "for Alexandre [the farmer who had destroyed the sugarcane plantings located in lands they disputed] he did not want justice, because he could enforce it with his own two hands." Illiterate farmers told their neighbors that they would pay the reparations for the damage caused by their invading cattle onto planted fields "with the tip of a knife," or that a coproprietor "better shorten" his steps and those of his goats on his way to his own roçado. Furthermore, some poor sertanejos emphasized their capacity to use violence—by carrying knives and machetes to planting fields, and destroying land improvements with the help of armed gangs of men—as a way to put limits on their neighbors' ability to challenge their intentions and use of contested lands.[42]

Through all of these actions, postures, and words, small farmers and ranchers manifested masculinities centered on violence as the only tool capable of enforcing their dominance and their designs on the use of contested lands or water. Moreover, just as in the case of young men who fought to cleanse offended honor or other sertanejos who engaged in brawls for reasons related to the state formation process as illustrated in Chapter 2, these men discursively exalted their masculine courage and their ability in the handling of weapons. It is likely that developing a reputation for bravery was the last recourse for sertanejos who managed to retain some landed property and livestock. It represented a means to obtain from neighbors and coproprietors respect for their claims to property, as these rivals might fear that daring and armed sertanejos could prove capable of violence. Yet in engaging in violence and bravado, these rural men contributed to a representation of themselves as the possessors of an aggressive masculinity. As we will see below, the practice of acts of violence by free poor men who joined bandit gangs and the celebration of famous bandits by popular poets also contributed to circulate and propagate a discourse on the "violent propensities" of the sertanejos.

Banditry and Honor

From the 1870s onward, the backlands of Ceará and other Northeastern provinces witnessed a significant intensification of banditry. Armed gangs of men who roved the sertão committing murders, stealing cattle, and pillaging fazendas were not, however, new to the sertão. Banditry had constituted a recurring problem since the late seventeenth century because of the fragility of the institutions of law, order, and justice under colonial rule. The weakness of the colonial state in the backlands translated into a virtual domination of the hinterlands by landowning clans who exercised ample private power through the use of violence and patronage. In turn, disputes for land or local power between rival family clans precipitated a series of bloody feuds that resulted in the formation of private, if short-lived, bands of kinsmen, their cowboys, and other dependants. These gangs avenged wrongdoings through theft, murder, and the pillage of property owned by their enemies or those associated with them. During the decades after independence, when severe political instability meshed with interfamilial rivalries, bandit activity became associated with struggles between political adversaries. Local potentates either organized armed gangs or hired bandits to attack the property and life of their political enemies.[43]

The bandit activity of the late nineteenth century sharply differed from that of the late colonial and early Imperial periods. Since the 1870s, professional bands of brigands, whose spheres of operation were wider than those of kin-related bandit gangs, became increasingly common in the interior. Thus, small and larger bands of *cangaceiros* (a term that came into use in the late nineteenth century and that denoted a professional bandit) lived off looting and robbery, extortion, and other illegal activities. Lasting anywhere from a few months to two years, and, in a few cases, ten to sixteen years, brigand bands such as the "Viriatos," "Brilhantes," and "Pereiros [*sic*]" caused widespread fear, as they attacked and murdered those who posed resistance to their actions and those whom they counted as their enemies. This type of bandit activity became even more visible during the Great Drought, when bands of armed men reportedly sacked fazendas, attacked food deposits where relief commissions stored foods, killed cattle, and even assaulted drought refugees. In some cases, these bandit groups provided private "services," such as murder or other assaults as requested by local notables who paid them or offered them protection from police and judicial prosecution.[44]

Some of the standard interpretations of the *cangaço* (a term that refers to the way of life of late-nineteenth- and early-twentieth-century professional bandits) recognize a link between banditry and issues of honor among the leadership of bandit gangs.[45] According to the scholarship, bandit chieftains typically came from middling or wealthy families who were experiencing downward mobility or had been defeated in their struggles for land, or political power by rival families. Often, the violent death of a relative in a long-standing feud sparked a bandit chief's first crime as an act that avenged the honor of their family. Persecuted by police authorities, whose presence gradually increased in the interior from the mid-nineteenth century, and unable to resume their normal lives, these men formed bandit gangs that led to lives of crime and violence.[46] As useful as this interpretation has been in establishing the significance of honor for elite and middling families in the interior, and the connections between familial honor and violence, the existing scholarship has yet to unveil the links between honor and banditry for the rank-and-file members of bandit gangs—by definition, the larger proportion of the bandit population.

But who were the followers of the famous cangaceiros, and why did they join the bands? Even though it is difficult to establish the social origins of the membership of bandit gangs, scattered sources indicate that most rank-and-file bandits were recruited among the poor. For instance, according to criminal records, José Alves and Gonçalo de tal, members of an unnamed group of bandits from Paraíba, who were at work in Jucás in 1877, were illiterate, and presumably poor, and declared farming as their occupation. In addition, both of them were eighteen years old at the time of their arrest. Police chief and provincial presidential reports from Ceará and other Northeastern provinces confirm that the common members of the bandit groups that emerged in the late nineteenth century came from the lower classes. A list based on these sources compiled by Hamilton Monteiro de Mattos shows that bandit gangs were composed of "common men," "miserable people," "run-away slaves," "deserters from the army and police forces," "unfortunate men," "men who have been dislocated by the Paraguayan War," "vagrants," "illiterates," "criminals," and the "unemployed."[47]

The deep social and economic dislocation that backlanders faced during these years and the lack of access to land, labor, water, and other resources necessary for survival left many economically uprooted men with few options for survival. Thus, a life of banditry attracted poor men with the promise of opportunity and perhaps even a degree of upward mobility. Through bandit activities men could at least include meat in their diets, and often partook in the distribution of money and other looted objects. The better-organized and larger bandit gangs at the turn of the twentieth century paid wages to the rank and file that reportedly were higher than those paid in more legal forms of employment. Moreover, as Linda Lewin has shown, although bandit gangs also had their own structures of patronage, bandit life, in all likelihood, exercised an attraction as an activity that demonstrated a degree of independence and autonomy.[48]

A search for material wealth was not the only incentive for poor sertanejos' adherence to the cangaço. According to Amaury de Souza, the confluence of two lines of development explains the rise in professional banditry in the backlands during the late nineteenth century, and the widespread participation of poor men in the bands. On the one hand, a decline in the patriarchal power of large landowners that resulted from broad social and economic change eroded their capacity both to sponsor violence and to provide protection to their dependants. Factors such as the emigration of poor men to the Amazon, the recruitment and return of soldiers from the Paraguayan War, the rise and fall of the cotton boom, and the Great Drought contributed to a rupture of social ties between people of different classes in the backlands. On the other hand, the expansion of the Imperial state that achieved only limited success in bringing order to the interior, challenged the private power of large landowners but failed to protect the masses of the rural population from violence. Caught between landlords and public authorities that often committed acts of aggression against the rural poor, men from this group sought refuge in bandit gangs as a form of protection. For poor men who were run-away slaves, deserters from the army, escapees from recruitment efforts, and for those who had had some run-ins with the law in one manner or another, protection was even more important. Then, it is not surprising that at least in one case, a deserter from the army who joined a known bandit from the area of Tamboril declared that, when he decided to travel with this bandit, he knew of his criminal way of life and the fact that the authorities were searching for him. Still, he felt that his own well-being was "more guaranteed, more secure" once he enjoyed the protection of a tough man.[49]

But beyond protection from state persecution and violence as well as aggression from landlords or enemies, free poor men who joined the cangaço derived masculine honor as a form of status from their bandit activities. For instance, an interview with a cangaceiro, although from a later period, demonstrates that involvement in bandit groups could bring masculine respect to poor sertanejos. Volta Seca, a man who had served as a cangaceiro in the band of the famous bandit Lampião, active in the interior of Bahia and other Northeastern states in the 1920s and 1930s, recalled his first years in the band, where he began working from the age of eleven on, in this manner: "I loved my new life. We were respected everywhere. Fearful sertanejos watched us pass by and that pleased me." In this particular case, a bandit life for this man had meant a change from dependence on his impoverished father's smallholding, and the selling of small quantities of beans, rice, and fruits in his youth, to a more independent way of life whereby he enjoyed the fear and admiration of others, as well as a good diet. Indeed, Volta Seca expressed how his involvement in banditry allowed him to shape his masculine identity, by declaring that sertanejos "saw in me a cangaceiro, a solid man, despite my young age." This example suggests that for poor men, and especially youths who had no other means to establish a masculine reputation, a life of banditry offered the possibility to obtain respect from other sertanejos, an admiration that could easily be confused with fear.[50]

Popular verses from cantadores confirm that the respect and social precedence that bandits, including the rank and file, enjoyed was closely associated with the fear their presence created among the people living in the villages and fazendas they passed by, precisely because of their capacity for violence, which was constructed as inherently male. For instance, in the following verses a popular poet expressed the fears that townspeople felt of Cabeleira, a late-eighteenth-century bandit from Pernambuco.

Fecha a porta, gente,	Close the door, people
Cabeleira aí vem:	Cabeleira is coming:
Matando mulheres,	Killing women,
Meninos também.	And children as well.[51]

Contemporary fiction provides further evidence of this association between respect and masculine competence in inflicting pain and spreading fear. In his 1876 naturalist novel *O Cabeleira*, Baturité-born writer Franklin Távora fictionalized the life story of this famous bandit. In Távora's narrative, when Cabeleira was a little boy, his father trained him in the expert use of a knife. Upon hearing Cabeleira's mother complaining that he was teaching the boy to be a murderer, the father exclaimed: "I will teach him to be courageous. I will teach him to use the knife and not to faint when he sees blood .... Don't you know that a murderer is respected and feared? Do you want to have a son whom nobody respects?" Thus, under certain circumstances, the sertanejos' emphasis on respect and masculine reputation could become indistinguishable from the masculine ability to produce pain and fear. As Cabeleira's father said, "[W]hoever is a man does not cry. Whoever is a man makes others cry."[52]

The respect accorded to members of bandit gangs was available to men regardless of class and age because the reputation of a cangaceiro depended on personal courage and competence in the use of weapons and not on his ability to sustain his family, his success as a farmer or rancher, his access to land, or his race. It is precisely for this reason that black males, caboclos, and other poor men of color who distinguished themselves in bands of cangaceiros were able to achieve masculine honor, despite the fact that race, along with other social notions, determined individual social position in the backlands. Thus, for example, five of the main comrades of Antônio Silvino, the famous cangaceiro who was active in Paraíba between 1897 and 1914, were men of color, whose deeds and bravery became legendary and were celebrated by popular poets.[53] In the following verses, the poet Francisco das Chagas Batista (1882–1930) praised the abilities of Moita Brava, the third companion of Silvino:

O terceiro é um mulato	The third one is a mulatto
Que acode por Moita Brava,	Known by the name of Moita Brava
Este cabra é mais valente	This cabra is more fearless
Do que um touro na cava;	Than a bull in an den
Muitas vezes o pai dele	Many times his father
Ao vê-lo se assombrava!	Was astounded when he observed him.[54]

As poor men joined the forces of the cangaço and relied on aggression and a capacity for violence to gain respect, they emphasized bravery, courage, and mastery in the use of weapons as the measures of a man. For instance, the verses above demonstrate that the manhood of Moita Brava was not in question, at least for popular poets, despite the fact that he was racially mixed, because of his bravery. Indeed, according to the verses, Moita Brava had proved his masculinity even to his father, by being courageous. Moreover, Billy Jaynes Chandler has shown that since the late nineteenth century, cangaceiros adopted a distinctive dress, which, in itself, became emblematic of a violent notion of honor. They wore the traditional Northeastern vaqueiro leather hats and indicated the bandit way of life by stitching them with gold or silver coins. Thus, cangaceiros appropriated the cowboy hat as a symbol of honor—a form of masculine reputation that sertanejo society had traditionally recognized as belonging to vaqueiros, who displayed courage in the physical handling of livestock. In addition, cangaceiros wore two ammunition belts over their shoulders, intersecting at the chest, which created an impressive and often menacing sight and gave them additional fire power. Some celebrated bandits such as Antônio Silvino provided the members of their bands with old uniforms that had belonged to National Guard or police soldiers. These cangaceiros then paraded in their uniforms and took pride in the golden bottoms or other insignias that showed recognition of their talent in the use of weapons, and thus of their masculine honor.[55]

Popular poets celebrated and romanticized the courageous deeds of bandits, the confluence of fear and admiration that qualified the respect that they elicited from the backlands population, and their enjoyment of such recognition. In the following verses, a cantador mythologized the life of Antônio Silvino by adopting the perspective of this famous cangaceiro as the narrator and by describing the commotion that Silvino's presence created, even in heaven and hell:

Cai uma banda do céu	A piece of the sky if falling,
Seca uma parte do mar,	A portion of the ocean is drying up,
O purgatório resfria,	Purgatory is getting cold,
Vê-se o inferno abalar. . .	Hell is in commotion
As almas deixam o degredo,	The souls leave their banishment
Corre o Diabo com medo,	The Devil runs in fear
O Céu Deus manda trancar!	God orders the doors to Heaven to be locked!
Admira todo o mundo	Everybody admires me
Quando eu passo em um lugar. . .	When I go through a place . . .
. . . os montes dizem aos caminhos:	. . .The mountains say to the roads:
—Deixai Silvino passar! . . .	—Let Silvino pass through! . . .[56]

Recurring themes in the popular poetry that celebrated the lives of famous cangaceiros of the late nineteenth century were the violent encounters between bandits and the police soldiers sent to arrest them, as well as the ultimate triumph of the cangaceiros over the representatives of the state. As

Chapter 2 illustrated, the consolidation of Imperial state power in the backlands included the gradual deployment of police and army units to patrol the
sertão in an effort to fight banditry and other forms of crime.Yet, the regulative capacity of the Imperial state was weak, and, consequently, attempts to
arrest bandits often ended in violence, as criminals resisted their capture and
state agents worked to beat cangaceiros into submission. Cantadores, sym-
pathetic to the cause of the bandits, depicted these violent confrontations as
masculine contests of honor.The following verses of a popular song from the
sertões of Rio Grande do Norte celebrated the honor of Jesuíno Brilhante,
a late-nineteenth-century bandit who died in combat with authorities:

Já mataram Jesuíno	They have killed Jesuíno
Acabou-se o valentão!	The courageous man is finished!
Morreu no campo da honra	He died in the field of honor
Sem se entregar à prisão . . .	Without turning himself to a jailing
	sentence . . .[57]

As these verses suggest, the honor of a bandit derived from his personal
courage in violently resisting capture.The popular poem entitled "Cantiga de
Vilela" mentioned above also shows that the measure of manhood for bandits
and their admirers was bravery and ability to kill men, especially those sent to
apprehend them. According to the "Cantiga," the gunman Vilela responded
to a police second lieutenant, who had gone to his house with 180 police
soldiers to take him to jail, with these words:

Seu Alfere Delegado,	Mister Second Lieutenant and Police
	Commissioner,
Largue de tanto zumzum,	Stop your blah blah blah,
Que o home que mata cem,	A man who can kill one hundred
Pode interá cente e um . . .	Can easily kill one hundred and one . . .
Eu hoje ainda não comi,	And today I have not even eaten yet,
Seu Alfere,	Mister Second Lieutenant,
Com você quebro o jejum!	With you I will break my fast![58]

The "Cantiga" exemplifies the extent to which the popular discourse created by cantadores on the bandits' capacity to elicit fear and to demonstrate
bravery depicted these qualities as "natural" to cangaceiros or as innate tendencies, akin to other instinctual behaviors, such as eating.

    But popular poets and bandits were not the only social actors responsible
for the production of a discourse that emphasized the "natural" aggression of
cangaceiros in particular, or of male sertanejos at large. In a paradoxical manner, state authorities, such as provincial presidents and police chiefs, as well
as local delegados and subdelegados—concerned as they were with bringing

order to the hinterlands—contributed to the elaboration and propagation of this discourse. As José Ernesto Pimentel Filho has demonstrated, in their correspondence and annual reports, these authorities constructed an image of free poor Cearense men as driven by "hot passions, strange hatreds, and the spirit of revenge." Moreover, in their view, the sertanejos were "barbarians," who often employed "brute force" in "horrendous and frequent" crimes. These evils were, in the authorities' analysis, "habitual," and had been present in the backlands population since time immemorial.[59] In this manner, state officials disseminated the representation of crime and aggression—including violent assertions of honor—as "natural tendencies" of poor men from the sertão.

Conclusions

During the verbal exchanges leading to the fight between Alexandre Rodrigues and Luís Pereira de Sousa examined above, both of these young men expressed what to contemporary readers might seem an absurd concern with whiskers—as the physical embodiment of a confrontational manhood—and a club—as a precious commodity whose possession was worth a deadly fight. Despite their own claims regarding their "natural" impulses to cleanse honor through bloodshed, the importance of clubs and whiskers for sertanejo males—even if shaped by cultural notions of honor—was not related to an essentialized violent masculinity. Instead, as this chapter has shown, the cultural value of weapons and of a man's strength in handling violence was reinforced within a context in which some male backlanders could only rely on aggression as the means to resolve the conflicts unleashed by the broad pressures of the last four decades of the nineteenth century, and to exercise a form of power or authority over others. Thus, rapidly impoverished young men employed culturally sanctioned forms of masculine challenge and aggression to establish status and prestige among their peers, as the loss of land, slaves, and livestock that affected their families since the 1860s had undermined their capacity to sustain honor claims contingent on economic success and property ownership. Likewise, male household heads who managed to retain smallholdings and cattle during these chaotic years resorted to interpersonal violence and bravado as the primary medium through which they sought to defend their landed patrimony. Facing the increasing failure of the old system of conventions between neighbors and coproprietors to guarantee property boundaries and their inability to use the expanding civil and criminal court system to settle their land and resource disputes, these small farmers and ranchers stabbed, wounded, and even killed their neighbors, in an effort to assert their rights to ownership and use of small plots of land and livestock. Moreover, as a growing number of destitute and, in all likelihood, young Cearense men turned to banditry in the absence of other viable occupations, they came to depend on aggression even for their survival.

In all these instances of violence, free poor men configured masculine spaces—whether in sambas, roças, villages, or cattle fields—in which they publicly tested their courage and their skills in the handling of weapons. And even though some of the competitive arenas of male socialization through which sertanejos derived a form of reputation received cultural sanction, the performance of violence within them was not only a cultural reflex. Instead, the winners in these contests managed to exercise authority, even if momentarily, over other men, to enforce their plans on the use of contested productive resources, and, in some cases, even to earn a living, within an environment of rigid hierarchy that ranked men according to race, wealth, and connections. Moreover, through these violent exchanges, as well as through the fights that poor men sustained as both sources and subjects of Imperial state power and the beatings designed to set up the boundaries of autonomous female behavior, these sertanejos manifested hegemonic masculinities that required aggression to uphold claims to authority or dominance. Clearly, in a context of urgent competition for survival, separation of families, geographical dislocation, and destitution, the range of strategies to defend patriarchy and to establish the privatized forms of masculine authority that were necessary to negotiate the social and material realities of backlands communities had become severely limited. Therefore, the reproduction of interpersonal masculine violence became the only available strategic response—creative and yet destructive—for many sertanejos to navigate their unsettling world.

The sertanejos' use of aggression and, just as important, their retelling of the details of fights and attacks that took place in public, contributed to reproduce a cultural discourse that exalted courage as the "natural" masculine endowment that guaranteed their honor and proved their manhood. In this discourse of masculinity, those who displayed fearfulness were perceived as the rightful targets of humiliation, since their fear exposed their lack of bravery and, consequently, of status and respectability. Other historical actors, besides the sertanejos who engaged in brawls, stabbings, and insults of other men, elaborated a discourse that praised violent hegemonic masculinities and approved the use of violence in the name of honor. Cantadores who visited fazendas and villages and collected the tales of bandits and tough men recirculated those stories and discursively applauded the perceived "natural" abilities of courageous men among audiences made up predominantly of young men. As careful observers of the ironies of their time, popular poets commented on the ineffectiveness of the Imperial state in subordinating bandits, and the ways in which state action, in fact, generated a measure of masculine aggression. In celebrating the daring of cangaceiros in facing and defeating the police and armed forces and in narrating the encounters between bandits and state representatives as contests for honorable manhood, cantadores contributed to broaden the reputation of tough men.

Curiously, police authorities at the municipal and provincial levels, and local male elites as judges and jury members in criminal courtrooms, also played a role in the diffusion of a discourse that sanctioned some forms of aggression among the sertanejos. Criminal courts staffed by jurors who subscribed to the belief that men enjoyed a right to exercise private vengeance and who exonerated some young men after they got caught perpetrating some of these acts, in effect, legitimized the use of violence to defend masculine honor. Anchored to the contradictory principles of the Imperial Criminal Code, the courts also sanctioned the notion that men lacked discernment and, more important, control over their capacity for violence. Paradoxically, provincial and municipal authorities generated a social-control discourse that criminalized the sertanejos as "naturally" aggressive and as the possessors of base passions and instincts that drove them to violence for the sake of honor. In all of these cases, as in the verses elaborated by cantadores and the insults launched by men during their fights, sertanejos constituted themselves and were constituted by others as "naturally" or inherently violent. This naturalizing discourse, in turn, concealed the mechanisms, including the process of state formation itself, as well the social, economic and environmental transformations that, in fact, had restricted many sertanejos' options to deal with conflict and establish honor and status without resorting to the use of violence and aggression.

Conclusion

"Fearles vaqueiro," "cabra macho," "jagunço," "sertanejo honrado." These easily recognizable images of rural men from the semiarid interior of the Northeast have abounded in the popular and scholarly imagination in Brazil since at least the late nineteenth century. At times reviled, praised, feared, and even pitied, the long-standing representation of the sertanejo macho creates an inherent association between the hinterlands, as a geographical and cultural space, and gender, through the intersection of Northeastern rurality and violent manhood. Nevertheless, the portrayal of belligerent backlands masculinity—even if politically useful in the regional elites' past disputes for resources and recognition at the national level—obscures the processes through which these forms of masculine identity were constructed in everyday life, and conceals the power struggles associated with gender in the region.[1] By contrast, this study has demonstrated that the hegemonic patterns of manhood that a stratum of free poor men in the backlands of Ceará manifested after 1845 were not only the result of a cultural prescription or past discourse—even if they were constrained by local cultural referents. Instead, they were constituted through the relations of power in which these men participated in an environment of conflict and urgency for survival. Thus, as free poor Cearense men negotiated access to productive resources, privileges over female kin and other women, positions of authority over slaves, peers, and some social superiors, and even the measure of control that state representatives exercised over their lives, they configured hegemonic masculinities centered on honor, and when not possible, centered on the practice of violence. Likewise, this book has shown that these patterns of masculinity were not as immutable and stable as the stereotype of the nordestino macho, or its broader-encompassing variety—the Latin American

macho—would imply. Instead of being frozen in time, the masculinities of
free poor men from Ceará—even those under which violence became the
main means for the domination of women and other men—were elaborated
and reinforced in social practice, including the use of aggression for symbolic
and material ends, especially during the conflictive years of the last third of
the nineteenth century.

This study has touched on several of the everyday experiences through
which free poor Cearense men derived the meanings of gender and honor.
Chief among them were the internal dynamics of family life, class and race relations, the development of strategies of survival and household reproduction,
arenas of male sociability, sexuality, state formation, discourse, and the practice
of bodily aggression. Nonetheless, this book does not claim to be an exhaus-
tive treatment of the history of gender, honor, and violence in Northeastern
Brazil, or even in Ceará during the years under study. Indeed, this work asks
as many questions as it answers and hopes to inspire the publication of more
document-based studies that will contribute to deconstruct the depiction
of aggression as an essential feature of sertanejo masculine identity, and to
replace it with a historically grounded understanding of the social construction of gender in the region. For instance, the research presented above has
demonstrated the ways in which the process of Imperial-state building in the
Cearense sertão, especially the expansion of police and criminal justice institutions and the redoubling of efforts to discipline free poor men, generated
disorder and violence and incited the reproduction of aggressive masculinities
among lower-class men. Nevertheless, an area that still needs investigation re-
lates to the question of how other political developments at the national level,
particularly the evolution of party politics, affected the practice of violence
and understandings about honor among men from this group. Judy Bieber's
study of politics and society in the São Francisco River region of northern
Minas Gerais shows that a significant effect of state centralization and the
creation of a national political party machine during the Imperial period
was precisely the exacerbation of political violence and the coercion of free
poor men in local elections in such peripheral areas as the *sertão mineiro*.[2] In a
similar manner, we must explore the ways in which regional and local politics,
including the alliances and the feuds between family clans that populate the
local histories of Northeastern intellectuals, were articulated into, instead of
isolated from, national-level party politics and ideological battles. In this sense,
Billy Jaynes Chandler's analysis of the sertão of the Inhamuns constitutes a
pioneer treatment of how the Carcarás and the Feitosas, the two leading families from that area of Ceará, organized themselves into Liberal and Conservative factions and disputed power all through the nineteenth century.[3] Yet, we

still need to account for how local elites and the poor alike understood the discourse of national party affiliation, and the ways in which participation in electoral fights, voting, and other political developments affected the constitution of masculine identities among lower-class men.

The workings of the system of rural patronage and the basis for the creation of patron-client ties between local notables and poor sertanejos are issues that speak directly to relations of power and domination—which become central in the constitution of masculinities—and that are in need of much more empirical research than they have received. The prevailing image of the Northeastern interior emphasizes the unchanging supremacy, based on the latifundia pattern of landholding, of cattle fazendeiros and other large landowners over the scores of dispossessed farmers, cowboys, day laborers, and other lower-class sertanejos. According to this popular representation, as well as much of the existing scholarly literature, this form of inequality promoted ties of patronage between the landed and the landless, and forced attitudes of dependence, submission, and loyalty from the poor to their powerful patrons. Nevertheless, as the research presented above has made clear, by the mid-nineteenth century, the structure of land tenure—at least in the studied municipalities from Ceará—revealed itself as a lot more complex than the enduring image of the backlands allows. Moreover, precisely because of the widespread existence of small and midsize holdings, a sizable stratum of poor families were able to develop autonomous, if still quite vulnerable, livelihoods based on small-scale farming and ranching, at least for a couple of decades. These findings, therefore, raise important questions: if latifundia did not characterize the hinterlands during all historical periods in all locations, what was the basis for the establishment of patron-client ties in backlands communities? What other forms of domination and power fostered the need for patron-client relations in specific communities? Studies by Joan Meznar and Peter Beattie make a persuasive case about how service in the National Guard and changes in military recruitment laws during the Imperial period forced men from the ranks of the honorable poor in Paraíba and Ceará to enter into relations of protection and loyalty from powerful patrons.[4] Yet, we still do not really understand how lasting these ties were and whether these relations intersected with other forms of class domination.

The viability of the system of rural patronage—that is, the manner in which patronage as an institution was affected by broad social and economic pressures—and the intersections between patronage, honor, and gender also need scholarly reconsideration from the perspective of change over time. While the well-known image of the semiarid hinterlands depicts patronage as an almost inherent feature of its seemingly fixed social landscape, several

scholars, including Roger Cunniff, Amaury de Souza, and Manuel Domingos, have suggested that the transformations and community pressures of
the late-nineteenth century contributed to the breakdown of patron-client
relations.[5] Although not directly investigating the question of patronage, my
examination of the rapidly changing conditions of this period appears to
validate the hypothesis that those years witnessed the emergence of a much
more complex, conflict-ridden, and mobile society, where the establishment
and maintenance of long-lasting patron-client bonds became increasingly
difficult and perhaps even untenable. Among the broad-ranging forms of
social change that appear to have eroded ties of patronage the following
stand out: the rapid subdivision of landholdings resulting from inheritance
and land sales that affected large landowning families; migrations of drought
refugees from other provinces who did not immediately establish ties with
powerful families; increasing dependence on agriculture and the consequent
competition for scarce resources among neighbors and coproprietors who
lived in a drought-prone environment; the gradual decline of slavery that
deprived wealthy and poor alike of an important source of labor; changes
in the international market for Northeastern cotton; and the onslaught of
the Great Drought in 1877, with its consequent short- and long-scale migrations, social displacement, and family separations. Yet, there are very few
studies, based on documentary evidence, detailing how patronage as an institution functioned under such tumultuous conditions and how free poor
people in the backlands re-created patron-client ties during times of hardship, conflict, and dislocation.[6] An examination of baptismal and marriage
records from parochial archives and of the practice of godparenting over time
could prove a productive beginning point for an exploration of the degree
of significance of this institution in shifting historical contexts and its importance in the constitution of gender identities among lower-class groups from
the interior.

One of the most significant costs of the obfuscation of gender in the
Northeastern backlands that has resulted from the apparently gender-neutral,
pervasive, and long-standing representation of the region itself as masculine and violent is the virtual absence of women—and especially lower-class
women—from the historical literature. The very few, and therefore, notable
exceptions to this trend are the works by Miridan Knox Falci, Joan Meznar,
and Otaviano Vieira, Jr., which treat aspects of the social history of interior
communities during the nineteenth century from the perspective of specific
groups of women.[7] Yet, the dearth of studies of poor women as gendered
subjects, influenced in no small degree by the lack of primary sources available to write their histories, remains puzzling, especially given the increasing

attention that women's and gender history have received in the Brazilian scholarship since the mid-1970s. It seems as if the denigration, or conversely, the idealization of sertanejo masculinity, and the consequent and unacknowledged assumption that patriarchy is an ingrained and natural backlands institution has rendered the study of women and of gender relations in the region a mute topic. Confronting this trend, this book constitutes an initial approximation to the experiences of historically situated sertanejas and the ways in which the social, economic, and political conditions of the second half of the nineteenth century conditioned relations of power between men and women, both within and outside households, and the practices through which women and men constituted gender identities within a specific milieu. The research presented above has demonstrated, for instance, that the social-economic and environmental dislocations of the post-1860s disrupted family life and effectively placed a large number of women in the position of household heads and main sources of sustenance for their children and other dependants. Nevertheless, local conceptualizations of gender hierarchy and male privilege did not keep pace with the broad-ranging social transformations of the period. Instead, these increasingly autonomous women gained the reputation of being dishonorable because of the absence of male figures in their lives, the obstacles they posed to the exercise of patriarchy, and their subversion of normative gender roles. Moreover, in that context, some free poor men resorted to the practice of violence against unattached sertanejas as one mechanism to enforce patriarchal prerogatives in their communities. Thus, this book accounts for at least some of the ways in which the marginalization of women, and especially autonomous females, was reproduced historically, and did not constitute a timeless feature of a masculinized hinterland terrain.

Still, my initial findings lead to other questions that remain in need of answers, especially if we are to continue making women and the workings of gender visible in the sertão. For instance, I have shown that one dimension of feminine gender identity among poor sertanejas who resorted to the criminal court system as a way to obtain judicial retribution against men who committed violent acts against them was to represent themselves, in their judicial depositions, as respectable, passive, and secluded. This discourse did not constitute simply a challenge to the qualification of autonomous women as dishonorable, since it was shaped by the intersection of local conceptualizations of ideal womanhood and the juridical process itself—including its linguistic conventions. Thus, the practice of criminal justice reinforced a discourse about femininity—the idea that only women who were honorable and recolhidas were worthy of being defended in court—which had implications for the normatization of gender roles and power imbalances between the sexes. But femininity, just like masculinity, is a situational, contingent, and variable construct, defined and redefined in social practice. Clearly, we should explore femininity in the backlands as it evolved from other types of relations, not only between women and political-legal institutions, such as the criminal courts, or between women and men within and outside households, but also in situations in which women remained mostly segregated from men. For instance, we need to analyze the ways in which the experiences of religiosity and mysticism have influenced the constitution of feminine identities among beatas and other female participants in millenarian groups—largely made up of female followers of male lay preachers—during the nineteenth and twentieth centuries. Indeed, examinations of the Catholic missions of Father Ibiapina during the 1860s and of the messianic movements of Canudos, Joaseiro, and Caldeirão—which included large populations of widows, orphans, and other poor females—would take on new meanings from the perspective of gender.[8]

My uncovering of the social-economic agency of free poor families, including their ownership of smallholdings, animals, slaves, and other property, also calls for further investigation into the legal and customary obstacles that sertanejas faced to control and maintain access to this patrimony, especially in absence of husbands or other male family members. Indeed, we still need to find out to what extent the processes through which smallholding families who became deprived during the calamitous last third of the nineteenth century were affected by gender, given what appears to be a prevalence of female headed households, at least in Ceará, during that period. It is true that women were legally capable of both holding and bequeathing wealth in Brazil. Yet, my own preliminary analysis into succession practices among the free poor of Ceará suggests that women from this group as widows faced gender-specific vulnerabilities to dispossession of family property. This vulnerability, in turn, was related to the intricacies of the community property regime that ruled marriages, the inheritance laws, and the system of guardianship of orphaned minors in place during the Imperial period.[9] Clearly, we need to develop studies, similar to those undertaken for the Southeast and coastal regions of the Northeast, of sertanejo women as property holders and transmitters of wealth, and of the ways in which inheritance laws and local conceptions of gender intersected in the practices of succession that affected their livelihoods after the death of their husbands.[10]

In a paper presented to the Conference on Latin American History in January of 1994, Donna Guy called for scholars of gender in Latin America to turn their attention in a sustained way to the study of patriarchy and machismo as historical concepts and to the investigation of their shifting meanings and uses from the vantage point of change over time. This type of analysis was needed, Guy pointed out, not only to further the agenda of feminist studies of gender but also to confront the popular and still widely circulating stereotype of machismo as a timeless feature of Latin American culture.[11] Although not the first in heeding Guy's advice, one of my hopes in writing this book has been to contribute to the collective efforts undertaken by scholars from a variety of fields since the late 1990s to challenge this enduring image through the study of the social constitution of distinctive models of masculinity in particular milieus in the region. Given the widespread acceptance in Brazil and elsewhere of the idea that the Northeastern backlands constitute the quintessential home of macho manhood, my analysis of the emergence of historically contingent, changing, and situational models of hegemonic masculinities in Ceará during the second half of the nineteenth century is particularly well placed to demonstrate the inadequacies of archetypical approaches to gender. Through my examination of the struggles for power and resources that took place in households, taverns, fazendas, villages, jails, and planted fields, this work has also illuminated the centrality of masculinity, and of gender relations, for understanding significant and often misunderstood aspects of the social, economic, and even political history of the backlands. Finally, my analysis of the ways in which a variety of material and symbolic conditions rewarded particular forms of masculinity—violent, abrasive, and domineering—in Ceará contributes to further our understanding of how and why the subordination of women and other forms of gender inequality were reproduced historically in a particular rural locality of Latin America.

Introduction

1. Euclides da Cunha's masterpiece *Rebellion in the Backlands* was originally published in his native Portuguese as *Os sertões,* in 1902.

2. The present Northeastern region of Brazil is constituted by nine states: Maranhão, Piauí, Ceará, Rio Grande do Norte, Paraíba, Pernambuco, Alagoas, Sergipe, and Bahia. Geographically it consists of two zones, the Eastern, humid and lush littoral, and to its west, the broad semiarid and drought-prone hinterlands. Nineteenth-century Brazilians, however, did not recognize the Northeast as a regional division. They simply divided the then provinces into those of the North and the South; see Melo, *O norte agrário,* 13.

3. On the elite discourse on civilization versus rural backwardness, see, for example, Greenfield *"Sertão* and *Sertanejo,"* "The Great Drought," and *Realities of Images;* and Skidmore, *Black into White.* On the ways in which intellectuals and politicians, including da Cunha, employed racial science to characterize the Northeast and its peoples during this period, see Blake, *The Vigorous Core,* 41-81. Other late-nineteenth-century Latin American intellectuals, among them Domingo Faustino Sarmiento, also saw in the so-called barbarism of rural men the main impediment for their nations to attain civilization; see *Civilización y barbarie.*

4. Da Cunha, *Rebellion,* 54, 77–79, 175, 408. For a discussion of how representations of masculinity serve to construct gendered images of the nation, see Horne, "Masculinity in Politics," 27–30.

5. See, for example, Facó, *Cangaceiros;* Barroso, *Heróes e bandidos;* Nonato, *Jesuíno Brilhante;* Chandler, "Brazilian Cangaceiros"; Moniz, *A guerra social;* Mattos, *Crise agrária;* and Queiroz, *O messianismo;* on sertanejos as "quick to become violent," see Levine, *Vale of Tears,* 62. The studies that focus on violence in backlands messianic communities, and on banditry and rebellion, have followed various interpretive frameworks, including Marxist, culturalist, and revisionist approaches. While on the whole they have regarded an unchanging social-economic structure as a major cause for violence in the region, they have also often argued that aggression in the sertão was exacerbated by a culture of honor.

6. Northeastern folk novels and popular poems that have circulated in the inexpensive pamphlets called *literatura de cordel* have often celebrated the domineering character and actions of infamous *cabras machos*, or manly backlanders. See Slater, *Stories on a String*; several motion pictures produced within the 1960s Cinema Novo movement focused on the timeless violent and/or revolutionary potential of male sertanejos and on their bizarre culture of aggression. See, for example, Glauber Rocha, *Deus e o Diabo na Terra do Sol*, 1963, and *Antônio das mortes*, 1969; Nelson Pereira dos Santos, *Vidas sêcas*, 1963; and Ruy Guerra, *Os fuzis*, 1964. On Cinema Novo, see, Johnson and Stam, *Brazilian Cinema*. For museum exhibits celebrating the courage of male sertanejos, see, for example, "Almanaques sertanejos," March 2008, Casa do carnaval da Prefeitura do Recife, Pernambuco; and "Vaqueiros," permanent exhibit, Centro Dragão do Mar de Arte e Cultura, Fortaleza, Ceará.

7. Albuquerque Júnior, *Nordestino*, "'Quem é froxo'"; see also "Weaving Tradition," and *A invenção do Nordeste*.

8. The Brazilian Imperial period was inaugurated in 1822 and ended with the collapse of the monarchy in 1889. That year also witnessed the birth of republican government in the form of the First Republic, a specific political arrangement that lasted until 1930.

9. Albuquerque Júnior, *Nordestino*, 31–44, 86–100, 149–202. For an analysis of the elaboration of a regional identity by politicians, scientists, intellectuals, civil servants, and social reformers from the Northeast, see Blake, *The Vigorous Core*.

10. Pierre Bourdieu elaborated his practice-based approach to gender in *Outline of a Theory of Practice* and in *Masculine Domination*.

11. The colonial captaincies were transformed into provinces in 1816.

12. The term *Cearense,* which is used throughout this study, refers to a resident of Ceará. As an adjective, the term also means having to do with or relative to Ceará.

13. The phrase "honor is cleansed only with blood," which inspired the title of this book, is a reflection on the cultural customs and morals of the sertanejos as presented by the Beato Romano, a character in Rachel de Queiroz's celebrated historical novel *Memorial de Maria Moura* (p. 101).

14. On "menacing" interior municipalities of Ceará, see Uchôa, *Anuário do Ceará*, 1: 149; on the stereotype of *machismo* as the defining feature of lower-class Latin American men, see n. 33, below.

15. My study of notions of honor among free poor sertanejos builds on a large body of works published during the last twenty years that demonstrate that constructions of gender in Latin America involved adherence to cultural concepts of honor not only among elites but also among poor and middle groups during the colonial and national periods; see, for example, Stern,

The Secret History; Chasteen, "Violence for Show"; Alonso, *Thread of Blood*; Chambers, *From Subjects to Citizens;* Caulfield, Chambers, and Putnam, *Honor*; Caulfield, *In Defense of Honor*; Beattie, *Tribute of Blood,* Meznar, "The Ranks of the Poor"; Klubock, *Contested Communities*; Putnam, *The Company They Kept*; Tinsman, *Partners in Conflict*; Garfield, "Tapping Masculinity"; and the relevant articles in Johnson and Lipsett-Rivera, *The Faces of Honor*.

16. This definition of honor is drawn from classical conceptualizations by Julian Pitt-Rivers in *The Fate of Shechem;* J. G. Peristiany in *Honour and Shame;* and from my own observation of the functioning of honor in the backlands of Ceará as expressed in an array of sources.

17. On latifundia as the main, and unchanging, landholding structure that has characterized the rural Northeast, see, for example, Menezes, *O outro Nordeste*; Monteiro, *Crise agrária*; Neves, *A multidão,* and "A lei de terras"; Alegre, "Fome de braços"; Andrade, *Land and People*; Leite, *O algodão*; Levine, *Vale of Tears*; Souza and Neves, *Seca*; Araújo, "O poder local no Ceará"; Chandler, *The Feitosas*; Greenfield, *Realities of Images*; Barreira, *Trilhas e atalhos do poder*; and Secreto, "(Des)medidos Quebra-quilos." See also Moura, "Andantes de novos rumos." For exceptions and critiques to this influential trend in the literature, see, for example, Barman, "The Brazilian Peasantry"; Palacios, *Campesinato e escravidão*; Martins, *Açúcar no sertão;* and Domingos, "The Powerful in the Outback."

18. Mattos de Castro, "Beyond Masters and Slaves," 465. Other works within this trend include, among others, Metcalf, *Family*; Faria, *A Colônia*; Mattos, *Das Cores;* Mahony, "Afro-Brazilians, Land Reform"; Barickman, *A Bahian Counterpoint;* Palacios, *Campesinato e escravidão;* Moura, *Saindo das sombras.*

19. Scott, "Gender," 1067–70; Dirks, Eley, and Ortner, *Culture/Power/ History,* 4–45.

20. See, for example, Bieber, *Power;* Kraay, *Race*; Kittleson, *Practice of Politics*; Mosher, *Political Struggle*; and McCreery, *Frontier Goiás.*

21. The functioning of Imperial politics at the provincial level in Ceará is a notoriously understudied topic. Exceptions to this overall trend are Montenegro, *Os partidos;* and Chandler, *The Feitosas.*

22. See, for example, Graham, *Patronage*; Viotti da Costa, *The Brazilian Empire*; Pang, *In Pursuit of Honor*; Beattie, *Tribute of Blood*; Kirkendall, *Class Mates*; and Kittleson, *Practice of Politics.*

23. In arguing that sertanejos reproduced dominant views of honor, I do not claim that they did not elaborate their own alternative understandings of honor, although I leave the study of such norms for future scholars. For studies on how subordinate groups elsewhere in Imperial Brazil reproduced seigniorial discourses for their own purposes, see, for example, Meznar, "The Ranks of the Poor"; Chalhoub, "Interpreting"; and Kittleson, *Practice*

of Politics. For an analysis of strategies, including the deployment of official or elite ideologies, that poor people used to negotiate citizenship rights in twentieth-century Rio de Janeiro, see Fischer, *A Poverty of Rights.* For research on how lower-class groups maintained alternative codes of honor while they publicly upheld elite versions of these codes, see, for example, Esteves, *Meninas Perdidas*; and Caulfield, *In Defense of Honor.*

24. See, for example, Chandler, *The Feitosas*; Bieber, *Power*; and McCreery, *Frontier Goiás.*

25. Connell, *Masculinities*, 67–86, and passim. On the usefulness of "hegemonic masculinities" as an approach to study Latin American men and masculinities, see the relevant articles in Gutmann, *Changing Men*; and Melhuus and Stolen, *Machos.*

26. Connell, *Masculinities*, 77; Tosh, "Hegemonic Masculinity," 49, 51.

27. The scholarly work that portrays the rural Northeast as dominated by large ranches also often depicts the scores of free poor, and mostly destitute, sertanejos as continuously subordinated, dependent, and exploited by large landowners; for references to this literature, see n. 17, above. Although not applying a gender framework, Joan Meznar in "The Ranks of the Poor" and Patricia Aufderheide in "Upright Citizens" have analyzed some of the hierarchies associated with notions of respectability and honor for free poor groups in Paraíba and Bahia, and therefore, are noteworthy exceptions to this pattern in the literature.

28. Connell, *Masculinities*, 84.

29. Williams, *Marxism,* 112. On the challenge, particularly by women, to hegemonic masculinities, see Connell, *Masculinities*, 77.

30. Notable exceptions to the scholarly neglect of sertanejas are Falci, "Mulheres"; Meznar, "Carlota Lucia," and "Orphans"; Vieira Jr., *Entre paredes e bacamartes*; Campos, "Mulher e universo mágico"; and Forti, *Maria do Juazeiro.*

31. Klubock, *Contested Communities*, 6.

32. Roseberry, *Anthropologies*, 42.

33. For useful critiques of the unitary Latin American macho cliché and its political and academic uses, see Gutmann, *Changing Men,* 1–25, and *Meanings of Macho,* 221–42; Navarro, "Against *Marianismo.*"

34. Lancaster, *Life Is Hard*, 19–20.

35. For studies that contribute to this collective effort, see, for example, Gutmann, *Meanings of Macho*, and *Changing Men*; Lancaster, *Life Is Hard*; Lumsden, *Machos;* Melhuus and Stolen, *Machos*; Irwin, *Mexican Masculinities*; Green, *Beyond Carnival*; Padilla, *Caribbean Pleasure Industry*; and Irwin, McCaughan, and Nassert, *The Famous 41.*

36. In emphasizing the ways in which the identities of free poor Cearense men as gendered subjects were formed within social practice, this

work does not posit that sertanejos lacked the ability, or agency, to define their self-identities. Instead, in accordance with Judith Butler's formulation in *Psychic Life of Power* (p. 2) that the "conditions of subjectivity" also "initiate and sustain our agency," I endeavor to account for how the social structures and cultural formations that shaped or constrained the sertanejos' gendered identities and strategies to deal with conflict also set the terms for their ability to exercise agency as subjects. For a discussion of the usefulness of Butler's insights to approach the problem of agency in Latin American gender studies, see Buffington, "Subjectivity."

37. The surviving land registries housed at the Arquivo Público do Estado do Ceará (hereafter, APEC) are in an advanced state of deterioration, which creates many difficulties in working with them. There are almost no complete registries, and sizable sections of each registry are completely destroyed. These facts forced me to work with the registries that were in a better state, particularly those from Russas, Icó, Ipu, and Santa Quitéria. These municipalities, in turn, lacked large collections of postmortem inventories. Thus, I verified the information from the land registries with that presented in estate inventories from Jucás, a township that possessed a greater number of complete and readable probate records. In working with the postmortem inventories from this township, I examined all the holdings for the period between 1830 and 1889 that were available for consultation at the APEC during my research trip in 2001–2. After a preliminary analysis, during which I excluded incomplete and unreadable records, as well as those that did not reveal rural livelihoods among the decedent wealthholders (that is, absence of indicators such as land, livestock, crops, and/or agricultural tools among the inheritable assets), I set out to build samples of postmortem inventories by decade, with the hopes of including the same number of documents in each set. Nevertheless, based on availability (the holdings for the 1860s and 1870s were much larger than those for other decades), I was able to collect information on 30 inventories for the 1830s, 30 for the 1840s, and 30 for the 1850s, while the sets for the 1860s and 1870s included 60 probate records each. The sample for the 1880s included 35 postmortem inventories. The end result was a core sample of 245 probate records.

38. Once again, the lack of availability of complete sets of documents for one or two municipalities at the APEC determined my choice to research the criminal cases from Jucás, Tamboril and Itapagé. While these municipalities do not possess readable land registries, they possess good collections of criminal cases for the entire period under study.

39. Nugent, "Frontiers and Empires," 171. I am grateful to Hal Langfur for pointing me to this useful analogy; for an insightful discussion of the limitations of criminal court cases as historical sources, see Caulfield, *In Defense of Honor,* 12–13.

40. The task of translating the popular poetry into English has been challenging, since cantadores used words with complex, regionally specific meanings that often do not have direct equivalents in English. I have not provided literal translations of the poetry, but rather, the translation that best conveys the overall sense of the verses.

41. On the origins, structure, and rules of the Northeastern desafio, see, for example, Cascudo, *Vaqueiros e cantadores*; and Bastide, *Sociologia*.

42. For a summary of the critiques, see, for example, Scribner, "Is a History of Popular Culture Possible?"

43. Darnton, *The Great Cat Massacre*, 6.

44. Ronald Chilcote in "The Politics of Conflict" found that while much of the late 1970s Northeastern popular poetry delved into stereotypical themes such as stories of kings and princesses, unexpected miracles, and romances, a substantial portion dealt with topics of contemporaneous political significance for the sertanejos. An interesting approach on how masculine desafios are inserted in the quotidian lives of popular subjects is discussed in Assunção, "Versos e cacetes."

Chapter 1

1. Ceará, Pres., *Relatório* (1865), 24.

2. For references to this literature, see n. 17 in "Introduction," this volume.

3. The term "socio-economic agency" comes from Hebe Mattos de Castro's critique of classic interpretations of rural Brazil that neglected the economic activities and social relations of free poor groups, as presented in "Beyond Masters and Slaves," 465. On sharecroppers and renters as tied, and therefore, subordinated to the economic and political interests of large landowners in the Cearense backlands, see, for example, Andrade, *The Land and People*, 162–63; Porto Alegre, "Vaqueiros," 1–29; Lemenhe, *As razões*, 57, 61; Leite, *O algodão*, 61–64; Ribeiro, *Penitência e festa*, 17–19; and Oliveira, *Elegia para uma re(li)gião*, 41. On the dependent situation of the rural poor in other hinterland areas of the Northeast, see, for example, Greenfield, *The Realities of Images*, 30–31; Levine, *Vale of Tears*, 91–93; and Meznar, "Deference and Dependence," 122–36. The stress by scholars of the Northeastern backlands on the dependence of free poor sertanejos on large landowners closely matches the classic plantation-centered understanding of rural relations and landholding structures in Brazil as developed in Prado Júnior, *Formação;* Furtado, *Formação;* and Freyre, *Casa-grande & senzala.*

4. On this point, an important exception is Meznar, who in "Deference and Dependence" analyzes labor arrangements among peasants from the Campina Grande district of Paraíba during the second half of the nineteenth century.

5. The following description of Ceará's geographic features and climatic system is based primarily on Sousa Brasil, *Ensaio estatístico,* 1: 9–50, 134–43; Alencar, *Dicionário geografico,* 2–189; Studart, "Geografia do Ceará," 3–124.

6. The following discussion of the colonization of Ceará, unless otherwise noted, is based on Abreu, *Caminhos antigos,* esp. 103–12 and 225–27; Girão, *Pequena história,* chs. 1–5; Théberge, *Esboço historico,* 1: 86–87; Girão, "Da conquista à implantação," 23–43; Schwartz, "Plantations and Peripheries," 98, 105; Furtado, *Formação,* chs. 10, 11; Prado Júnior, *Formação,* 63; and Girão, "Bandeirismo Baiano," 5–20.

7. *Tapuias* was a generic designation for various nomadic indigenous groups living in the dry interior of Ceará, among them the Cariris, Tarairiús, and Tremembés, who did not belong to the Tupi linguistic group. The meaning of the word *Tapuia* in the Tupi language was simply "enemy." See Oliveira, *A fortificação,* 61–62; Studart Filho, "Notas históricas," 53–103.

8. On the development and retraction of charqueadas, see, for example, Girão, *As oficinas;* and Nobre, *As oficinas.*

9. A study of the distribution of sesmarias in the captaincy of Ceará reveals that of the total of 2,378 land grants awarded between 1679 and 1822, 2,162, or 91 percent, were requested to develop cattle ranching; seventy-six, or 3 percent, to engage in agriculture and ranching; and 140, or 5.8 percent, to set up agricultural establishments. Pinheiro, "Mundos em confronto," 31. See also Lemenhe, *As razões,* 10–11.

10. Araújo, *Povoamento;* Pinheiro, *O Cariri.*

11. Girão, *História econômica,* 207, 215.

12. On the end of the cotton boom in Brazil, see Ellison, *The Cotton Trade,* 80–88; population estimates for these years are available in Lemenhe, *As razões,* 57.

13. Cunniff, "The Great Drought," 13.

14. Freire Alemão, "Papéis," 339.

15. On sesmaria sizes, see Chandler, *The Feitosas,* 10–11; for names of sesmaria owners and the numbers of land grants they received, see Pompeu Sobrinho, *Sesmarias cearenses,* 6–7.

16. Pompeu Sobrinho, *Sesmarias cearenses,* 50, 52, 196.

17. Linda Lewin, in her two-volume work *Surprise Heirs,* describes changes in the application and the letter of inheritance law in Portugal and Brazil between 1750 and 1847. These transformations affected mainly the rights to succession of some categories of illegitimate children.

18. Burton, *Explorations,* 2: 432; on subdivision of sesmarias in backlands districts, see Araújo, *A morte do sertão,* 200–211; see also Aquino, *Aspectos históricos,* 50, 62–63; Bandeira, *O feudo;* and Joffily, *Notas,* 119; for a comparative perspective on subdivision of landholdings in the ranching districts of Rio Grande do Sul during the nineteenth century, see Chasteen, "Background to Civil War."

19. Chandler, *The Feitosas*, 10–12, 126–27; on fragmentation of land in other regions of Brazil, see Barickman, *A Bahian Counterpoint*, 105–8; Mattoso, *Bahia*, 462–63; Graham, *Caetana Says No*, 85–94.

20. Sampaio, "Formação territorial," 6–9.

21. Almeida, *Codigo Philippino.*

22. See, for example, Diegues Junior, *População e Propriedade*, 22–23; Dean, "Latifundia"; and Naro, "Customary Rightholders."

23. On land occupation in Milagres and Baturité, see Of. 32, December 21, 1861, Of. 34, December 30, 1861, Ofs. Gov. Prov. Ceará ao Ministério da Agricultura, 1861–72, ala 19, est. 404, liv. 144, APEC; on difficulties migrants faced in finding land by the late 1850s, see Sousa Brasil, *Ensaio estatístico*, 1: 296, 380. For a description of migrations to Crato and Icó, see Of. 213, December 31, 1853, Ofs. ao Ministro dos Negocios da Justiça, ala 19, est. 404, liv. 133, APEC.

24. RT, Freg. Santa Quitéria, 1855, liv. 33, entries 193 and 197, APEC.

25. Jucás, Inv., 2, 87: 1–25, 1830–45; Jucás, Arrol., 1, 39: 1–10, 1826–56, APEC; Freire Alemão, "Papéis," 246. On the continuous subdivision of landholdings during the second half of the nineteenth century, see Chapters 3 and 4, this volume.

26. RT, Freg. Nossa Senhora do Rosário da Vila de São Bernardo, 1855, liv. 28; RT, Freg. Cidade do Icó, 1858, liv. 12; RT, Freg. Santa Quitéria, APEC.

27. On the depth of properties, see Jucás, DT, 2, 69-A: 5, 1850; Jucás, DT, 2, 69-A: 17, 1869; Jucás, DT, 2, 69-A:19, 1864, APEC; see also Sampaio, "Formação territorial," 6; Cunniff, "The Great Drought," 16–18.

28. While land size is relative and dependent on other conditions, including availability of water sources, type of soil, and nearness to transportation routes, I have relied on Lewin's consideration of rural properties of less than 100 hectares in the caatinga-agreste of Paraíba in the 1920s as small for agriculture, and on Catharine LeGrand's assessment of farms of up to 100 hectares as small in the Colombian coffee frontier during the nineteenth century. See Lewin, *Politics and Parentela*, 72–73; and LeGrand, *Frontier Expansion*, 222; on small sizes of ranching properties in the Cearense backlands, see Chandler, *The Feitosas*, 129–30; for the Southern Brazilian borderlands, see Chasteen, "Background to Civil War," 746.

29. Sousa Brasil, *Ensaio estatístico*, 2: 56–57, 69, 193.

30. RT, Freg. Santa Quitéria, entries 406, 422, 432, 434, 447, 494, 539, 565, 707, 708, 903–6, 908, 922, 924–26, 961–63, 965, 988–91, APEC; Macêdo, *O clã de Santa Quitéria*, 26, 32, 38.

31. RT, Freg. Cidade do Icó, entries 59, 4, 72, APEC; on land prices, see Sousa Brasil, *Ensaio estatístico*, 1: 379; Jucás, Arrol., 1: 39, 26, 1852; Jucás, Arrol., 2: 40, 6, 1858, APEC.

32. RT, São Gonçalo da Serra dos Cocos, Comarca do Ipu, in RT, Freg. Senhora de Santa Ana da Telha, liv. 35, APEC.

33. It is impossible to determine the number of families with joint claims over one landholding. Civil cases for another municipality show a range of two to seventeen families of proprietors of the same sítio, engaging in common judicial action. For example, Jucás, DT, 2, 69-A: 5, 1837; Jucás, DT, 2, 69-A: 10, 1864; and Jucás, DT, 2, 69-A: 14, 1867; Jucás, Cr., 1, 12: 14, 1846 (this is a civil case mistakenly filed in criminal case package), APEC. For further discussion on the common practice of joint landholding, see Chapter 3, this volume.

34. The total number of postmortem inventories consulted for the period between 1830 and 1859 is ninety. These calculations are based on the seventy-seven inventories from the sample that listed landed property as an inheritable asset.

35. During the initial occupation of areas of the interior, *patrimônios* were set up for the construction and upkeep of churches. They included usually large tracts of lands, donated by one or several families of parishioners. These lands were then leased to several foreiros, who owed *foros,* or perpetual lease payments, to the administrator of the patrimônio. Nobre, *História de Morada Nova,* 1: 113.

36. Jucás, Cív., 1-A, 2: 35, 1875; Jucás, Cív., 1-A, 2: 28, 1873; and Jucás, Cív., 1-A, 2: 41, 1876; Tamboril, Cív., 1, 1: 18, 1871, APEC. On the burdens of rent payment for manioc and cereals rendeiros, see *Cearense,* December 11, 1857, 2.

37. Alves, *História das sêcas,* 107; Koster, *Travels,* 1: 441; Freire Alemão, "Papéis," 293.

38. Pinheiro, *O Cariri,* 122–23.

39. See, for example, Dean, "Latifundia," 612–13; Naro, "Customary Rightholders," 485–517; and Graham, *Patronage,* 21–24; on de Mornay's description of moradores as "tenants at will" in Pernambuco, see Barickman, *A Bahian Counterpoint,* 119.

40. This description of the expansion of the Cearense economy is based primarily on Guabiraba, *Ceará,* 13–41; Sousa Brasil, *Ensaio estatístico,* 1: 296–359, and "Desenvolvimento," in Ceará, Pres., *Falla* (1886), 36–57; Girão, *História econômica,* 218–19; Cunniff, "The Great Drought," 81, 103; and Campos, *Crônica.*

41. The agricultural export economy of Brazil as a whole expanded rapidly during these years; coffee ascended to the position of the leading export crop, and production of sugar increased, despite decreasing prices. Moreover, other products such as cotton and rubber gained importance from the mid-nineteenth century onward. Furtado, *Formação,* ch. 25; Eisenberg, *The Sugar Industry.*

42. On the second cotton boom in the Northeast, see Stein, *The Brazilian Cotton*, esp. ch. 4.

43. Brazil, *Recenseamento da população*, 4: 176.

44. Brígido Santos, *Anais da Câmara dos Deputados* 14 (1879): 538, quoted in Pinheiro, "A organização do mercado," 60; Sousa Brasil, "Desenvolvimento," in Ceará, Pres., *Falla* (1886), 42.

45. On family labor employed by smallholding families, see Chapter 3, this volume.

46. Depictions of small farmers' cultivation of cereals and manioc are available in Freire Alemão, "Papéis," 211; Gardner, *Travels*, 234; on the commercial cultivation of breadstuffs, see Cunniff, "The Great Drought," 21; on self-sufficiency in farinha and bean production, see Guabiraba, *Ceará*, 36; on the abandonment of manioc and cereals, see "A questão alimentícia II," *Cearense*, December 11, 1857, 2; "A questão alimentícia III," *Cearense*, December 15, 1857, 2.

47. Alencastre, "Memoria," 66; Stein, *The Brazilian Cotton*, 47–48; for a discussion of cotton varieties, see Cunniff, "The Great Drought," 84; on cotton as the "poor man's crop," see Sousa Brasil, "Desenvolvimento," in Ceará, Pres., *Falla* (1886), 33; on cotton as a "fever," see, for example, Theophilo, *História*, 26.

48. Theophilo, *História*, 27; Fiuza Pequeno, *Revista da Associação Comercial do Ceará*, número comemorativo do Centenário da Independência, 1922, quoted in Girão, *História econômica*, 388.

49. Leite, *O algodão*, 66.

50. On the traditional interpretation, see Menezes, *O outro Nordeste*; Araújo, "O poder local," among others.

51. Paulet, "Descripção," 79; Gardner, *Travels*, 234; on miúdos, see Guabiraba, *Ceará*, 32.

52. Although postmortem inventories are drawn in the name of single individuals, I use these sources to analyze free poor families' strategies of survival and access to landholding in Ceará for the following reasons: in most cases the documents make it clear that the decedent wealthholders relied on the labor of all able-bodied family members to survive and even accumulate resources to purchase land or slaves. In addition, the Portuguese marriage system in place in Brazil until the adoption of the Civil Code in 1916 established complete community property unless a prenuptial agreement was signed. On community property, see Lewin, *Surprise Heirs*, 1, ch. 1; and Nazzari, *Disappearance of the Dowry*, 142–43. The following discussion of the economic activities of smallholders of one and two plots is based on analysis of the forty-four postmortem inventories that included land as an inheritable asset from a total sample of sixty postmortem inventories from the 1860s from Jucás.

53. The sources do not provide specific information on what the weight of these crop sacks was.

54. See, for example, Ceará, Pres., *Relatório* (1865), 8; Ceará, Pres., *Relatório* (1867), 8; and Mello, "Excursões," 80–169. The older historiography argues that slavery was, for the most part, incompatible with ranching, small-scale production of cotton, and the other economic activities in the sertão; see, for example, Furtado, *Formação;* Prado Júnior, *Formação;* and Andrade, *Land and People.* However, the newer research on various districts of Northeast Brazil has begun to challenge this argument. See, for example, Mott, *Piauí colonial;* Versiani and Vergolino, "Slaveholdings in the Nineteenth-Century Brazilian Northeast"; Funes, "Negros no Ceará," 103–32; Nobre, *O Ceará;* and Campos, *Revelações.*

55. Funes, "Negros no Ceará," 107.

56. These calculations and the following discussion of slaveholding according to wealth derive from analysis of a total sample of 120 postmortem inventories from Jucás from the period between 1840 and 1869. Of these, 30 date from the 1840s, 30 from the 1850s, and 60 from the 1860s.

57. According to the information from postmortem inventories, slaveholding among all wealth groups in Jucás was on small scale. No more than a handful of individuals in this municipality in the mid-nineteenth century owned more than seven slaves; in some cases, inventoried families owned only shares on the value of slaves, which were the result of subdivision of slave property among legal heirs. These findings closely match the results of recent research on Brazil as a whole, beginning with the pioneering article by Schwartz, "Patterns of Slaveholding," 55–86; see also Luna and Costa, "Posse de escravos em São Paulo," 211–21; Barickman, *A Bahian Counterpoint;* and Bergard, *Slavery.*

58. Jucás, Arrol., 1, 39: 31, 1853; and Jucás, Arrol., 2, 40: 10, 1859. See also, for example, Jucás, Inv., 2, 87: 20, 1837; Jucás, Inv., 3, 88: 8, 1847; Jucás, Inv., 3: 88, 22, 1862; Jucás, Inv., 3: 88: 24, 1862, APEC.

59. This practice has been documented for the region of Brejo do Campo Seco of the sertão of Bahia during the first half of the nineteenth century. See Santos Filho, *Uma comunidade rural,* 267–87; for postmortem inventories featuring poor families who had borrowed from municipal elites, see, for example, Jucás, Arrol., 5, 43: 29, 1883; and Jucás, Arrol., 5, 43: 48, 1885, APEC.

60. Jucás, Arrol., 1, 39: 31, 1853; Jucás, Arrol., 5, 43: 23, 1882; on other merchants from Icó, as well as Aracati and Fortaleza as sources of credit, see, for example, Jucás, Inv., 4, 89: 3, 1866; Jucás, Inv., 4, 89: 9, 1867; Jucás, Inv., 4, 89:14, 1867; Jucás, Inv., 4, 89: 45, 1869; and Jucás, Inv., 4: 89: 48, 1869, APEC; on credit practices in Baturité, see Sousa Brasil, "Desenvolvimento," in Ceará, Pres., *Falla* (1886), 30; and Freire Alemão, "Papéis," 341.

61. Brazil, *Recenseamento da população,* 4: 172.

62. Brígido Santos, *Anais da Câmara dos Deputados* 14 (1879): 538, quoted in Pinheiro, "A organização do mercado," 59.

63. Freire Alemão, "Papéis," 200, 211, 245; "Situação agrícola da comarca de Crato," *Araripe,* April 2, 1859, 1–2; *Cearense,* May 23, 1872, 1.

64. Souza, "The Cangaço," 109–31; Pessar, *From Fanatics to Folk,* ch. 1; Cunniff, "The Great Drought," 155. See also Domingos, "The Powerful in the Outback."

65. On the "insubordination" of sertanejos, see Bezerra, *Notas de viagem,* 153; Paulet, in his "Descripção" (p. 63), described the resistance of freed blacks to work for others; works by foreign visitors impressed with the "laziness" of the backlanders include Avé-Lallemant, *Viagem,* 1: 341; Gardner, *Travels,* 190; Burton, *Explorations,* 2: 399. Koster noted that sertanejos were not as "docile" as the "peasantry" that lived in the coastal sugar districts of the Northeastern provinces. See *Travels,* 2: 91; on gender differences in "lazy" attitudes, see Freire Alemão, "Papéis," 210.

66. On the provincial elites' proposals to solve the labor crisis and on the Companhia de Trabalhadores, see Pinheiro, "A organização do mercado," 61–64; 88–98; examples of civil and criminal cases against poor free farmers who violated labor contracts are Tamboril, Cív., 3, 6: 23, 1869; Jucás, Cr., 3, 14: 3, 1871; Tamboril, Cr., 2, 5: 22, 1864, APEC. For a discussion of the elite discourse at the provincial and national levels on the sertanejo population as an obstacle to civilization, see Greenfield, "*Sertão* and *Sertanejo,*" and "The Great Drought." On the efforts by Pernambuco elites to transform the free poor into productive laborers, see Blake, *The Vigorous Core,* 20–48.

67. On the ideology of vagrancy, see Souza, *Desclassificados do ouro;* and Kowarick, *Trabalho e vadiagem.*

68. Kittelson, *Practice of Politics,* ch. 1.

69. "Situação agrícola da comarca do Crato," *Araripe,* April 2, 1859, 1–2.

70. Barbosa, "Entre a barbárie e a civilização," 74.

Chapter 2

1. Jucás, Cr., 3:14, 43, 1874, APEC.

2. On the ways in which the masculine worlds of war and politics in Europe and the United States have not been analyzed from a gender perspective, see Dudink and Hagermann, "Masculinity in Politics"; and Horne, "Masculinity in Politics." The lack of gendered analysis of independence movements and citizenship practices in postcolonial Latin America is analyzed in Díaz, *Female Citizens,* 9–15.

3. Horne, "Masculinity in Politics," 22, 36.

4. Scott, "Gender," 1053–75.

5. On the similar social makeup of the political class, see, for example,

Carvalho, *A construção da ordem;* Barman, *The Forging of a Nation;* Pang and Seckinger, "The Mandarins of Imperial Brazil"; Barman and Barman, "The Role of the Law Graduate"; and Kirkendall, *Class Mates.*

6. Viotti da Costa, *The Brazilian Empire,* 53–77; Graham, *Patronage,* 103–9.

7. According to the 1824 Constitution, voters needed a minimum annual income of Rs. 100$000 (an 1846 electoral law raised this annual income to Rs. 200$000) to exercise this right. Voters could make choices only for electors (free men with double the annual income of voters), who then cast ballots for elected deputies for the national chamber (free men who possessed an income of Rs. 400$000, according to the 1824 regulation). Graham, *Patronage,* 102–4. On the contradictory aspects of Brazilian liberalism, see, for example, Viotti da Costa, *The Brazilian Empire;* Bieber, *Power,* ch. 4; and Kittelson, *Practice of Politics,* 4–5.

8. On the lack of a national identity and unity by the time of independence, see Barman, *The Forging of a Nation;* Carvalho, *A construção da ordem;* on early rebellions during the Imperial period, see Mosher, *Political Struggle;* and Ribeiro, *A liberdade em construção.*

9. Bethell and Carvalho, "Brazil from Independence," 3: 679–746; on the judge and jury system, see Flory, *Judge and Jury.*

10. Kraay, *Race,* ch. 8; on the National Guard as an institution that promoted ties of patronage, see Meznar, "The Ranks of the Poor."

11. On the popular agendas of lower-class rebels, see Assunção, "Elite Politics"; Kraay, "The Bahian Sabinada"; Cleary, "Race and Cabanagem"; Chasteen, "Cabanos and Farrapos"; Naro, "The 1848 Praieira Revolt"; Mosher, *Political Struggle,* ch. 3; Ricci, "A Cabanagem"; Dias, "Movimentos sociais"; on slave flight and rebellion in the Northeast, see Reis, *Slave Rebellion;* Carvalho, *Liberdade.* For an analysis of Imperial-period rebellions in Ceará, see Montenegro, *Ideologia.*

12. On the difficulties in determining the nomenclature and dates of emergence of the Liberal and Conservative parties, see Mosher, *Political Struggle,* 138–39; on the similar conservative ideology among Liberals and Conservatives, see Needell, *The Party of Order;* Mattos, *O tempo saquarema.*

13. Kittelson, *Practice of Politics,* 4–5.

14. Flory, *Judge and Jury,* 171–74.

15. On the goals of the ruling elites during the second half of the nineteenth century, see Carvalho, *Teatro de sombras;* Needell, *The Party of Order;* Mattos, *O tempo saquarema.*

16. On universal suffrage's theoretical promise of equality among men, see Landes, "Republican Citizenship"; on the ideology of the seigniorial class, see Chalhoub, "Interpreting," 89; on the honorable designations of elite men, see Graham, *Patronage,* 33; on women's status in civil law, see Caulfield, *In Defense of Honor,* 23–24.

17. Tosh, "Hegemonic Masculinity," 48.

18. Kraay, *Race,* 203, 185.

19. Beattie, *Tribute of Blood*; see also Meznar, "The Ranks of the Poor."

20. On dominant elites' need to assert their understandings of masculinity through government policies in another Latin American context, see Díaz, *Female Citizens,* 12–13.

21. On private power in the Cearense backlands, see Macêdo, *O clã dos Inhamuns,* and *O bacamarte*; and Chandler, *The Feitosas.* For Paraíba, see Lewin, *Politics and Parentela,* ch. 1.

22. Chandler, *The Feitosas,* ch. 4; Macêdo, *O bacamarte,* 41–79; Víctor, *Chefes,* 26–28.

23. Ceará, Pres., *Falla* (1836), 1; Nogueira, *Os Presidentes,* 3: 2; on laws to curb political banditry during Alencar's years, see Law 8, 1835; Law 51, 1836; Law 86, 1837; Ceará, *Leis Provinciais,* 1: 10, 55–56, 142–43; on the difficulties in organizing and deploying the corps, see Ceará, Pres., *Falla* (1836), 2; Souza, *História militar,* 88–90, 114; Holanda, *Polícia Militar,* 1: 35–37; on the Cabanagem rebellion, see Cleary, "Race and Cabanagem."

24. Classic arguments on the successes and failures of state efforts to subordinate the private power of landowning family clans are presented in Holanda, *Raízes do Brasil*; Vianna, *Instituições políticas,* Freyre, *Casa-grande & senzala,* and *Sobrados e mucambos;* Nunes Leal, *Coronelismo.*

25. On increasing provincial budgets, see Ceará, *Leis Provinciais,* 3: 141–50, 221–28, 371–76, 413–20, 506–69; "Relatório Insp. Thesouraria," in Ceará, Pres., *Relatório* (1865); "Bal. receita e despesa," in Ceará, Pres., *Falla* (1885), 29; on partisan politics among municipal notables, see Chandler, *The Feitosas,* ch. 3; and Montenegro, *Os partidos,* 36–56.

26. Montenegro, *Os partidos,* 26–27; Chandler, *The Feitosas,* 46–78.

27. The Criminal Code established that persons who did not secure honest occupations after a first warning form a justice of the peace were to be incarcerated for a minimum of eight and a maximum of twenty-four days. The Code of the Criminal Procedure prescribed that those rearrested for vagrancy, as well as beggars, habitual drunks, prostitutes who disturbed public peace, and ruffians who upset public tranquility with insults, were required to sign a *termo de bem viver,* or a pledge of good behavior, with local police officials. If these public offenders violated the termo, which in the case of vagrants required them to obtain employment within fifteen days, they were subject to three years of imprisonment. See arts. 295, 296, Vasconcellos, *Codigo criminal,* 115–16; Vasconcellos, *Roteiro,* 45–46.

28. On social control and vagrancy in Ceará, see, for example, Ceará, Pres., *Relatório* (1867), 10; "Relatório Chefe da Polícia," in Ceará, Pres. *Relatório* (1871), 4; and "Secr. Polícia do Ceará," in Ceará, Pres., *Fala* (1887), 4–5; on the discourse on the moral failings of the sertanejo, see

Pimentel Filho, "A produção do crime," ch. 3; on the social composition of the Cearense elite, see Paiva, *A elite*, 175–77; on authorities' concern over vagrancy among the poor elsewhere in Brazil, see Souza, *Desclassificados do ouro;* Kowarick, *Trabalho e vadiagem*; Huggins, *Slavery to Vagrancy;* Kittelson, *Practice of Politics*, ch. 1; Chalhoub, *Trabalho*.

29. On localized rebellions during the second half of the nineteenth century, see Mattos, *Crise agrária,* 117–50; Barman, "The Brazilian Peasantry"; Secreto, "(Des)Medidos Quebra-quilos"; on the authorities' perceptions of the violent "nature" of the lower classes in Ceará, see Pimentel Filho, "A produção do crime," ch. 3.

30. Ceará, Pres., *Relatório* (1851), 9; Ceará, Pres., *Falla* (1876), 16; Ceará, Pres., *Fala* (1887), 24.

31. On the state of the police detachment of Tamboril, see Tamboril, Cr., 6, 9: 9, 1875, APEC. For the interior in general, see, for example, "Relatório Com. Corpo da Polícia," in Ceará, Pres., *Relatório* (1869), 1–2; and Ceará, Pres., *Relatório* (1872), 18.

32. On the reliance on army personnel to perform policing tasks in Brazil, see Beattie, *Tribute of Blood*, 135; and Kraay, "O cotidiano," 240–41; on insufficient personnel for policing functions, see, for example, Ceará, Pres., *Relatório* (1867), 14; and Ceará, Pres., *Falla* (1878), 12–13.

33. Police officials had full jurisdiction to investigate, press charges, and judge crimes that the Criminal Code punished with up to three months in jail or with fines of up to 100 mil-réis. Vasconcellos, *Roteiro*, 55–57. The crime of use of illegal weapons was punishable by fifteen to sixty days in prison. Art. 297, Vasconcellos, *Codigo criminal*, 116–17.

34. Ceará, Pres., *Relatório* (1865), 7; "Relatório Chefe da Polícia," in Ceará, Pres., *Falla* (1877), 14; Ceará, Pres., *Fala* (1887), 20.

35. The word *cabra* (literally, "the goat") refers to an individual of mixed-race, the product of a combination of Indian, white, and African ancestry. In addition, it denotes indeterminacy in the racial categorization of a person of color and can have the pejorative connotation of half-caste. In the Northeast, the word can also imply masculine bravery and aggressiveness. *Dicionário eletrônico Houaiss da língua portuguesa* (CD-ROM, version 1.0, 2001), s.v. *cabra*.

36. Chandler noted, in *The Feitosas* (p. 93), that adding *de tal* to a given name in official documents indicates that a person's last name was not known, or perhaps more commonly, that his or her social status, and that of their family, was so insignificant that it was not worth mentioning.

37. Tamboril, Cr., 1, 4: 1, 1843, APEC.

38. Hebe Mattos in *Das cores* (pp. 93–103) demonstrates that references to race and color disappeared from criminal and civil records in Southeast locales by the mid-nineteenth century. She attributes this silence about race

to the demographic increase of free blacks and mixed-raced individuals and
the incorporation, during the first half of the nineteenth century, of people
of color into the experiences of freedom, including slave and property ownership. Racial designations in criminal and civil cases in Ceará follow the
same patterns observed in Mattos's work.

39. See, for example, Itapagé, Cr., 3, 26: 2, 1873; and Tamboril, Cr., 5:
8, 20, 1873, APEC.

40. Ceará, Pres., *Relatório* (1861), 2; Ceará, Pres., *Fala* (1887), 10; on the
judicial reform of 1871, see Holloway, *Policing*, ch. 6.

41. See, for example, Ceará, Pres., *Falla* (1878), 18; and Ceará, Pres.,
Falla (1880), 12–13.

42. Ceará, Pres., *Relatório* (1869), 12–13; Ceará, Pres., *Relatório* (1867),
11; Ceará, Pres., *Falla* (1868), 7–10; Ceará, Pres., *Falla* (1880), 12–13.

43. Law 454, 1848, arts.1–4, in Ceará, *Leis Provinciais*, 2: 42–43; on
the numbers and state of prisons in the interior, see Ceará, Pres., *Relatório*
(1851), 6–7; Ceará, Pres., *Falla* (1869), 18; Ceará, Pres., *Falla* (1880), 7–8;
Ceará, Pres., *Relatório* (1881), 32–34; on the rationale behind the provision
of relief help in exchange of labor, see Greenfield, *Realities of Images,* ch. 1.

44. "Relatório das prisões," in Secr. Polícia do Ceará ao Ministério da Justiça,
1858, 1, APEC; on the Tamboril cadeia, see Tamboril, Cr., 6, 9: 9, 1875, APEC;
Ceará, Pres., *Fala* (1887), 21–22.

45. Jucás, Cr., 1, 12: 33, 1864. See also Jucás, Cr., 5, 16: 36, 1876; and
Tamboril, Cr., 2, 5: 8, 1861, APEC.

46. On recommendations on the management of in flagrante arrests, see
Ceará, Pres., *Fala* (1887), 4; on the process of legal verification of in flagrante arrests, see Vasconcellos, *Roteiro*, 52; problems with these arrests are
recorded in Jucás, Cr., 2, 13: 1, 1867; Jucás, Cr., 2, 13: 19, 1870; and Jucás,
Cr., 5, 16: 7, 1876, APEC.

47. Ceará, Pres., *Falla* (1878), 12–13.

48. "Relatório Chefe da Polícia," in Ceará, Pres., *Fala* (1887), 11–13.

49. On similar practices of Imperial state formation in a frontier context,
see McCreery, *Frontier Goiás*, chs. 1 and 2.

50. Holloway, *Policing*, 36–37; on the assimilation of criminals into the police
corps, see "Rel. Com. Corpo da polícia," in Ceará, Pres., *Relatório* (1871), 1; for
similar practices in Mexico, see Vanderwood, *Disorder*, ch. 5. Daily wages for
police praças were Rs. $500 in 1860, about half of what they were in cotton-
picking activities at the peak of the cotton boom. See Ceará, *Leis Provinciais*, 3:
402; on wages paid during the cotton boom, see Chapter 4, this volume.

51. Beattie, *Tribute of Blood*, 141.

52. On lack of popular regard for praças in the backlands, see Meznar,
"The Ranks of the Poor." See also the descriptions of the character
Capríuna, an army soldier, in Olímpio, *Luzia-Homem*, 12–13.

53. "O Cego Sinfrônio," in Mota, *Cantadores*, 52.

54. Tamboril, Cr., 5, 8: 25, 1872, APEC.

55. Vasconcellos, *Roteiro*, 53; Ceará, Pres., *Fala* (1887), 4.

56. See, for example, Ceará, Pres., *Fala* (1868), 18; "Relatório Com. da Polícia, in Ceará, Pres., *Relatório* (1869), 2–3; and "Relatório Secr. da Polícia," in Ceará, Pres., *Relatório* (1872), 4; on foreign travelers' observations of army soldiers in the backlands, see, for example, Burton, *Explorations*, 2: 388; and Gardner, *Travels*, 255. On indiscipline and lack of training of army soldiers in Bahia, see Kraay, "O cotidiano," 247–50.

57. Tamboril, Cr., 7, 10: 22, 1876; Ofs., April 17, 1879, May 18, 1879, Secr. Polícia do Ceará, Ofs. expedidos, 1878–80; ala 19, est. 393, caixa 12, APEC.

58. Tamboril, Cr., 5, 8: 16, 1874, APEC.

59. Tamboril, Cr., 3, 6: 18, 1867; Tamboril, Cr., 4, 7: 15, 1871. See also Tamboril, Cr., 5, 8: 1, 1871; Tamboril, Cr., 5, 8: 2, 1867; Tamboril, Cr., 6,9: 9, 1875, APEC.

60. See, for example, "Relatório Secr. da Polícia," in Ceará, Pres., *Relatório* (1872), 5; "Relatório Chefe da Polícia," in ibid. (1874), 4–5; and Ceará, Pres., *Falla* (1876), 5.

61. "Relatório Com. Polícia do Ceará," in Ceará, Pres., *Relatório* (1869), 2; Ceará, Pres., *Falla* (1870), 15.

62. Kraay, *Race,* 213.

63. On arrests for possession and use of illegal weapons, see, for example, Ceará, Pres., *Relatório* (1861), 2; "Relatório Chefe da Polícia," in Ceará, Pres., *Falla* (1883), 2; Jucás, Cr., 1, 12: 19, 1861; Jucás, Cr., 2, 13: 18, 1870; Jucás, Cr., 3, 14: 10, 1872; Jucás, Cr., 4, 15: 27, 1871; and Jucás, Cr., 5, 16: 38, 1872, APEC; on the legal basis of confiscation of weapons, see arts. 297, 298, Vasconcellos, *Codigo criminal*, 116–17; on the sertanejos' practice of carrying weapons, see Tamboril, Cr. 1, 4: 19, 1857; Tamboril, Cr., 2, 5: 1, 1860, APEC; "Relatório Chefe da Polícia," in Ceará, Pres., *Falla* (1870), 4; "Relatório Chefe da Polícia," in Ceará, Pres., *Relatório* (1871), 5; for the regulations of sertanejos' clothing, see Ceará, Pres., *Falla* (1880), 6.

64. Jucás, Cr., 2, 13: 18, 1870, APEC.

65. See, for example, Jucás, Cr., 3, 14: 11, 1870; Tamboril, Cr., 5, 8: 18, 1873, APEC; and Ceará, Pres., *Relatório* (1861), 1; on the use of weapons by trustworthy civilians, see Vasconcellos, *Roteiro,* 62.

66. Jucás, Cr., 3, 14: 10, 1872, APEC.

67. Itapagé, Cr., 3, 26: 2, 1873, APEC.

68. Tamboril, Cr., 2, 5: 1, 1860, APEC.

69. On the war's causes, consequences, and human cost, see Costa, *A espada de Dâmocles*; Doratioto, *Maldita Guerra;* Whighman, *The Paraguayan War;* Kraay and Whighman, *I Die with My Country.*

70. Beattie, *Tribute of Blood*, ch. 2.

71. Ibid., 8, 41; Ceará, Pres., *Falla* (1870), 17. See also Morais, "Metamorfoses," 49–77.

72. Kraay, "Patriotic Mobilization," 60–80.

73. Ramos, "Por trás de toda fuga," 134, 140–46.

74. Kraay, "Patriotic Mobilization," 60–80; Beattie, *Tribute of Blood*, chs. 1–2; on the influence of private power on recruitment practices in Rio de Janeiro, see Izecksohn, "Recrutamento militar."

75. Of. 784, November 5, 1868; Of. 802, November 11, 1868; Of. 842, November 23, 1868, Of. 861, November 21, 1868; Major Recrutador do Crato ao Chefe da Polícia, February 20, 1868, Secr. Polícia do Ceará, Ofs. Expedidos, ala 19, est. 393, caixa 7. See also Ceará, Pres., *Relatório* (1867), 12; Tamboril, Crime, 3, 6: 14, 1867, APEC.

76. "Correspondência," *Constituição*, September 30, 1865, 1; see also "Recrutamento e designação," *Constituição*, February 1, 1866, 1; "Recrutamento e designação," *Constituição*, August 30, 1865, 1–2; *Pedro II*, October 5, 1867, 1. On recruitment and elections elsewhere in Brazil, see Beattie, *Tribute of Blood*, 70–73; Graham, *Patronage*, 92–93.

77. See, for example, "Recrutamento," *Cearense*, September 1, 1866, 2; and Ramos, "Por trás de toda fuga," 87–88; on recruitment in Jardim, see Of. 784, Secr. Polícia do Ceará, Ofs. Expedidos, ala 19, est. 393, caixa 7, APEC. On municipal elites' use of partisan journals to denounce rival parties' corruption and violence in the sertão of Minas Gerais, see Bieber, "A 'Visão do Sertão.'"

78. Chandler, *The Feitosas*, 70–72.

79. This profile is based on personal data of twenty-three police soldiers featured in criminal cases from Tamboril and Jucás between 1850 and 1889.

80. This profile is based on a small sample of seven army praças featured in criminal cases for these two municipalities between 1850 and 1889.

81. Kraay, "O cotidiano," 241–43, and *Race,* 198–99; Beattie, *Tribute of Blood,* 153–55; Brazil, *Recenseamento da população,*4: 172.

82. Tamboril, Cr., 7, 10: 22, 1876, APEC; Kraay, *Race,* 213–14.

83. Tamboril, Cr., 5, 8: 18, 1843, APEC.

84. See, for example, Jucás, Cr., 3, 1: 41, 1874, APEC; "Relatório Secr. da Polícia," in Ceará, Pres., *Relatório* (1872), 2; Relatório Chefe da Polícia," in Ceará, Pres., *Falla* (1876), 5; Ceará, Pres., *Falla* (1877), 6; "Relatório Secr. Polícia do Ceará," in Ceará, Pres., *Falla* (1883), 2; and Ceará, Pres., *Fala* (1887), 6–8.

85. See, for example, Jucás, Cr., 4, 15: 23, 1875, APEC; and Ceará, Pres., *Falla* (1885), 6.

86. Inspector de Saco ao Delegado de Sobral, February 19, 1868, Secr. Polícia do Ceará, Ofs. Expedidos, ala 19, est. 393, caixa 7, APEC.

87. See, for example, Tamboril, Cr., 1, 4: 3, 1851; Tamboril, Cr., 2, 5: 6, 1860; Jucás, Cr., 5, 16: 10, 1870; and Jucás, Cr., 4, 15: 27, 1871, APEC.

88. Tamboril, Cr., 1, 4: 3, 1851, APEC.

89. Connell, *Masculinities,* 84.

90. Tamboril, Cr., 5, 8: 11, 1873; Jucás, Cr., 5, 16: 1877; Tamboril, Cri., 9, 12: 5, 1878, APEC.

91. On the erosion of patronage ties, see, for example, Souza, "The Cangaço"; Cunniff, "The Great Drought," 30, 155; and Pessar, *From Fanatics to Folk,* ch. 1.

92. Jucás, Cr., 3, 14: 19, 1874; Itapagé, Cr., 1, 24: 26, 1867, APEC.

93. Graham, *Patronage,* 256–57.

94. "Justificação de Inocêncio Francisco dos Santos," filed in Itapagé, Cr., 1, 24: 13, 1862; see also "Justificação de João Borges da Cruz," filed in Itapagé, Cr., 1, 24: 7, 1860, APEC.

95. "Azulão," in Mota, *Cantadores,* 93.

96. I am thankful to Peter Beattie for pointing me toward the connection between Nonato's assertions that he was not a "loafer," masculinity, and the discourse on vagrancy.

97. On the significance of autonomy and access to property as values that differentiated the free poor from slaves, see Mattos, *Das cores,* 45–46; and Faria, *A Colônia.*

98. Jucás, Cr., 3, 14: 29, 1868. See also Jucás, Cr., 3, 14: 5, 1871; Jucás, Cr., 5, 16: 41, 1877; Jucás, Cr., 6, 17: 6, 1877, APEC.

99. Jucás, Cr., 3, 14: 43, 1874, APEC; on judicial definition of vagrancy, see Vasconcellos, *Roteiro,* 106.

100. According to criminal procedure as explained in Filgueiras Junior, *Codigo do Processo* (1: 62), the defendants' and plaintiffs' "ascendants, descendants, husband or wife, relatives to the second degree, and slaves" could not serve as witnesses in criminal cases, as well as minors younger than fourteen years of age.

101. Ibid., 1: 60–62; Tamboril, Cr., 1, 4: 2a, 1845; Tamboril, Cr., 4, 7: 18: 1879; Jucás, Cr., 4, 15: 16, 1875; see also Tamboril, Cr., 1, 4: 2b, 1846, APEC. For similar assessments of poor people's moral quality as witnesses in twentieth-century Rio de Janeiro, see Fischer, "Slandering Citizens."

102. Fischer, *Poverty of Rights,* 102.

103. Holloway, *Policing,* 1–27; on the partial modernization of criminal law in Imperial Brazil, see Caulfield, *In Defense of Honor,* 21–26.

104. Bieber, *Power,* 204.

105. On the ways in which subordinate groups in Brazil reproduced the seigniorial logic of domination, for their own purposes, see Chalhoub, "Interpreting," 85–105. See also Meznar, "The Ranks of the Poor."

Chapter 3

1. These popular verses were included in Oliveira Paiva's novel *Dona Guidinha do Poço* (p. 76), originally published in literary magazines in Fortaleza in 1894 and 1895. A first edition of the complete novel was published in 1952.

2. See, for example, "Moralidade em facecias," in Mota, *Violeiros,* 125; "Azulão," "Jacó Passarinho," "Luís Dantas Quesado," and "O Anselmo," in Mota, *Cantadores,* 51–52, 59, 92, 114, 164; "Desafio de Neco Martins com Francisco Sales," in Seraine, *Antologia do folclore,* 52; "Martelo de Romano com Inácio," in Lessa, *Inácio da Catingueira,* 49; and "Cancioneiro do folk-lore pernambucano," 430.

3. Leonardo Mota, in his anthology *Cantadores* (pp. 80, 93, 149), provides biographical information about late-nineteenth- and early-twentieth-century cantadores from the Northeast. The information reveals that they were often poor; many were blind, and therefore, could not easily engage in other economic activities. Those who were not blind were, in some cases, former slaves who survived through a combination of subsistence agriculture and payments for private and public performances.

4. Koster, *Travels,* 1: 230; Gardner, *Travels,* 161–62; Ceará, Pres., *Falla* (1870), 7; "Relatório Secr. da Polícia," in Ceará, Pres., *Falla* (1883), 2; Araripe Júnior, *Luizinha,* 78. *Luizinha*—a naturalist novel—was written in 1873, while Alencar Araripe occupied the post of district judge in Maranguape.

5. On the code of honor as cultural heritage in the Northeast and elsewhere in rural Brazil, see, for example, Queiroz, *O messianismo;* Levine, *Vale of Tears,* esp. ch. 2; Reesink, *The Peasant,* 46–49. See also A. C. de M. Souza, *Os parceiros;* and da Cunha, *Rebellion.* Folkloric studies on Northeastern banditry also emphasize the code of honor as part of the culture of the backlands; see, for example, Daus, *O ciclo épico,* 56–57; Cascudo, *Vaqueiros e cantadores;* Barroso, *Heróes e bandidos;* and Nonato, *Jesuíno Brilhante.* See also Queiroz, *Os cangaceiros.*

6. Andrade, *Land and People,* 158; Ceará, *Coleção das Leis,* resolução 2136 and 2115, quoted in Campos, *Crônica,* 80; on the use of grazing fields by owners of joint landholdings, see Garcez, *Fundos de pasto,* 21–37; on informal arrangements for use of the range, see Alves, *História das sêcas,* 95.

7. Ceará, Pres., *Falla* (1878), 20.

8. Jucás, Inv., 4, 89: 9, 1867, APEC.

9. For ordinances on loose livestock and draft animals, see, for example, Law 536, 1850, "Posturas do Ipu," Art. 10; Law 646, 1854, "Posturas de Barbalha," Art. 14; and Law 645, 1854, "Posturas de Crato," Art. 50, in Ceará, *Leis provinciais,* 2: 204, 450, 444. For ordinances on land clearing

and fences between landed properties, see, for example, Law 538, 1850, "Posturas de Granja," Art. 54; Law 647, 1854, "Posturas de Santa Cruz," Art. 35; and Law 699, 1854, "Posturas de Telha," Art. 24, in ibid., 2: 217, 456, 555.

10. See, for example, Jucás, Cr., 1, 12: 27, 1863; Jucás, Cr., 2, 13: 9, 1869; Jucás, Cr., 3, 14: 21, 1873; and Jucás, Cr., 7, 10: 15, 1877, APEC.

11. On the shortage of land for open-range grazing, see Sousa Brasil, *Ensaio estatístico*, 1: 380; on the transfer of cattle to serras during droughts, see, for example, Ceará, Pres., *Falla* (1878), 21; Ribeiro, *Jaguaribe*, 3: 12–14; and Theophilo, *História*, 90.

12. Cunniff, "The Great Drought," 55–61; Theophilo, *História*, 27; Sousa Brasil, "Desenvolvimento," in Ceará, Pres., *Falla* (1886), 12.

13. See, for example, Law 662, 1854, "Posturas de Pereiro," Art. 51, in Ceará, *Leis Provinciais*, 2: 481.

14. See, for example, Jucás, Cr., 6, 17: 19, 1877; and Tamboril, Cr., 4, 7: 23, 1872, APEC.

15. Paulet, "Descripção," 242.

16. Law 536, 1850, "Posturas do Ipu," arts. 17, 34; Law 645, 1854, "Posturas de Crato," Art. 64; Law 646, 1854, "Posturas de Barbalha," Art. 21 in Ceará, *Leis Provinciais*, 2: 204, 206, 447, 451.

17. The word *dona* denoted a title or the informal address of respectability accorded to women of the elites.

18. Ofs., January 25, 1859, January 28, 1859, Secr. da Polícia a diversas autoridades, 1859. Fundo Secr. da Polícia, ala 19, est. 414, liv. 326, fls.12, 14, APEC.

19. See, for example, Jucás, Cr., 1, 12: 11, 1864; Jucás, Cr., 27, 1865; Jucás, Cr., 2.13: 9, 1871; Jucás, Cr., 5.16: 17, 1877; and Tamboril, Cr., 7, 10: 19, 1876, APEC.

20. Ofs., January 19, 20, 1859, Secr. da Polícia a diversas autoridades, 1859, ala 19, est. 414, liv. 326, fls. 9, 10, APEC.

21. See, for example, Jucás, Cr., 1, 12: 4, 1865; Jucás, Cr., 1, 12: 35, 1864; Jucás, Cr., 2, 13: 14, 1870; Jucás, Cr., 2, 13: 15, 1870; Jucás, Cr., 3, 14: 6, 1866; Tamboril, Cr., 2, 5: 19, 1864; and Tamboril, Cr., 2, 5: 19b, 1864, APEC. On violent conflict among neighbors and proprietors of joint land-holdings, see Chapter 6, this volume.

22. On the legal codification of men as household heads and their functions, see Deere and León, "Liberalism," 647; on men as household heads in the sertão, see Vieira Jr., *Entre paredes e bacamartes*, 253. See also Johnson, *Sharecroppers*, 99.

23. RT, São Gonçalo da Serra dos Cocos, Comarca do Ipu, in RT, Freg. Senhora de Santa Ana da Telha, liv. 35; for Lourença Maria de Mourais, see

entries 590, 592 and 593; for Maria Rodrigues de Oliveira and Rita Duartes de Azevedo, entries 819 and 820, APEC.

24. Despite royal regulations that required *sesmeiros,* or land grantees, to have their lands judicially demarcated, in practice, few of them carried such delimitations. This created problems even during the colonial period, since the lack of surveys resulted in the overlapping designation of the same lands in sesmarias of different grantees. See Dean, "Latifundia," 606–25; Sampaio, "Formação territorial," 6.

25. This discussion is based on analysis of fifteen cases of land demarcation for the municipality of Jucás, from the years 1837 to 1885, and on two others of contested demarcation. Jucás, DT, 2.69-A, 1834–1938, 3–21; Jucás, Cív., 1-A, 2: 30, 1874; Tamboril, Cív., 1, 1: 35, 1864, APEC.

26. Garcez, *Fundos de pasto,* 21–37; Godoi, *O trabalho da memória,* 44–51, 60.

27. On joint landholding as a strategy to confront land subdivision, see Chandler, *The Feitosas,* 126–27; RT, Freg. Santa Quitéria, liv. 33, entries 257–69, APEC.

28. RT, Freg. Santa Quitéria, entries 284–92, APEC.

29. RT, São Gonçalo da Serra dos Cocos, APEC.

30. According to Godoi in *O trabalho da memória* (pp. 84–85), joint landholding was common among squatters in some regions of Piauí during the nineteenth and early twentieth centuries.

31. On the regulation of shared lands in patrimônios, see ibid.; on renting lands, along with others, in the same landholding, see Itapagé, Cr., 1, 29: 9, 1861. See also, for example, Jucás, Cív., 1-A, 2: 28, 1873; Jucás, Cív., 1-A, 2: 41, 1876; Tamboril, Cív., 1, 1: 18, 1871, APEC.

32. On posses and the implications of the lack of a land policy for land occupation patterns in the empire until 1850 and after, see Dean, "Latifundia," 606–25; and Smith, *Propriedade,* 99–149.

33. Mattos, *Das cores,* 74–81; Naro, "Customary Rightholders," 485–517.

34. Motta, *Nas fronteiras do poder,* 142, 162–67. See also McCreery, *Frontier Goiás,* 160.

35. For an insightful analysis of how land legislation in Brazil has promoted conflict, violence, and encroachments by both poor and elite alike, since the colonial period and into the present, see Holston, "The Misrule of Law."

36. See, for example, Jucás, Cív., 1A, 2: 9, 1866; Jucás, Cr., 1, 12: 4, 1865; Jucás, Cr., 1, 12: 35, 1864; Jucás, Cr., 2, 13: 14, 1870; and Tamboril, Cr., 5, 8: 3, 1873, APEC. These practices were common in the backlands of Paraíba as well. See Joffily, *Notas,* 210.

37. See, for example, Tamboril, Cr., 6, 9: 11, 1875, APEC.

38. Jucás, Cr., 2, 13: 14, 1870, APEC.

39. Aulete Caldas, *Diccionario contemporâneo da língua portuguesa* (Lisboa: Imprensa Nacional, 1881), s.v. *senhor*.

40. Jucás, Cr., 3, 14: 6, 1866, APEC.

41. Tamboril, Cr., 4, 7: 23, 1870, APEC.

42. Caldas, *Diccionario*, s.v. *proprietário*.

43. Tamboril, Cr., 4, 7: 23, 1872, APEC. Caldas, *Diccionario*, s.v. *possuidor*.

44. On the lack of land titles among local notables in the backlands of Ceará, see Chandler, *The Feitosas*, 127–28; for Paraíba, see Meznar, "Deference and Dependence," 120–21.

45. Sousa Brasil, *Ensaio estatístico*, 1: iii.

46. Itapagé, Cr., 3, 26: 12, 1874, APEC.

47. Ibid.

48. Vasconcellos, *Codigo criminal*, 105–6.

49. This information is drawn from a total of twenty dano cases from Jucás and Tamboril. Of these cases, twelve featured literate plaintiffs and one featured an illiterate supplicant. In seven of them, the literacy of the plaintiffs could not be determined. Data on literacy for the defendants is as follows: seven were literate, six were illiterate, and seven were undetermined. Taking the information on literacy as a proxy for class, this information indicates that literate and, presumably wealthier, landholders were comparably more able to take up property damage issues in criminal courts than the poor. For further discussion on class accessibility to the courts, see Chapters 2 and 6, this volume.

50. Itapagé, Cr., 3, 26: 12, 1873; Tamboril, Cr., 7, 10: 7, 1876, APEC.

51. Jucás, Cr., 1, 12: 11, 1853, APEC.

52. Itapage, Cr., 1, 24: 1, 1852. APEC.

53. Ibid.

54. For understandings about water as communal property in another backlands context, see Godoi, *O trabalho da memória*, 67.

55. Jucás, Cr., 2, 13: 2, 1867, APEC.

56. A provincial law of 1841 established the obligatory registration of cattle brands. Ordinances from several municipalities required that all persons who, for any reason, transported cattle with marks other than their own carry with them official notes from police authorities with the name of the stock seller and his or her brand. Tamboril, Cr., 1, 4: 16, 1843, APEC.

57. Julio, *Terra e povo*, 173; Barroso, *Terra de sol*, 201; Tamboril, Cr., 2, 5: 12, 1862; Tamboril, Cr., 3, 6: 8, 1865, APEC.

58. Koster, *Travels*, 1: 234–35; Tamboril, Cr., 1, 4: 9, 1859, APEC.

59. Tamboril, Cr., 3, 5: 2, 1865.

60. On the difficulties that free poor people faced to initiate criminal and civil suits, see Chapter 6, this volume.

61. On the solidity of the sertanejos' word, see "O Cego Sinfrônio," in

Mota, *Cantadores*, 46; on being a "cabra of strong words (*orações fortes*)," see Tamboril, Cr, 5, 8: 14, 1874, APEC.

62. Paiva, *Dona Guidinha do Poço*, 76.

63. For a summary of the literature on honor and patriarchy in Latin America and the Mediterranean, see Stern, *The Secret History*, ch. 2.

64. See, for example, Metcalf, "Fathers and Sons," and *Family*; Nazzari, *Disappearance of the Dowry*, and "An Urgent Need to Conceal"; Lewin, *Politics and Parentela*, ch. 3, and "Who Was 'o Grande Romano'?"; and Borges, *The Family in Bahia*, 225–26. On regulation of marriage choices and honor in Spanish America, see, for example, Martínez-Alier, *Marriage, Class and Colour*; Socolow, "Acceptable Partners"; Seed, *To Love*; Gutiérrez, *When Jesus Came;* Twinam, *Public Lives*; and Van Deusen, *Between the Sacred and the Worldly*.

65. See, for example, Chambers, *From Subjects to Citizens*; Putnam, *The Company They Kept;* and Kittelson, *Practice of Politics*.

66. On inheritance laws in colonial and nineteenth-century Brazil, see Lewin's two-volume work *Surprise Heirs;* on the 1847 legal reforms that curtailed the inheritance rights of some natural children, see ibid., 2: 163–263.

67. Sousa Brasil, *Ensaio estatístico*, 1: 314.

68. For a comparative analysis of legitimacy rates in rural, agricultural areas and in urban and mining areas of the Brazilian Southeast during the eighteenth and nineteenth centuries as presented by the existing historiography, see Faria, *A Colônia*, 55.

69. On higher rates of illegitimacy in mining regions, see, for example, Costa, *Vila Rica*, 227; and Marcílio, *A cidade de São Paulo*, 157–59.

70. Faria, *A Colônia*, 52–54; on the constitution of families as a precondition for developing agrarian activities among the free poor in the Southeast, see Mattos, *Das cores*, 60.

71. On the shortage of priests and the work of visiting vicars in the interior of Ceará and the Northeast during the nineteenth century, see Gardner, *Travels*, 213–14; Chandler, *The Feitosas*, 145; Levine, *Vale of Tears*, 31; and Santos Filho, *Uma comunidade rural*, 187. On the fluid relationship between concubinage and marriage, see Kuznesof, "Sexual Politics."

72. *Araripe*, October 16, 1858, quoted in Pinheiro, *O Cariri*, 123; Freire Alemão, "Papéis," 246. On land subdivision along the middle São Francisco River, see Burton, *Explorations*, 2: 432.

73. On epidemics and mortality rates, see Chapter 4, this volume.

74. RT, Freg. Cidade do Icó, 1858, liv. 12, entries 28–39, APEC.

75. Jucás, Inv. 7, 92: 12, 1889, APEC.

76. Jucás, Arrol., 1, 39: 39, 1855.

77. Tamboril, Cr., 2, 5: 5, 1861, APEC; *Araripe*, October 16, 1858, quoted in Pinheiro, *O Cariri*, 123.

78. Schneider, "Of Vigilance and Virgins," 16–21.

79. For a discussion of rapto among upper classes in the Northeast, see Falci, "Mulheres," 266–67; for a more general discussion of rapto and seduction in Brazil in the colonial period, see Silva, *Sistemas de casamento*, 75–80.

80. Arts. 226, 227; Vasconcellos, *Codigo criminal*, 93; Lewin, *Surprise Heirs*, 2: 243.

81. See, for example, Tamboril, Cr., 1, 4: 15, 1855; and Jucás, Cr., 1, 12: 24, 1865, APEC.

82. See, for example, Jucás, Cr., 1, 12:24, 1865; Jucás, Cr., 2, 13: 20, 1869; and Tamboril, Cr., 1, 4: 18, 1857, APEC.

83. Jucás, Cr., 3, 14: 13, 1872, APEC.

84. Queiroz, *Memorial de Maria Moura*; Freire Alemão, "Papéis," 286.

85. Vieira Jr., *Entre paredes e bacamartes*, 267–68.

86. Jucás, Cr., 5, 16: 30, 1871; see also Itapagé, Cr., 1, 24: 2, 1852, APEC.

87. "O Anselmo," in Mota, *Cantadores*, 178.

88. Freire Alemão, "Papéis," 210. Sir Richard Burton, in his *Explorations* (2: 432), observed that free poor women from the sertões of Bahia and Minas Gerais gave birth to ten to twenty-five children, not of all whom lived.

89. Calculations based on a sample of thirty postmortem inventories from Jucás, corresponding to the period between 1850 and 1859. Jucás, Inv., 3, 88: 1846–66; Jucás, Arrol., 1, 39: 1826–56; Jucás, Arrol., 2, 40: 1856–64, APEC.

90. Recent studies that analyze the survival strategies of free poor people who participated in regional markets for foodstuffs and other crops during the colonial period and the nineteenth century emphasize the centrality of the family as the basis for their agricultural production. See, for example, Faria, *A Colônia*, 153–58; Metcalf, *Family*, ch. 5; and Mattos, *Das cores*, 60–61.

91. For a useful discussion of the sexual and technical division of labor and their interactions with material local conditions, see Deere and León, "Peasant Production"; on masculine and feminine tasks in field work in the present-day backlands of Pernambuco, see Rebhun, *The Heart*, 174.

92. This and the following discussion of family labor is based, unless otherwise noted, on descriptions of life in the sertão found in Galeno, *Lendas*, 1: 32; Koster, *Travels*, 1: 214, 229; Pinheiro, *O Cariri*, 118, 120; Freire Alemão, "Papéis," 212, 219; Meznar, "Deference and Dependence," 44, 152, 165; and Jucás, Cr., 5, 16: 19, 1876, APEC. See also Falci, "Mulheres," 250; and Cunniff, "The Great Drought," 86. On family labor in peasant households in the Northeast from the 1950s onward, see Garcia Junior, *O sul*.

93. Theophilo, *Historia*, 27.

94. Barickman, *A Bahian Counterpoint,* 163–68; and Meznar, "Deference and Dependence," 163–65. See also Jucás, Cr., 3, 14: 13, 1872, APEC.

95. On men's decision-making regarding the commercialization of cotton and produce, see, for example, Tamboril, Cív., 1, 1: 5A, 1875; Tamboril, Cív., 2, 2: 105, 1876; Jucás, Cr., 2, 13: 1870; and Jucás, Cr., 3, 14: 3, 1871, APEC; on women's marketing of small animals, see Marson, "Imagens da condição feminina," 238; for similar contemporary practices, see Rebhun, *The Heart,* 174.

96. On women "helping their husbands out" in agricultural field work, see, for example, Itapagé, Cr., 3, 26: 1, 1873, APEC; and Theophilo, História, 77–78; on women's and children's work in tobacco farming as easy and less strenuous, see Sousa Brasil, *Estado do Ceará,* 97.

97. See, for example, Socolow, *The Women,* 66–72; and Stern, *The Secret History,* 87–91. See also Graham, "Honor among Slaves," and *Caetana Says No;* and Chambers, *From Subjects to Citizens.*

98. See, for example, Itapagé, Cr., 9, 32: 12, 1884, APEC.

99. "O Anselmo," in Mota, *Cantadores,* 166.

100. Tamboril, Cr., 7, 10: 20, 1876, APEC.

101. Vieira Jr., *Entre paredes e bacamartes,* 250.

102. Tamboril, Cr., 5, 8: 22, 1873, APEC.

103. "Relatório Chefe da Polícia," in Ceará, Pres., *Falla* (1870), 2.

104. The ambiguous language used to describe women's status in the available documentation attests to the fluidity in conjugal relationships and their public perceptions in Ceará. Criminal cases referred to women who appear as adulteresses with the term *mulher de* to indicate they were engaged in some form of stable relationship with a man, but without providing any additional proofs of marriage or consensual partnership. According to the *Dicionário Houaiss,* the use of the word *mulher* (literally, woman) to indicate both conjugal partner and wife in Brazil dates back to the sixteenth century. The *Dicionário Houaiss* also notes that *mulher* has the meaning of girlfriend, and generally constant sexual partner of a man. *Dicionário eletrônico Houaiss da língua portuguesa* (CD-ROM, version 1.0, 2001), s.v. *mulher.*

105. Jucás, Cr., 5, 16: 19, 1876, APEC.

106. Mota, *Violeiros,* 216.

107. Itapagé, Cr., 6, 29: 6, 1873; Itapagé, Cr., 10, 33: 5, 1885, APEC; on the right of household heads to punish his dependents as permitted by civil laws during the colonial and Imperial periods, see Graham, *Caetana Says No,* 46.

108. Bourdieu, *Outline of a Theory of Practice,* 15, 60–61.

109. Connell, *Masculinities,* 82.

Chapter 4

1. Theophilo, *História*, 109.
2. Lewin, "The Oligarchical Limitations," 120.
3. Benjamin, "Thesis," 257.
4. See, for example, Taussig, "Terror as Usual," 3–20; and Scheper-Hughes, *Death*, ch. 6.
5. "Recrutamento e designação," *Constituição*, February 1, 1866, 1; "Recrutamento e designação," *Constituição*, August 30, 1865, 1–2; "Recrutamento," *Cearense*, September 1, 1866, 2; *Pedro II*, October 5, 1867, 1; "Recrutamento e designação," *Constituição*, August 30, 1865, 1.
6. Ramos, "Por trás de toda fuga," 163; Galeno, "A esmola" and "O recruta," in *Lendas*, 2: 67–69; 200–205.
7. On the burst of the Brazilian cotton boom in the late 1860s and early 1870s, see Stein, *The Brazilian Cotton*, 45.
8. Cunniff, "The Great Drought," 94, 81.
9. Theophilo, *História*, 27.
10. Ibid., 27–28.
11. See, for example, Freire Alemão, "Papéis," 341. Interest rates in Ceará are available in Sousa Brasil, "Desenvolvimento," in Ceará, Pres., *Falla* (1886), 30; and "Relatório Associação Comercial," in Ceará, Pres., *Relatório* (1872), 6.
12. On business transactions between illiterate sertanejos and merchant-lenders, see Girão, *História econômica*, 387–88.
13. See, for example, Tamboril, Cív., 1,1: 5A, 1875; Tamboril, Cív., 1, 1: 6, 1875; Tamboril, Cív., 1, 1: 13, 1873; Tamboril, Cív., 2, 2: 105, 1876; and Tamboril, Cív., 2, 2: 19, 1876, APEC; on small cotton farmers' loss of landed property and animals to their creditors, see Theophilo, *História*, 28.
14. On periodic droughts in Ceará and their dates, see Studart, *Datas e factos*; Alves, *História das sêcas*.
15. On the exploitative and inadequate nature of the relief system during the Great Drought, see Greenfield, *Realities of Images*.
16. Ceará, Pres., *Falla* (1878), 43.
17. Of. May 16, 1877, Co. Soc., Jucás, Ofs. expedidos e recebidos; Of. October 23, 1878, Ofs. Expedidos, Câm. Mun. São Mateus, ala 20, est., 431, caixa 80, APEC.
18. On scarcity of food and elevated prices, see, for example, *Cearense*, March 11, 1877, 2; *Cearense* April 18, 1877, 3; *Cearense*, August 9, 1877, 2; and *Cearense*, September 14, 1877, 2; on migrations by retirantes, see Cunniff, "The Great Drought," chs. 3, 5. See also Villa, *Vida e morte*, ch. 2.
19. Cunniff, "The Great Drought," 127, 130, 155.
20. *Cearense*, July 8, 1877, 2.

21. On the 1832 reservoir law, see Campos, *Crônica,* 87; on the number of açudes built with the assistance of provincial funds, see Cunniff, "The Great Drought," 63–64.

22. For example, an observer described the "notable" reservoir that an influential family of agrarian entrepreneurs built in Pacatuba for a total price of Rs. 54:000$000 during the 1860s. Another traveler noted a large açude near Icó that cost his owner, a major in the National Guard, Rs. 80$000. Mello, "Excursões," 88; Freire Alemão, "Papéis," 294. A list of fifty-four private reservoirs built throughout the whole municipality of Jucás by 1882 also reveals an overwhelming concentration of ownership of large reservoirs among wealthy families; thirty-four of the fifty-four dams listed belonged to members of the Silva Pereira and Oliveira Bastos families, two of the most politically dominant and economically well-off families from the township. Among these owners, it is possible to identify past town council presidents, councilmen, one police deputy, two National Guard commandants, and several men who had served as jury members in criminal proceedings. Of. January 17, 1882, Câm. Mun., Ofs. Expedidos, São Mateus, ala 20, est. 431, caixa 80, APEC.

23. See, for example, Of. 19, January 20, 1859; and Ofs. Souré January 25, 28, 1859, Secr. Polícia com diversas autoridades prov., 1859, ala 19, est. 414, liv. 326, fls. 9, 10, 12,14, APEC; on conditioning the use of water, see "Situação Agrícola da Comarca do Crato," *Araripe,* April 2, 1859, 2.

24. See, for example, Alves, *História das sêcas,* 215; and Of. January 23, 1885, Câm. Mun., Ofs. Expedidos, Tamboril, ala 20, est. 431, caixa 86, APEC.

25. Theophilo, *História,* 89.

26. Sousa Brasil, "Desenvolvimento," in Ceará, Pres., *Falla* (1886), 21 (for the findings of the 1877 report); Ceará, Pres., *Falla* (1878), 43.

27. On relief programs during the drought and the birth of the drought industry, see Cunniff, "The Great Drought," ch. 4; Greenfield, *Realities of Images.*

28. On dams built by retirantes, see, for example, Ceará, Pres., *Falla* (1880), 44; on the location of those dams, see, for example, "Correspondência do Interior, Assaré," *Cearense,* September 14, 1877; and "Correspondência do Interior, Cruz," *Cearense,* October 14, 1877, 4.

29. Cunniff, "The Great Drought," 282, 283, 295.

30. On the end of the transatlantic trade and the internal slave trade after 1850, see Conrad, *The Destruction of Brazilian Slavery,* esp. chs. 1–3.

31. Bethell and Carvalho, "Brazil from Independence," 3: 758.

32. Estimates available in Funes, "Negros no Ceará," 107; Nascimento, "Síntese histórica," 172–74; Brazil, *Recenseamento da população,* 4: 172.

33. Prime working-age slaves include young adult slaves, both male and

female, between the ages of sixteen and twenty-eight. Slave prices are based on appraisals found in postmortem inventories from Jucás.

34. These calculations are based on a total sample of 155 postmortem inventories from Jucás. Of this total, 60 correspond to the period between 1860 and 1869, 60 to the years between 1870 and 1879, and 35 to the period between 1880 and 1889. Of the total number of inventories analyzed for the 1860s, 24 percent listed slaves as inheritable wealth. This figure decreased to 20 percent during the 1870s and to nearly 6 percent during the 1880s.

35. Slenes, "The Demography and Economics," 191–97, 616.

36. These calculations of landholding capacity by family are based on the 128 postmortem inventories that included land as an inheritable asset from the total sample of 155 inventories from Jucás for the period between 1860 and 1889.

37. Chapter 6 in this volume will discuss in detail violent conflict for land during the years between 1860 and the late 1880s; on sertanejos who were unable to recover their lands after the Great Drought, see, for example, Ceará, Pres., *Relatório* (1881), 41.

38. See, for example, Jucás, Inv., 5, 90: 16, 1870; and Jucás, Inv., 5, 90: 22, 1872, APEC.

39. These calculations derive from analysis of the sample of 185 postmortem inventories for Jucás from the period between 1850 and 1889. Even though there are no studies on inflation in the interior of the Northeast, works on other regions indicate that inflation was on the rise, especially between 1850 and 1870. Mircea Buescu in *300 anos de inflação* (pp. 173, 176, 195) presents an index for consumer goods in the city of Rio de Janeiro, and points to an 84 percent increase in prices between 1850 and 1870. Kátia Mattoso in *Bahia* (ch. 29) calculated a 90 percent rise in prices of basic goods in the city of Salvador in the same years. See also Onody, *A inflação brasileira*, 117.

40. Jucás, Arrol., 3, 41: 5, 1857; Jucás, Inv., 4, 89: 39, 1868; Jucás, Arrol., 4, 42: 16, 1875, APEC.

41. See, for example, Shammas, "The Determinants of Personal Wealth," 677; and Frank, *Dutra's World*, 39.

42. This analysis is based on the total sample of 185 postmortem inventories from Jucás for the period between 1850 and 1890. Of these, 30 correspond to 1850–59, 60 to the years between 1860 and 1869, 60 to the period between 1870 and 1879 and 35 to 1880–89.

43. See, for example, Jucás, Cr., 2, 13: 1, 1867; Jucás, Cr., 5, 16: 1870; Jucás, Cr. 4, 15: 13, 1875; and Tamboril, Cr., 2, 5: 6, 1860, APEC.

44. "Mapa dos recrutas que são remetidos pelo Delegado de Polícia de Sobral," Secr. Polícia do Ceará, Of. Expedidos, ala 19, est. 393, caixa 7, APEC; Beattie, *Tribute of Blood*, 58.

45. Studart, *Climatologia,* 38, 54–57.

46. Studart, *Datas e factos,* 2: 179–80; Studart, *Climatologia,* 59.

47. See, for example, "Relatório Insp. Saúde Pública," in Ceará, Pres., *Falla* (1870), 2; Ceará, Pres., *Relatório* (1872), 21; Ceará, Pres., *Falla* (1874), 14; and Ceará, Pres., *Falla* (1886), 5.

48. Cunniff, "The Great Drought," 105.

49. Ibid., 213.

50. According to Maria Luisa Marcílio's article "A etnodemografia" (pp. 2–11), infant mortality was already considered a major public health concern in Brazil in the mid-nineteenth century; on mortality rates, see also Mattoso, *Bahia,* 158. Because of the difficulties in research on this topic, studies with precise information on infant mortality rates during these years are scarce. For the most part, the existing literature presents estimates of mortality rates only among abandoned children in urban areas.

51. Of. October 29, 1877, Co. Soc., Jucás, Ofs. expedidos e recebidos; see also Of. November 14, 1877, Co. Soc., Jucás, Ofs. expedidos e recebidos, APEC.

52. Villa, *Vida e morte,* 49.

53. Studart, *Climatologia,* 72.

54. According to the *Ordenações Filipinas,* outstanding debts needed to be paid from the remaining estate of a deceased before the drawing of a partilha when there were at least two surviving successors. Almeida, *Codigo Philippino,* liv. II, tít. LII, Art. 5, 484.

55. Jucás, Inv, 4, 89: 44, 1869, APEC.

56. Jucás, Inv., 4, 89: 14, 1867, APEC.

57. Sousa Brasil, "Desenvolvimento," in Ceará, Pres., *Falla* (1886), 9.

58. See, on average wages at the provincial level, Sousa Brasil, *Ensaio estatístico,* 1: 392–93; on wages in coffee-producing areas, Freire Alemão "Papéis," 200; and, for wages in cotton farms, Theophilo, *História,* 27. Average wages in Jucás are included in Of. October 27, 1884, Ofs. Expedidos, Câm. Mun. São Mateus, ala 20, est. 431, caixa 80, APEC.

59. Freire Alemão, "Papéis," 200.

60. Theophilo, *História,* 27–28.

61. The average wages paid in the interior, as detailed in Sousa Brasil's 1886 report "Desenvolvimento" (p. 9), are comparable to those that Freire Alemão reported in 1859.

62. The increase in food prices in Ceará during the second half of the nineteenth century was part of a broader pattern observed in Brazil as a whole; see Slenes, "Os múltiplos de porcos," 467–68; and Stein, *Vassouras,* 48–49. Katia Mattoso's study *Bahia* (pp. 564–67) reveals rising prices of basic foods such as farinha, beef, beans, and rice, especially during the late 1860s and throughout the 1870s in Bahia. See also Buescu, *300 anos;* and Onody,

A inflação. In the absence of true price series for the interior of Ceará and of a set of nationally comparable prices series, it is difficult to assess to what extent food prices in the interior of Ceará diverted from escalating prices elsewhere in Brazil. Nevertheless, it is likely that the factors that Mattoso has found significant in precipitating high food prices in Bahia, especially periodic droughts, epidemics, and rapid demographic growth, were at play in Ceará as well, where similar conditions existed. These factors, in turn, might account for an even more severe increase in prices in the interior of the Northeast as compared to other Brazilian regions.

63. "A questão alimentícia II," *Cearense*, December 11, 1857, 2; "A questão alimentícia III," *Cearense,* December 15, 1857, 1; "A questão alimentícia IV," *Cearense*, December 22, 1857, 1.

64. Guabiraba, *Ceará*, 67; Cunniff, "The Great Drought," 105.

65. Cunniff, "The Great Drought," 104; Of. August 30, 1877, Of. November 3, 1877; Jucás, Co. Soc., Ofs. expedidos e recebidos, APEC.

66. On road construction in Baturité and other northern municipalities, see Oliveira, *A estrada de ferro*, 37–38.

67. Sousa Brasil, *Ensaio estatístico*, 1: 393–94; Freire Alemão, "Papéis," 264; Tamboril, Cr., 1, 4: 22, 1859, APEC.

68. On the cotton planting and harvesting seasons, see Andrade, *Land and People,* ch. 5; Alencastre, "Memoria," 66; on labor for sugar production, see "Relatório Insp. Thesoureria Provincial," in Ceará, Pres., *Relatório* (1865), iv.

69. Freire Alemão, "Papéis," 199.

70. Galeno, "No Cafezal," in *Lendas*, 2: 137–41, 243; "Azulão," in Mota, *Cantadores*, 94.

71. Brazil, *Recenseamento da população,* 4: 176.

72. Ibid., 18, 75, 120.

73. Ibid., 176.

74. Girão, *História econômica*, 393–94.

75. Benchimol, *O Cearense*, 39–40, and, for the numbers of Northeasteners arriving in Manaus, 61. Benchimol also argues that as a result of the Great Drought and other droughts of the 1890s and early twentieth century, Cearenses emigrated as families and not as single individuals. On the scant migration of Cearense women to the Amazonian region of Acre during the 1870s, see Wolff, *Mulheres,* 51. For a more general discussion of isolated migrant rubber tappers during the crest of the rubber boom, see Oliveira Filho, "O Caboclo e o Brabo," 101–40.

76. Anderson, *Colonization*, 120–23.

77. On colonization programs and the presence of Cearenses, see Penteado, *Problemas*, esp. 58–68; Weinstein, *The Amazon Rubber Boom*, 114–24; Anderson, *Colonization*, 118–23.

78. Personal communication from Barbara Weinstein.

79. Wolff, *Mulheres*, 52.

80. Galeno, "O emigrante," in *Lendas*, 2: 228.

81. For a discussion of the intensification of banditry in the 1870s, see Chapter 6, this volume.

82. Connell, *Masculinities*, 84–85. See also Vigoya, "Contemporary," 27–57.

83. "O Anselmo," in Mota, *Cantadores*, 179.

84. "Azulão," in ibid., 94. According to the *Dicionário Houaiss*, the word *moça* means a girl who has entered into puberty, menstruates, and therefore is considered ready to get married. The same dictionary notes that one of the meanings of mulher is a woman who is no longer a virgin. *Dicionário eletrônico Houaiss da língua portuguesa* (CD-ROM, version 1.0, 2001), s.vv. *moça*, *mulher*.

85. Tamboril, Cr., 5, 8: 22, 1873, APEC.

86. In her article "Carlota Lucia" (p. 43), Joan Meznar mentions that one of the multiple outcomes of drought-related dislocation was women's separation from undesirable husbands.

87. Ceará, Pres., *Relatório* (1872), 5.

88. Tamboril, Cr., 7, 10: 6, 1877, APEC.

89. See, for example, Ceará, Pres., *Falla* (1874), 6; and "Relatório Secr. da Polícia," in Ceará, Pres., *Fala* (1887), 5.

90. See, for example, Tamboril, Cr. 6, 9: 19, 1876, APEC; and "Boa terra é o Cariri," in Seraine, *Antologia do folclore*, 70.

91. Galeno, "A desgraça," in *Lendas*, 2: 22.

92. Paiva, *Dona Guidinha do Poço*, 20, 33.

93. *Cearense*, August 2, 1877, 4; *Cearense,* August 14, 1877, 2; on body postures associated with honor and dishonor, see Stern, *The Secret History,* 161–77.

94. *Cearense*, June 10, 1877, 7; *Cearense,* September 8, 1877, 2; *Cearense,* September 30, 1877, 3.

95. Ibid., November 29, 1877, 3.

96. According to the 1824 Constitution, free people were not to suffer any form of physical punishment or whipping. Moreover, despite the fact that the Brazilian Parliament banned whipping of army soldiers in 1831, this practice continued to take place all the way into the second half of the nineteenth century. See Holloway, *Policing*, 60; Beattie, *Tribute of Blood*, 9; Kraay, "O cotidiano dos soldados," 250.

97. Jucás, Cr., 5, 16: 41, 1877, APEC.

98. See, for example, *Cearense*, September 30, 1877, 2; Of. March 17, 1879; Of. June 23, 1879; and Of. August 25, 1879, Secr. Polícia do Ceará, Ofs. expedidos, 1878–80, ala 19, est. 393, caixa 12, APEC.

99. Galeno, "O jornaleiro," in *Lendas*, 2: 124.

100. On recruitment and enlisted military service as a source of dishonor, see, for example, Beattie, *Tribute of Blood*; Meznar, "The Ranks of the Poor."

101. Galeno, "O recruta," in *Lendas*, 2: 202.

102. See, for example, Cunniff, "The Great Drought"; Greenfield, *Realities of Images*; Albuquerque Júnior, "Palavras que calcinam," 111–20; Souza and Neves, *Seca*; and Landim, *Seca*. For a recent revisionist study of the connections between the construction of a Northeastern regional identity and the creation of social and labor legislation to improve conditions in the region between 1870 and 1940, see Blake, *The Vigorous Core.*

Chapter 5

1. While it is difficult to determine the date of this poetic contest, the reference to Romano do Teixeira's attendance indicates that it took place sometime during the second half of the nineteenth century. According to Linda Lewin's research on this famous bard as presented in "Who Was 'o Grande Romano'?" (pp. 129–79), Romano was born in Paraíba in 1835 and died in 1891. Moreover, he was already a celebrated popular poet during the early 1870s; for the narrative of the encounter between Jerônimo and Zefinha, see "O Cego Sinfrônio," in Mota, *Cantadores,* 41–47.

2. A *viola* is a small guitar, typical of the Northeastern backlands, that cantadores use to accompany their sung poetry.

3. "O Cego Sinfrônio," in Mota, *Cantadores*, 42.

4. Galeno, *Lendas*, 1: 34; Della Cava, *Miracle*, 19; see also Hoornaert, *Crônicas*, 75. On orphans and abandoned children in the backlands during the second half of the nineteenth century, see Meznar, "Orphans," 499–515.

5. See, for example, Theophilo, *História*, 109; Câmara, *Fatos e documentos*, 118.

6. Cunniff, "The Great Drought," 235, 237.

7. Ibid., 236, 238; Brazil, *Recenseamento da população*, 4: 176.

8. According to a legal complaint filed by Maria Magdalena de Jesús, from Tamboril, she was "a poor, destitute woman, considered a widow since she was abandoned by her husband, three years ago." Tamboril, Cr., 9, 12: 19, 1878, APEC. On separated or abandoned women calling themselves widows in late-colonial Mexico, see Stern, *The Secret History*, 262.

9. Beattie, *Tribute of Blood*, 132–33.

10. Palazzi, "Work and Residence," 216–28; on debates about the place of the single woman, or "la femme soule," in French society after World War I, see Roberts, *Civilization*, 149–211.

11. For instance, based on manuscript parish censuses, Donald Ramos in "Single and Married Women" (p. 265) established that in the agrarian area of Ca-

choeira do Campo, Minas Gerais, 35.1 percent of all households were headed by women in 1838. Elizabeth Kuznesof found 31.4 percent female-headed households in three rural parishes around the city of São Paulo in 1836 in her study "Household Composition" (p. 86). B. J. Barickman and Martha Few identified 27.8 percent of female-headed households in two rural parishes of the Bahian Recôncavo, the hinterland immediately adjacent to the city of Salvador, in "Ana Paulinha" (pp. 169–201). Other studies that have identified considerable rates of female-headed households include Figueredo, *Barrocas Famílias*, 139–40; Metcalf, *Family*, 145; Faria, *A Colônia*, 53.

12. The 1762 manuscript census of Oeiras is published in Falci, "A cidade de Oeiras do Paiuí" (pp. 255–91). Based on the same census, Luiz Mott in *Piauí Colonial* (p. 83) demonstrates that single women and widows headed households located in more rural areas, where the main economic activities were cattle ranching and subsistence agriculture.

13. Samara and Sousa, "Morar e viver," 61.

14. Galeno, "A costureira," "A lavandeira," and "A engomadeira, " in *Lendas*, 2: 25–28, 63–67, 111–14; for references to laundresses and ironing women working in the interior of Ceará and other Northeastern provinces, see Pinheiro, *O Cariri*, 119–20; and Burton, *Explorations*, 2: 358.

15. Galeno, "A lavandeira," in *Lendas*, 2: 65.

16. Ibid., 2: 67.

17. This percentage is calculated from a total of fifty-two women that appear as witnesses, defendants, and plaintiffs in criminal proceedings in Jucás and Tamboril between 1865 and 1889.

18. Brazil, *Recenseamento da população*, 4: 176; Theophilo, *História*, 26; Tamboril, Cr., 3, 6: 5a, 1865, APEC.

19. Jucás, Inv. 4, 89: 28, 1868. See also Jucás, Inv. 7, 92: 2, 1887, APEC.

20. On the choice of cultivation of crops compatible with family labor, and particularly tobacco, over more labor-, land-, and capital-intensive crops, such as sugar, by poor free female household heads in Bahia, see Barickman and Few, "Ana Paulinha," 170–94.

21. Brazil, *Recenseamento da população*, 4: 176.

22. Olímpio, *Luzia-Homem*, 11, 16–17, 42.

23. Secreto, "Ceará, a fábrica," 59.

24. Ceará, Pres., *Falla* (1876), 5.

25. Beattie discusses at length the parliamentary and public debate regarding the passing of the Recruitment Law of 1874, and its broader implications in *Tribute of Blood* (chs. 3, 4). On resistance to the law as a protest from the honorable poor in the Northeast, see Meznar, "The Ranks of the Poor," 335–51.

26. Secreto, "Ceará: a fábrica," 59; on widows' and orphans' plight in Fortaleza, see Samara and Sousa, "Morar e viver," 50–51.

27. See, for example, Freire Alemão, "Papéis," 210; Galeno, *Lendas*, 1: 33–34; Bezerra, *Notas*, 247.

28. See, for example, Theophilo, *História*, 104; Olímpio, *Luzia-Homem*, 4; see also the discussion of prostitution during the Great Drought in Villa, *Vida e morte*, 65–68.

29. The Brazilian legal inheritance practice regulated by the *Ordenações Filipinas* established the *tutorias* system as a way to protect the material possessions and guarantee the well-being of orphans who were minors by making provisions for the minors' guardianship by the time of passing of one of their parents. Under the system, legally appointed guardians were required to take charge of orphans and teach them skills that would make possible their survival after they reached legal majority. Guardians were also required to deposit a yearly stipend in the municipal treasury that was to be given to the orphans by the time they reached legal age, or married. On the workings of the tutorias system in the Northeast, see Meznar, "Orphans," 499–515.

30. Galeno, *Lendas*, 1: 34–35.

31. See Kuznesof, "Sexual Politics," 241–60. For twentieth-century Rio de Janeiro, see Caulfield, *In Defense of Honor;* and Esteves, *Meninas perdidas*.

32. Stern, *The Secret History*, 261.

33. In listing prostitution as an occupation this is an unusual source, since other censuses, such as the 1872 national census, do no include prostitution as an occupation. Samara, "Mão-de-obra feminina," 18.

34. Freye, *Casa-grande & senzala*. The work has been translated into English as *The Masters and the Slaves*.

35. A scholar who advanced this perspective is A. C. de M. Souza, "The Brazilian Family" (pp. 291–312). See also Holanda, *Raízes do Brasil;* and Prado Júnior, *Formação*. For an examination of how the revisionist scholarship produced since the 1960s, in fact, merged Freyre's and Cândido's findings into a "traditional view" of the patriarchal extended family as the predominant arrangement in slaveholding Brazil, see Barickman, "Revisiting the *Casa-grande*."

36. See, for example, Corrêa, "Repensando a família patriarcal"; Marcílio, *A cidade de São Paulo*; Costa, *Vila Rica*; Samara, *As mulheres*; Ramos, "Marriage and the Family," 200–225, and "Single and Married Women," 261–82; Kuznesof, *Household Economy*; and Dias, *Power*.

37. See, for example, Samara, *As mulheres*, and "Tendências atuais," 25–36; Dias, *Power;* and Ramos, "Marriage and the Family," 201–25. Several scholars have critiqued the revisionist scholarship's reliance on analysis of household composition and structure as a way to understand the functioning of patriarchy; see, for example, Vainfas, *Trópico dos pecados*, 110; Barickman, "Revisiting the *Casa-grande*"; and Faria, *A Colônia*, 48–49. For a thought-

ful discussion on the need to historicize the concept of "patriarchal family" and the reasons for its appearance and application, see Albuquerque Júnior, *Nordestino*, 134–48.

38. Stern, *The Secret History*, 266; Franco, *Plotting Women*.

39. "O Anselmo," in Mota, *Cantadores*, 176.

40. Ibid., 175–77.

41. Julian Pitt-Rivers in *The Fate of Shechem* (p. 44) notes that women can be seen as dishonorable if they engage in actions or occupations that society deems as proper to men.

42. Scribes in criminal cases used the common phrase "lives off her own work" to describe these women's occupations, but did not specifically declare what their occupations were. Tamboril, Cr., 4, 7: 18, 1871, APEC.

43. Jucás, Cr., 3, 14: 42, 1874; see also Tamboril, Cr., 4, 7: 18, 1871, APEC. On the bad reputation of seamstresses and other female workers in São Paulo, see Dias, *Power*, 135–36.

44. On unmarried and widowed women with children as outside of the norms of ordered communities in Paraíba, see Meznar, "Deference and Dependence," 42.

45. Socolow, "Women and Crime," 4–5; for similar findings in late-colonial Mexico, see Stern, *The Secret History*, ch. 3.

46. Connell, *Masculinities*; Gutmann, *Meanings of Macho;* Stern, *The Secret History*.

47. Only in one of these cases the attackers were relatives of the victim and in another, they were the victim's neighbors.

48. Jucás, Cr., 4, 15: 19, 1875; Jucás, Cr., 4, 15: 7, 1875; Tamboril, Cr., 3, 6: 1, 1865; Jucás, Cr., 6, 17: 2, 1868; another case of a woman who refused a man's sexual advances and consequently was flogged is Jucás, Cr., 5, 16: 9, 1876, APEC.

49. See, for example, Jucás, Cr., 3, 14: 36, 1873; Jucás, Cr., 3, 14: 40, 1874; Jucás, Cr., 6, 17: 1, 1875; Jucás, Cr., 6, 17: 29, 1881; and Tamboril, Cr., 6, 9: 16, 1876, APEC.

50. Jucás, Cr., 4, 15: 7, 1875; Tamboril, Cr., 9, 12: 19b, 1881, APEC.

51. Behar, "Sexual Witchcraft," 178–206; Jucás, Cr., 4, 15: 19, 1875, APEC.

52. Women as wives, consensual partners, sisters, and even mothers of men were surrogate victims of violence directed to their loved ones when those who had issues of contention (including land disputes, nonpayment of debts or indemnities for destruction of property) sought to settle with violence and did not find them in their homes. As Chapter 3 in this volume has shown, wives and female consensual partners suffered domestic violence at the hands of their husbands or male partners. In addition, young girls received disciplinary floggings from their fathers. See, for example, Tamboril,

Cr., 1, 4: 9, 1848; Tamboril, Cr., 2, 5: 10, 1863; Tamboril, Cr., 3, 6: 5a, 1865; Tamboril, Cr., 3, 6: 24, 1870; Tamboril, Cr., 6, 9: 2, 1875; Jucás, Cr., 2, 13: 12, 1870; and Jucás, Cr., 5, 16: 17, 1872, APEC.

53. Jucás, Cr., 4, 15: 7, 1875; Tamboril, Cr., 6, 9: 16, 1876; Tamboril, Cr., 9, 12: 19b, 1881, APEC.

54. Itapagé, Cr., 5, 28: 14, 1875; Jucás, Cr., 6, 17: 29, 1881, APEC.

55. Koster, *Travels*, 1: 230; on the silence of Cearense women in the presence of their husbands during the mid-twentieth century, see Benchimol, *O Cearense*, 63.

56. Tamboril, Cr., 9, 12: 19b, 1881; Jucás, Cr., 1, 12: 39, 1864, APEC.

57. On miscarriage and death as a result of flogging, see, for example, Jucás, Cr., 4, 15: 14; and Jucás, Cr., 4, 15: 19, 1875; on rape, see, for example, Jucás, Cr., 6, 17: 2, 1868; and Tamboril, Cr., 2, 5: 13b, 1865, APEC.

58. Foucault, "Docile Bodies," in Rabinow, *The Foucault Reader*, 179–87; on masculine contests of violence as vehicles to claim or defend honor, see Pitt-Rivers, *The Fate of Shechem*, 4–5.

59. "Azulão," in Mota, *Cantadores*, 81.

60. For a theoretical discussion on male bodily performance, sociability, and the constitution of hegemonic masculinities, see Connell, *Masculinities*, 60–64; for the Cearense cases, see Jucás, Cr. 3, 14: 40, 1874; and Jucás, Cr., 4, 15: 19, 1875, APEC.

61. Jucás, Cr., 6, 17: 2, 1868; Jucás, Cr., 6, 17: 4, 1876, APEC.

62. Jucás, Cr., 4, 15: 14, 1875; Jucás, Cr., 6, 17: 29, 1881, APEC.

63. Jucás, Cr., 1, 12: 39, 1864, APEC.

64. See, for example, Jucás, Cr., 3, 14: 44, 1872; and Tamboril, Cr., 9, 12: 24, 1881; on female insolence, Itapagé, Cr., 4, 27: 4, 1875, APEC.

65. Itapagé, Cr., 3: 26, 1, 1873, APEC.

66. Tamboril, Cr., 2, 5: 13b, 1865, APEC.

67. Tamboril, Cr., 9, 12: 24, 1881, APEC.

68. Vasconcellos, *Codigo criminal;* Filgueiras Junior, *Codigo do Processo*; on the Imperial criminal laws' grounding on liberal legal philosophies, see Caulfied, *In Defense of Honor*, 21–25.

69. Vasconcellos, *Codigo criminal*, 87–89.

70. Ibid., 87.

71. Ibid., 89–91.

72. Vasconcellos, *Roteiro dos delegados,* 83–89.

73. Itapagé, Cr., 3, 26: 14, 1873, APEC.

74. Findlay, "Courtroom Tales," 201–22.

75. On the "house" and the "street" as a metaphorical distinction between the contrasting spaces of order, hierarchy, gender, and honor, see the classical elaboration by Freyre, in *Sobrados e mucambos* (1: 33–48); and the application of these contrasting images to contemporary Brazil in Da Matta,

Carnavais (pp. 71–75). Historical analyses that incorporate this metaphor include Graham, *House and Street;* and Beattie, *Tribute of Blood.*

76. Vasconcellos, *Codigo criminal*, 13–14.

77. Ibid., 92–93; on the implications of references to "honesty" in the code, see Caulfield, *In Defense of Honor*, 24–25.

78. On the contradiction between liberal philosophy and the inclusion of the concept of honor and private vengeance in the Criminal Code—a contradiction that, in fact, ensured the continuation of gender and social hierarchies, see Caulfied, *In Defense of Honor*, 23.

79. Tamboril, Cr., 9, 12: 24, 1881, APEC; Vasconcellos, *Codigo criminal*, 15; on defense of a person's rights as an extenuating circumstance, see 10–12.

80. Itapagé, Cr., 9, 12: 19b, 1881, APEC; Vasconcellos, *Codigo criminal*, 15.

81. Itapagé, Cr., 9, 32: 10, 1883, APEC; Vasconcellos, *Codigo criminal*, 13, 15–16.

82. Jucás, Cr., 5, 16: 20, 1876, APEC.

83. Findlay, "Courtroom Tales," 218.

84. Tamboril, Cr., 2, 5: 13b, 1868, APEC; Vasconcellos, *Codigo Criminal*, 86–87.

85. See, for example, Jucás, Cr., 6, 17: 29, 1881, APEC.

86. Findlay, "Courtroom Tales," 201–4.

87. Tamboril, Cr., 9, 12: 21, 1881; Itapagé, Cr., 3, 26: 14, 1873, APEC; Vasconcellos, *Codigo criminal*, 15–16.

88. See, for example, Tamboril, Cr., 2, 5: 13b, 1865; and Jucás, Cr., 6, 17: 2, 1868, APEC.

89. See, for example, Tamboril, Cr., 1, 4: 12, 1854; Tamboril, Cr., 2, 5: 13b, 1865; Jucás, Cr., 6, 17: 4, 1868; Jucás, Cr., 3, 14: 17, 1872; and Jucás, Cr., 2, 13: 5, 1868, APEC.

90. Connell, *Masculinities*, 84.

91. Ibid., 76.

Chapter 6

1. "Luís Dantas Quesado," in Mota, *Cantadores*, 114.

2. For references to this literature, see n. 5 and n. 6 in "Introduction" and n. 5 in Chapter 3, this volume.

3. A notable exception to the overall lack of historicization of the idea of the sertanejo macho is the discursive analysis by the Brazilian scholar Albuquerque Júnior, *Nordestino.*

4. Hall, *Representation*, 41–51; Parker, "Gentlemanly Responsibility," 126.

5. Itapagé, Cr., 9, 32: 7, 1883, APEC.

6. Historical works on honor and violence among poor men in Latin America include, among others Stern, *The Secret History*; Johnson, "Dangerous Words"; Chasteen, "Violence for Show"; Boyer, "Honor among Plebeians." See also Chambers, *From Subjects to Citizens*, ch. 5; and Kittelson, *Practice of Politics*, ch. 3. On the classic conceptualizations of honor in contemporary Mediterranean societies, see Pitt-Rivers, *The Fate of Shechem*; Peristiany and Pitt-Rivers, *Honor and Grace*; and Peristiany, *Honour and Shame*. On the paradoxical use of dueling by politicians and journalists in turn-of-the-twentieth-century Mexico and Uruguay, see Picatto, "Politics"; and Parker, "Gentlemanly Responsibility."

7. Stern, *The Secret History*, 171.

8. Ibid., 177.

9. See, for example, Tamboril, Cr., 5, 8: 7, 1872; and Tamboril, Cr., 6, 9: 14A, 1876, APEC. On sambas and desafios as spaces of male sociability, see da Cunha, *Rebellion*, 102.

10. Da Cunha, *Rebellion*, 99–101.

11. Alonso, *Thread of Blood*, 80–81.

12. Tamboril, Cr., 6, 9: 14A, 1876; Itapagé, Cr., 3, 26: 9, 1874, APEC.

13. Johnson, "Dangerous Words," 127–51.

14. Jucás, Cr., 4, 15: 18, APEC.

15. On racial constructs in the backlands, see Lewin, "Who Was 'o Grande Romano'?" 129–79.

16. Tamboril, Cr., 3, 6: 18, 1866, APEC.

17. Itapagé, Cr., 11, 34: 19, 1888, APEC.

18. Itapagé, Cr., 2, 25, 1871, APEC.

19. Itapagé, Cr., 9, 32: 7, 1883, APEC.

20. See, for example, Jucás, Cr., 4, 15: 6, 1872; Tamboril, Cr., 2, 5: 13, 1862; Tamboril, Cr., 7, 10: 22, 1876; Itapagé, Cr., 3, 26: 9, 1874; Itapagé, Cr., 11, 34: 19, 1888, APEC; and Art. 18, nos. 3, 4, 6 and 8, Vasconcellos, *Codigo criminal*, 15, 16.

21. Itapagé, Cr., 3, 26: 9, 1874, APEC; Art. 18, nos. 3, 4 and 6, Vasconcellos, *Codigo criminal*, 15.

22. Itapagé, Cr., 9, 32: 7, 1883; Jucás, Cr., 4, 15: 13, 1875, APEC.

23. Itapagé, Cr., 3, 26: 8, 1874; Art. 18, no 9, Vasconcellos, *Codigo criminal*, 16.

24. Olímpio, *Luzia-Homem*, 130–31.

25. "O cego Sinfrônio," in Mota, *Cantadores*, 48.

26. Maximiliano, *Viagem*, 2: 427, 457. See also da Cunha, *Rebellion*, 102.

27. Tamboril, Cr., 7, 10: 15, 1877, APEC.

28. Tamboril, Cr., 6, 9: 17, 1876. See also, for example, Jucás, Cr., 1, 12:4, 1865; Jucás, Cr., 2, 13: 14, 1870; Jucás, Cr., 2, 13: 15, 1870; and Tamboril, Cr., 2, 5: 19, 1864, APEC.

29. This discussion is based on analysis of fifteen cases of land demarcation for the municipality of Jucás, from the years 1837 to 1890, and two other cases of contested demarcation. Jucás, DT, 2, 69-A, 1834–1938, Procs. 3 to 21; Jucás, Cív., 1-A, 2: 30, 1874; Tamboril, Cív., 1, 1: 35, 1864, APEC.

30. In the absence of other class markers in criminal cases, this study relies on illiteracy, along with other characteristics, as proxies for poverty. From a collection of thirty-two civil suits related to land issues from the municipalities of Jucás and Tamboril between 1850 and 1889, only two cases were initiated by illiterate farmers and ranchers. These civil suits are included in the following packages: Tamboril, Cív., 1, 1, 1853–75; Tamboril, Cív., 2, 2, 1876–84; Jucás, Cív., 01-A, 2, 1837–79; Jucás, DT, 2, 69-A, 1834–1938, APEC.

31. "Luís Dantas Quesado," in Mota, *Cantadores*, 118.

32. Tamboril, Cív., 1, 1: 27, 1853; Jucás, Cív., 01-A, 2: 32, 1875, APEC; Bezerra, *Notas*, 166.

33. Jucás, DT, 2, 69-A: 14, 1867; Jucás, DT, 2, 69-A: 16, 1869, APEC.

34. Vasconcellos, *Codigo criminal*, 105–6.

35. Vasconcellos, *Roteiro*, 83–85.

36. Jucás, Cr., 2, 3: 15, 1870, APEC.

37. Jucás, Cr., 2, 13: 15, 1870; see also Jucás, Cr., 1, 12: 35, 1864, APEC.

38. From a total of twenty property damage cases from Jucás and Tamboril for the years 1865 to 1889, twelve featured literate plaintiffs and one featured an illiterate supplicant. In seven of them, the literacy of the plaintiffs could not be determined. Data on the literacy of the defendants is as follows: seven were literate, six were illiterate, and seven were undetermined.

39. Jucás, Cr., 1, 12: 4, 1865, APEC.

40. See, for example, Tamboril, Cr., 2, 5: 19, 1864; Tamboril, Cr., 3, 6: 9, 13, 1866; and Jucás, Cr., 4, 15: 26, 1875, APEC; on sentences prescribed for the crime of dano, see Vasconcellos, *Codigo criminal*, 106.

41. Jucás, Cr., 01, 12: 4, 1865; see also Tamboril, Cr., 7, 10: 7, 1876; and Jucás, Cr., 2, 13: 22, 1871. For ear-cutting as retaliation, see Tamboril, Cr., 5, 8: 14, 1874, APEC.

42. Tamboril, Cr., 5, 8: 14; Tamboril, Cr., 4, 7: 19, 1871; Jucás, Cr., 1, 12: 27, 1863, APEC; see also the case of the illiterate farmers from the Rodrigues and Ferreira families of Jucás who worked in the fields with weapons, and gang-destroyed roças claimed by Major Francisco de Abreu Barros in Jucás, Cr., 3, 14: 6, 1866, APEC.

43. On family feuds and violence in the seventeenth and eighteenth centuries in Ceará and elsewhere in the Northeast, see, for example, Macêdo, *O clã dos Inhamuns*, and *O bacamarte dos Mourões*; and Chandler, *The Feitosas*; on the colonial origins of banditry in the Northeast, see, for example, Queiroz, *Os Cangaceiros*, 43–55; Souza, "The Cangaço," 109–31; and Chandler, *The*

Bandit King, ch. 1. See also Hobsbawm, *Primitive Rebels,* ch. 2; and Lewin, "The Oligarchical Limitations."

44. On the professionalization of bandit gangs in the late nineteenth century, see, for example, Queiroz, *Os Cangaceiros,* 199–213; Souza, "The Cangaço," 109–31; Chandler, "Brazilian Cangaceiros," 97–112; Lewin, "The Oligarchical Limitations"; and Pericás, *Os Cangaceiros.* On the activities of bandit gangs in late-nineteenth-century Ceará, see Of. 453, September 22, 1879, Secr. Polícia do Ceará, Ofs. expedidos, 1878–80, ala 19, est. 393, caixa 12, APEC; Ceará, Pres., *Falla* (1878), 5; Ceará, Pres., *Falla* (1880), 5; and Ceará, Pres., *Relatório* (1881), 41.

45. Another line of analysis of Northeastern banditry, and more broadly, Latin American forms of banditry, addresses the question of whether or not these brigands can be considered "social bandits" in the sense that Eric Hobsbawm gave to the term in his influential work *Primitive Rebels* and in his *Bandits.* Examples of the revisionist scholarship are the articles by Chandler and Lewin published in the 1987 collection *Bandidos: The Varieties of Latin American Banditry,* edited by Richard Slatta, which represents a comprehensive and empirical critique to Hobsbawm's model. For a useful critique of the revisionist scholarship and for suggestions on other approaches to understanding peasant social action in Latin America, see Joseph, "On the Trail."

46. On the elite or middling social origins of bandit chieftains, see Queiroz, *Os Cangaceiros,* 43–55; Chandler, "Brazilian Cangaceiros," 100–101; Fausto, "Social and Political Structure," 805; Barroso, *Heróes e bandidos,* 49–53; Nonato, *Jesuíno Brilhante,* 8–15.

47. Jucás, Cr., 6, 17: 24, 1877; Jucás, Cr., 5, 16: 37, 1877, APEC; Mattos, *Crise agrária,* 71–72.

48. On living conditions, wages, and feelings of autonomy of bandits, see, for example, Souza, "The Cangaço," 116, 125; and Lewin, "The Oligarchical Limitations," 139–43.

49. Souza, "The Cangaço," 109–23; Tamboril, Cr., 5, 8: 20, 1874, APEC.

50. Billy Jaynes Chandler, in *The Bandit King* (pp. 214–17), analyzes the social origins of Lampião's bandits and shows that most came from the small-property-owning classes of the backlands. Interestingly, most of them ranged in age between eighteen and thirty-five years. See also Queiroz, *Os Cangaceiros,* 160–61.

51. "Romance do Cabeleira," in Mello, *Estórias e lendas,* 76.

52. Távora, *O Cabeleira,* 46.

53. The workings of race among the rank-and-file members of bandit gangs are not fully investigated in this study, but it is a topic worthy of further research.

54. "Antônio Silvino," in Barroso, *Heróes e bandidos,* 242–47.

55. Chandler, "Brazilian Cangaceiros," 99; "Antônio Silvino," in Barroso, *Heróes e Bandidos,* 228; Hobsbawm, *Primitive Rebels,* ch. 2.

56. Cascudo, *Vaqueiros e cantadores,* 119.

57. Nonato, *Jesuíno Brilhante,* 78.

58. "O Cego Sinfrônio," in Mota, *Cantadores,* 52.

59. Pimentel Filho, "A produção do crime," 153–57.

Conclusion

1. On the rhetorical deployment of the image of the sertanejo macho as a strategy by regional elites to confront their loss of resources and power at the national level during the early twentieth century, see Albuquerque Júnior, *Nordestino,* 31–44, 86–100, 149–202.

2. Bieber, *Power,* 143–59, 199–206.

3. Chandler, *The Feitosas,* 46–78.

4. Meznar, "The Ranks of the Poor"; Beattie, *Tribute of Blood.*

5. Souza, "The Cangaço," 109–31; Cunniff, "The Great Drought," 155; Domingos, "The Powerful in the Outback"; Pessar, *From Fanatics to Folk,* ch. 1.

6. Chandler, *The Feitosas;* Meznar, "Deference and Dependence." See also Lewin, *Politics.*

7. Falci, "Mulheres"; Meznar, "Carlota Lucia," and "Orphans"; Vieira Jr., *Entre paredes e bacamartes.*

8. While there is a voluminous literature on messianic movements in the Northeast, and some studies consider the roles of women in those communities, very few of them analyze beatas as gendered subjects. Exceptions to this trend are Campos, "Mulher e universo mágico"; and Forti, *Maria do Juazeiro.*

9. Santos, "Disempowering Women."

10. For example, Nazzari, *Disappearance of the Dowry;* Metcalf, "Women and Means," and "Fathers and Sons"; Mattoso, *Família e sociedade.*

11. Guy, "Future Directions," 1–9.

Archives and Manuscript Collections

Arquivo Público do Estado do Ceará, Fortaleza, Ceará (APEC)
  Seção Histórica
  Seção Cartórios
Biblioteca da Academia Cearense de Letras, Fortaleza, Ceará
  Setor Livros Raros
Biblioteca do Instituto do Ceará, Fortaleza, Ceará
  Coleção Barão de Studart
  Coleção História dos Municípios
Biblioteca Nacional, Rio de Janeiro (BNRJ)
  Acervo de Periódicos
  Acervo Manuscritos
  Acervo Obras Raras
Biblioteca Pública Governador Menezes Pimentel, Fortaleza, Ceará
  Setor de Periódicos
  Setor Obras Raras
  Setor Ceará
Library of Congress, Washington, DC (LC)
  Geography and Map Division
  Hispanic Division
  Rare Book and Special Collection Division
Oliveira Lima Library, Catholic University of America, Washington, DC (OLL)

Newspapers

Cearense.
Pedro II.
Constituição.
Araripe.

Published Primary Sources

Alemão, Francisco Freire. "Papéis da Expedição ao Ceará." *Anais da Biblioteca Nacional* 81 (1961): 195–347.

Alencar, Alvaro Gurgel de. *Dicionário geografico, historico e descriptivo do estado do Ceará*. Ceará: Typographia Moderna, 1903.

Alencastre, José Martins Pereira de. "Memoria chronologica, histôrica e corographica da provincia do Piauí." *RIHGB* 20, 1 (1857): 5–164.

Almeida, Candido Mendes de. *Codigo Philippino ou Ordenações e Leis do Reino de Portugal*. 5 vols., 14th ed. Rio de Janeiro: Typographia do Instituto Philomathico, 1870.

Araripe Júnior, Tristão de Alencar. *Luizinha*. Rio de Janeiro: José Olympio Editora, 1980; reprint, Rio de Janeiro: Tipografia Vera-Cruz, 1878.

Avé-Lallemant, Robert. *Viagem pelo norte do Brasil, no ano de 1859*. Translated by Eduardo de Lima Castro. 2 vols. Rio de Janeiro: Instituto Nacional do Livro, 1961 [1860].

Bezerra, Antonio. *Notas de viagem*. Fortaleza: Imprensa Universitária, 1965 [1884].

Brasil, Thomaz Pompeu de Sousa. *Ensaio estatístico da provincia do Ceará*. 2 vols. Fortaleza: Typographia de B. de Mattos, 1863.

———. *Estado do Ceará na exposição de Chicago*. Fortaleza: Typographia da Republica, 1893.

Brazil, Directoria Geral de Estatística. *Recenseamento da população do Império do Brazil a que se procedeu no dia 1o de Agosto de 1872*. 21 vols. Rio de Janeiro: 1873–76.

Brígido João. *Ceará: Homens e factos*. Rio de Janeiro: Typographia Besnard Freres, 1919.

Burton, Richard. *Explorations of the Highlands of Brazil*. 2 vols. New York: Greenwood Press Publishers, 1969; reprint, London: Tinsley Brothers, 1869.

"Cancioneiro do folk-lore pernambucano." *RIHGB* 70, 166 (1908): 429–55.

Carvalho, Jáder de, ed. *Antologia de João Brígido*. Fortaleza: Editora Terra do Sol, 1969.

Cavalcante, José Pompeu de Albuquerque. *Chorographia da provincia do Ceará*. Rio de Janeiro: Imprensa Nacional, 1888.

Ceará. *Compilação das Leis provinciais do Ceará*. 3 vols. Rio de Janeiro: Typographia Universal de Laemmert, 1863.

Ceará. Provincial President. *Relatório* or *Falla . . . à Assembléa Legislativa Provincial do Ceará* (title varies), 1836–89.

Da Cunha, Euclides. *Rebellion in the Backlands*. Translated by and with introduction by Samuel Putnam. Chicago: University of Chicago Press, 1944.

———. *Os Sertões*. 5th. ed. Rio de Janeiro: Editora Record, 2002.

Falci, Miridan Britto. "A cidade de Oeiras do Paiuí." *RIHGB* 47 (April–June 2000): 255–91.

Filgueiras Junior, Araujo. *Codigo do Processo do Imperio do Brasil*. 2. vols. Rio de Janeiro: Eduardo & Henrique Laemmert, 1874.

Galeno, Juvenal. *Lendas e canções populares*. 2 vols. Fortaleza: Imprensa Universitária do Ceará, 1965 [1864].

Gardner, George. *Travels in the Interior of Brazil*. New York: AMS Press, 1970; reprint, London: Reeve Brothers, 1846.

Hoornaert, Eduardo. *Crônicas das Casas de Caridade fundadas pelo padre Ibiapina*. Fortaleza: Museu do Ceará-Secretaria da Cultura do Estado do Ceará, 2006.

Joffily, Irinêo. *Notas sobre a Parahyba*. Rio de Janeiro: Typographia do Jornal do Commercio, 1892.

Koster, Henry. *Travels in Brazil*. 2 vols., 2d ed. London: Longman, Hurst, Rees, Orme and Brown, 1817.

Maximiliano, Príncipe de Wied-Neuwied. *Viagem ao Brasil, nos anos de 1815 a 1817*. 2 vols. Translated by Edgar Sussekind de Mendonça and Flávio Poppe de Figuereido. 2d ed. São Paulo: Companhia Editora Nacional, 1958.

Mello, Marcondes Homem de. "Excursões pelo Ceará, S. Pedro do Sul e S. Paulo." *RIHGB* 34 (1872): 80–169.

Mota, Leonardo. *Cantadores: Poesia e linguagem do sertão cearense*. 3d ed. Fortaleza: Imprensa Universitária do Ceará, 1960.

———. *Violeiros do norte: Poesia e linguagem do sertão nordestino*. 4th ed. Rio de Janeiro: Livraria Editora Cátedra, 1976.

Nogueira, Paulino. *Os presidentes do Ceará durante a monarquia*. 5 vols. Fortaleza: Typographia Studart, 1889.

Olímpio, Domingos. *Luzia-Homem*. Fortaleza: ABC Fortaleza, 1999 [1903].

Paiva, Manoel de Oliveira. *Dona Guidinha do Poço*. 2d ed. Fortaleza: ABC Fortaleza, 2001 [1952].

Paraíba. Provincial President. *Relatorio . . . à Assembléa Legislativa da Parahyba do Norte* (title varies), 1857, 1875.

Paulet, Antonio José da Silva. "Descripção geografica abreviada da capitania do Ceará." *RIHGB* 60 (1897): 75–101.

"Roteiro de Maranhão a Goiás pela Capitania do Piauí." *RIHGB* 57 (1897): 60–161.

Sarmiento, Domingo Faustino. *Civilización y Barbarie: Vida de Juan Facundo Quiroga*. Santiago: Imprenta del Progreso, 1845.

Sobrinho, Thomas Pompeu. *Sesmarias cearenses (distribuição geográfica)*. Fortaleza: SUDEC, 1972.

Studart, Barão de. *Datas e factos para a historia do Ceará*. 2 vols. Fortaleza: Typographia Studart, 1896.

———. *Climatologia, epidemias e endemias do Ceará*. Fortaleza: Typographia Minerva, 1909.

———. "Geografia do Ceará." *RIC* 31 (1924): 3–124.

Studart, Guilherme. *Notas para a história do Ceará*. Lisboa: Typografia Recreio, 1892.

Távora, Franklin. *O Cabeleira*. Fortaleza: ABC Editora, 2001 [1876].

Théberge, Pedro. *Esboço historico sobre a provincia do Ceará*. 3 vols. Fortaleza: Typographia Imparcial de Francisco Perdigão, 1869.

Theophilo, Rodolpho. *História da secca do Ceará, 1877 a 1880*. Fortaleza: Typographia do Libertador, 1883.

Vasconcellos, J. M. P. de. *Roteiro dos delegados e subdelegados da polícia*. Rio de Janeiro: Typografia de J. Villeneuve e comp., 1857.

———. *Codigo criminal do Império do Brasil*. Rio de Janeiro: Eduardo & Henrique Laemmert, 1859.

Secondary Sources

Abreu, João Capistrano de. *Caminhos antigos e povoamento do Brasil*. Rio de Janeiro: Sociedade Capistrano de Abreu, 1930.

Albuquerque Júnior, Durval Muniz de. "Palavras que calcinam, palavras que dominam: a invenção da seca do Nordeste." *Revista Brasileira de História* 15, 28 (1995): 111–20.

———. "'Quem é froxo não se mete': Violência e masculinidade como elementos constitutivos da imagem do nordestino." *Projeto História (PUCSP)* 19 (1999): 173–88.

———. *A invenção do Nordeste e outras artes*. 2d ed. Recife: Fundação Joaquim Nabuco, Editora Massangana, 2001.

———. *Nordestino: Uma invencão do falo—uma história do gênero masculino (Nordeste, 1920–1940)*. Maceió: Edições Catavento, 2003.

———. "Weaving Tradition: The Invention of the Brazilian Northeast." *Latin American Perspectives* 135, 31, 2 (March 2004): 42–61.

Alegre, Maria Sylvia Porto. "Fome de braços—questão nacional. Notas sobre o trabalho livre no Nordeste no século XIX." *Revista de Ciências Sociais UFC* 20/21, 1/2 (1989/1990): 105–42.

———. "Vaqueiros, agricultores, artesãos: Origens do trabalho livre no Ceará colonial." *Revista de Ciências Sociais UFC* 20/21, 1/2 (1989/1990): 1–29.

Alonso, Ana María. *Thread of Blood: Colonialism, Revolution, and Gender on Mexico's Northern Frontier*. Tucson: University of Arizona Press, 1995.

Alves, Joaquim. *História das sêcas: Séculos XVII a XIX*. Fortaleza: Edições do Instituto do Ceará, 1953.

Anderson, Robin. *Colonization as Exploitation in the Amazon Rain Forest, 1758–1911*. Gainesville: University Press of Florida, 1999.

Andrade, Manoel Correia de. *The Land and People of Northeast Brazil*. Translated by Dennis V. Johnson. Albuquerque: University of New Mexico Press, 1980.

———, ed. *Movimentos populares no Nordeste do periodo regencial*. Recife: Editora Massangana, 1989.

Aquino, Aécio Villar de. *Aspectos históricos e sociais da pecuária na caatinga paraibana*. Mossoró: Escola Superior de Agricultura de Mossoró, 1987.

Araújo, Antônio Gomes de. *Povoamento do Cariri*. Fortaleza: Imprensa Universitária, 1973.

Araújo, Douglas. *A morte do sertão antigo no Seridó: O desmoronamento das fazendas agropecuaristas em Caicó e Florânia (1970–90)*. Fortaleza: Banco do Nordeste Brasileiro, 2006.

Araújo, Maria do Carmo. "O poder local no Ceará." In *História do Ceará*, ed. Simone de Souza, 109–26. Fortaleza: Edições Demócrito Rocha, 1995.

Assunção, Matthias Rohrig. "Elite Politics and Popular Rebellion in the Construction of Post-colonial Order. The Case of Maranhão Brazil (1820–41)." *Journal of Latin American Studies* 31 (1999): 1–38.

Aufderheide, Patricia. "Upright Citizens in Criminal Records: Investigations in Cachoeira and Geremoabo, Brazil, 1780–1836." *The Americas* 38, 2 (October 1981): 173–84.

Bandeira, Luiz Alberto Moniz. *O feudo: A Casa da Torre de Garcia d'avila: Da conquista dos sertões à independência*. Rio de Janeiro: Civilização Brasileira, 2000.

Barbosa, Ivone Cordero. "Entre a barbárie e a civilização: o lugar do sertão na literatura." In *Uma nova história do Ceará*, ed. Simone de Souza, 56–75. Fortaleza: Edições Demócrito Rocha, 2000.

Barickman, B. J. *A Bahian Counterpoint: Sugar, Tobacco, Cassava and Slavery in the Recôncavo, 1780–1860*. Stanford: Stanford University Press, 1998.

———. "Revisiting the *Casa-grande*: Plantation and Cane-Farming Households in Early Nineteenth-Century Bahia." *HAHR* 84, 4 (2004): 619–59.

Barickman, B. J., and Martha Few. "Ana Paulinha de Queirós, Joaquina da Costa, and Their Neighbors: Free Women of Color as Household Heads in Rural Bahia (Brazil), 1835." In *Beyond Bondage: Free Women of Color in the Americas*, ed. David Barry Gaspar and Darlene Clark Hines, 169–201. Urbana: University of Illinois Press, 2004.

Barman, Roderick. "The Brazilian Peasantry Reexamined: The Implications of the Quebra-Quilo Revolt, 1874–1875." *HAHR* 57, 3 (1977): 401–24.

———. *Brazil: The Forging of a Nation, 1798–1852*. Stanford: Stanford University Press, 1988.

Barman, Roderick, and Jean Barman. "The Role of the Law Graduate in the Political Elite of Imperial Brazil." *Journal of Inter-American Studies and World Affairs* 18, 4 (1976): 423–50.

Barreira, César. *Trilhas e atalhos do poder: Conflitos sociais no sertão*. Rio de Janeiro: Rio Fundo Editora, 1992.

Barroso, Gustavo. *Heróes e bandidos (os cangaceiros do Nordeste)*. Rio de Janeiro: Livraria Francisco Alves, 1917.

———. *Terra de sol (natureza e costumes do Norte)*. Rio de Janeiro: Livraria Francisco Alves, 1930.

Bastide, Roger. *Sociologia do folclore brasileiro*. São Paulo: Anhambi, 1959.

Beattie, Peter. *The Tribute of Blood: Army, Honor, Race, and Nation in Brazil, 1864–1945*. Durham: Duke University Press, 2001.

Behar, Ruth. "Sexual Witchcraft, Colonialism and Women's Power." In *Sexuality and Marriage in Colonial Latin America*, ed. Asunción Lavrin, 178–206. Lincoln: University of Nebraska Press, 1989.

Benchimol, Samuel. *O cearense na Amazônia: Inquérito antropogeográfico sôbre um tipo de imigrante*. Rio de Janeiro: SPVEA, 1965.

Benjamin, Walter. "Thesis on the Philosophy of History." In *Illuminations*, ed. Hannah Arendt, 253–64. New York: Schoken Books, 1968.

Bergard, Laird. *Slavery and the Demographic and Economic History of Minas Gerais, Brazil, 1720–1888*. Cambridge: Cambridge University Press, 1999.

Bethell, Leslie. "The Independence of Brazil." In *The Cambridge History of Latin America*. 11 vols., ed. Leslie Bethell, 3: 157–96. Cambridge: Cambridge University Press, 1985.

Bethell, Leslie, and José Murilo de Carvalho. "Brazil from Independence to the Middle of the Nineteenth Century." In *The Cambridge History of Latin America*. 11 vols., ed. Leslie Bethell, 3: 679–746. Cambridge: Cambridge University Press, 1985.

Bieber, Judy. *Power, Patronage, and Political Violence: State Building on a Brazilian Frontier, 1822–1889*. Lincoln: University of Nebraska Press, 1999.

———. "A 'Visão do Sertão': Party Identity and Political Honor in Late-Imperial Minas Gerais, Brazil." *HAHR* 81, 2 (2001): 309–42.

Blake, Stanley E. *The Vigorous Core of Our Nationality: Race and Regional Identity in Northeastern Brazil*. Pittsburgh, PA: University of Pittsburgh Press, 2011.

Borges, Dain. *The Family in Bahia, Brazil, 1870–1945*. Stanford: Stanford University Press, 1992.

Bourdieu, Pierre. *Outline of a Theory of Practice*. Translated by Richard Nice. Cambridge: Cambridge University Press, 1977.

———. *Masculine Domination*. Translated by Richard Nice. Stanford: Stanford University Press, 2001.

Boyer, Richard. "Honor among Plebeians." In *The Faces of Honor*, ed. Lyman Johnson and Sonya Lipsett-Rivera, 152–78. Albuquerque: University of New Mexico Press, 1998.

Buescu, Mircea. *300 anos de inflação*. Rio de Janeiro: APEC Editora, 1973.

Buffington, Robert M. "Subjectivity, Agency, and the New Latin American History of Gender and Sexuality." *History Compass* 5, 5 (2007): 1640–60.

Burkholder, Mark. "Honor and Honors in Colonial Spanish America." In *The Faces of Honor*, ed. Lyman Johnson and Sonya Lipsett-Rivera, 18–44. Albuquerque: University of New Mexico Press, 1998.

Butler, Judith. *The Psychic Life of Power: Theories in Subjection*. Stanford: Stanford University Press, 1997.

Câmara, José Aurélio Saraiva. *Fatos e documentos do Ceará provincial*. Fortaleza: Imprensa Universitária da UFC, 1970.

Campos, Alzira Lobo de Arruda. "Mulher e universo mágico: Beatas e curandeiras." *História* (Universidade Estadual Paulista) 12 (1993): 29–47.

Campos, Eduardo. *Revelações da condição de vida dos cativos do Ceará*. Fortaleza: Secretaria de Cultura e Desporto, 1984.

———. *Crônica do Ceará agrário: Fundamentos do exercício agronômico*. Fortaleza: Stylus, 1988.

Carvalho, José Murilo de. *A construção da ordem: A elite política imperial*. Brasília: Ed. Universidade de Brasília, 1981.

———. *Teatro de sombras: A política imperial*. São Paulo: Vértice, 1988.

Carvalho, Marcus Joaquim M. de. *Liberdade: Rotinas e rupturas do escravismo no Recife, 1822–1850*. Recife: Editora Universitária da UFPE, 2001.

Cascudo, Luis da Câmara. *Vaqueiros e cantadores*. Porto Alegre: Edição da Livraria Globo, 1941.

Castro, Hebe Maria Mattos de. *Ao sul da história: Lavradores pobres na crise do trabalho escravo*. São Paulo: Brasiliense, 1987.

———. "Beyond Masters and Slaves: Subsistence Agriculture as a Survival Strategy in Brazil during the Second Half of the Nineteenth Century." *HAHR* 68, 3 (1988): 461–89.

Caufield, Sueann. *In Defense of Honor: Sexual Morality, Modernity and Nation in Early Twentieth-Century Brazil*. Durham: Duke University Press, 2000.

———. Sarah Chambers and Lara Putnam, eds. *Honor, Status and the Law in Modern Latin America*. Durham: Duke University Press, 2005.

Chalhoub, Sidney. *Trabalho, lar e botequim: O cotidiano dos trabalhadores no Rio de Janeiro da belle époque*. São Paulo: Brasiliense, 1986.

———. "Interpreting Machado de Assis: Paternalism, Slavery, and the Free Womb Law." In *Honor, Status and the Law in Modern Latin America*, ed. Sueann Caulfield, Sarah Chambers, and Lara Putnam, 87–108. Durham: Duke University Press, 2005.

Chambers, Sarah. *From Subjects to Citizens: Honor, Gender and Politics in Arequipa, Peru, 1780–1854*. University Park: Pennsylvania State University, 1999.

Chandler, Billy Jaynes. *The Feitosas and the Sertão dos Inhamuns: The History of a Family and a Community in Northeast Brazil, 1700–1930*. Gainesville: University of Florida Press, 1972.

———. *The Bandit King: Lampião of Brazil*. College Station: Texas A&M University Press, 1978.

———. "Brazilian Cangaceiros as Social Bandits: A Critical Appraisal." In *Bandidos: The Variety of Latin American Banditry*, ed. Richard Slatta, 97–112. New York: Greenwood Press, 1987.

Chasteen, John Charles. "Background to Civil War: The Process of Land Tenure in Brazil's Southern Borderland, 1801–93." *HAHR* 74, 4 (1991): 737–60.

————. "Cabanos and Farrapos: Brazilian Nativism in Regional Perspective, 1822–1850." *Locus* 7, 1 (Fall 1994): 31–46.

————. "Violence for Show: Knife Dueling on a Nineteenth-Century Cattle Frontier." In *The Problem of Order in Changing Societies*, ed. Lyman Johnson, 47–64. Albuquerque: University of New Mexico Press, 1990.

Chilcote, Ronald. "The Politics of Conflict in the Popular Poetry of Northeast Brazil." *Journal of Latin American Lore* 5, 2 (1979): 205–31.

Cleary, David. "'Lost Altogether to the Civilised World': Race and *Cabanagem* in Northern Brazil, 1750 to 1850." *CSSH* 40, 1 (January 1998): 109–35.

Connell, R. W. *Masculinities*. Berkeley: University of California Press, 1995.

Conrad, Robert. *The Destruction of Brazilian Slavery, 1850–1888*. 2d ed. Malabar, FL: Krieger Publishing Co., 1993.

Corrêa, Mariza. "Repensando a família patriarcal brasileira (notas para o estudo das formas de organização familiar no Brasil)." In *Colcha de retalhos: Estudos sobre a família no Brasil*, ed. Maria Suely Kofes de Almeida et al., 13–38. São Paulo: Brasiliense, 1982.

Costa, Emília Viotti da. *The Brazilian Empire: Myths and Histories*. Rev. ed. Chicago: University of Chicago Press, 1985.

Costa, Iraci del Nero da. *Vila Rica: População (1719–1826)*. São Paulo: IPE-USP, 1979.

Costa, Wilma Peres. *A espada de Dâmocles: O exército, a guerra do Paraguai e a crise do império*. São Paulo: Editora Hucitec, 1996.

Da Matta, Roberto. *Carnavais, malandros e heróis: Para uma sociologia do dilema brasileiro*. 2d ed. Rio de Janeiro: Zahar, 1981.

Darnton, Robert. *The Great Cat Massacre and Other Episodes in French Cultural History*. New York: Random House, 1985.

Daus, Ronald. *O ciclo épico dos cangaceiros na poesia popular do Nordeste*. Translated by Raquel Teixeira Valença. Rio de Janeiro: Fundação Casa de Rui Barbosa, 1982.

Dean, Warren. "Latifundia and Land Policy in Nineteenth-Century Brazil." *HAHR* 51, 4 (November 1971): 606–25.

Deere, Carmen Diana, and Magdalena León. "Peasant Production, Proletarianization, and the Sexual Division of Labor in the Andes." *Signs* 7, 2 (Winter 1981): 338–60.

————. "Liberalism and Married Women's Property Rights in Nineteenth-Century Latin America." *HAHR* 85, 4 (November 2005): 627–78.

Della Cava, Ralph. *Miracle at Joaseiro*. New York: Columbia University Press, 1970.

Dias, Claudete Maria Miranda. "Movimentos sociais do século XIX: Resistência e luta dos Balaios no Piauí." In *Formas de resistência camponesa: Visibilidade e diversidade de conflitos ao longo da história*, ed. Márcia Motta and Paulo Zarth, 199–218. São Paulo: Editora UNESP, 2008.

Dias, Maria Odila Silva. *Power and Everyday Life: The Lives of Working Women in Nineteenth-century Brazil.* Translated by Ann Frost. New Brunswick: Rutgers University Press, 1995.

Díaz, Arlene. *Female Citizens, Patriarchs, and the Law in Venezuela, 1786–1904.* Lincoln: University of Nebraska Press, 2004.

Diegues Junior, Manoel. *População e propriedade da terra no Brasil.* Washington, DC: Secretaria Geral, Organização dos Estados Americanos, 1959.

Dirks, Nicholas, Geoff Eley, and Sherry B. Ortner, eds. *Culture/Power/History: A Reader in Contemporary Social Theory.* Princeton: Princeton University Press, 1994.

Domingos, Manuel. "The Powerful in the Outback of the Brazilian Northeast." *Latin American Perspectives* 135, 31, 2 (March 2004): 94–111.

Doratioto, Francisco. *Maldita Guerra: Nova história da Guerra do Paraguai.* São Paulo: Companhia das Letras, 2002.

Dudink, Stefan, and Karen Hagermann. "Masculinity in Politics and War in the Age of Democratic Revolutions, 1750–1850." In *Masculinities in Politics and War: Gendering Modern History,* ed. Stefan Dudink, Karen Hagermann, and John Tosh, 3–21. Manchester: Manchester University Press, 2004.

Dudink, Stefan, Karen Hagermann, and John Tosh, eds. *Masculinities in Politics and War: Gendering Modern History.* Manchester: Manchester University Press, 2004.

Duncan, Julian S. *Public and Private Operation of Railways in Brazil.* New York: Columbia University Press, 1932.

Eisenberg, Peter. *The Sugar Industry in Pernambuco: Modernization without Change, 1840–1910.* Berkeley: University of California Press, 1974.

Ellison, Thomas. *The Cotton Trade of Great Britain.* London: Cass, 1886.

Esteves, Martha Abreu de. *Meninas perdidas: Os populares e o cotidiano do amor no Rio de Janeiro da belle époque.* Rio de Janeiro: Paz e Terra, 1989.

Facó, Rui. *Cangaceiros e fanáticos.* Rio de Janeiro: Civilização Brasileira, 1963.

Falci, Miridan Knox. "Mulheres no sertão nordestino." In *História das mulheres no Brasil,* ed. Mary del Priore, 241–77. São Paulo: Editora Contexto, 1997.

Faoro, Raimundo. *Os donos do poder.* 5th ed. Porto Alegre: Globo, 1979.

Faria, Sheila de Castro. *A Colônia em movimento: Fortuna e família no cotidiano colonial.* Rio de Janeiro: Nova Fronteira, 1998.

Fausto, Boris. "Brazil: The Social and Political Structure of the First Republic, 1889–1930." *The Cambridge History of Latin America.* 11 vols., ed. Leslie Bethell, 5: 779–829. Cambridge: Cambridge University Press, 1985.

Figueiredo, Luciano Raposo de Almeida. *Barrocas famílias: Vida familiar em Minas Gerais no século XVIII.* São Paulo: Hucitec, 1997.

Findlay, Eileen J. "Courtroom Tales of Sex and Honor: *Rapto* and Rape in Late-Nineteenth Century Puerto Rico." In *Honor, Status, and Law in*

Modern Latin America, ed. Sueann Caulfield, Sarah Chambers, and Lara Putnam, 201–22. Durham: Duke University Press, 2005.

Fischer, Brodwyn. "Slandering Citizens: Insults, Class, and Social Legitimacy in Rio de Janeiro's Criminal Courts." In *Honor, Status, and Law in Modern Latin America*, ed. Sueann Caulfield, Sarah Chambers, and Lara Putnam, 176–200. Durham: Duke University Press, 2005.

———. *A Poverty of Rights: Citizenship and Inequality in Twentieth-Century Rio de Janeiro*. Stanford: Stanford University Press, 2008.

Flory, Thomas. *Judge and Jury in Imperial Brazil, 1808–1871: Social Control and Political Stability in the New State*. Austin and London: University of Texas Press, 1981.

Forti, Maria do Carmo Pagan. *Maria do Juazeiro: A beata do milagre*. São Paulo: Annablume, 1999.

Franco, Jean. *Plotting Women: Gender and Representation in Mexico*. New York: Columbia University Press, 1989.

Franco, Maria Sylvia de Carvalho. *Homens livres na ordem escravocrata*. São Paulo: Instituto de Estudos Brasileiros, 1969.

Frank, Zephyr. *Dutra's World: Wealth and Family in Nineteenth-Century Rio de Janeiro*. Albuquerque: University of New Mexico Press, 2004.

Freyre, Gilberto. *Sobrados e mucambos: Decadência do patriarcado rural e desenvolvimento do urbano*. 2 vols., 3d ed. Rio de Janeiro: José Olympio Editora, 1961.

———. *The Masters and the Slaves (Casa-grande & senzala): A Study in the Development of Brazilian Civilization*. Translated by Samuel Putnam. 2d. rev. ed. Berkeley: University of California Press, 1986.

———. *Casa-grande & senzala: Formação da família brasileira sob o regime da economia patriarcal*. 43d ed. Rio de Janeiro: Record, 2001.

Funes, Eurípedes Antônio. "Negros no Ceará." In *Uma nova história do Ceará*, ed. Simone de Souza, 103–32. Fortaleza: Edições Demócrito Rocha, 2000.

Furtado, Celso. *Formação econômica do Brasil*. 7th ed. São Paulo: Companhia Editora Nacional, 1967.

Garcez, Angelina Nobre Rolim. *Fundos de pasto: Um projeto de vida sertanejo*. Bahia: Instituto de Terras da Bahia, 1987.

Garcia Junior, Raul Afrânio. *O sul: Camiho do roçado: Estratégias de reprodução camponesa e transformação social*. Brasília: Editora Universidade de Brasília, 1989.

Garfield, Seth. "Tapping Masculinity: Labor Recruitment to the Brazilian Amazon during World War II." *HAHR* 86: 2 (2006): 275–308.

Girão, Raimundo. "Bandeirismo baiano e povoamento do Ceará." *RIC* 62 (1940): 5–20.

———. *História econômica do Ceará*. Fortaleza: Editora Instituto do Ceará, 1947.

———. *Pequena história do Ceará*. 4th ed. Fortaleza: Edições UFC, 1984.

Girão, Valdice Carneiro. *As oficinas ou charqueadas no Ceará*. Fortaleza: Imprensa Oficial do Ceará, 1984.

————. "Da conquista à implantação dos primeiros núcleos urbanos na capitania do Siará Grande." In *História do Ceará*, ed. Simone de Souza, 23–43. Fortaleza: Fundação Demócrito Rocha, 1995.

Godoi, Emília Pietrafesa de. *O trabalho da memória: Cotidiano e história no sertão do Paiuí*. Campinas: Editora da UNICAMP, 1999.

Graham, Richard. *Patronage and Politics in Nineteenth-Century Brazil*. Stanford: Stanford University Press, 1990.

Graham, Sandra Lauderdale. *House and Street: The Domestic World of Servants and Masters in Nineteenth-Century Rio de Janeiro*. New York: Cambridge University Press, 1989.

————. "Honor among Slaves." In *The Faces of Honor*, ed. Lyman Johnson and Sonya Lipsett-Rivera, 201–28. Albuquerque: University of New Mexico Press, 1998.

————. *Caetana Says No: Women's Stories from a Brazilian Slave Society*. Cambridge: Cambridge University Press, 2002.

Green, James M. *Beyond Carnival: Male Homosexuality in Twentieth-Century Brazil*. Chicago: University of Chicago Press, 1999.

Greenfield, Gerald Michael. "The Great Drought and Elite Discourse in Imperial Brazil." *HAHR* 72, 3 (1992): 375–400.

————. "*Sertão* and *Sertanejo*: An Interpretative Context for Canudos." *Luso-Brazilian Review* 30, 2 (1993): 25–36.

————. *The Realities of Images: Imperial Brazil and the Great Drought*. Philadelphia: American Philosophical Society, 2001.

Guabiraba, Célia. *Ceará: A crise permanente do modelo exportador, 1850–1930*. Fortaleza: Instituto da Memória do Povo Cearense, 1989.

Gutiérrez, Ramón A. *When Jesus Came, the Corn Mothers Went Away: Marriage, Sexuality and Power in New Mexico, 1500–1846*. Stanford: Stanford University Press, 1991.

Gutmann, Matthew, ed. *The Meanings of Macho: Being a Man in Mexico City*. Berkeley: University of California Press, 1996.

————. *Changing Men and Masculinities in Latin America*. Durham: Duke University Press, 2003.

Guy, Donna. "Future Directions in Latin American Gender History." *The Americas* 51, 1 (July 1994): 1–9.

Hall, Stuart, ed. *Representation: Cultural Representations and Signifying Practices*. London: Sage Publications, 1997.

Hobsbawm, Eric. *Primitive Rebels: Studies in Archaic Forms of Social Movement in the 19th and 20th Centuries*. New York: Norton and Co., 1959.

————. *Bandits*. New York: Pantheon, 1969.

Holanda, João Xavier de. *Polícia militar do Ceará: Origem, memória e projeção*. 2 vols. Fortaleza: Imprensa Oficial do Ceará, 1987.

Holanda, Sérgio Buarque de. *Raízes do Brasil.* 26th ed. São Paulo: Companhia das Letras, 1995.

Holloway, Thomas. *Policing Rio de Janeiro: Repression and Resistance in a 19th-Century City.* Stanford: Stanford University Press, 1993.

Holston, James. "The Misrule of Law: Land and Usurpation in Brazil." *CSSH* 33, 4 (October 1991): 695–725.

Horne, John. "Masculinity in Politics and War in the Age of Nation-states and World Wars, 1850–1950." In *Masculinities in Politics and War: Gendering Modern History,* ed. Stefan Dudink, Karen Hagermann, and John Tosh, 22–40. Manchester and New York: Manchester University Press, 2004.

Huggins, Martha Knisely. *From Slavery to Vagrancy in Brazil: Crime and Social Control in the Third World.* New Brunswick: Rutgers University Press, 1985.

Irwin, Robert McKee. *Mexican Masculinities.* Minneapolis: University of Minnesota Press, 2003.

Irwin, Robert McKee, Edward McCaughan, and Michelle Rocío Nasser, eds. *The Famous 41: Sexuality and Social Control in Mexico, c. 1901.* New York: Palgrave Macmillan, 2003.

Izecksohn, Vitor. "Recrutamento militar no Rio de Janeiro durante a Guerra do Paraguai." In *Nova História Militar Brasileira,* ed. Celso Castro, Vitor Izecksohn, and Hendrik Kraay, 179–208. Rio de Janeiro: Editora FGV, 2004.

Johnson, Allen. *Sharecroppers of the Sertão: Economics and Dependence on a Brazilian Plantation.* Stanford: Stanford University Press, 1971.

Johnson, Lyman. "Dangerous Words, Provocative Gestures, and Violent Acts: The Disputed Hierarchies of Plebian Life in Colonial Buenos Aires." In *The Faces of Honor,* ed. Lyman Johnson and Sonya Lipsett-Rivera, 127–51. Albuquerque: University of New Mexico Press, 1998.

Johnson, Lyman, and Sonya Lipsett-Rivera, eds. *The Faces of Honor: Sex, Shame and Violence in Colonial Latin America.* Albuquerque: University of New Mexico Press, 1998.

Johnson, Randal, and Robert Stam, eds. *Brazilian Cinema.* Exp. ed. New York: Columbia University Press, 1995.

Joseph, Gilbert. "On the Trail of the Latin American Bandits: A Reexamination of Peasant Resistance." *Latin American Research Review* 25, 3 (1990): 7–53.

Julio, Silvio. *Terra e povo do Ceará.* Rio de Janeiro: Livraria Carvalho Editora, 1936.

Kirkendall, Andrew. *Class Mates: Male Student Culture and the Making of a Political Class in Nineteenth Century Brazil.* Lincoln: University of Nebraska Press, 2002.

Kittelson, Roger. *The Practice of Politics in Post-Colonial Brazil: Porto Alegre, 1845–1895.* Pittsburgh, PA: University of Pittsburgh Press, 2006.

Klubock, Thomas Miller. *Contested Communities: Class, Gender, and Politics in Chile's El Teniente Copper Mine, 1904–1951.* Durham: Duke University Press, 1998.

Kowarick, Lúcio. *Trabalho e vadiagem: A origem do trabalho livre no Brasil.* São Paulo: Editora Brasiliense, 1987.

Kraay, Hendrik. "'As Terrifying as Unexpected': The Bahian Sabinada, 1837–1838." *HAHR* 72, 4 (1992): 501–27.

———. *Race, State, and Armed Forces in Independence-Era Brazil, Bahia, 1790s–1840s.* Stanford: Stanford University Press, 2001.

———. "O cotidiano dos soldados na guarnição da Bahia (1850–89)." In *Nova História Militar Brasileira,* ed. Celso Castro, Vitor Izecksohn, and Hendrik Kraay, 237–68. Rio de Janeiro: Editora FGV, 2004.

———. "Patriotic Mobilization in Brazil: The Zuavos and Other Black Companies." In *I Die with My Country: Perspectives on the Paraguayan War, 1864–1870,* ed. Hendrik Kraay and Thomas Whigman, 60–80. Lincoln: University of Nebraska Press, 2004.

Kraay, Hendrik, and Thomas Whighman, eds. *I Die with My Country: Perspectives on the Paraguayan War, 1864–1870.* Lincoln: University of Nebraska Press, 2004.

Kuznesof, Elizabeth Anne. "Household Composition and Headship as Related to Changes in Mode of Production: São Paulo 1765 to 1836." *CSSH* 22, 1 (1980): 78–108.

———. *Household Economy and Urban Development: São Paulo, 1765 to 1836.* Boulder, CO: Westview Press, 1986.

———. "Sexual Politics, Race and Bastard-bearing in Nineteenth-century Brazil: A Question of Culture or Power." *Journal of Family History* 16, 3 (1991): 240–60.

Lancaster, Roger. *Life Is Hard: Machismo, Danger, and the Intimacy of Power in Nicaragua.* Berkeley: University of California Press, 1992.

Landes, Joan B. "Republican Citizenship and Heterosocial Desire: Concepts of Masculinity in Revolutionary France." In *Masculinities in Politics and War: Gendering Modern History,* ed. Stefan Dudink, Karen Hagermann, and John Tosh, 96–115. Manchester: Manchester University Press, 2004.

Landim, Teoberto. *Seca: A estação do inferno.* 2d ed. Fortaleza: Editora UFC, 2005.

Lavrin, Asunción, ed. *Sexuality and Marriage in Colonial Latin America.* Lincoln: University of Nebraska Press, 1989.

Leal, Victor Nunes. *Coronelismo, enxada e voto: O município e o regime representativo no Brasil.* Rio de Janeiro: Revista Forense, 1949.

LeGrand, Catharine. *Frontier Expansion and Peasant Protest in Colombia, 1830–1936.* Albuquerque: University of New Mexico Press, 1986.

Leite, Ana Cristina. *O algodão no Ceará: Estrutura fundiária e capital comercial, 1850–1880.* Fortaleza: Secretaria da Cultura e Desporto do Estado do Ceará, 1994.

Lemenhe, Maria Auxiliadora. *As razões de uma cidade: Conflito de hegemonias.* Fortaleza: Stylus Comunicações, 1991.

Lessa, Orígenes. *Inácio da Catingueira e Luís Gama: Dois poetas negros contra o racismo dos mestiços.* Rio de Janeiro: Fundação Casa de Rui Barbosa, 1982.

Levine, Robert. *Vale of Tears: Revisiting the Canudos Massacre in Northeastern Brazil, 1893–1897.* Berkeley: University of California Press, 1992.

Lewin, Linda. "The Oligarchical Limitations of Social Banditry in Brazil: The Case of the 'Good' Thief Antonio Silvino." *Past and Present* 82 (February 1979): 116–46.

———. *Politics and Parentela in Paraíba: A Case Study of Family-Based Oligarchy in Brazil.* Princeton: Princeton University Press, 1987.

———. "Who Was 'o Grande Romano'? Genealogical Purity, the Indian 'Past' and Whiteness in Brazil's Northeast Backlands, 1750–1900." *Journal of Latin American Lore* 19 (1996): 129–79.

———. *Surprise Heirs.* 2 vols. Stanford: Stanford University Press, 2003.

Lumsden, Ian. *Machos, Maricones and Gays: Cuba and Homosexuality.* Philadelphia: Temple University Press, 1996.

Luna, Francisco Vidal, and Iraci del Nero da Costa. "Posse de escravos em São Paulo no início do século XIX." *Estudos econômicos* 13, 1 (January–April 1983): 211–21.

Macêdo, Nertan. *O bacamarte dos Mourões.* Fortaleza: Editora Instituto do Ceará, 1966.

———. *O clã dos Inhamuns.* 2d ed. Fortaleza: Edições A Fortaleza, 1967.

———. *O clã de Santa Quitéria.* 2d ed. Fortaleza: Editora Renes, 1980.

Mahony, Mary Ann. "Afro-Brazilians, Land Reform, and the Question of Social Mobility in Southern Bahia." *Luso-Brazilian Review* 34 (1997): 59–79.

Marcílio, Maria Luisa. *A cidade de São Paulo: Povoamento e população, 1750–1850.* São Paulo: Pioneira/ EDUSP, 1973.

———. "A etnodemografia da criança abandonada na história do Brasil, séculos 18 e 19." *Latin American Population History Bulletin* 28 (Fall 1998): 2–11.

Marson, Izabel Andrade. "Imagens da condição feminina em 'Travels in Brasil' de Henry Koster." *Cadernos Pagu* 4 (1995): 219–42.

Martínez-Alier, Verena. *Marriage, Class and Colour in Nineteenth-Century Cuba: A Study of Racial Attitudes and Sexual Values in a Slave Society.* Cambridge: Cambridge University Press, 1974.

Martins, Mônica Dias. *Açúcar no sertão: A ofensiva capitalista no nordeste do Brasil.* São Paulo: Annablume, 2008.

Mattos, Hamilton Monteiro de. *Crise agrária e luta de classes: O Nordeste brasileiro entre 1850–1889.* Brasília: Horizonte Editora, 1980.

Mattos, Hebe Maria. *Das cores do silêncio: Os significados da liberdade no Sudeste escravista. Brasil, século XIX.* 2d ed. Rio de Janeiro: Nova Fronteira, 1998.

Mattos, Ilmar Rohloff de. *O tempo saquarema.* São Paulo: Hucitec, 1987.

Mattoso, Kátia de Queirós. *Família e sociedade na Bahia do século XIX.* São Paulo: Corrupio, 1988.

————. *Bahia, século XIX: Uma província no Império.* Rio de Janeiro: Nova Fronteira, 1992.

McCreery, David. *Frontier Goiás, 1822–1889.* Stanford: Stanford University Press, 2006.

Melhuus, Marit, and Kristi Anne Stolen, eds. *Machos, Mistresses, Madonnas: Contesting the Power of Latin American Gender Imagery.* New York: Verso, 1996.

Mello, Anísio. *Estórias e lendas do Norte e Nordeste.* São Paulo: Livraria Editora Iracema, 1961.

Melo, Evaldo Cabral de. *O norte agrário e o Império, 1877–1889.* Rio de Janeiro: Editora Nova Fronteira, 1984.

Menezes, Djacir. *O outro Nordeste: Formação social do Nordeste.* Rio de Janeiro: José Olympio Editora, 1937.

Metcalf, Alida. "Fathers and Sons: The Politics of Inheritance in a Colonial Brazilian Township." *HAHR* 66, 3 (1986): 455–84.

————. "Women and Means: Women and Family Property in Colonial Brazil." *Journal of Social History* 24, 2 (Winter 1990): 277–98.

————. *Family and Frontier in Colonial Brazil: Santana de Parnaíba, 1580–1822.* Berkeley: University of California Press, 1992.

Meznar, Joan. "The Ranks of the Poor: Military Service and Social Differentiation in Northeast Brazil, 1830–1875." *HAHR* 72, 3 (1992): 335–51.

————. "Orphans and the Transition from Slave to Free Labor in Northeast Brazil: The Case of Campina Grande, 1850–1888." *Journal of Social History* 27, 3 (Spring 1994): 499–515.

————. "Carlota Lucia de Brito: Women, Power, and Politics in Northeast Brazil." In *The Human Tradition in Modern Latin America,* ed. William Beezley and Judith Ewel, 41–52. Wilmington, DE: Scholarly Resources, 1997.

Moniz, Edmundo. *A guerra social de Canudos.* Rio de Janeiro: Civilização Brasileira, 1978.

Montenegro, Abelardo. *Fanáticos e cangaceiros.* Fortaleza: Editora Henrique Galeno, 1973.

————. *Os partidos políticos do Ceará.* Fortaleza: Edições UFC, 1980.

Montenegro, João Alfredo de Sousa. *Ideologia e conflito no Nordeste rural (Pinto Madeira e a revolução de 1832 no Ceará).* Rio de Janeiro: Tempo Brasileiro, 1976.

Morais, Fábio André da Silva Morais. "Metamorfoses da guerra: O recrutamento de menores para a Armada Imperial na Compahia de Aprenzides Marinheiros do Ceará durante a guerra contra o Paraguai (1865–1870)." In *Documentos: Revista do Arquivo Público do Ceará,* 4: 49–77. Fortaleza: Secretaria da Cultura do Estado do Ceará, 2006.

Mosher, Jeffrey. *Political Struggle, Ideology and State Building: Pernambuco and the Construction of Brazil, 1817–1850.* Lincoln: University of Nebraska Press, 2008.

Mott, Luiz. *Piauí colonial: População, economia e sociedade.* Teresina: Projeto Petrônio Portella, 1985.

Motta, Márcia Maria Menendes. *Nas fronteiras do poder: Conflito e direito à terra no Brasil do século XIX*. Rio de Janeiro: Vício de Leitura, 1998.

Moura, Denise Soares de. "Andantes de novos rumos: A vinda de migrantes cearenses para fazendas de café paulistas em 1878." *Revista Brasileira de História* 17, 34 (1997): 119–32.

———. *Saindo das sombras: Homens livres no declínio do escravismo*. Campinas: Area de Publicação CMU/Unicamp, 1998.

Naro, Nancy Priscilla. "Customary Rightholders and Legal Claimants to Land in Rio de Janeiro, Brazil, 1870–1890." *The Americas* 48, 4 (April 1992): 485–517.

Nascimento, F. S. "Síntese histórica da escravidão negra." In *História do Ceará*, ed. Simone de Souza, 167–84. Fortaleza: Edições Demócrito Rocha, 1995.

Navarro, Marysa. "Against *Marianismo*." In *Gender's Place: Feminist Anthropologies of Latin America,* ed. Rosario Montoya, Lessie Jo Frasier, and Janice Hurtig. New York: Palgrave Macmillan, 2002.

Nazzari, Muriel. *The Disappearance of the Dowry: Women, Families, and Social Change in São Paulo, Brazil (1600–1900)*. Stanford: Stanford University Press, 1991.

———. "An Urgent Need to Conceal: The System of Honor and Shame in Colonial Brazil." In *The Faces of Honor*, ed. Lyman Johnson and Sonya Lipsett-Rivera, 103–26. Albuquerque: University of New Mexico Press, 1998.

Needell, Jeffrey D. *The Party of Order: The Conservatives, the State, and Slavery in the Brazilian Monarchy, 1831–1871*. Stanford: Stanford University Press, 2006.

Neves, Frederico de Castro. *A multidão e a história: Saques e outras ações de massas no Ceará*. Rio de Janeiro: Relume Dumará, 2000.

———. "A lei de terras e a lei da vida: Iransformações do mundo rural no Ceará do século XIX." *Estudos de História, França* 8, 2 (2001): 37–58.

Nobre, Geraldo da Silva. *História de Morada Nova, 1876–1976*. 2 vols. Fortaleza: Gráfica Editorial Cearense, 1976.

———. *As oficinas de carne no Ceará: Solução local para uma pecuária em crise*. Fortaleza: Gráfica Editorial Cearense, 1979.

———. *O Ceará em preto e branco*. Fortaleza: 1988.

Nonato, Raimundo. *Jesuíno Brilhante, o cangaceiro romântico, 1844–1879*. Rio de Janeiro: Editora Pongetti, 1970.

Nugent, Walter. "Frontiers and Empires in the Late Nineteenth Century." In *Trails: Toward a New Western History,* ed. Patricia N. Limerick, Clyde Millner II, and Charles Ranking, 161–81. Lawrence: University of Kansas Press, 1991.

Oliveira, André Frota de. *A estrada de ferro de Sobral*. Fortaleza: Expressão Gráfica e Editora, 1994.

———. *A fortificação holandesa de Camocim*. Fortaleza: Expressão Gráfica e Editora, 1995.

Oliveira, Francisco de. *Elegia para uma re(li)gião: SUDENE, Nordeste, planejamento e conflictos de classe*. Rio de Janeiro: Paz e Terra, 1977.

Oliveira Filho, João Pacheco de. "O caboclo e o brabo: Notas sobre duas modalidades de força de trabalho na expansão da fronteira Amazônica no século XIX." *Encontros com a civilização brasileira* 11 (May 1979): 101–40.

Onody, Oliver. *A inflação brasileira (1820–1958)*. Rio de Janeiro: 1960.

Padilla, Mark. *Caribbean Pleasure Industry: Tourism, Sexuality, and AIDS in the Dominican Republic*. Chicago: University of Chicago Press, 2007.

Paiva, Maria Arair Pinto. *A elite política do Ceará Provincial*. Rio de Janeiro: Tempo Brasileiro, 1979.

Palacios, Guillermo. *Campesinato e escravidão no Brasil: Agricultores livres e pobres na Capitania Geral de Pernambuco (1700–1817)*. Translated by Walter Sotomayor. Brasília: Editora Universidade de Brasília, 2004.

Palazzi, Maura. "Work and Residence of 'Women Alone' in the Context of a Patrilineal System (Eighteenth- and Nineteenth-Century Northern Italy)." In *Gender, Kinship, Power: A Comparative and Interdisciplinary History*, ed. Mary Jo Maynes, Ann Waltner, Birgitte Soland, and Urike Strasser, 216–28. New York: Routledge, 1996.

Pang, Eul Soo. *In Pursuit of Honor and Power: Noblemen of the Southern Cross in Nineteenth-Century Brazil*. Tuscaloosa: University of Alabama Press, 1988.

Pang, Eul-Soo, and Ron Seckinger. "The Mandarins of Imperial Brazil." *CSSH* 14, 2 (1972): 215–44.

Parker, David. "'Gentlemanly Responsibility' and 'Insults of a Woman': Dueling and the Unwritten Rules of Public Life in Uruguay, 1860–1920." In *Gender, Sexuality and Power in Latin America since Independence,* ed. William French and Katherine Elaine Bliss, 109–32. Lanham, MD: Rowman and Littlefield, 2007.

Penteado, Rocha. *Problemas da colonização e de uso da terra na região Bragantina do estado do Pará*. Lisboa: Junta de Investigações de Ultramar, 1968.

Pericás, Luis Bernardo. *Os cangaceiros: Ensaio de interpretação histórica*. São Paulo: Boitempo, 2010.

Peristiany, J. G., ed. *Honour and Shame: The Values of Mediterranean Society*. Chicago: University of Chicago Press, 1966.

Peristiany, J. G., and Julian Pitt-Rivers, eds. *Honor and Grace in Anthropology*. Cambridge: Cambridge University Press, 1992.

Pessar, Patricia. *From Fanatics to Folk: Brazilian Millenarianism and Popular Culture*. Durham: Duke University Press, 2004.

Picatto, Pablo. "Politics and the Technology of Honor: Dueling in Turn-of-the-Century Mexico." *Journal of Social History* 33, 2 (Winter 1999): 331–54.

Pinheiro, Francisco José. "Mundos em confronto: Povos nativos e europeos na disputa pelo território." In *Uma nova história do Ceará*, ed. Simone de Souza, 17–55. Fortaleza: Edições Demócrito Rocha, 2000.

Pinheiro, Irineu. *O Cariri, seu descobrimento, povoamento, costumes*. Fortaleza: R. Senador Pompeu, 1950.

Pitt-Rivers, Julian. *The Fate of Shechem, or the Politics of Sex: Essays in the Anthropology of the Mediterranean*. Cambridge: Cambridge University Press, 1977.

Prado Júnior, Caio. *Formação do Brasil contemporâneo: Colônia*. São Paulo: Martins Editora, 1942.

Putnam, Lara. *The Company They Kept: Migrants and the Politics of Gender in Caribbean Costa Rica, 1870–1960*. Chapel Hill: University of North Carolina Press, 2002.

Queiroz, Maria Isaura Pereira de. *O messianismo no Brasil e no mundo*. São Paulo: Dominus Editôra, 1965.

———. *Os cangaceiros*. São Paulo: Duas Cidades, 1977.

Queiroz, Rachel de. *Memorial de Maria Moura*. São Paulo: Editora Siciliano, 1992.

Rabinow, Paul, ed. *The Foucault Reader*. New York: Pantheon Books, 1984.

Ramos, Donald. "Marriage and the Family in Colonial Vila Rica." *HAHR* 55, 2 (1975): 200–245.

———. "Single and Married Women in Vila Rica, Brazil, 1754–1838." *Journal of Family History* 16, 3 (1991): 261–82.

Rebhun, L. A. *The Heart Is Unknown Country: Love in the Changing Economy of Northeast Brazil*. Stanford: Stanford University Press, 1999.

Reesink, E. B. *The Peasant in the Sertão: A Short Exploration of His Past and Present*. Leiden: Institute of Cultural and Social Studies, 1981.

Reis, João José. *Slave Rebellion in Brazil: The Muslim Uprising of 1835 in Bahia*. Translated by Arthur Brakel. Baltimore: Johns Hopkins University Press, 1993.

Ribeiro, Gladys Sabina. *A liberdade em construção: Identidade nacional e conflitos anti-lusitanos no Primeiro Reinado*. Rio de Janeiro: Relume Dumará, 2002.

Ribeiro, Josiane. *Penitência e festa: As missões do Padre Ibiapina no Ceará*. Fortaleza: Expressão Gráfica e Editora Ltda., 2006.

Ribeiro, Waldir Uchôa. *Jaguaribe, minha terra*. 3 vols. Fortaleza: Premius Editora, 2001.

Ricci, Magda. "A Cabanagem, a terra, os rios e os homens na Amazônia: O outro lado de uma revolução (1835–1840)." In *Formas de resistência camponesa: Visibilidade e diversidade de conflitos ao longo da história*, ed. Márcia Motta and Paulo Zarth, 153–70. São Paulo: Editora UNESP, 2008.

Roberts, Mary Louise. *Civilization without Sexes: Reconstructing Gender in Postwar France, 1917–1927*. Chicago: University of Chicago Press, 1994.

Roseberry, William. *Anthropologies and Histories*. New Brunswick: Rutgers University Press, 1989.

Samara, Eni de Mesquita. "Tendências atuais da história da família no Brasil." In *Pensando a família no Brasil*, ed. Carneiro Almeida and Paula Gonçalves, 25–36. Rio de Janeiro: Espaço e Terra, 1987.

———. *As mulheres, o poder e a família: São Paulo, século XIX*. São Paulo: Marco Zero, 1989.

Samara, Eni de Mesquita, and José Weyne de Freitas Sousa. "Morar e viver no Nordeste do Brasil: Fortaleza, séc. XIX." *Trajetos: Revista de História UFC* 4, 7 (2006): 41–67.

Santos Filho, Lycurgo. *Uma comunidade rural do Brasil antigo (aspectos da vida patriaral no sertão da Bahia nos séculos XVIII e XIX)*. São Paulo: Companhia Editora Nacional, 1956.

Santos, Martha S. "On the Importance of Being Honorable: Masculinity, Survival, and Conflict in the Backlands of Northeast Brazil, Ceará, 1840s–1890." *The Americas* 64, 1 (July 2007): 35–57.

Scheper-Hughes, Nancy. *Death without Weeping: The Violence of Everyday Life in Brazil*. Berkeley: University of California Press, 1992.

Schneider, Jane. "Of Vigilance and Virgins: Honor, Shame and Access to Resources in Mediterranean Societies." *Ethnology* 10, 1 (January 1971): 1–24.

Schwartz, Stuart. "Patterns of Slaveholding in the Americas: New Evidence from Brazil." *AHR* 87, 1 (February 1982): 55–86.

———. *Sugar Plantations in the Formation of Brazilian Society: Bahia, 1550–1835*. Cambridge: Cambridge University Press, 1985.

———. "Plantations and Peripheries, c. 1580–1750." In *Colonial Brazil*, ed. Leslie Bethell, 64–144. New York: Cambridge University Press, 1987.

Scott, Joan Wallach. "Gender: A Useful Category of Historical Analysis." *American Historical Review* 91, 5 (December 1986): 1053–75.

Scribner, Bob. "Is a History of Popular Culture Possible?" *History of European Ideas* 10, 2 (1989): 175–91.

Secreto, María Verónica. "Ceará, a fábrica de trabalhadores: Emigração subsidiada no final do Século XIX." *Trajetos: Revista de História UFC* 2, 4 (2003): 47–65.

———. "(Des)Medidos Quebra-quilos e outros quebras nos sertões nordestinos (1874–1875)." In *Formas de resistência camponesa: Visibilidade e diversidade de conflitos ao longo da história*, ed. Márcia Motta and Paulo Zarth, 219–40. São Paulo: Editora UNESP, 2008.

Seed, Patricia. *To Love, Honor and Obey in Colonial Mexico: Conflicts over Marriage Choice, 1574–1821*. Stanford: Stanford University Press, 1988.

Seraine, Florival. *Antologia do folclore cearense*. Fortaleza: Imprensa Universitária-UFC, 1983.

Shammas, Carole. "The Determinants of Personal Wealth in Seventeenth-Century England and America." *Journal of Economic History* 37, 3 (September 1977): 675–89.

Silva, Maria Nizza da. *Sistemas de casamento no Brasil colonial*. São Paulo: Editora da Universidade de São Paulo, 1984.

Skidmore, Thomas. *Black into White: Race and Nationality in Brazilian Thought*. Durham: Duke University Press, 1993.

Slater, Candace. *Stories on a String: The Brazilian Literatura de Cordel*. Berkeley: University of California Press, 1989.

Slenes, Robert. "Os múltiplos de porcos e diamantes: A economia escrava de Minas Gerais no século XIX." *Estudos econômicos* 18, 3 (September–December 1988): 449–95.

Smith, Roberto. *Propriedade da terra e transição: Estudo da formação da propriedade privada da terra e transição para o capitalismo no Brasil.* São Paulo: Editora Brasiliense, 1990.

Socolow, Susan Migden. "Acceptable Partners: Marriage Choice in Colonial Argentina, 1778–1810." In *Sexuality and Marriage in Colonial Latin America,* ed. Asunción Lavrin, 209–51. Lincoln: University of Nebraska Press, 1989.

———. "Women and Crime, Buenos Aires, 1757–97." In *The Problem of Order in Changing Societies,* ed. Lyman Johnson, 1–18. Albuquerque: University of New Mexico Press, 1990.

———. *The Women of Colonial Latin America.* Cambridge: Cambridge University Press, 2000.

Souza, Amaury de. "The Cangaço and the Politics of Violence in Northeast Brazil." In *Protest and Resistance in Angola and Brazil,* ed. Ronald Chilcote, 109–31. Berkeley: University of California Press, 1972.

Souza, Antonio Cândido de Mello. "The Brazilian Family." In *Brazil: Portrait of Half a Continent,* ed. Lynn Smith and Alexander Marchant, 291–312. New York: Dryden Press, 1951.

———. *Os parceiros do Rio Bonito: Estudo sôbre o caipira paulista e a transformação dos seus meios de vida.* 2d ed. São Paulo: Duas Cidades, 1971.

Souza, Eusebio de. *História militar do Ceará.* Fortaleza: Editora Instituto do Ceará, 1950.

Souza, Laura de Mello. *Desclassificados do ouro: A pobreza mineira no século XVIII.* Rio de Janeiro: Edições Graal, 1982.

Souza, Simone de, ed. *História do Ceará.* Fortaleza: Edições Demócrito Rocha, 1995.

———, ed. *Uma nova história do Ceará.* Fortaleza: Edições Demócrito Rocha, 2000.

Souza, Simone de, and Frederico de Castro Neves, eds. *Seca.* Fortaleza: Edições Demócrito Rocha, 2002.

Stein, Stanley. *The Brazilian Cotton Manufacture.* Cambridge: Harvard University Press, 1975.

———. *Vassouras: A Brazilian Coffee County, 1850–1900: The Roles of Planter and Slave in a Plantation Society.* Princeton: Princeton University Press, 1985 [1958].

Stern, Steve. *The Secret History of Gender: Women, Men and Power in Late Colonial Mexico.* Chapel Hill: University of North Carolina Press, 1995.

Studart Filho, Carlos. "Notas históricas sobre os indígenas cearenses." *RIC* 43 (1931): 53–103.

Taussig, Michael. "Terror as Usual: Walter Benjamin's Theory of History as a Stage of Siege." *Social Text* 23 (Fall–Winter 1989): 3–20.

Tinsman, Heidi. *Partners in Conflict: The Politics of Gender, Sexuality and Labor in the Chilean Agrarian Reform, 1950–1973*. Durham: Duke University Press, 2002.

Tosh, John. "Hegemonic Masculinity and the History of Gender." In *Masculinities in Politics and War: Gendering Modern History*, ed. Stefan Dudink, Karen Hagermann, and John Tosh, 41–60. Manchester: Manchester University Press, 2004.

Twinam, Ann. *Public Lives, Private Secrets: Gender, Honor, Sexuality and Illegitimacy in Colonial Spanish America*. Stanford: Stanford University Press, 1999.

Uchôa, Waldery. *Anuário do Ceará: História do Ceará e dos municípios*. 2 vols. Fortaleza: 1953.

Vainfas, Ronaldo. *Trópico dos pecados: Moral, sexualidade e Inquisição no Brasil*. Rio de Janeiro: Campus, 1989.

Van Deusen, Nancy. *Between the Sacred and the Worldly: The Institutional and Cultural Practice of Recogimiento in Colonial Lima*. Stanford: Stanford University Press, 2001.

Vanderwood, Paul. *Disorder and Progress: Bandits, Police and Mexican Development*. 2d ed. Wilmington, DE: Scholarly Resources, 1992.

Vianna, Oliveira. *Instituições políticas brasileiras*. 3d. ed. Rio de Janeiro: Distribuidora Record, 1974 [1948].

Víctor, Hugo. *Chefes de polícia do Ceará*. Fortaleza: Typografia Minerva, 1943.

Vieira Jr., A. Otaviano. *Entre paredes e bacamartes: História da família no sertão (1780–1850)*. Fortaleza: Edições Demócrito Rocha; Hucitec, 2004.

Vigoya, Mara Viveros. "Contemporary Latin American Perspectives on Masculinity." In *Changing Men and Masculinities in Latin America*, ed. Matthew Gutmann, 27–57. Durham: Duke University Press, 2003.

Villa, Marco Antonio. *Vida e morte no sertão: História das secas no Nordeste nos séculos XIX e XX*. São Paulo: Editora Atica, 2000.

Weinstein, Barbara. *The Amazon Rubber Boom, 1850–1920*. Stanford: Stanford University Press, 1983.

Whighman, Thomas. *The Paraguayan War: Causes and Early Conduct*. Lincoln: University of Nebraska Press, 2002.

Williams, Raymond. *Marxism and Literature*. Oxford: Oxford University Press, 1977.

Wolff, Christina Scheibe. *Mulheres da floresta: Uma história. Alto Juruá, Acre (1890–1945)*. São Paulo: Hucitec, 1999.

Unpublished Dissertations and Papers

Assunção, Matthias Rohrig. "Versos e cacetes: Desafios masculinos na cultura afro-fluminense." Paper presented at the IX Congress of the Brazilian Studies Association-BRASA, New Orleans, March, 2008.

Aufderheide, Patricia Ann. "Order and Violence: Social Deviance and Social Control in Brazil, 1780–1840." Ph.D. diss., University of Minnesota, 1975.

Cunniff, Roger Lee. "The Great Drought: Northeast Brazil, 1877–1880." Ph.D. diss., University of Texas at Austin, 1970.

Meznar, Joan Ellen. "Deference and Dependence: The World of Small Farmers in a Northeastern Brazilian Community, 1850–1900." Ph.D. diss., University of Texas at Austin, 1986.

Naro, Nancy Priscilla Smith. "The 1848 Praieira Revolt in Brazil." Ph.D. diss., University of Chicago, 1981.

Pimentel Filho, José Ernesto. "A produção do crime: Violência, distinção social e economia na formação da província cearense." Ph.D. diss, Universidade de São Paulo, 2002.

Pinheiro, Francisco José. "A organização do mercado de trabalho no Ceará." Master's thesis, Universidade Federal de Pernambuco, 1990.

Ramos, Xislei Araújo. "'Por trás de toda fuga nem sempre há un crime': O recrutamento 'a laço' e os limites da ordem no Ceará (1850–1875)." Master's thesis, Universidade Federal do Ceará, 2003.

Samara, Eni de Mesquita. "Mão-de-obra feminina, oportunidades e mercado de trabalho no Brasil, século XIX." Paper presented at the International Congress of the Latin American Studies Association, Washington, DC, 1995.

Sampaio, Yony. "Formação territorial do Nordeste." Paper presented at the International Congress of the Latin American Studies Association, Guadalajara, April 1997.

Santos, Martha S. "'*Sertões Temerosos* (Menacing Backlands)': Honor, Gender, and Violence in a Changing World. Ceará, Brazil, 1845–1889." Ph.D. diss., University of Arizona, 2004.

———. "Disempowering Women: Widows, Property Rights, and Inheritance in the Brazilian Backlands of Ceará, 1845–1889." Paper presented at the 56th Annual Conference of the Rocky Mountain Council for Latin American Studies, Santa Fe, New Mexico, March 2009.

Slenes, Robert. "The Demography and Economics of Brazilian Slavery: 1850–1888." Ph.D. diss., Stanford University, 1976.

Versiani, Flávio, and José Vergolino. "Slaveholdings in the Nineteenth-Century Brazilian Northeast: Sugar Estates and the Backlands." Paper presented at the XIII Congress of the International Economic History Association, Buenos Aires, July 2002.

CPSIA information can be obtained
at www.ICGtesting.com
Printed in the USA
LVHW101613190323
741978LV00011B/147/J